© Lars Klove

JAKE BERNSTEIN was a senior reporter on the International Consortium of Investigative Journalists team, which broke the Panama Papers story. In 2017, the project won the Pulitzer Prize for Explanatory Reporting. Bernstein earned his first Pulitzer Prize in 2011 for National Reporting, for coverage of the financial crisis. He has written for *The New York Times, The Washington Post, Bloomberg, The Guardian, ProPublica,* and *Vice,* and has appeared on the BBC, NBC, CNN, PBS, and NPR. He was the editor of *The Texas Observer* and is the coauthor of *Vice: Dick Cheney and the Hijacking of the American Presidency.*

THE LAUNDROMAT

INSIDE THE PANAMA PAPERS,
ILLICIT MONEY NETWORKS,
AND THE GLOBAL ELITE

JAKE BERNSTEIN

PICADOR

HENRY HOLT AND COMPANY

NEW YORK

picadorusa.com • instagram.com/picador
twitter.com/picadorusa • facebook.com/picadorusa

Picador® is a U.S. registered trademark and is used by Macmillan Publishing Group, LLC, under license from Pan Books Limited.

For book club information, please visit facebook.com/picadorbookclub or email marketing@picadorusa.com.

Designed by Kelly S. Too

The Library of Congress has cataloged the Henry Holt edition as follows:

Names: Bernstein, Jake, author.
Title: Secrecy world : inside the Panama papers investigation of illicit
    money networks and the global elite / Jake Bernstein.
Description: First edition. | New York : Henry Holt and Company, [2017] |
    Includes index.
Identifiers: LCCN 2017035225 (print) | LCCN 2017037165 (ebook) |
    ISBN 9781250126696 (ebook) | ISBN 9781250126689 (hardcover)
Subjects: LCSH: Panama Papers. | Tax evasion. | Tax havens. | Political
    corruption. | Money laundering. | Financial disclosure. | Finance,
    Public—Corrupt practices.
Classification: LCC HV6341 (ebook) | LCC HV6341. B47 2017 (print) |
    DDC 364.16'8–dc23
LC record available at https://lccn.loc.gov/2017035225

Picador Movie Tie-in ISBN 978-1-250-75440-0

Our books may be purchased in bulk for promotional, educational, or business use. Please contact your local bookseller or the Macmillan Corporate and Premium Sales Department at 1-800-221-7945, extension 5442, or by email at MacmillanSpecialMarkets@macmillan.com.

First published as *Secrecy World* by Henry Holt and Company, LLC

First Picador Movie Tie-in Edition: November 2019

10 9 8 7 6 5 4 3 2 1

To Eve, without whom this book would not exist.
Your wisdom and beauty light my day.

CONTENTS

PROLOGUE

In the spring of 2015, a prosperous shipping-company executive in Mexico faced a problem. He wanted to buy a $585,000 town house in Seattle for his sister and ten-year-old niece. It was not the distance that posed a challenge. His sister was embroiled in a divorce. The executive did not want the house to become part of the dispute. He also hoped to minimize any taxes on the transaction. Finally, the ownership of the house needed to revert back to him should his sister die.

He contacted a law firm in Panama that handled such matters. The firm had decades of experience helping people all over the world hide their money and disguise their most intimate affairs. Mostly it sold anonymous shell companies based in tax havens. Sometimes, as in this case, it went a bit further.

The executive flew to Panama. A car picked him up at the airport and took him to the firm's offices. Nothing about the firm's outward appearance indicated it was a massive global operation with hundreds of employees scattered throughout the world. Its headquarters was in a squat office building on an unassuming mixed residential and commercial side street in Panama City. The firm owned many of the houses on the street, but that was not immediately obvious.

The new client met with one of the firm's top lawyers and explained what he hoped to accomplish. The lawyer asked for and received proper documentation from the client that established his identity, including copies of his passport and bank statements. The scheme the lawyer devised was not particularly complex by the standards of a wealth management industry that is accustomed to mixing and matching multiple legal structures and countries to safeguard the riches of its clients. This transaction was a small one. Of questionable ethics, but by all appearances completely legal.

The strategy began with a Delaware limited liability company. It would be the entity to buy the house. The law firm contacted an outfit in Delaware that procured companies in the state on its behalf. To establish a company based in Delaware required minimal information. Anyone, anywhere in the world, could create one. As long as the company did no business in Delaware, it was not required to file any information about its activities or reveal who really owned it. The company only had to list a "member," but that could be another company or legal entity.

The ability of foreigners to hide their activities through companies in Delaware and other states was the cause of considerable consternation by governments around the world, including the United States. The same year the Mexican businessman set up his company, the U.S. Treasury issued a report in which it expressed "particular concern" about Eurasian organized crime figures using U.S. shell companies to conduct their illegal activities. The worry was exacerbated by the sheer number of anonymous companies the United States was pumping out. In 2015, Delaware alone produced more than 128,000 LLCs.

The executive had a name in mind for his company. He wanted to call it The Cherry Group, but a Delaware company with that name already existed. He settled for Cherry Group USA LLC. The company cost little more than $300 to summon into existence but the law firm charged $1,260 in total to make it active with all the appropriate books and records. The executive paid promptly.

But the Delaware company by itself was not sufficient for the executive's needs. If he owned it directly, it would be clear to the soon-to-be ex-husband and the U.S. government who actually purchased the house. The lawyer suggested a Panamanian foundation that would legally own the Delaware company.

The law firm gave the executive a choice of names for the foundation, Vanora or Eleus. It had already created the foundations two months earlier, before the firm was even aware of this particular client. Two women, who were actually low-paid employees of the firm, ostensibly controlled the foundations. In actuality they served as figureheads for thousands of companies and foundations. Their existence was a shield behind which the actual owner could hide. The executive chose Vanora and paid $3,950 to buy the foundation.

By this time, a lawyer from another firm in the United States had also been brought in to help shepherd the transaction. His retainer was $3,500. The executive made plans to fly to Seattle to buy the house. But his real estate broker informed him of a hitch: He could not purchase the home in the name of Cherry Group USA because the company was owned by the foundation, not him. This was easily remedied. The two low-paid employees of the Panamanian law firm simply signed a document saying that as the controlling members of Vanora Foundation, they authorized him to buy the house. The law firm was willing to provide this service because the executive was paying for the house in cash, so there was no risk the Panamanians would be stuck with the mortgage.

This was only one of thousands of transactions the law firm facilitated in 2015. Its name was Mossack Fonseca. Unbeknownst to the firm, at the same time it was helping someone secretly buy a house in Seattle, its data was being siphoned off and given to reporters. The resulting global journalism investigation, the Panama Papers, afforded an unprecedented look into the operations of an underground economy through which trillions of dollars flow annually.

This river of cash exists in a largely unregulated place known as the secrecy world. It's an alternate reality available only to those who can afford the trip. In the secrecy world, wealth is largely untouchable by government tax authorities and hidden from the view of criminal investigators. Through the secrecy world, family dynasties are nurtured, their fortunes—often acquired illicitly—laundered and passed on to heirs. It's a place where capital always triumphs over labor and the well-to-do are free to ignore the laws that govern their fellow citizens.

Global private wealth has steadily increased in recent years, from $121.8 trillion in 2010 to $166.5 trillion in 2016. An estimated 8 percent of the world's household financial wealth is held in the secrecy world. The wealthy individuals who control this money appear disproportionately reluctant to contribute back to their native countries. One recent study of three Scandinavian nations found that personal tax avoidance among the population at large was about 3 percent. But for those in the top 0.01 percent—each of whom had more than $40 million in assets—a staggering 30 percent stiffed the taxman. Not surprisingly, the ease by which wealth is transferred through the secrecy world has become a major contributor to global inequality.

The effects are everywhere around us. Money hijacked by the secrecy world is no longer available to pay for infrastructure, build schools, or police communities. It has led to the spiraling cost of real estate in major cities such as New York, Los Angeles, Miami, and London. The wealthy eager to park their money in safe assets are bidding up prices by grabbing properties in these places. They often buy through anonymous companies that keep their identities secret from tax collectors at home and abroad. In the last quarter of 2015, the buyers of 58 percent of all property purchases in the United States worth more than $3 million were LLCs. They spent a total of $61.2 billion.

The biggest abusers of the secrecy world are multinational corporations. They base their operations in places that provide minimal taxes and maximum secrecy like Delaware, the Cayman Islands, and Luxembourg. After they were exposed, Mossack Fonseca's principals insisted they were no different from these corporations. They were simply behaving the way accountants, bankers, lawyers, and trust companies operate every day.

They were right.

1

NAZIS AND RADICAL PRIESTS

Against the backdrop of a brilliant blue sky, a disembodied voice, vaguely recognizable from the world of advertising, declares: "All our dreams can come true, if we have the courage to pursue them."

The quotation launches an eighteen-minute corporate video to celebrate the thirty-fifth anniversary of the Panamanian law firm Mossack Fonseca. Filmed in 2012, the video tells the sanitized origin story of a pair of visionaries who built a global empire selling secrecy.

The firm started as two people and grew to almost six hundred employees with forty-two offices around the world. Its Panama headquarters operated twenty-four hours a day, churning out anonymous companies, a product as versatile as it was desirable. Each company was an empty corporate shell waiting to be filled. It could do practically anything: hold a bank account, own a mansion, enter into complex business transactions. Best of all, it was near impossible to discover who owned it.

The video doesn't dwell much on this wonder product. Instead it's a paean to the law firm's ambition and cutting-edge technical achievements.

"One thing is for sure," states the narrator, "we are the leaders when it comes to utilizing technology in order not only to meet but to anticipate our clients' needs."

Jürgen Mossack, the firm's senior partner, is the star—the man, the video's narrator states, "who has been in the forefront of making technology a priority attending to our clients." The video recounts how for Mossack's forty-ninth birthday in 1997 the firm retired its original IBM computer system—"state of the art at the time"—and replaced it with a customized Oracle software database.

Mossack delivers a curt opening statement from a formless brown easy chair as bland as its occupant's demeanor. The senior partner's smooth brow highlights close-set eyes and a tight mouth that relaxes into a frown. What the video does not reveal is a quiet reserve, a protective layer like the anonymity of the companies he sells, which serves as a way to keep his feelings hidden.

"My vision is that our company and its various different divisions become an organization that is really, really, not only well respected but that which is an organization similar to perhaps, Microsoft," Mossack says, before adding, "in a much smaller scale, of course."

The video forecasts a limitless horizon. "I believe this group will endure and we will still be here as a sound and strong firm in thirty, sixty, or ninety more years," says the firm's cofounder, Ramón Fonseca.

The usually gregarious and charming Fonseca appears stilted and uncomfortable while delivering his short statement. Hair streaked gray and slicked back, his skin a colorless office pallor, he peers at the camera as if suspicious of its intentions.

His performance, like the video itself, is slightly off-kilter—a mimic of what big companies do—like a boy wearing his father's suit. In another scene, the IT director, who joined the firm while still a university student in Panama, looks into the camera and remembers the joy of experiencing snow and air travel for the first time.

Yet the accomplishment to which the video testifies is undeniable: Mossack and Fonseca built a factory that flooded the planet with more than 210,000 anonymous companies, trusts, and foundations. Rather than Microsoft, they became the McDonald's of secrecy, selling cheap products that offered limited economic nourishment while clogging the world's financial arteries with tax evasion and some-times even criminality.

THE MOSSACK FONSECA story begins in war-torn Germany, in the ashes of Hitler's Third Reich.

In March 1945, two months before Germany's unconditional sur-render, U.S. forces captured Erhard Mossack, a corporal in the Waffen-SS Skull and Crossbones division. Only twenty-one years old, Erhard had already lived a full life. He joined the Hitler Youth at fifteen and enlisted in the SS three years later. He saw action in Russia and was wounded in Czechoslovakia. While the Waffen-SS had a gruesome reputation for massacres, no evidence has emerged that Erhard took part.

Nine months after his capture, Erhard and seven other POWs stole a truck and escaped from a prison camp near Le Havre, France. They had almost made it to the German border when a French sentry sur-prised them. Erhard and two comrades fled. At Cologne, they sepa-rated, melting into the population. Germany was a battered and contested land, with the Soviets and the Americans actively recruit-ing former Nazis to repurpose them as agents in the coming Cold War. Former SS officers such as Erhard, when not choosing sides, secretly banded together for mutual aid.

These comrades helped Erhard locate a physician skillful at remov-ing the telltale tattoo of his blood group, stenciled under the left arm of most Waffen-SS. The tattoo was a dangerous giveaway to occupi-ers hunting for former Nazis. The small scar the doctor left behind was one of the few successful actions Erhard took in the year after his prison break. Almost everything that followed, as detailed in a report by the Federal Bureau of Investigation stamped "secret," reads like a clandestine comedy of errors.

Erhard found work as a farmhand. That spring, a former Nazi pro-paganda official attempted to enlist him in the German Communist Party. Erhard rejected the offer. Two months later, a man who claimed to be a former high official in the Nazi Party came to the farm. He told the gullible Erhard that he toured Germany as a traveling salesman, all the while quietly building a network of secret agents. He offered the former corporal a choice: join a covert organization for the Soviets or one to restore fascist rule to Europe. Erhard pledged his support for the latter option.

Why did ex-Nazis peddling dreams of future glory find Erhard such a promising mark? A U.S. Army intelligence assessment provides a clue: "[Erhard] has had a very extensive, but superficial political education and is thoroughly indoctrinated with Nazi ideology. A typical [Hitler Youth] leader, he still lives in his world of Nazi slogans and is a striking example of German youth under HITLER."

In late May 1946, Erhard fell in with another former SS officer bent on reconstituting the Reich. Erhard explained he'd already committed to one underground organization. Nonetheless, he accompanied the man home to obtain forged papers. Late that night, U.S. Army intelligence roused Erhard and took him into custody. His new friend had betrayed him.

After first refusing to talk, Erhard told his army interrogator the convoluted tale of his life on the lam, characterizing his apparent willingness to join German underground organizations as a ruse. He was gathering information, he said, to barter with army intelligence to escape punishment for the Le Havre prison break.

The interrogator was skeptical.

"His alleged motive in doing this—to win the good graces of the US Authorities by acting as an informant for [us]—is open to question and may well simply constitute a shrewd attempt to get out of an awkward situation," states the interrogation report.

After his release, Erhard married and scraped together a living as a small-time journalist and author. In March 1948, his first child, Jürgen, was born. Three more children followed over the next decade. Soon after the birth of the last one, Erhard uprooted his family and moved to Panama.

In the early 1960s, there was much to recommend Panama to a former Nazi ideologue. It was a country with a mercantile bent, controlled by a white oligarchy and stratified along class, racial, and geographic lines. Located on the isthmus connecting North and South

America, it never produced much itself. Yet its strategic value as a crossroads, with less than forty miles between the Atlantic Ocean on one coast and the Pacific on the other, gave rise to a merchant class that grew rich off the despoiling of the Americas. Along with the descendants of the Spanish colonial elite, Germans and their institutions also had deep roots in Latin America, making it a beacon for former Nazis following Germany's defeat.

According to a declassified Central Intelligence Agency report, Erhard contacted the agency in 1963, offering to peddle information about Communist Cuba, but the files don't detail what relationship, if any, he maintained with American intelligence. Erhard found employment with Lufthansa and dabbled in different jobs. Jürgen, thirteen years old at the time of the family's arrival, spoke neither Spanish nor English at first. Only able to communicate among themselves, the family stuck together. Self-conscious about the language barrier and naturally shy, Jürgen found it hard to make friends. "It was kind of difficult," he recalls with typical understatement. Still, the Mossacks had an immigrant's zeal to succeed. His seven-year-old brother was first in his class within six months, Jürgen proudly notes.

Jürgen Mossack's upbringing, isolated by language and his father's Nazi past, taught him to keep secrets, instilling a wariness he carried his entire life. People mistook his shyness for callousness, which he didn't discourage, as he discovered that a little intimidation could be useful. "He'd look at you with cold eyes like you were nothing," says a subordinate of their initial encounters. However, the same employee quickly learned that if there was a problem that needed solving, Mossack, rather than his partner, Fonseca, was the one to approach.

At one of the law firm's occasional company retreats, another employee recalls a facilitator conducting a trust-building exercise. Unaware that she had chosen the leader of the firm, the facilitator blindfolded Mossack, who was then led around by a junior employee. Upon the conclusion of the exercise, the facilitator asked Mossack how he had felt. Did he trust his guide? Mossack replied he didn't like the exercise at all. "I don't trust anybody," he reportedly said.

Mossack studied to become a lawyer at a small private Catholic university in Panama. In his practice, he became an expert in maritime law. By the early twentieth century, Panama began to offer itself as a place to register foreign ships. With the Panamanian flag on their vessels, shipowners could avoid taxation and circumvent regulations such as labor protections and boat safety standards that their native countries demanded. The extractive industries (petroleum, minerals, precious metals) were first to discover these benefits, with Standard Oil registering its fleet of tankers in Panama in 1919.

After graduating law school in 1973, Mossack went to work for one of Panama's top firms, Arosemena, Noriega & Castro, helping to establish its London office. After only a couple of years, he quit, frustrated with the firm's refusal to recognize his contributions and pay him accordingly. Mossack returned to Panama in 1977 and gambled on his own ambition, opening a law office as a sole practitioner. "It was a real nail-biting time," Mossack recalls. "I never knew if I would make enough to provide for my family."

In those early days, Ramón Fonseca, a recent law graduate himself, stopped by to wish him luck.

To this day, Fonseca idolizes Mossack for his vision, toughness, and organizational ability. He admits that his older partner, who stands six foot three and sports a perpetually dour expression, looks forbidding, but he insists Mossack is really just "a big teddy bear." Others who know Mossack echo the sentiment, saying that under the gruff exterior beats "a heart of gold."

When they first met, the two men didn't immediately recognize how much they shared in common. Both were outsiders, yet close enough to Panama's small circle of wealth and power to feel the distance that much more acutely. Each felt he was smarter than those he envied. Each harbored a similar drive to make his mark. Years later, Fonseca would explain in an interview that his greatest desire when starting out was not to be a sheep like everyone else. The sheep are not happy, he said, they never travel the world.

Fonseca always dreamed expansively, pursuing overlapping careers as a businessman, fiction writer, and politician. Born in 1952, Ramón Enrique Fonseca Mora, known to childhood friends as "Yike" (pronounced YEE-kay, short for Enrique), is the grandson of Costa Rica's first ambassador to Panama on his father's side and a dentist-turned-insurrectionist on his mother's. He proudly claims a family history of passionate political activism, often directed at the United States, with which Panama has a long and complicated history. It dates back to the country's separation from Colombia in 1903, in a "revolution" instigated by the United States, which was eager to secure favorable terms for building a canal across the isthmus. The resulting treaty turned the new Panamanian republic into a de facto protectorate of the United States, giving America absolute control over the future canal and the right to intervene in Panama's domestic affairs, while paying a pittance for the privilege. This arrangement became a focal point for Panamanian grievances: Non-Americans couldn't travel freely inside the Canal Zone. Local workers received lower pay. Outside the Canal Zone, Americans held top positions in the Panamanian government and English encroached on Spanish as the favored language.

Fonseca's maternal grandfather, Ramón Mora, was among those who rebelled against this second-class status in their own country. Mora had attended Swarthmore College and then studied dentistry at the University of Pennsylvania. His 1921 graduation photo shows a bespectacled youth, head framed by jug ears, thickset lips pursed and unsmiling as he gazes solemnly into the camera. Back in Panama, still in his early twenties, Mora helped found an anticorruption, anti-Yankee organization called Community Action. When not at his dentistry, he also ran an opposition newspaper and built a successful rum distillery.

In 1931, Mora, revolver in hand, was among a small group of young men who staged a successful coup against the Panamanian government of Florencio Arosemena. To keep the peace, the United States made minor concessions. Mora became agricultural and public works secretary. He lasted nine months before Community Action's pick for the presidency, Harmodio Arias Madrid, removed him. The dentist watched from the sidelines as Arias, and then his brother Arnulfo, both of whom had participated in the coup, assumed control. They pursued a populist agenda: Women received the vote, a social security system was created, antiforeigner rhetoric escalated. In 1940, Arnulfo Arias, who openly sympathized with the Nazis and Mussolini, won the presidency. A year after his election, the National Police (under the approving eye of the United States) deposed him.

The pattern repeated itself over the next forty years, with Arias winning three presidential elections, only to see the armed forces depose him each time. After a victory in 1968, he and his Panamañista Party served only eleven days before the National Guard stepped in. The coup gave rise to General Omar Torrijos, a charismatic populist who espoused a "dictatorship with a heart."

At the time of the coup, the sixteen-year-old Fonseca was a budding activist who later entertained thoughts of becoming a priest and "saving the world." There had been a priest in almost every generation of the Mora family going back centuries. Fonseca dropped out of university after a year, attracted by the reformist zeal of the Jesuits. The priests were secretly running workshops where university students could connect with other members of civil society interested in social reform. Through the Jesuits, Fonseca met Father Héctor Gallego, a charismatic thirty-year-old Catholic cleric from Colombia. Gallego practiced liberation theology, which taught that the Church's responsibility to the poor included helping them to improve their economic and political situation.

Gallego worked in an isolated rural parish called Santa Fé in the Panamanian province of Veraguas. Today, it can be reached from Panama City by road in about four and half hours. In the early seventies, it was an all-day bone-jarring journey on a jeep donated by the Americans. The isolated farmers in Santa Fé lived in feudal conditions, toiling for large landowners. Most of the population had no clean water, and the Catholic Church estimated that 50 percent of the children suffered from malnutrition. At Gallego's invitation, Fonseca moved to Santa Fé, where the priest put him to work on several projects, including burying the babies who had died from hunger and poor sanitation.

Relations between the local landowners and the radical priest soured after Gallego helped the farmers form a cooperative. The landowners and the military launched a campaign of harassment, which culminated at about midnight on June 9, 1971, when two soldiers from the local army base kidnapped Gallego.

The story of what happened next took on the power of myth. Soldiers hustled Gallego onto a helicopter. Hovering above the jungle over the island of Coiba, sixteen miles off Panama's Pacific coast, they pushed him out. The gentle priest fell from the sky and vanished into the dense canopy, martyred for helping the poor.

Father Gallego's disappearance had a profound impact on Fonseca. The archbishop of Panama, Mark McGrath, urged him to study for the priesthood as a way to keep Gallego's message alive. Fonseca agreed, then gave up when he realized his appetite for women proved an insurmountable obstacle. Instead, he returned to university to study law but continued his activism. Panamanian students had long led protests against American control of the canal, which American soldiers sometimes met with violence. After the coup, students also demonstrated against the dictatorship. Fonseca joined the protests, becoming a student leader. His grandmother kept a ladder against the garden wall behind her house in case the police came calling and her grandson needed a speedy exit.

Yet even deep into adulthood, Gallego's death haunted Fonseca. "When somebody disappears it's worse than burying him; it's not finished," he says. "I have been looking for him my whole life."

In 1988, Seymour Hersh reported in the *New York Times* that Gallego had survived the fall, at least for a few days. Intercepted communications purportedly revealed the chief of army intelligence, General Manuel Noriega, joking how he'd learned it was better to kill your victim before tossing him from a helicopter. Almost ten years later, a former soldier approached Church authorities with information about a clandestine grave where several people including Gallego had allegedly been dumped. An exhumation recovered a jumbled collection of bones but a DNA test proved inconclusive.

Fonseca, by now a successful lawyer, offered to have a private DNA test performed. While one missing man was positively identified, the priest was not. For years, Fonseca kept a box of mixed human remains under his office desk at Mossack Fonseca, the suspected bones of his former mentor resting by his feet. In 2015, the public ministry took them back. They still await a proper examination and burial.

A year before he died, an ailing Noriega told Gallego's sister another version of what had occurred in 1971. The death-by-helicopter story that had transfixed the world was a lie. Noriega's final account was more prosaic, although no less brutal. After his kidnapping, the priest was driven to Panama City, with the goal of sending him into exile. Along the way, he jumped out of the moving jeep and punctured a lung. His captors then beat him severely. By the time he arrived in Panama City, Gallego was barely alive. After several agonizing days, he died and his body was dumped into a mass grave. Fonseca suspects that the possible remains of his old mentor have yet to receive a new DNA test because those connected to the original crime continue to maintain influence in Panama.

Upon completion of his law degree in 1976, Fonseca left Panama to attend classes at the London School of Economics. The United Nations recruited him before he could complete his studies. They needed Central American lawyers to fill their quota system. In the UN, Fonseca envisioned an opportunity to save the world on a good salary. He accepted a position with the United Nations Conference on Trade and Development in Geneva, but within a few years he had soured on his employer.

"I lost my idealism inside the UN bureaucracy," he says. Fonseca watched in dismay as those around him hijacked the organization's global mission in order to enrich themselves. Bosses turned official business trips into junkets. Salvation came in the guise of a Geneva attorney. In a meeting, she kept staring at him.

"Are you Panamanian?" she asked excitedly during a break. "Tell me you are a Panamanian lawyer!"

The attorney had been searching for someone to create Panamanian companies for her clients. In Fonseca, she found her man.

According to Panama's corporate statutes, only a Panamanian lawyer could register a Panamanian company, but the lawyer could do so on behalf of anybody. Since 1927, Panama had allowed foreigners to buy anonymous companies in the country and did not require the names of the owners or shareholders to be made public. Companies did not need to file annual financial reports. While the companies had to have directors, who were publicly listed, these directors were not required to be the companies' owners. The registration fee was minimal, and a company could be created in as little as a week. The government did not take an interest in what these foreigners did with their Panamanian companies, which paid no tax as long as they made their money outside of Panama. The 1927 law turned the country into one of the world's first "offshore" jurisdictions—a place where foreigners could take advantage of low or no taxes with minimal regulation.

Panama's corporation law was based on American corporate legislation from Delaware, New Jersey, and Arkansas. It was the state of Delaware, in fact, that created the template for most of the tax havens that followed. In the nineteenth century, Delaware was torn between a desire to compete for business with the corporation creation laws of neighboring states, particularly New Jersey, and concern over the corruption that might follow. Corporations were already seen in America as a source of financial instability and unchecked power, because they allowed individuals to engage in speculation and escape accountability for their misdeeds.

At first, Delaware permitted only certain local industries, such as fruit production, to create companies, and their monetary size was capped. By 1875, company formation in Delaware was limited to an act of the state legislature or approval by a judge who determined whether the entity was lawful and would not harm the community. This attempt to tamp down on corruption instead drove incorporation practices in a different direction. A cabal of lobbyists formed. For a fee, they guaranteed they could round up enough votes in the Delaware legislature for clients who wanted to create a new company. In 1899, Delaware passed a General Corporation Law patterned on New Jersey's but offering a lower tax rate to entice businesses to incorporate there. Gone were the state legislature and the judges. The new law also protected Delaware-based companies from liability and empowered them to conduct business in any state or place in the world. They only needed to avoid business activity in Delaware itself.

The Geneva attorney was Fonseca's doorway into the secrecy world, acting as his sponsor and making introductions. She called the companies "chickens." The business was simple—hatch the chickens in Panama and collect the annual fee as the registered agent.

Fonseca says that while employed by the UN, he referred the work to a cousin in Panama, who agreed to give the companies back to Fonseca if he returned home.

The final blow to Fonseca's career at the United Nations came from a seemingly innocuous offer. He was notified that he had become eligible for burial in a section of a Geneva cemetery reserved for the UN. As a perk to employees, the UN helped defray the costs. Fonseca suddenly saw his whole life play out as a bureaucrat, right up until the moment they shoveled the dirt over his casket.

In 1982, after six years at the UN, he quit and moved back to Panama to open his own law practice, retrieving from his cousin the companies created during his UN years. Fonseca created a Panamanian holding company, Michiana International, to handle the registration business. His new clientele included one of the richest men in the world: Adnan Khashoggi, the Saudi billionaire arms dealer. (The Geneva attorney had helped Fonseca land Khashoggi as a client.)

Khashoggi embraced the benefits of offshore tax havens, particularly as places to register his yachts, floating pleasure palaces where he entertained friends and influenced business prospects. Fonseca's Michiana International registered at least three of Khashoggi's boats, including his most opulent creation, the *Nabila*.

Named after Khashoggi's daughter, the *Nabila* cost around $85 million (roughly $250 million in today's dollars) to build and outfit. The 292-foot yacht could travel eighty-five hundred miles without refueling and store three months of food for one hundred people. It had a hair salon, a surgery, and a patisserie on board. Tucked away among the five levels and one hundred rooms were quarters for a crew of fifty-two. Movie stars, musicians, and the megawealthy danced in its disco. Bathrooms were hewn from single pieces of onyx. Khashoggi's personal suite had a tortoiseshell ceiling and featured a ten-foot-wide bed, behind which lay a secret passageway for paramours. Portly, short, and balding, Khashoggi kept a bevy of high-end prostitutes on call. The yacht was a self-contained mobile world, ideal for a hyper-controlling, reality-bending, glam-loving billionaire. When creditors repossessed the *Nabila* in 1988, Donald Trump bought it.

All that sizzle was in service of the sale. Khashoggi acted as a middleman for arms deals and commodities trades, taking a healthy commission on each transaction. Inside the *Nabila*'s staterooms, Middle Eastern royalty, Fortune 500 company executives, Swiss bankers, and government functionaries wheeled and dealed. When necessary, the yacht motored into international waters to complete contracts free of government constraint such as tax obligations.

A few years after Fonseca returned to Panama, a transaction involving another Khashoggi yacht brought Ramón Fonseca and Jürgen Mossack together as lawyers for the first time. As Fonseca tells it, Khashoggi had sold a yacht to a sheikh who was Mossack's client. As part of the deal, the sheikh wanted a helipad on the boat. The two lawyers worked out the details. In the process, they established a rapport.

Khashoggi had an unsavory reputation, but neither Panamanian lawyer appeared to show any hesitation in working with him. In the mid-1970s, U.S. congressional hearings had exposed Khashoggi's involvement in a massive multicountry corporate bribery scheme orchestrated by the defense contractor Northrop, which had poured tens of millions of dollars into the bank accounts of foreign officials to win contracts. Northrop had paid Khashoggi $106 million as a consultant between 1970 and 1975. The hearings showed that at least $450,000 of that found its way into bribes for two Saudi generals.

In Panama, moral flexibility was a professional selling point. The country's lawyers and bankers had made Panama a destination for the criminal class. Torrijos's regime had grown increasingly corrupt, transforming the country into an offshore banking hub. By law, Panamanian banks could not release any information about account holders, even to the government. This blanket of company and bank secrecy attracted the unscrupulous. Then in 1981, in what many believe was a political assassination, Torrijos perished when his airplane crashed in western Panama. With him went the stability of the country.

Manuel Noriega, who had been head of intelligence for Torrijos, quickly maneuvered his way into power. Noriega accelerated the turn toward corruption, transforming Panama into a one-stop financial service provider for the Colombian drug cartels. Billions of dollars from cocaine shipments to the United States and Europe were stashed and laundered through Panama City. International condemnation followed.

Fonseca joined a civil society movement full of Rotarians and Lions Club members opposed to Noriega. He and Mossack began to discuss combining their law offices to protect themselves from pressure that might come from the dictator. The merger also made sense from a business perspective. They conducted similar practices. Combined, they had about five thousand companies under registration. This provided a steady income through annual fees.

"It was more ideal to have a single, stronger firm to be able to resist any political difficulties," says Mossack, "and a single practitioner could never aspire to have big clients, unless you were a firm."

In July 1986, Mossack and Fonseca held a cocktail soiree at the Union Club in Panama City as the firm's coming-out party. Long a watering hole of the Panamanian oligarchy, Fonseca was a member of the club because of his ambassador grandfather. "We were connected to the elite but without the money," he says, laughing at the memory.

The thirty-fifth-anniversary video features a photo of the two men at the party, dressed in suits, drinks raised in salutes to each other. Fonseca beams. Even Mossack is smiling into the camera as they toast to the future.

2

TROPICAL PARADISES

The ferry from Saint Thomas passes verdant islands, skimming over turquoise waters where pirates plied their trade. After about an hour, it crosses Sir Francis Drake Channel and reaches Road Town on the island of Tortola. Ramón Fonseca didn't know what awaited him when he took the ride in the autumn of 1986.

Shortly after joining forces, Mossack and Fonseca began to look for a new base for their companies. Panama was in turmoil. General strikes roiled the country, and the U.S. intelligence services publicly denounced Noriega's cooperation with drug cartels. It seemed likely the government would default on its International Monetary Fund and World Bank loans, isolating Panama internationally. The unrest tainted the new firm's main product, Panamanian companies.

"You have CNN showing demonstrations in the streets, the camera focusing on burning tires, it was not good for business," recalls Mossack.

The two lawyers studied a map of the world looking for a jurisdiction in which to launch their enterprise. They needed a place that offered company incorporations, with low or no taxes on foreign holdings, government-enforced secrecy, a stable political system, and minimal competition from other providers. It had to be close to

Panama for ease of travel and efficient enough to produce tens of thousands of companies.

In other words, they needed a tax haven. Power to create a corporation stems from the government. Without the complicity of a tax haven, firms like Mossack Fonseca cannot exist. The best tax havens from the perspective of offshore providers have similar qualities: They feature a business-friendly political culture, functioning legal systems, and limited economic competition. The offshore industry provides much-needed revenue for the government through the assessment of registration and other fees related to company incorporations. In exchange, the industry receives state support and protection.

As usual, Delaware offered the model. The state is a staunch defender of its revenue from company incorporations, which accounts for a sizable proportion of its budget. While actual industry practitioners in Delaware are few, they have an outsize control over the political process, writing the legislation that governs the industry and protecting its prerogatives in Congress.

Fonseca was fighting off a bad cold as his boat approached Tortola, too sick to contemplate those who had preceded him. Christopher Columbus stumbled upon the archipelago in 1493, naming the islands "Saint Ursula and her 11,000 Virgins," later abridged to the Virgin Islands. According to Catholic legend, Saint Ursula was a princess who, with her virginal handmaidens, set out on a pilgrimage to the Hun-besieged town of Cologne. They were not welcome. The Huns beheaded the virgins, and their leader killed Ursula with a bow and arrow.

At twenty-one square miles, Tortola is the largest and most populated of the more than forty volcanic outcroppings the English acquired in 1662, known today as the British Virgin Islands, and, in financial circles, the BVI. Beyond importing slaves and planting crops for export, the British did little to develop this territorial backwater on the outer edges of the empire. Demands for independence began in 1949 and culminated almost twenty years later with a constitution establishing a two-tiered government. Locals, called "Belongers," elect a legislative council, who in turn select a chief minister. The Belongers oversee domestic laws, keep the peace, and raise revenue.

The British Crown appoints a governor to monitor affairs and handle foreign policy. Queen Elizabeth's name graces bridges and parks, and her image is hung in schools and government buildings. When the Queen visited in 1966, she was chauffeured around in a Lincoln convertible that for years afterward was on display at the Smuggler's Cove Beach Bar.

The BVI's origins as a tax haven date to the mid-1970s, when Paul Butler, a Wall Street tax attorney, contacted Harney Westwood & Riegels, then the only practicing law office in the territory. Butler was an expert on double tax treaties, which are designed to avoid taxing the same income in multiple jurisdictions. He creatively employed one such treaty between the United States and the Netherlands Antilles on behalf of his clients. Under the double tax treaty, the United States did not tax companies based in the Antilles. In turn, the Antilles did not tax foreign investments. U.S. companies with subsidiaries in the Antilles could thus avoid being taxed by either government. Still, Butler found the Dutch language barrier formidable.

The BVI enjoyed a similar arrangement with the United States. As a member of the United Kingdom, it fell under a 1945 double tax treaty created to boost the American and British postwar economies. The BVI also had a functioning government and a literate population. It operated under common law appealable all the way to the Privy Council in London. And the islanders spoke English.

With a phone call, Butler discovered the locals were all too happy to help his clients take advantage of the treaty to avoid taxes in their homelands. Tax *avoidance* is what a government authority sanctions as appropriate, usually after a corporation, lawyer, or accountant pushes the boundaries of what's acceptable. Tax *evasion* occurs when the activity violates the law, either blatantly or after a ruling by a court or governmental entity. The difference between tax avoidance and tax evasion, it has been said, "is the thickness of a prison wall."

A cottage industry began. Butler's biggest customer was Citicorp. In 1978, he created Citicorp Overseas Finance Corporation, based in the BVI. The subsidiary raised money in Europe and then lent it tax-free to Citicorp in the United States. Butler also established a BVI corporation for two wealthy Saudis so they could escape paying hefty taxes on the dividends from hundreds of millions of dollars of stock in U.S. companies.

But Butler's schemes proved too successful. U.S. Treasury officials objected to the revenue loss. Despite Butler's pleas as the island's unpaid lobbyist in Washington, the United States rescinded the tax treaty in 1982.

By then, the BVI was addicted to the income. There was little else available. Limited rainfall restricted agriculture on the islands. Many Belongers commuted to Saint Thomas, in the U.S. Virgin Islands, for work. A fledgling tourist trade yielded a bit more than $42 million in 1985, around 50 percent of the gross domestic product that year. The only other significant economic activity came from drug trafficking, which could not be taxed. Butler's innovative schemes had brought a small measure of prosperity. But now, with one stroke of the pen, the United States had eliminated the equivalent of the country's education budget.

"Something had to be done to replenish the coffers," said Lewis Hunte, attorney general of the BVI at the time.

Butler suggested a new route. Together with Hunte and the Harneys lawyers—subsequently known as the "Gang of Five"—he crafted legislation to permit the BVI to mint "international business companies" as the Panamanians did.

Mindful of its competition, the BVI added improvements to the Delaware template. As with Delaware, the BVI did not collect information on who owned the companies. Its public registry featured the company name and the name of the firm that registered it. The BVI company had to issue shares and have at least one company director, as in Panama. However, unlike Panama, there was no public registry of directors, making the identity of the company owners even more secret. And nonlawyers could create companies as long as they had a General Trust License from the BVI.

The BVI law passed in 1984. The Gang of Five had built the perfect company formation machine. It was primed and ready to pump out companies to nourish trade and connect communities throughout the world. But when they flipped the switch, nothing much happened.

No flood of company incorporations followed. The law went largely unused, until Ramón Fonseca arrived in Road Town two years later.

As he stepped onto Tortola, Fonseca saw a sparsely developed village. Only one taxi was parked at the ferry dock. There were no traffic lights, Fonseca remembers, instead a roundabout with a tractor tire in the middle.

Fonseca's prospecting trip had come at the suggestion of the Trident Trust Company, an American financial firm based in Saint Thomas. Trident suggested that Fonseca contact Richard Peters, a member of the Gang of Five, to learn more about the BVI's new company creation law. Fonseca instructed the taxi driver to take him to the center of town. It was a short trip. The taxi deposited him on a narrow two-way street. Chickens and goats wandered the cobblestones. Rough wooden dwellings lined the roadway.

In 1986, THERE were slightly more than twelve thousand people in all of the British Virgin Islands—and around nine thousand of them on Tortola. The bonds of kinship on a small island are iron-strong. In the BVI, the wise never speak ill of their neighbors, lest it get back to them. Road Town was a close-knit community that viewed outsiders with suspicion, and so Fonseca needed a way to win the trust of the Belongers. Once they experienced the benefits of working with Mossack Fonseca, their loyalty would follow.

Tax havens are remarkably cohesive communities. The financial services industry dominates. Local elites follow the cash, joining the industry or servicing it in other ways. Business interests and the political establishment become intertwined. Once the industry is established, the social controls that already exist in small, isolated communities activate on behalf of the industry. Locals accept a certain degree of corruption in the interest of keeping the money flowing. Those who resist are cowed into silence, ostracized, and—if they persist—sometimes imprisoned or exiled.

The BVI forms part of a system of British tax havens. These vestiges of the British Empire include the BVI, the Cayman Islands,

Bermuda, the Channel Islands, and Turks and Caicos. Farther afield but part of the same tax haven family are former English possessions like the Bahamas, Belize, Cyprus, Singapore, and the Seychelles.

Among these jurisdictions, one of the oldest and most venerable is Jersey, an island off the coast of Normandy in the English Channel, less than an hour's plane ride from London. Jürgen Mossack remembers visiting the island for conferences to learn about the offshore industry during his residence in the UK in the 1970s. Jersey operates as an extension of the City of London's financial district.

John Christensen was an economic adviser to Jersey in the early 1990s. Raised in a local upper-crust family, he cooperated with a *Wall Street Journal* exposé of a banking scandal that implicated the island's most powerful politician. Parliamentary committees opened investigations into Christensen's department, he believes, to drown him in work and destroy his reputation. Friends and family abandoned him. An older brother, who worked in a Jersey trust company, refused to speak with him for nearly twenty years.

The saying on Jersey, Christensen recalls, was, "If you don't like it here, there's a boat in the morning."

FONSECA FOUND RICHARD Peters, the lawyer Trident recommended, in his office on Tortola's main street. Peters directed him to Cyril B. Romney, the BVI's chief minister, to inquire about a business license to create companies. Romney had sponsored the 1984 company incorporation law, and, after listening to Fonseca, he promised to review the matter and get back to him.

After his meeting with Romney, Fonseca encountered Keith Flax, a local jeweler who was also speaker of the legislative council and a close friend of both Romney and Peters. It didn't take long for the Panamanian and the Belonger to recognize they shared a special bond. Both were members of the ancient order of Freemasons. Dating to the Industrial Revolution in England, Freemasonry appropriated the symbols of craft guilds like the stonemasons to forge a fraternal order kept alive through esoteric rituals and Masonic lodges.

Fonseca had tapped into an underground network—a secret society within a secret society—that exists in tax havens, particularly the British ones. Knowledge of Freemasonry, its signs, symbols, and rites, often serves as a doorway into closed cultures. It provides instant solidarity and an opportunity for government and business interests to network privately. John Christensen says he was approached multiple times on Jersey to join one lodge or another. He always declined the offer. Holding no particular animus toward Freemasonry or the elite hobnobbing in the lodges, Christensen nonetheless viewed it all as slightly creepy.

Flax invited Fonseca to a meeting at the Saint Ursula Masonic Lodge. Fonseca remembers traveling deep into the jungle to get there. At last they arrived at a clearing where he encountered one of the most beautiful Masonic temples he had ever seen. As he watched the gathering, Fonseca's cold asserted itself. He began to cough uncontrollably. Mortified, he tried to stifle the hacking. Seemingly out of nowhere, Cyril Romney appeared by his side. He patted Fonseca on the back. "I know you're nervous," the chief minister said. "Don't worry, you're getting the license."

The firm soon hired Keith Flax's wife, Rosemarie, to run the Tortola office. She had experience working for a trust company. More important, she was well connected among her fellow Belongers. When Keith Flax built a three-story building, he rented the top floor to Mossack Fonseca, which was becoming known as "Mossfon," for short. Flax named the sky blue building "aKaRa," a mash-up of the couple's first initials and those of their three daughters.

In the beginning, Mossfon sold companies in the BVI for as little as $750. The business was simple: The person buying the company was usually an intermediary—a lawyer, accountant, or banker—who acted on behalf of the actual customer, known as the "ultimate beneficial owner." Sometimes the buyer wanted to purchase a preexisting company. An older vintage company conferred respectability, making it look as if it had a history. Mossfon kept a stock of these "shelf companies" available for an additional fee.

The beneficial owner now had decisions to make. Who would be the shareholder of the company? As an added layer of secrecy, many jurisdictions, including Panama and the BVI, allowed companies to issue "bearer shares." These share certificates were pieces of paper and whoever physically possessed them owned the company. Bearer shares could be used to transfer assets completely anonymously. They were favorite tools of money launderers and one of Mossfon's more popular offerings.

Finally, the owner needed to choose directors. For an extra $100, Mossfon provided another layer of secrecy by arranging for the services of a company director. These stand-ins, known in the trade as "nominees," appeared on paper as corporate officers who controlled the company. In reality, they served only to hide the identity of the beneficial owner, who often covertly controlled the company through a secret power-of-attorney agreement. Nominee directors are a corporate compliance charade commonly practiced throughout the offshore industry.

The nominee directors created new opportunities for Mossfon to profit. When the company wanted to perform an act—open a bank account, move money, sign a contract, make a purchase—the nominee directors had to hold a meeting (usually only on paper) and provide their signatures to make it official. Every signature was another $45 in the Mossfon coffers.

In the early days, Mossack and Fonseca, members of their small staff, and even their relatives served as nominee directors for the companies they registered. Before the partners quit acting as nominees themselves, they served as directors for thousands of companies. Later, as the Mossfon company-creation factory cranked up, the firm required scores of nominees. While the service was lucrative for the firm, Mossfon paid the employees who performed it poorly. Mossfon's most prolific directors were corporate officers for tens of thousands of companies. Some even worked for multiple registered agents. Adelina Mercedes Chavarria de Estribi was a director of over one hundred Mossfon companies and more than twenty-seven thousand Panamanian registered companies overall.

As part of their job, the nominees signed hundreds of blank forms. These blanks became legal corporate documents and resolutions. Mossfon provided the signed blanks to their offices around the world. The signatures were in different places on the empty page, depending on what the document would ultimately become—for example, on the bottom for a share certificate or in the middle to resign from a company. It was of no consequence that the nominees never saw the filled-in documents to which their signatures were affixed. They exercised no real authority over the company. For the fiction of an active company officer to work as a business concept, it had to be efficient— hence the signed blanks.

"The signed blank documents allow [clients] to open bank accounts and carry out business transactions without the need to wait one or two weeks for documents to arrive," Fonseca explained to a Mossfon employee in Europe. "All our competitors do the same thing in Geneva and therefore, we are obliged to do so."

Once Mossfon created the company, it went into a file, forgotten, until a year passed and it was time to send an invoice to renew the registration. In 1985, the annual reregistration fee was $150.

There were any number of ways an offshore company could be used legally, even to avoid taxes. Corporations had been doing it for generations. Companies based in a tax haven allowed for the efficient operation of a business that crossed multiple jurisdictions, reducing levies and liabilities. Individuals wanted the same service for the same reasons. Anonymous companies also shield assets, allowing a businessman or politician to hide a mistress and minimize unwelcome attention from covetous relatives and potential kidnappers. From the perspective of Mossack and Fonseca, the service they offered was one of selling privacy. BVI companies also proved irresistible to the criminal class. An anonymous company was the perfect vehicle to move or conceal the proceeds of illegal activity.

Within a year of Mossfon's arrival in the BVI, another Panamanian law firm, Morgan and Morgan, set up shop. More firms followed. Rising living standards in the developing world began to expand the market for offshore companies. What was once the domain of the superrich became accessible to the merely wealthy. Company incorporations catering to a new global elite took off, launching a boom period for the BVI.

In Mossfon's early years, the Caribbean was awash in drug money. It's impossible to quantify the impact of money laundering from drug trafficking on Mossfon's business, although it was likely significant. The drug trade added an anything-goes flavor to Tortola. Martin Kenney, a Canadian lawyer and fraud investigator, remembers visiting the island during this period because he needed information from one of the dozens of trust companies working out of the BVI. The firm that held the information was run by a bartender, who operated his trust company from a fax machine behind the bar. Busy serving up rum punches, the bartender gestured to the stack of papers piled next to the fax machine and invited Kenney to find the documents himself.

"It was like the three monkeys back then," says Kenney of offshore client vetting. "See nothing. Hear nothing. Say nothing."

ANONYMOUS COMPANIES SOON surpassed the more traditional secrecy vehicle, the trust. The concept of the trust dates to feudal England. Knights setting out for the Crusades entrusted their estates to stewards to safeguard them while they were spilling blood in foreign lands. The steward, usually an adult male relative or friend, took custody of the assets. It was a tidy mechanism for landholders to escape taxes and inheritance complications. At a time when wills had a shaky legal foundation, trusts, with after-death directives, allowed a wealthy man to pass assets to a mistress or a favored child. Prohibitions against leaving property to women could be circumvented. Trusts ensured the family business went to an intelligent daughter rather than an idiot son.

A legal deed spelled out the relationship between the steward, called the trustee, and the person relinquishing the assets, known as the "settlor." Governments did not register or approve the trustee relationship. It was a private contract, an inexpensive way to create an impenetrable wall of secrecy. By entrusting the assets to a trustee, one could have the benefits of ownership without the duties and liabilities. Officially, the assets of the trust no longer belonged to the settlor but to the trustee. Taxes were levied where the trust was based, which helped British-formed tax havens flourish. Trust laws guaranteed stiff penalties for violations of confidentiality. In Panama, anyone violating trust secrecy could be sanctioned with a $50,000 fine or up to six months in prison.

However, for the sales force at Mossfon, trusts had a major flaw: Their customers did not trust the trustee. In Britain and America, well-placed trustee firms went back generations. When it came to safeguarding assets, they had sterling reputations. Furthermore, trust equity law was well established; courts recognized and understood trusts. These institutional protections did not exist in emerging markets such as Latin America, China, and Eastern Europe—the very places where Mossfon sought to grow.

In those regions, corruption and impunity drove people to Mossfon in search of anonymous companies. Far from expecting their own governments and legal systems to safeguard their wealth, they feared government functionaries might steal their money—if the clients weren't doing the thieving themselves. Lack of confidence in their own institutions extended to foreign ones, and with some justification. In Jersey and other tax havens, courts had poked holes in the validity of asset transfers, calling certain trust arrangements a "sham." Many of Mossfon's beneficial owners had gone to considerable trouble to spirit money away from their home countries. The idea of turning their hard-won cash over to a third party to place in an unregistered financial structure, protected only by a legal system in which they had little faith, was naturally unappealing.

IN 1989, MOSSFON added another tax haven to its menu, the Bahamas, whose proximity to the United States had long made it a destination for Americans trying to escape taxes. President Franklin Roosevelt sent a letter to Congress in 1937, complaining that Americans were using the Bahamas, Panama, and Newfoundland to avoid paying taxes. Citizens had formed sixty-four offshore companies in the Bahamas to escape their civic responsibilities, the president complained. "When our legitimate revenues are attacked, the whole structure of our Government is attacked," he wrote. " 'Clever little schemes' are not admirable when they undermine the foundations of society."

The Mafia used the Bahamas as a staging area for bootlegging during Prohibition. The first premier of the Bahamas, Sir Roland Symonette, grew rich smuggling whiskey. After Fidel Castro shut down the Mob's outpost in Cuba in 1959, Mafia strategist Meyer Lansky looked to the islands. He found a ready partner in Symonette, one of a group of local elites known as the Bay Street Boys, because they met at a downtown club on Bay and Charlotte Streets in Nassau. Together they concocted a system of government-backed offshore banking and company formation that laundered money and helped multinationals and individuals evade taxes.

Mossfon was already entering a crowded market in the Bahamas. By 1990, according to the Bahamas public registry, there were more than one hundred agents who were registering companies there. "This seems like an easy business but it is very difficult," says Jürgen Mossack. "The competition is always there." Low margins and intense competition required constant improvement to survive. In the offshore business, this primarily meant easier and faster company incorporations.

As more incorporators crowded into the BVI and the Bahamas, Mossfon looked to increase its business elsewhere. The United States pointed the way. As a specialist in maritime law, Mossack was familiar with the Liberian ship registry. Since the 1950s, Liberia had registered ships under its own flag but the public registry was never based in Africa. Rather, the registry resided in a suite of offices in New York City. It was created by a former U.S. secretary of state in conjunction with corporate interests like Shell Oil. The Liberians readily assented in return for a cut of the proceeds.

Mossack thought, if the Americans could have a monopoly by running their own public registry, why couldn't Mossfon?

The partners sent the recently widowed manager of their Jersey office, an American named Nancy Broadhurst, to the South Pacific. Her instructions were to find a friendly country that would allow itself to be used as an exclusive jurisdiction for Mossfon companies.

"She disappeared for a week, literally disappeared in Papua New Guinea," remembers Fonseca. "We were really worried. We thought maybe she had been eaten by cannibals or something."

Broadhurst had gone prospecting at an offshore conference in

Papua New Guinea. One day at the conference she was sitting at the hotel bar and struck up a conversation with a neighbor on the stool beside her. She told him she'd been sent out by the bosses in Panama to find a magical land to serve as a new location for offshore companies. Her new friend listened with interest. We can do that, he told her. Her bar mate, Frank Lui, was the premier of the island nation of Niue.

A sparsely populated coral outcrop situated in the middle of nowhere, Niue is 1,500 miles northeast of New Zealand. It's currently about 103 square miles in size, but rising sea levels threaten to shrink its landmass. Europeans first laid eyes on the place in 1774, when the locals repeatedly prevented Captain James Cook from landing there, prompting him to dub it "Savage Island." New Zealand annexed it in 1901 but approved self-government for Niue under an association agreement in 1974. As New Zealand's ward, Niue received a stipend, but the money wasn't enough to make ends meet, according to Mossack. When Broadhurst met Lui, the island's leaders were already investigating converting to a tax haven to create additional income for its approximately five hundred inhabitants.

Broadhurst traveled to Panama and joined a group of Mossfon lawyers to draft an incorporation law for Niue. They largely copied the BVI law—which had itself been copied from Delaware—and customized it for Niue, adding some innovations of their own. For example, the law allowed company names in Chinese characters and the Russian Cyrillic alphabet, which the BVI did not. The Niue International Business Company Act passed in 1994. Later that year, the firm took Frank Lui to Hong Kong as part of a road show to sell the jurisdiction to the Chinese. They advertised the island as the "Jewel in the Crown of the South Seas."

With the registry located in Mossfon's offices, the firm could crank out a Niue company in under an hour, at whatever price the firm determined. Mossfon's offices around the world had the blank documents and the official seals, pre-signed by the Niue deputy registrar, who happened to be a Mossfon employee. All they had to do was check with Panama to ensure the name was available, get the International Business Company number, pull up the correct template, and print.

"We could control the process, control the quality and the speed," said Mossack.

All that control did not prevent Mossfon's Niue companies from being used by criminals. James Ibori, the governor of Nigeria's oil-rich Delta State, opened a Niue company called Stanhope Investments while still holding office, using it to buy expensive properties in London. In 2012, prosecutors in the UK convicted Ibori of fraud and corruption, sentencing him to thirteen years in prison. Gary Porritt employed his Niue company, Gold Star, to make it appear as if an outside company was buying shares in his South African investment company, to artificially prop up its value, according to prosecutors. In Argentina, the father and son Hugo and Mariano Jinkis operated a network of offshore companies that U.S. prosecutors alleged were used to pay bribes in exchange for multimillion-dollar television contracts to broadcast soccer matches. The Mossfon files show that one of these companies, Cross Trading, based in Niue, purchased the rights for Ecuadorian soccer matches for $111,000 and then quickly flipped them to the Ecuadorian broadcaster Teleamazonas for $311,170.

Niue never equaled the success of the BVI. Despite the ease of incorporation, the island was always a tough sell to many potential customers. "If you think people didn't know where the BVI was, try explaining to them where this empty spot in the middle of the Pacific Ocean was," said Mossack.

By 1994, THE BVI hosted 136,112 companies. This represented 47.7 percent of the total share of offshore company formation worldwide. Even though there were thirty-nine firms registering companies in the BVI, Mossfon accounted for more than 10 percent of all the companies created.

Inconspicuous-looking from the outside, the Akara Building served as the principal business address for economic activities that spanned the globe, a temple of financial secrecy. Road Town grew up around it. The offshore business accounted for almost half of the BVI government's revenue, making it one of the most prosperous small island nations in the developing world. Every Belonger who wanted a job had one. Financial service professionals from countries throughout the world came to Road Town to sell companies and offshore structures. The BVI's population had more than doubled from where it was when Fonseca first arrived.

Success carried a cost. Privately, locals talk wistfully of a paradise lost, a culture changed forever. They describe the old BVI as unspoiled, a place of leisurely rhythms, friendly neighbors, Saturday open-air markets, and pristine beaches. The financial service workers brought traffic, bustle, high prices. Today, the new BVI is a place where the affluent pay others to stand in the long lines at banks and government offices. Criticizing the financial services industry is viewed as disloyal. People drop their voices and look around before expressing disapproval.

The old Saint Ursula Masonic Lodge is gone, too. Ramón Fonseca's memory of that visit is gauzy with nostalgia. In reality, the lodge was only about half a mile from the main road. While it may have been surrounded by the bush when he arrived, today it's off a street filled with disheveled houses and small businesses. A new, larger Saint Ursula's temple has replaced the quaint wooden building that once enchanted Fonseca. Behind the new lodge rises a modern office building. Among its tenants are company formation agents.

3

NAME OF THE GAME

With the additions of the BVI, the Bahamas, and Niue, Mossfon had tax-haven homes for its companies. What it needed next was a way to get its product into the hands of more customers—lots more customers. Taking a page from McDonald's, Mossack and Fonseca decided the answer was to franchise. They would identify big sellers and turn them into Mossfon distributors. In return for exclusive rights to handle Mossfon's products in their area, the franchisee received the companies at a slight discount. Jürgen Mossack reasoned that this could expand their market with a limited outlay of resources from the firm.

Beyond sales, there was another benefit to this network of intermediaries. Selling through middlemen added a layer between Mossfon and the product's end user, the beneficial owner of the company. Mossfon depended on the middlemen to ensure that the companies were used legally. If the beneficial owner of the company turned out to be a crook, Mossfon could claim that the franchisee or the lawyer, accountant, or banker failed to vet the buyer properly. The name of the game was avoiding blame. In practice, though, off-loading responsibility to middlemen proved tricky. Culpability is remarkably sticky, and vile deeds are hard to keep buried. It did not help that Mossfon willingly ventured into direct involvement with questionable activities when the partners thought the financial reward outweighed the risk.

In 1993, Ramón Fonseca came to New York looking for a company formation agent to develop the U.S. market. He found John Gordon. Earnestly intelligent but socially awkward, Gordon had graduated from the State University of New York at Albany in 1981, with a degree in psychology. He took a job as a process server, but after two years of earning minimum wage, Gordon branched out into company formations, which mostly meant filing incorporation papers with the state government in Albany for lawyers in New York City.

Mossfon's courtship of Gordon included a weekend at Jürgen Mossack's beach house on the lush island of Contadora. Mossack flew Gordon there from Panama City in his Cessna. The two men fished off Mossack's yacht. After a twenty-minute struggle, the gangly Gordon, with an assist from Mossack, landed a thirty-four-inch amberjack. Next, Gordon traveled to the BVI, happy to escape the Albany winter. He stayed in Mossfon's apartment in Road Town. Staff took him snorkeling off Norman Island, the inspiration for Robert Louis Stevenson's *Treasure Island*. The VIP treatment worked. In March 1994, Mossfon announced that Gordon's company, USA Corporate Services, would be the firm's exclusive franchisee for the United States.

For Gordon, the partnership with Mossfon seemed like a good way to break into the international incorporation market. It turned out to be tougher than he imagined. His new business partners became impatient at the slow pace of sales. At first Fonseca was charming, but lurking under the surface was a temper when he didn't get his way. Gordon explained that Americans who wanted companies for legitimate purposes could get them in Delaware. Law-abiding Americans didn't need Mossfon. USA Corporate Services took out advertisements in the *Economist* magazine and hawked its financial products at offshore conferences, but it was a challenge to make the arrangement profitable. Increasingly, Gordon relied on foreign clients.

In early 1997, Ian Tuppen and Subhash Singh approached Gordon with a proposal to open Mossfon companies in the Bahamas, held through bearer shares. After they became customers, Gordon referred them to the Royal Bank of Scotland and assumed the bank had properly vetted its clients. In fact, it appears no one looked too closely at the business plan, which relied on pirating Microsoft Office software. Less than two years later, the British press would describe the scheme as one of the largest counterfeit software cases in the country's history. A subsequent court case revealed the two had raked in as much as £2.5 million (about $6 million today) off the counterfeiting. The men used the money to fund a lavish lifestyle. Tuppen lived in a mansion in Hampshire. Singh drove a yellow Porsche.

Tuppen and Singh had a UK-based company called Backslash Distributors, but they wanted to run their operation out of a tax haven. Through Gordon and Mossfon, the two men created a company called Bahamas Software Agency in March 1997. Mossfon provided nominees to serve as Bahamas Software's corporate officers. When anyone on the outside looked for the directors, they would see only Mossfon nominees; Tuppen and Singh remained hidden. Secretly, power of attorney over the company was given to Singh. The Royal Bank of Scotland promptly opened a bank account for the company.

Two months later, Tuppen and Singh arranged for Bahamas Software to buy Backslash for £120,000, essentially selling the company to themselves. Mossfon was an integral part of the deal, since the nominee directors serving as the company's officers had to sign off and agree to release the funds. Mossfon charged only a few hundred dollars for the signatures. As part of the transaction, Tuppen and Singh sent the company books and records for Backslash Distributors to the Mossfon office in the Bahamas for safekeeping.

Three months after Tuppen and Singh created Bahamas Software, the company faxed a handwritten letter to Mossfon. It asked the firm to type the document on Bahamas Software company letterhead, have the Mossfon directors sign it, and then send it to Backslash Distributors. From the outside, it was impossible to know that the men were actually sending a letter to themselves. The heading read: "RE: PROBLEMS WITH SOURCE OF BONA FIDE PRODUCT." The letter began, "Having spent some considerable time perusing the books and records for which we acknowledge receipt, and having also considered problems with the quality of product which we have, for some time, been sourcing for you, which you have brought to our attention, it is with regret that we hereby direct the following actions." Bahamas Software then instructed Tuppen and Singh to destroy their stock of software, cease any trading, and send all records to the Bahamas.

When Mossfon received the handwritten letter for its directors to sign, the firm should have known it was being asked to do something improper. From the outside, anyone investigating Backslash Distributors would think its new owner, Bahamas Software, was disassociating itself from past problems. In reality, it was a ploy designed to evade responsibility for the activities of Backslash Distributors. Nonetheless, Jürgen Mossack authorized the head of the Bahamas office to sign the letter. However, he instructed her not to use her own name. Instead she was only to write her title, "assistant secretary."

"Mr. Mossack do not want your signature in such document," a lawyer in Panama wrote to the head of the Bahamas office.

Mossfon also demanded that Gordon approve the letter. After consulting with Singh, he did so.

A week later, Mossfon sent a fax to Gordon, explaining that Jürgen Mossack had reached his limit. After Mossfon collected its money for signing the misleading letter, the senior partner wanted out. "He instructs us to resign as Directors after the execution of the document, as it seems that it will be little bit dangerous," wrote a Mossfon lawyer in Panama.

The firm told Gordon to notify Tuppen and Singh of the resignations and to ask them to appoint their own directors. There the matter stood until a year later, when the massive piracy operation came to the attention of Microsoft and the authorities.

"The two were idiots," recalls Gordon. "They put up a billboard in the middle of London advertising their products."

The Hampshire fraud squad raided the homes of the two men. The London *Sunday Times* reported the police seized thousands of copies of pirated Microsoft software and two shrink-wrapping machines.

Armed with an urgent injunction from the High Court in London, Microsoft's lawyers went to the Bahamas to try to pierce the secrecy encasing the scheme. At this point, Mossfon discovered its directors hadn't resigned from the company after all, as neither Gordon nor the firm had followed through with the appropriate resolutions to make it official. Each had believed the other had the responsibility to do so.

In response to a Microsoft request for information, Gordon sent a panicked fax to Panama. He had lost touch with Tuppen and Singh. Gordon urged Mossfon to tell Microsoft's lawyers the nominee directors had officially resigned lest they bring "more unwanted and unneeded attention to all of us." Doing it himself, he feared, would expose him to legal liability. By this point, getting rid of the directors wasn't going to stop Microsoft's lawyers. Gordon remembers meeting with them the day he relocated his office from Albany to New York City. Everybody, including Mossfon, had lawyered up. Gordon says he turned over all the company records in his possession.

What the Microsoft attorneys really wanted were the books and records that Backslash had sent to Mossfon for safekeeping. Tuppen signed a letter authorizing Mossfon to disclose the records. Four days later, the head of Mossfon's Bahamas office told Microsoft that Tuppen himself had telephoned the firm and told it to destroy the documents. Since the request had been over the phone, there was no written confirmation. Tuppen appears to have denied the conversation occurred. Microsoft's attorneys were incredulous. "We would have thought that as a Director of Bahamas Software Agency Limited, you were under an obligation to retain these documents," they wrote to Mossfon. And indeed, they were. Mossfon's own procedures required it to retain records for six years.

By the end of 1999, an English civil court ordered Tuppen and Singh to pay £3 million in costs and compensation, which bankrupted the men. Even so, they proclaimed their innocence. Two years later, police dropped criminal charges, for lack of evidence.

The Microsoft case was an early warning that delegating customer vetting to others was perilous. Whatever distance the firm gained from selling through intermediaries brought with it a lack of control over their activities. At the end of the day, law enforcement and civil litigants approached Mossfon as the registered agent, not the franchisee. But the firm appears to have paid little heed at the time to this danger. Business was booming. In addition to adding franchisees,

Mossfon expanded its own network of company offices. It also began to involve itself more directly with its customers.

THE PARTNERS PUT Ramsés Owens, a young legal dynamo with a ready smile, in charge of the firm's trust company, Mossfon Trust. Owens had joined Mossfon straight from the University of Panama law school, where he graduated summa cum laude. Mossack and Fonseca understood that the firm's customers did not trust trusts, but perhaps their new associate could turn around the division. He dove into the work with undisguised joy. Mossfon Trust became a place for clients "who are in need of more complicated solutions," as one of Owens's assistants explained to a customer in the United States.

Owens mixed and matched company structures and tax haven jurisdictions to create tailor-made offshore solutions that allowed "the highest possible degree of protection of our clients' interests regarding protection of their patrimony and confidentiality." These were clients like Juan Eljuri Antón, one of the richest men in Latin America, whose family business had established more than a dozen companies with Mossfon. Owens helped Eljuri structure a reinsurance deal that appears to have legally cut his tax burden from 25 percent to 1 percent for certain assets. Alabama representative Oliver Wesley Long also worked with Mossfon Trust; prior to being elected he asked for help setting up an offshore bank account in Panama that would have no reporting requirements in the United States. He wrote the firm, "The two things this accomplishes is no red flags to the IRS upon us transferring money to you, and a safe haven for money in times of trouble either martially [sic] or in business." Owens also advised the men behind Fidentia, a South African investment firm, how to hide their financial activities. Fidentia went on to loot a survivors' fund set aside to pay for school and medicine for tens of thousands of children who had lost their parents in the mines.

Owens also became the go-to guy for Mossfon matters large and small. The partners asked him to show USA Corporate's John Gordon around when the American first came to Panama City. Owens took

Gordon to General Noriega's former headquarters and pointed out the pockmarks from the bullets U.S. troops had fired in 1989, when they ousted the strongman. After the trip to the former barracks, Owens brought Gordon to the Panama Canal, where he recited "The Star-Spangled Banner" from memory. The New Yorker was impressed. Owens was the only person Gordon had ever met who knew all the stanzas, not just the verse people sing at sporting events.

As a student, Owens had participated in the civil society demonstrations against Noriega. He proudly kept the X-rays that show where his wrist was injured by police. For years President Ronald Reagan had countenanced Noriega's alliances with money launderers and drug traffickers because the dictator was an ally in the fight against the Sandinistas. After the fall of the Berlin Wall, Noriega's usefulness diminished. The December 1989 invasion ended years of economic and social turmoil in Panama but left the country's banking secrecy and tax haven status intact.

A brilliant legal tactician, Owens had a quick wit matched by a puppy's eagerness to please. An Isle of Man newspaper report of an Owens speech promoting Panamanian shell companies noted that alongside his PowerPoint presentations, the lawyer "likes to break into a little salsa to liven up the proceedings." He frequently closed his email communications with "*un abrazo*"—a hug—or "*un gran abrazo*," if feeling particularly friendly. Over more than twenty years at Mossfon, he bestowed thousands of electronic hugs on correspondents around the world. His name is associated with 73,010 emails in the Panama Papers and 97,178 documents overall.

Owens and those who worked for him promised their clients they would make them disappear. "You are an invisible man. A product of our imagination," wrote one associate to a prospect. "The main purpose of this company is that one. That a third party (us) will be in charge of the company and its assets and you will be completely disconnected from the company. With this scheme, if your creditors try to get your assets, there will be no connection with you."

For Owens, the secrecy world posed a never-ending series of intellectual challenges, a delightful puzzle to solve. But on particularly delicate matters, at least in the beginning, he took his cue from Jürgen

Mossack and Ramón Fonseca. After a tax-evasion scandal in Costa Rica implicated a client, Fonseca asked Owens to investigate. In a memo, Owens laid out the facts: Costa Rica gave tax credits to exporters. Unscrupulous companies falsely inflated the amount they exported to get undeserved credits. Some companies claimed to export hundreds of millions of obviously fraudulent items like "shark fins" and "gallstones." These were "clear tricks," wrote Owens, in open contempt at the sloppiness of the schemes. Mossfon's client, on the other hand, had genuine exports of canned tuna, but to reduce its tax burden, the company routed invoices through a Mossfon-created BVI subsidiary, a place where it did no actual business.

"We must take into account that the re-billing is something 'legal,' although it may be interpreted as 'legally immoral,'" wrote Owens.

He recommended that the partners continue working with the client, "a very good customer . . . because 95% of our work is casually to sell vehicles to avoid paying taxes."

The firm kept the customer.

IN 1995, OWENS and Mossfon received another tool to help clients hide their money. Panama's national assembly passed a foundation law. The new Panama foundation provided most of the benefits of a trust but without the loss of control that troubled Mossfon's clients.

The original inspiration for using foundations to hide money came from Europe. After World War I, the European principality of Liechtenstein found itself in a tight spot. Only twice the size of Manhattan, with a population of less than twelve thousand, it was completely landlocked. A tiny country in a tough neighborhood, Liechtenstein created a safe haven for the private wealth of Europe's elite—earning their protection—through strict secrecy laws, low taxation, and favorable corporate structures. In 1926, the principality tweaked the legislation of an already existing Swiss family foundation law, creating a financial vehicle that anyone outside of Liechtenstein could use to secretly transfer money.

The Liechtenstein foundation had similarities to companies and trusts. Like a company, it was a stand-alone legal entity that was registered with the government. Yet unlike a company, it didn't have members, shares, or technically even owners. As with a trust, the creator, often called a "founder," moved assets to a separate entity, the foundation. Yet instead of a trustee, there was a foundation council that acted on written guidelines from the founder. For a nonresident of Liechtenstein, there was almost no official record of a foundation's activities. The identity of the ultimate beneficiary was not publicly recorded. Accounting records were not required. Taxes were minimal. Secrecy was near absolute.

The Panamanians made their foundations even more flexible, opaque, and cost effective. In Liechtenstein, the foundation council had to have a local professional as a member. If the foundation did commercial business, annual financial audits were required. Panama did away with these requirements. A Panamanian foundation was prohibited from engaging in commercial activities "on a regular basis," but it could collect dividends, rents, and royalties, and it could hold shares and own properties.

The government fees for Liechtenstein foundations were based on a proportion of the assets. In Panama, it didn't matter how much the foundation held in assets; the country charged a flat annual franchise tax of $250. Most important, Panama allowed for a new role, that of a "protector." According to Mossfon, this person was "usually the client himself or someone he trusts." The protector essentially oversaw the foundation council, which functioned as the public face of the foundation, and had the power to remove its members. In this way, the founder never relinquished control.

The Panamanian statute ensured that everybody involved was insulated from liability and shrouded in secrecy. Mossfon told prospective customers that the members of the foundation council, protectors, supervisory bodies, and anyone else connected to a foundation were "required to maintain strict confidentiality, even after its termination." Failure to do so was a criminal offense that could result in a fine of up to $50,000 or up to six months in prison.

Owens put Panamanian foundations to work for the unscrupulous gang behind the South African Fidentia fraud. Mossfon created companies in Panama, the BVI, and the Seychelles for Fidentia, each of which was owned by a foundation, with names like "Attila Hun" and "Mitas." The beneficiary was a limited liability company based in the United Kingdom. The stated purpose was to avoid paying taxes to the South African government.

With the Fidentia middleman Steven Goodwin, Owens went quite a bit further. Goodwin had bribed a fund manager to obtain investments for the firm while pocketing millions for himself. Owens created a private foundation for Goodwin to hold property in the United Kingdom. When a receiver took over Fidentia after its executives looted the survivors' fund for the miners' orphans, Goodwin fled to Australia. Still, he needed Owens to safeguard his cash. He flew the Panamanian lawyer to New York, where the two men met at the Sheraton New York Times Square Hotel, along with an Australian lawyer friend of Goodwin's. For three hours, they discussed Fidentia's problems, including by that time the arrests of its top executives. Owens's self-serving verdict: Goodwin was not involved in any way whatsoever. The real blame for Goodwin's predicament lay with the South African media, which was exaggerating his role in the Fidentia scandal. Goodwin was clearly a victim of circumstance, contemporaneous notes of the meeting concluded.

Despite being convinced of Goodwin's innocence, Owens urged the South African to better protect his assets. They decided to create an addendum to the foundation's original agreement to pass ownership of Goodwin's assets to his Australian lawyer friend for safekeeping. Mossfon and Owens would retain $25,000 to do the work. To cement the revised agreement, Goodwin, the lawyer, their wives, and Owens had dinner at a pricey Manhattan steak house known for its Gatsby-era bordello-like decor. Beneath portraits of scantily clad burlesque stars, Owens made a show of paying for the meal. Goodwin insisted on picking up the check.

Four months after the meeting, South African authorities issued an arrest warrant for Goodwin. The South African press dubbed him the "missing man." But Mossack Fonseca continued its relationship with the now fugitive until he was apprehended at Los Angeles International Airport by U.S. Customs and Immigration agents on a warrant from Interpol. Goodwin fought extradition for almost a year before accepting return to South Africa, where he signed a plea deal to serve ten years in jail. While never employed directly by Fidentia, Goodwin admitted to laundering approximately $11 million for the firm.

Sometimes, even a foundation did not provide enough secrecy. In those cases, Owens recommended adding a charity to the mix. Mossfon did not invent this idea. For decades, trust operators used charities as fake beneficiaries to avoid government scrutiny and further hide the identity of actual owners. With Mossfon foundations, the firm suggested the client name the Red Cross or the World Wildlife Fund as a beneficiary. These charities were ideal. They had high profiles and local chapters in nearly every country. Seeing the named beneficiary, tax authorities might give the foundation a pass, believing it to be a charitable enterprise. The nonprofits themselves had no inkling they were beneficiaries. The "protector" of the foundation would then replace the fake beneficiary with another name, sending Mossfon the real instructions in a sealed envelope. The final instructions would be opened only upon the client's death. At that point, the true beneficiary would be revealed. "In this manner officially and truthfully we know only the name of the first beneficiary," Owens explained to a client. "Nevertheless, the Protector will always be able to replace such envelope or the name of the substitute."

THE MORE WORK Mossfon performed directly for a beneficial owner, the more risk it ran if the customer turned out to be a criminal. Even if Mossfon did nothing but create a company through an intermediary, there was still no guarantee it could sidestep fallout. The firm learned this unsetting truth when it belatedly discovered its involvement with one of the world's most bloodthirsty drug traffickers.

Rafael Caro Quintero, the founder of the Guadalajara cartel, may have been Mexico's first narcotics billionaire. He owed his fortune to transporting Colombian cocaine and growing marijuana and opiates. In late 1984, Enrique "Kiki" Camarena, a U.S. Drug Enforcement Administration undercover agent, infiltrated Caro Quintero's thriving marijuana business. He led the DEA to "El Bufalo," a massive pot plantation in northern Chihuahua, where they found more than a thousand acres of plants. Mexican soldiers destroyed product likely worth several billion dollars. Consumed by fury and paranoia, Caro Quintero lashed out. An American novelist from Minneapolis and a dental student from Fort Worth were among the first to die. In January 1985, the two friends mistakenly walked into the Crazy Lobster, a restaurant Caro Quintero owned in Zapopan, outside Guadalajara. The drug kingpin was having a private party inside. The revelers kidnapped the students, who they may have suspected were DEA agents. They tortured them in the kitchen with knives and ice picks before burying their bodies in a local park. One of them was still alive when they put him in the ground.

The following month, Caro Quintero's men grabbed Camarena after he left the American consulate in Guadalajara. They burned the thirty-seven-year-old ex-Marine with cigarettes and beat him with a tire iron for two days in a secret chamber behind one of Caro Quintero's mansions. A doctor was on call to keep the DEA agent alive during the ordeal. Before Mexican authorities discovered Camarena's mutilated body, Caro Quintero boarded a Falcon executive jet and left the country.

That March, he traveled to Costa Rica, where he did business with José Maria Pla Horrit, a local lawyer with a crooked clientele. A few years earlier, when the U.S. government wanted to serve an indictment on the fugitive financier Robert Vesco for looting a mutual fund of hundreds of millions of dollars, the U.S. embassy suggested they deliver the papers to Pla Horrit, one of Vesco's attorneys. In the early days, Mossack provided Panamanian companies to Pla Horrit and several other Vesco associates.

On April 4, Costa Rican authorities arrested Caro Quintero for criminal acts related to narcotics trafficking. During his time in the Central American nation, he alternated among the four properties he owned, dined at the best restaurants, and traveled around in a limousine. Despite the publicity surrounding the arrest, Pla Horrit managed to stay in the background. About a week after Caro Quintero's extradition to Mexico, Pla Horrit registered the first of two Panamanian companies on the drug lord's behalf with Jürgen Mossack. Wanting maximum secrecy, he paid Mossack to act as a director of the company. Mossack appears not to have known the real identity of the beneficial owner. At least one of the companies held a sprawling mansion on the outskirts of the Costa Rican capital, San José.

In 1989, a Mexican judge sentenced Caro Quintero to forty years in prison, the country's then maximum. U.S. authorities later accused the drug kingpin of continuing his business while behind bars. The Treasury Department sanctioned Caro Quintero's friends and relatives for investing his considerable fortune in legitimate businesses. With his client in prison and the properties confiscated, Pla Horrit stopped paying Mossfon. The companies fell into limbo. Pla Horrit died on Christmas Eve in 2004.

A year later, a Mossfon lawyer sent an email to the partners. The president and the secretary-general of the Costa Rican National Olympic Committee had visited the office with a thorny problem. The Costa Rican government had given the committee Caro Quintero's mansion for its new headquarters, but the committee couldn't acquire legal title because the drug lord technically still held it through Mossfon's Panamanian company.

The Olympic Committee wanted Mossack, as a director of the company, "to donate" the property to the committee to avoid a complicated judicial process. Giving away property that still technically belonged to one of the world's most fearsome drug traffickers seemed ill-advised to Mossack. The firm decided that the Mossfon directors would resign their positions. The Costa Ricans would have to solve their legal issues on their own.

"Pablo Escobar was a child nursing at his mother's breast compared to R. Caro Quintero!" Mossack explained in Spanish in an email, referring to the notorious Colombian drug kingpin. "I don't want to be among those he will visit after he leaves prison."

Mossack's instincts for self-preservation proved prescient. On August 9, 2013, a judge in Guadalajara unexpectedly released Caro Quintero on a technicality, with twelve years remaining on his sentence. Before the United States could extradite him, he disappeared. As of this writing, his name sits atop the DEA's list of fugitives.

4

RISE OF THE GLOBAL BANKSTERS

An offshore company without a bank account is of limited utility. A bank is necessary for any significant financial activity to take place. For more than a century the gold standard for secrecy in banking was Switzerland, where bankers could be counted upon not to reveal an account holder's identity or expose a customer's transgressions. In fact, it was against Swiss law for a banker to reveal private information about his clients. The Swiss banks did not care if the origin of the money was legitimate or nefarious. Account holders bore the responsibility for paying their taxes and obeying the law, not the bankers who hid their money. But if Swiss account holders wanted to spend large sums while keeping their money secret, an anonymous company was the way to go. Flexible Swiss bankers created offshore companies for their account holders. They were among Mossfon's best customers and contributed to making Geneva the firm's most profitable office.

Among Mossfon's best banker clients, HSBC stood out. The bank and the law firm grew together symbiotically, riding a wave of financial globalization, both legal and illegal. They shared a casual approach to customer vetting and a profit-first mind-set. HSBC ordered more than twenty-three hundred companies from Mossfon over the lifetime of the law firm. It bought inactive shelf companies in bulk.

When a customer needed one, the banker alerted Mossfon to transfer control.

Their collaboration began in the early 1980s, before Jürgen Mossack and Ramón Fonseca joined forces, through Antoni Guerrero, a Geneva-based South American businessman. Despite having no legal training, Guerrero recognized the value of being a middleman. He acquired companies from Ramón Fonseca for Geneva's bankers and lawyers. After the partners formed Mossfon, the firm became Guerrero's main conduit to anonymous companies.

Guerrero's top banking client was Luxembourg-based Safra Republic Holdings, which operated a successful Swiss private bank. Republic's thirty thousand high-net-worth clients included bagmen for corrupt African leaders, Chinese princelings, Middle Eastern royalty, the Russian mafia, crooked diamond merchants, and money launderers. Most wanted the secrecy afforded by offshore companies. Republic specialized in absolute discretion, minimal questions, and concierge service—the kind of hands-on tight-lipped Swiss banking caricatured in a thousand spy novels.

Guerrero was a great salesman and a terrible businessman. He had a habit of collecting the registration renewal fees from customers but not actually renewing the companies. Only when the customer needed the company to act would Guerrero pay up. His cavalier approach to customer affairs may have been a factor in his abrupt departure from Geneva. After an unexpected trip to Panama in 1998, Guerrero returned to the office in Switzerland and told his assistant Adrian Simon that he had sold the business to Mossfon. Simon was not entirely surprised by the spur-of-the-moment decision. Guerrero had half-joked that he was so nervous about customers coming after him, he slept with his passport under his pillow.

Fonseca traveled to Geneva to clean up the mess Guerrero left behind. He put Simon, a former translator and schoolteacher from Spain, in charge. The Spaniard solidified relationships with prized clients like Republic, which was going through its own transformation.

Republic's founder, Edmond Safra, was in the process of selling his financial empire to HSBC. The billionaire scion of a Syrian banking dynasty, Safra referred to Republic Holdings and its twin, Republic National Bank of New York, the third-largest retail bank in the New York metropolitan area, as his children. They were big boys, with a combined $56 billion in assets under management and clients in eighty countries.

Safra was one of the last connections to old-school relationship banking. His forefathers had financed camel caravans in the Ottoman Empire. His bankers kept the secrets of dangerous men. He frequently traveled with an entourage of well-armed Israeli bodyguards. Superstitious, paranoid, and suffering from Parkinson's disease, Safra was reluctantly ceding the field to a corporation that was more machine than flesh and blood.

On December 3, 1999, before Safra could complete Republic's sale to HSBC, one of his nurses, a former U.S. Army medic and Green Beret, set a fire inside a waste basket in his Monte Carlo penthouse. The nurse then yelled a warning that armed assailants were loose inside the home. According to police, it was a misguided stunt to impress Safra by rescuing him from a fictitious attack. Instead, the alarm sent the sixty-seven-year-old banking tycoon and another nurse fleeing into a steel-reinforced lavatory that doubled as a safe room. As the fire spread inside the penthouse, police banged on the walls, urging Safra to come out. Not even the cell phone pleas of his wife, Lily, could coax the terrified mogul to open the door. When the rescuers finally breached the bunker bathroom, they found Safra and a Filipina nurse dead of smoke inhalation, their bodies blackened by soot.

Safra's bizarre death cast a pall over the $10 billion HSBC deal under way, but did not stop it. As mourners eulogized Safra at a Geneva synagogue, the U.S. Federal Reserve approved the sale.

Republic's culture had deep roots in Switzerland, where willful blindness was both tradition and law. Switzerland's bank secrecy dates at least to the early years of the twentieth century. After surrounding countries raised taxes, wealthy French and German citizens rushed to hide money in neighboring Switzerland. Swiss banks then feasted on the turmoil afflicting Europe around World War I. As the financial services industry grew more powerful, it strengthened its grip. Initially, it was a civil offense for bank officials and others to divulge information about account holders. In 1934, Switzerland made it a crime, punishable by three years in jail. Tax evasion, on the other hand, remained a civil infraction.

True to its colonial roots, HSBC changed little about the manner in which Republic operated, lest reform hinder profits. The Hongkong and Shanghai Banking Corporation had opened for business in 1865, five years after Anglo-French forces looted and burned the Summer Palace and defeated the Xianfeng Emperor in the Second Opium War. British merchants created the bank to fund foreign trade and based it in Hong Kong, itself wrested from China in the First Opium War. HSBC earned a reputation as excessively conservative, secretive, and arrogant. The bank could ignore its negative image in Hong Kong thanks to cozy government relations, nonexistent disclosure requirements, and a malleable press.

In 1993, HSBC moved its headquarters to London and tried to shake its conservatism by binge buying other banks. HSBC hoped the Republic acquisition would vault it to the top of the bank rankings, known as the league tables. The view at the time was that bigger was better, and many banks grew through a feeding frenzy of mergers and acquisitions. How to mesh disparate banking cultures or manage the sprawling multinationals that resulted received insufficient attention.

HSBC's executives saw an emerging class of global rich as the bank's path to prosperity. The superwealthy were increasingly stateless. They banked in Geneva. Lived in London and New York. Shopped in Paris and Milan. And they held their assets through offshore companies registered in places like the British Virgin Islands. HSBC executives were reading the telltale signs of a new age of inequality, even if they didn't recognize it as such. Governments were retreating from providing their citizens pension and health obligations, an HSBC strategy report observed. The stateless rich balked at paying taxes in their home countries, to which they felt little allegiance. It made sense to them to base their operations inside tax havens and to bank in Switzerland, where discretion was woven into the country's DNA. These trends represented an opportunity for the wealth management industry.

HSBC recognized but ignored the dangers inherent in the Republic acquisition. Rumors that the bank served the criminal class had long dogged Republic. The accusations went beyond the normal reputation of Swiss bankers as handmaidens to the unscrupulous. By the end of the 1990s, there were plenty of facts in the public domain. Republic actively dealt in murky commodity businesses such as diamonds and gold favored by the underworld. Republic was implicated in Manuel Noriega's money-laundering activities in Panama. It had voluntarily disclosed to the U.S. Department of Justice that the Russian mafia was using its correspondent banking services. While a number of these scandals involved multiple banks, Republic's name kept resurfacing.

HSBC code-named its plan to buy Republic "Project Gold." Rather than look inside Republic directly, it opted to perform initial due diligence via public filings. HSBC feared takeover talk would alarm Republic's executive management team, which it wanted to capture intact. After green-lighting the acquisition, HSBC likely did a standard prepurchase audit. If the review exists, its contents have never been made public.

Stephen Green, Baron Green of Hurstpierpoint, an HSBC board member at the time, admitted while testifying before a committee of the House of Lords in 2015 that the bank had been aware that there were going to be issues with Republic. Those tasked with the mechanics of merging the two institutions noted that Republic's executives had a troubling habit of disregarding written directives from regulators.

Still, HSBC made few changes. Dedicating the resources needed to fix Republic immediately would have washed away the short-term benefits of the acquisition. Transforming institutional culture is costly. It requires new procedures and personnel.

The deal was finalized a month after Safra's funeral. HSBC's $9.84 billion purchase of Republic doubled its private banking business overnight, increasing assets under management to $122 billion. Prior to his death, Safra had shaved $450 million off the asking price when HSBC discovered that Republic had known about a Japanese Ponzi scheme run through its trading accounts but failed to promptly notify regulators. U.S. regulators eventually slapped the bank with a $700 million fine.

Even with the fine, the deal quickly produced the money pot HSBC envisioned. In 1999, its global private banking operation had earned pretax profits of $180 million. A year after the Safra banks came online (along with another smaller acquisition, Crédit Commercial de France), profits soared to $440 million.

Mossfon turned out to be an ideal partner for HSBC. Adrian Simon didn't pester bankers with questions, he simply filled their orders. "The banks knew why they wanted to buy companies and for whom," Simon says.

Mossfon was interwoven with Republic/HSBC at every level, from clients to customer relations to top executives. Underpinning Safra's private banking empire were the relationship managers, who brought in the customers and kept them happy. Their importance was such that Safra had given them ample space to operate. The relationship managers helped their clients acquire Mossfon companies.

Under Safra, and even more so after HSBC acquired Republic, the bank's relationship managers became de facto Mossfon salesmen. They knew when a client needed an offshore company. The relationship managers didn't just juggle figures, the Swiss newspaper *Le Temps* observed, the good ones acted as "therapist, lightning rod, friend." With discretion came access. As the guardians of secret money, the bankers maintained an intimate relationship with their clients, hopping on trains or planes when beckoned, even vacationing together. While a multimillionaire and his Swiss banker discussed the client's financial affairs over espresso in say, Saint Moritz, their wives shopped together.

Sexism was the norm, a form of male intimacy that bonded banker and client. One relationship manager wrote in a private note in his client's file that the account holder's wife was in Cyprus, and "she is not up to date with the account," so communicate only by his cell phone. Swiss journalists found that customers were often more afraid of their wives finding their money than tax authorities. If the wife did manage to collect from a divorce, the client could count on the sympathetic ear and helping hand of his banker. In one case, a Belgian diamond merchant informed his relationship manager he now owed his wife $700,000 from an amicable divorce. He then asked if the banker could set up an offshore company for her.

Republic's Swiss private bank was housed in the former Grand Hôtel Bellevue, a majestic edifice constructed at the beginning of the twentieth century, located in an exclusive shopping district on Geneva's tony lakefront drive. The building boasted spectacular views of the lake's famous Jet d'Eau. Inside, among the marble, wood paneling, and staircases with finely wrought iron railings were four departments or "desks" that covered different parts of the world and, in some cases, distinct business lines. The most notorious desk among the four was MEDIS, short for Mediterranean, Europe, and Israel. "The MEDIS accounts were disproportionately more often the subjects of requests from Swiss authorities in relation to criminal charges," noted David Garrido, the head of the Swiss bank's legal compliance department. Captained by Judah Elmaleh, a charming Moroccan Jew, MEDIS handled the diamond trade.

Mossfon and the bank shared a collection of wealthy Jewish diamond merchants as customers. These were men who had grown rich plundering African resources while fending off prosecution. Among them was the Israeli billionaire Daniel Gertler, whose involvement with blood diamonds through his close friendship with the Democratic Republic of Congo's corrupt and bloodthirsty president, Joseph Kabila, made him the subject of multiple government inquiries.

The Mossfon files show at least 130 companies controlled or connected to another Israeli billionaire, Benjamin "Beny" Steinmetz. His relationship with Republic/HSBC dated to at least 1997. Steinmetz has courted controversy from Sierra Leone to Washington, DC. In 2016, he was arrested in Israel over a bribery allegation that involved a Mossfon company and a contract to mine iron ore in the West African country of Guinea.

Another diamond client of HSBC and Mossfon, Mozes Victor Konig, fled his native Belgium in 1999, before he could be arrested. Konig was part of an organized criminal group that used a hotel investment to launder money from criminal activities. He had multiple companies with Mossfon that in turn maintained bank accounts with Republic/HSBC. One of them, Front Trading Consultants, kept $114 million in its account at one point. Interpol issued an alert for his arrest for unlawful circulation of precious metals, among other crimes.

HSBC executives themselves were Mossfon customers. Michael Geoghegan began his HSBC career in 1973 as a teenager and became its go-to guy on foreign operations—and later, the bank's CEO. In 1997, Geoghegan created three companies with Mossfon, through a Jersey subsidiary of Midland Bank, another HSBC acquisition. Midland didn't usually create companies, a Mossfon lawyer explained, but "this was a special case for their senior executive." One of the companies, BVI-based Shireburn Limited, held a house in London's posh Kensington neighborhood, near the Royal Albert Hall. The Michael Geoghegan Settlement Trust, of which Geoghegan was the beneficiary, owned Shireburn. The trust owned the company. The company owned the house, which in turn leased it to, among others, Geoghegan himself.

Stuart Gulliver succeeded Geoghegan as HSBC's chief executive officer in 2010. Gulliver had started his career as a relationship manager in 1981, before quickly becoming HSBC's head of trading. He owned a Panama-based Mossfon company, Worcester Equities. Initially he held the company through bearer shares. Then Gulliver canceled the shares and made the shareholder the Worcester Foundation. The British newspaper the *Guardian* reported that until 2003, Gulliver used the company to receive his HSBC bonuses. Gulliver claimed he paid all his taxes on the money but needed the secrecy to hide the size of his compensation from his colleagues.

Mossfon and HSBC both strove to be number one in their respective industries, no matter what. A desire to be wealthy and important also animated Jeffrey Tesler, one of their most infamous shared clients. Tesler's business dealings with Jürgen Mossack began in 1982, when he was a small-time real estate attorney in the two-man London firm of Kaye Tesler & Co. Mossack created a Panamanian company for Tesler with the upmarket name of Cavendish International. The company was short-lived, but the relationship was not.

Through his law practice, Tesler met wealthy Nigerians keen to buy property in the United Kingdom. The clients then asked for additional legal help. Tesler soon gained a reputation as well connected in Nigeria. This caught the attention of Western firms looking to do business in the notoriously corrupt country. Among them was M. W. Kellogg Company, which hired Tesler as an adviser on a fertilizer plant project.

In 1989, Nigeria announced plans to build the Bonny Island Natural Liquefied Gas Project, a massive and costly natural gas facility in the Niger River delta. M. W. Kellogg and several other firms established a joint venture to bid on construction contracts for the project, but they hired the wrong middleman. Their efforts foundered. Then they tried Tesler. He spent two months shuttling between Britain and Nigeria, shepherding discussions between the joint venture and Nigerian government officials to determine the amount in bribes needed to win the first contract. The figure arrived upon was $60 million. It was a down payment. The scheme lasted years.

The Mossfon documents, along with HSBC files acquired by the French newspaper *Le Monde*, reveal Tesler to have been an adroit manipulator of the secrecy world. In September 1995, six months after Tesler entered into his first agreement with the joint venture, a law office in Jerusalem registered a Bahamas company for Tesler. He eventually moved the company to Mossfon. Ownership was held through bearer shares. It was the first of many such companies.

In 1997, Tesler opened his first accounts with HSBC. The same year, the U.S. multinational firm Halliburton acquired Kellogg and merged it with Brown & Root, a similar company it already owned. Under Halliburton, the Nigerian bribery scheme continued. Former U.S. secretary of defense (and future vice president) Dick Cheney was Halliburton's CEO at the time. Cheney was no stranger to offshore companies. In the mid-1990s, he and his wife, Lynne, did a series of Wyoming real estate transactions with Jura Nominees S.A., which, according to notarized Teton County documents, was based in the British Virgin Islands.

There is no evidence of the existence of a Jura Nominees S.A. in the British Virgin Islands public registry. Mossfon did create a company called Jura Nominees S.A. in Panama in 1984, but it went inactive five years later. The Cheneys purchased a residential property from Jura Nominees S.A. (BVI) and sold a separate property to the company as well. Wyoming real estate documents identify the director of Jura Nominees S.A. (BVI) as Ian James Ffrench, a Geneva-based attorney and one of Mossfon's oldest clients.

Jeffrey Tesler disbursed money from the joint venture for the Nigeria project in a variety of ways. Mostly, he wired it from bank accounts in Geneva to Nigerian officials hiding behind their own offshore companies. Sometimes the process was more involved. In one instance in August 2002, Tesler arranged for a million dollars in one-hundred-dollar bills to be delivered in a pilot's briefcase to a fancy hotel in Abuja, Nigeria. The ruling People's Democratic Party wanted to spread the loot around in advance of upcoming elections. The following April, $500,000 in Nigerian currency provided by Tesler was left for a party official to fetch from a vehicle in a Nigerian hotel parking lot. That month, the People's Democratic Party scored an overwhelming victory in the polls in an election marked by violence, vote rigging, and fraud.

In 2003, French prosecutors began to dig into the Nigerian scheme. U.S. prosecutors followed. They concluded that the joint venture had given Tesler more than $130 million to bribe Nigerian government officials. The payments leveraged about $6 billion in engineering and construction work for the Western firms, including the Halliburton subsidiary now known as Kellogg, Brown & Root.

By the time American authorities closed in, Tesler operated at least six offshore companies with Mossfon, some created with HSBC. In addition to the one in the Bahamas, he also had companies in the BVI, Gibraltar, Samoa, the Seychelles, and Panama. When Swiss authorities froze twelve of Tesler's bank accounts, five of them were with HSBC.

Tesler involved his wife and daughters as bank account owners and company directors. His daughter was part owner of HSBC bank accounts that contained more than $35 million when she was a twenty-one-year-old psychology student in London. Tesler's activities with HSBC and Mossfon continued despite the investigation and even after U.S. prosecutors indicted him in 2009.

In 2010, Nigeria also indicted Dick Cheney in the multimillion-dollar bribery scheme. Cheney, a notorious micromanager, claimed not to know about the bribery. The charges were dropped after Halliburton paid $35 million in a settlement.

Despite investigations on two continents, HSBC and Mossfon stood by Tesler. Notes in one of his HSBC account files indicate the bank was aware of the legal issues, though Mossfon's files offer no acknowledgment of the widening scandal.

Tesler's lawyer tried to argue that norms had changed and that his client's bribery activities weren't particularly illegal in the mid-1990s when they first started. But by 1998, both the United States and the United Kingdom had signed a Convention on Combating Bribery of Foreign Public Officials in International Business Transactions. Tesler confessed to a judge that he became infatuated with his influential role as paymaster: "I relished the opportunity to talk with prominent government officials and leaders of multinational corporations." The judge, unmoved, sentenced Tesler to twenty-one months in prison, calling him "a gatekeeper of corruption."

Two years after Tesler was sentenced to prison, one of his companies canceled his wife and daughter's shares and issued them to a Mossfon-controlled foundation, also used by a Russian billionaire, Rashid Sardarov, a long-standing client of Mossfon. Sardarov used one of his offshore companies to purchase 108 square miles in Namibia for a hunting reserve.

HSBC WAS FAR from the only bank doing business with Mossfon. More than five hundred banks registered nearly 15,600 shell companies with the firm over its lifetime.

In the early days, Mossfon held to the self-serving belief that the banks screened their customers. "If a bank asked you for a company, you assumed there couldn't be anything wrong with it," said Jürgen Mossack.

In fact, in the case of HSBC, the bank conducted little if any review. Its risk management was ineffectual and marginalized. If a relationship manager brought in a client whom the bank's risk management found objectionable, the conflict was submitted to a due diligence committee. This committee was dominated by members of the various desks and almost always decided in favor of keeping the client.

F. David Ford, the head of compliance for Republic in Switzerland, Luxembourg, Monaco, Paris, Guernsey, and Gibraltar, also sat on the due diligence committee. He advised senior management on anti-money-laundering matters. Broad-faced and boyish-looking, Ford had been a U.S. Navy officer in the Judge Advocate General's Corps before joining the Department of Justice. For six years, as senior legal adviser for the criminal division of the Office of International Affairs, he worked with European partners on extraditions and legal assistance requests, maintaining friendly relations with the Geneva prosecutor's office. After HSBC bought Republic, the new owner kept Ford on staff and expanded his role to include full responsibility for anti-money-laundering controls. While Ford worked for HSBC, his wife was employed by the U.S. Justice Department, in the International Affairs Office, a fact he says was properly disclosed.

Ford's efforts were ineffective at best. To his colleagues, Ford's actual job, which did not seem to involve much compliance work, was a matter of speculation. "Nobody seemed to know what he did but everyone was afraid of him," said one former HSBC supervisor, who requested anonymity because he still worked in the industry.

Many of Ford's colleagues believed he was back-channeling information on Republic and HSBC's customers to U.S. intelligence, although Ford denies the allegation. The rumor even surfaced in a Swiss newspaper. The CIA refuses to provide documents on Edmond Safra because the information is classified. Nonetheless, if the CIA was involved with HSBC somehow, it would not come as a surprise. Both the CIA and the KGB were early purveyors of the secrecy afforded by Swiss banks and tax havens.

Somewhere in Geneva was a covert CIA listening post where a young Edward Snowden once worked as a National Security Agency contractor. Snowden told the *Guardian* how CIA operatives worked to compromise Swiss bankers to gain information. As with Fonseca's experience in Geneva, Snowden's time in Switzerland left him disillusioned. It was during his stint in Geneva that he first thought about exposing government secrets, Snowden said.

The CIA discovered its own need for secret bank accounts early in its existence. A secret account offered the answer to a simple problem: How to pay its covert operatives? In 1952, the agency's disbursements had grown to such an extent that it became unwieldy to hand-carry the amounts of cash required. It needed a bank account that could be kept hidden. In long bureaucratic meetings with the monetary branch of the finance division, CIA officials debated what to do. By the end of 1953, they had devised a plan.

The agency enlisted a banker at Washington, DC–based Riggs Bank who was already in its confidence. The inside man ensured that everything proceeded smoothly. An operative using a fake identity opened an account. In case that person died unexpectedly, the agency created "Twin Declarations of Trust," according to a declassified secret CIA document detailing the arrangements. The first declaration, establishing CIA ownership of the account, was the most important. It was legally binding but politically toxic.

"In the event of decease or extreme mismanagement this document could be used by the Agency to establish government control over the funds," reads a memorandum on the project from December 1953, "although of course this would blow the account and that particular situation could conceivably be so embarrassing that the Agency would not want to disclose its ownership."

The second Declaration of Trust did not mention the CIA or the United States government. The name of the true owner was left blank. "This document is designed for obtainment of control without disclosing United States Government interest," the memo explained. "Supposedly a pseudo could be inserted as the true 'owner' and the account transferred." The pseudonymous account holder would sign a separate side agreement with the agency admitting he did not actually own the money in the account.

By the mid-1980s, the CIA's involvement had expanded into tax havens, as David Fischer, the U.S. ambassador to the Seychelles, discovered. Located in the Indian Ocean off the coast of Somalia, the

Seychelles served as a stop on the slave trade and a listening post during the Cold War, but its biggest impact on the global economy has been as a tax haven. The island's ruler, France-Albert René, seized power in a coup in 1977 and held it for thirty years. He turned the country into a hub for offshore banking and money laundering. The Gambino crime family in New York and gunrunners in Libya, among others, washed cash in the Seychelles. In an oral history taken by the Association for Diplomatic Studies and Training, Ambassador Fischer related how police fished the body of a Mafia soldier out of the swamps of New Jersey in 1984. Among the dead man's possessions was an address book that contained President René's private telephone number.

Ambassador Fischer was once a CIA officer in Africa himself, and on a trip home he met with his former chief of station in Tanzania. After lunch at the agency's Langley headquarters, his colleague walked him to the parking lot. The man stopped and looked around to ensure nobody was listening. He then told Fischer that all the diplomatic cables the ambassador sent from the Seychelles were "blue streaked," which meant they had been marked for the attention of the CIA director, William Casey, as being highest priority. His former colleague had no idea why.

Later, as Ambassador Fischer and his staff dug deeper into the criminal activities flowing through the Seychelles, including Mafia and Middle Eastern use of the island's banks for money laundering, the local CIA station chief showed him a strange message Langley sent. It was for the station chief's eyes only, from Director Casey, and read: "You are hereby instructed never to report, never to use any assets or any resources to pursue anything regarding international fraudulent banking operations in the Seychelles."

In 1998, Mossfon began registering companies in the Seychelles. It would become one of the firm's more popular jurisdictions, eventually accounting for more than fifteen thousand companies.

5

HOW TO BEAT THE GAME

Thousands of people jammed London's Business Design Centre for Shorex 1997, billed as "the Premier Offshore Exhibition and Conference." Targeted at financial intermediaries, offshore professionals, and high-net-worth individuals, eighty exhibitors advertised their services, including Mossack Fonseca, USA Corporate Services, the Central Bank of Cyprus, and the BVI Financial Services agency. For offshore professionals, it was a "must be there" event.

There was nothing covert about the sales pitch for secrecy in London that year. More than half the world's wealth was controlled offshore, noted Philippe Gelin, the managing director of Shorex. This was a "forum in which professionals in the offshore industry can openly market their services," he proclaimed.

More than fifty countries were represented, but a small group of Americans stood out. Whispers followed them as they scrutinized the display booths. The United States Internal Revenue Service had come to Shorex.

Agent Joe West had convinced his IRS bosses to send him and three others to learn about the industry. A gathering of offshore providers—where intermediaries brazenly marketed tax evasion—it didn't get any better, thought West.

"I was a kid in a candy store," he recalls.

The reactions of attendees to the agents ran from fear to befuddlement. As word of their presence spread, some conference goers gave them a wide berth. West watched as a presenter at one seminar, after being told the IRS was in the audience, altered his presentation on the fly. A Cyprus exhibitor explained to the agents how he could help them hide their money—even after they held up their conference badges identifying themselves as IRS agents. He was so excited to be at Shorex for the first time that he didn't care.

The government men hit every exhibitor table, collecting bundles of materials to bring back to headquarters. They would use the information in one of the most far-reaching and innovative investigations in IRS history. West's story reveals both the possibilities and the limitations of the government's fight against offshore tax evasion. It also helps explain why the U.S. government ignored Mossfon's activities for so many years.

The progeny of a mixed marriage between an African American airman stationed in Japan during the Korean War and a Japanese secretary at the military installation, Joseph C. West was born in 1953. He had the typical upbringing of a military brat, attending six different high schools and living everywhere from New Jersey to Guam. After two years of active service in the navy, West attended a public university in New Jersey on the GI Bill. In 1978, his uncle, an IRS agent, convinced him to join the agency to get some training while he finished his MBA and certified public accounting degrees. Excellent grades landed him in the IRS's highly coveted international section, focusing on multinational companies. At the age of twenty-five, West had stumbled into a calling.

Tall and handsome, with a broad face and a deep brown complexion, West had long encountered resistance because of his looks. From an early age, adults counseled him that despite his keen intellect, he needed to temper his expectations. A black man could only go so far, his father told him. A guidance counselor suggested technical school. When he proved adept at finding audit violations, IRS superiors asked for his informant, unable to accept that he'd discovered the problems on his own. West stubbornly pushed himself to excel and reacted impatiently to opposition, trampling bureaucratic niceties and arguing with authority figures with whom he disagreed.

West recalls a fellow agent telling him once that the best way to survive in the IRS was not to take any initiative. You would only get in trouble if you stuck your head out. No one was ever fired for lackluster performance. West was horrified. The words haunt him still. He would discover that the agency's struggles to curb offshore tax evasion had as much to do with self-sabotage and lack of will as anything else.

In 1972, six years before West joined the agency, an IRS investigation into offshore abuses had ended in disaster. The investigation, known as Operation Tradewinds, employed a confidential informant, Norman Casper, to probe the Bahamas-based Castle Bank and Trust Company. Casper lured a Castle Bank manager to Miami on the pretext of a tryst. The banker was unaware that his date was a former policewoman participating in a sting operation. While the two were out on the town, Casper rifled the banker's briefcase and found a list of 306 offshore account holders. The names included Hugh Hefner, Tony Curtis, members of the band Creedence Clearwater Revival, and the Pritzker family, who owned the Hyatt Hotel chain. Casper also uncovered links to President Richard Nixon and his Key Biscayne pal Bebe Rebozo.

The dog had finally caught the car, which promptly ran over it. The brass criticized the evidence collection. Few prosecutions resulted. Nixon's IRS commissioner quashed the investigation. Those in the IRS who participated in Operation Tradewinds had their careers sidelined. By 1976, IRS officials labeled the whole investigation a bust. For years, any agent who dared to look into the offshore world risked professional suicide. Future grand jury investigations were discouraged. It would be more than a decade before the IRS focused on offshore tax abuse again.

In the mid-1980s, West joined a team auditing Wheaton Industries, a century-old glassmaker located in Millville, New Jersey. Wheaton produced bottles for everything from cosmetics to pharmaceuticals. The company transformed southern New Jersey into a commercial glass-manufacturing mecca, becoming one of the area's largest

employers. Millville, population twenty-five thousand, was the quin-
tessential company town. Frank Wheaton Jr., the grandson of the
firm's founder, was its "Glass King."

The audit, which took years, revealed a multinational company
run like a family business, where relatives were paid off the books
through gifts of cars, boats, and other assets. In the end, whatever
violations the firm committed paled in comparison to what Frank
Wheaton himself was doing. To hide his income, Wheaton operated
bank accounts in at least three offshore jurisdictions, including the
Bahamas and Panama. He ran an offshore business empire based in
multiple tax havens through a network of undeclared trusts and anonymous companies.

When West found hints of this offshore activity, his superiors at
the IRS tried to dissuade him from pursuing the offshore trail. It
wasn't worth the effort, they said, pointing to the challenge all such
cases present of proving that the taxpayer controlled the trusts and
anonymous offshore companies. West would never find the documentation to establish that Wheaton secretly managed his offshore
empire, his superiors warned. It was a classic Catch-22. In order to get
the records, you needed the records. To obtain a court order to force
Wheaton to produce documents, the IRS had to convince a judge the
documents existed. Wheaton denied his control over the companies
and trusts, and no public documents existed to the contrary.

West needed no reminding he was on the clock. The statute of limitations was short, three years at the time, although more if an agent
could prove fraud. Not a lot of time to peel back multiple layers of
offshore secrecy. Management judged auditors by how fast they worked
and how much money they brought in. Failure to complete a case
before the statute of limitations expired could damage an auditor's
career. West convinced his direct managers to let him try anyway.

"They couldn't walk away because everybody knew this guy was
doing it," West says.

In his quest to understand the schemes, West traveled to the Bahamas to interview the trust manager at the Royal Bank of Scotland. The
manager informed him that Wheaton was not the owner of record of
the companies in question. However, West spoke with distributors

who ordered bottles from Wheaton's offshore companies directly from Frank Wheaton. During the audit, West also spent a lot of time in Millville, where he earned a reputation as a straight shooter. Soon folks in town came forward with gossip. With a stenographer in tow, West put Wheaton Industries executives under oath, saving Wheaton's longtime personal secretary for last. (By this time, the company's board had grown weary of Wheaton's rule bending and fired him.)

In her testimony, the secretary recalled that Wheaton had personally dictated instructions for his offshore companies. West asked her how she'd recorded the information. On steno pads, she answered. It turned out she'd kept them all.

West finally had enough evidence to issue a summons to Wheaton demanding his books and records. When Wheaton refused to comply, the IRS took the matter to a judge, who upheld the request. By the end of his audit, West had amassed ninety boxes of documents that conclusively proved his case. Armed with the evidence, the IRS eventually levied millions of dollars in fines and back taxes. West's direct superiors had risked their careers to give him the space he required to complete his audit. Still, not everyone at the IRS was happy over how much time and resources it took.

As West scored court victories, IRS attorneys with whom he worked commended him; he had essentially created a textbook on how to do an offshore tax exam. His district director recognized the potential. Individual audits wouldn't catch or deter offshore abuses. An agent needed to identify a multitude of Americans hiding taxable income offshore and expose enough of them to send a signal to the rest. Scared and excited at the same time, West suggested a deep-dive research project into how the offshore industry functioned. His managers in New Jersey agreed.

"You have to know their industry as well as they know it," West says. "Once you figure out the techniques, it's not hard to figure out a class of people who are using them."

The U.S. government had not entirely ignored the problem. The Senate Permanent Subcommittee on Investigations under Delaware Republican senator William Roth issued a stinging report in 1985 titled "Crime and Secrecy: The Use of Offshore Banks and Companies." Its conclusions were stark. Despite overwhelming evidence of dirty money in their banking systems, tax havens chose instead to "systematically obstruct U.S. law enforcement investigations." The stonewalling eroded public trust in the U.S. justice system and left massive amounts of tax revenue uncollected. The report contributed to the passage in 1986 of legislation that for the first time made money laundering a federal crime.

West found a guide and kindred spirit in Jack Blum, a Washington lawyer and IRS consultant who had advised on the Wheaton case. Blum had arranged for the PBS documentary program *Frontline* and the BBC to surreptitiously tape John Mathewson, the chairman of a Cayman Islands bank, Guardian Bank and Trust, as he described the various ways to hide and access offshore money. The broadcasts prompted a Department of Justice investigation.

Blum connected West with others in the government who recognized the scale of the problem. West made the rounds, including stops at the Federal Reserve Bank of New York, the State Department, the Treasury Department, and even the National Security Agency. These were agencies that seldom spoke to one another, but they all talked with West.

Blum had also worked on the most explosive scandal involving offshore finance of the period, the investigation into the Bank of Credit and Commerce International (BCCI). Founded by a Pakistani businessman, the Luxembourg-based BCCI grew from $200 million in assets at its inception in 1972 to $2.2 billion in just five years. Huge influxes of cash kept the wheels spinning, with much of the money coming from the Middle East and drug cartels. Government investigations beginning in the late 1980s revealed BCCI's inner workings, and the media feasted on lurid tales of the bank's involvement with criminals, terrorists, and the CIA. Not surprisingly, Mossfon counted key BCCI shareholders as clients.

Kamal Adham, a native of Turkey and the former head of Saudi Arabia's intelligence service, was a Mossfon customer and a BCCI shareholder. Fortune had smiled on Adham when Saudi king Faisal chose his sister as a wife, bringing him into the kingdom's inner circle. He was known as the "godfather of Middle East Intelligence," in part because of his alliance with the CIA—a relationship that continued long after he left office in 1979 to focus on business. Jürgen Mossack's law office created companies for Adham beginning as early as 1982. He ultimately had at least five Mossfon companies, mostly based in Panama.

Middle Eastern elites like Adham didn't need Mossfon's structures to hide from a local tax collector. Rather, they created companies for cross-border trading, to escape liability and to disguise their activities from jealous relatives and prying foreigners. Adham even inherited a few of his Mossfon companies from others in the Middle East as payment for still-secret deals. The transfers show up in the Mossfon files simply as resolutions changing the power of attorney to Adham.

The Saudi spymaster received more than $323 million in loans from BCCI and owned about 2.9 percent of the bank. Another large shareholder, Abdul Raouf Khalil, the Saudi intelligence liaison to the United States, was a director of at least two Mossfon companies in the 1980s. The leading shareholder of the bank was the emir of Abu Dhabi, Sheikh Zayed bin Sultan Al Nahyan, whom Mossfon helped buy large swaths of London real estate through multiple anonymous companies registered by the firm.

After regulators yanked its license in 1991, BCCI went into receivership. Seven years later, Mossfon received correspondence from an English solicitor asking to reactivate several of Adham's companies, which were claimants to what was left of the carcass of BCCI. Adham died a year later, in 1999, of a heart attack, but his Mossfon structures outlived him. In 2000, almost a year after his death, the manager of Adham's office requested the firm shutter another of the spymaster's companies.

As Blum familiarized West with BCCI's offshore machinations, West also met with representatives of the Organisation for Economic Co-operation and Development (OECD), an international body consisting of the world's leading industrialized nations, which in 1998 had launched a crusade against "harmful tax practices."

The OECD identified four behaviors it said defined a country as a tax haven: if the nation had low or no taxation; if it ring-fenced its offshore industry by forbidding the use of its financial products domestically; if its activities lacked transparency; and if it resisted information exchanges with other nations. The OECD identified forty-seven tax havens worldwide that fit its criteria. Those who failed to reform risked being blacklisted with potential economic sanctions to follow.

The OECD released its first blacklist of thirty-five countries in June 2000. Notably missing from the list were three of the world's biggest secrecy jurisdictions: Switzerland, Luxembourg, and the United States, where Delaware annually churned out more than a hundred thousand anonymous companies. All three were founding members of the OECD.

West watched with interest as the OECD blacklisted seven Pacific island countries, including Niue. The islands had gained reputations as money-laundering sink holes. The spread of offshore banks, ostensibly based on sparsely populated atolls, alarmed the major powers. These banks served as conduits for cleaning dirty money and funneling it into the global financial system. Evidence substantiated the concern. A direct line of Russian mafia cash ran from the Pacific islands to the 1990s New York banking scandals involving Republic National Bank, among others.

A seemingly infinite number of ways existed for an offshore bank to facilitate money laundering. All it took was a basic understanding of the financial system and a flexible bank. The bank could move money between financial institutions and accounts, muddying its trail. Currency trades, particularly if backdated, allowed for large losses or gains. Account holders could place opposing bets on the stock market that canceled each other out. The bets produced no profits but provided a paper trail to legitimize the money.

For the criminal class and the merely circumspect, offshore banks seemed too good to be true. "Can this Niue bank locate its offices in Niue while it's being ran [sic] in Hong Kong (remote control)?" asked one Chinese prospective Mossfon client in disbelief.

The tiny Micronesian island of Nauru was one of the worst offenders. In 1999, the Russian Finance Department claimed that 90 percent of Russian banks maintained sixty-six hundred offshore subsidiaries in Nauru. The island was all of 8.1 square miles, but billions of dollars in Russian capital flowed through it every month. West added Nauru to his list of targets.

Nauru's biggest promoter was Jerome Schneider, who advertised books he'd written with titles like *Hiding Your Money* and *How to Own Your Own Private International Bank* in airline in-flight magazines and the *Wall Street Journal*. Even Mossfon recognized Schneider as trouble. The firm advised its offices to "be very careful" with companies that came through Schneider or his associates. "We do not want to be involved in any way with J. Schneider, who has been in several intn'l scandals," the general comments memo read.

Schneider ran a lucrative business selling Nauru bank licenses at $60,000 a pop. Eventually the Russians realized if they went to Nauru themselves, they could get the same license for $5,000. An identical problem confronted Mossfon, which charged $25,000 for a Niue bank license. After Niue undercut Mossfon's price, the Panamanians didn't sell many banking licenses there.

Mossfon's Niue incorporation business hit its peak in 1999, with nearly two thousand companies that year. After that, the OECD blacklist soured the business from a reputational standpoint, making Niue companies less appetizing. Hearings in the U.S. Congress singled out Niue for its Russian activities. Then in January 2001, the Bank of New York and Chase Manhattan embargoed all money transfers to the country. The prime minister of Niue suggested that if the OECD countries really wanted his nation to stop its offshore business, it needed to make up the difference in the island's annual budget. The $1.6 million Mossfon was paying Niue accounted for 80 percent of the government's revenue. Jürgen Mossack went to New Zealand to reassure the government that Mossfon's Niue operations were harmless, but the foreign minister refused to meet him.

West identified Mossfon as a major player in the offshore business but decided to give the firm a pass. Intermediaries such as Mossfon were not deemed low-hanging fruit. What worried West was the possibility that as a law firm, its activities might be protected by attorney-client privilege. While many inside the U.S. government believe that the privilege does not cover commercial transactions a nonlawyer performs—such as incorporating a company—the failure-averse IRS has long been leery of testing that theory in court. It also faced legal hurdles in getting information from a foreign intermediary like Mossfon without a leak or a whistle-blower.

West's research pinpointed four questions to master in order to effectively prosecute offshore tax evasion. The first involved how the taxpayer entered the offshore world. Who was the intermediary who set up the structures and the sales pitch that brought the parties together? Second, how did the taxpayer move his money offshore? As with money laundering, an endless number of variations existed. Businessmen could route transactions via the Bahamas or other tax havens and skim profits into offshore bank accounts. They could falsify invoices to pay their offshore company or associates for services that never occurred. Another tactic involved selling assets to the offshore company at a loss, which not only transferred money but also provided a tax write-off. Third, West had to prove that the taxpayer covertly controlled the secret companies, trusts, and foundations. And finally, how did the taxpayer get the offshore money home? There is no benefit to having tax-free cash if it's not accessible. West realized you did not need to own something to enjoy it. The title to any asset—a car, a yacht, real estate—could be held offshore and then leased back to the owner.

West visited John Mathewson, the Guardian Bank chairman exposed by Blum and public television's hidden cameras. Mathewson had cooperated with the government to avoid a lengthy prison sentence stemming from money laundering, tax evasion, and fraud charges. He told West how Guardian Bank offered a surefire way to repatriate offshore cash. It was a strategy West also saw advertised in the brochures he collected at Shorex.

Mathewson explained that his bank would issue credit cards to its customers. As long as they had sufficient cash in their account, they could draw down on the now tax-free money anywhere in the world simply by using the cards. Nobody tracked these purchases. Credit cards connected to an offshore bank were standard practice in the industry. When clients asked Mossfon to recommend a bank for their anonymous companies, credit cards were one of the criteria the firm considered.

West saw an opportunity. The credit cards might be issued by foreign banks but the transaction records went through company servers based in the United States. He visited the credit card companies to learn how the process worked. The companies anonymized the transactions and then stored them, some in more modern formats than others. Visa, for example, kept its records on eight-track tape.

The IRS agent prepared a report for his managers and presented a lengthy menu of ideas for how to attack offshore abuses, from looking at credit cards to concentrating on the firms that created the companies, like Mossfon. His bosses in New Jersey selected one: credit cards.

He then laid out a bold plan of action. West chose a tactic the IRS utilized infrequently at the time, the John Doe summons. The Internal Revenue Code gave the agency authority to issue a summons to third parties to investigate unknown individuals, "so-called John Does," who the agency believed deserved scrutiny. The bar for convincing a judge to allow such a fishing expedition was understandably high. The IRS needed to show that the information could not be readily obtained from other sources. It also had to make a strong case that the evidence collected would in fact lead to a group of people who had failed to comply with the law.

West suspected there were tens of thousands of Americans who were using offshore credit cards to avoid taxes. The brass at the IRS told him they could only handle five hundred cases. He filed this information away and tried not to let the lack of enthusiasm from his higher-ups demoralize him.

He focused on the major credit card companies: Visa, Mastercard, and American Express. The last two had servers on the East Coast. At the time, the agency was bifurcated by geography. West's management was ready to go forward, but in order to target Visa, he needed the approval of the IRS on the West Coast. It moved more slowly. Despite the delay, the New Jersey–led effort continued.

On October 18, 2000, the IRS filed John Doe summonses in U.S.

District Court in Miami seeking approval to ask for records from Mastercard and American Express. West and Blum provided declarations for the affidavit. The agency's request was for records from cards issued in three dozen countries, including Panama, the BVI, and Switzerland. A judge approved the request less than two weeks later. Next, the IRS served the companies. That process took months. The companies worried about customer privacy, but the data did not come with names. Company lawyers argued that the information was difficult, if not impossible, to retrieve. West had consulted the technical gurus at the credit card companies; they had already told him it could be done.

As the matter crawled forward, Michigan Democratic senator Carl Levin picked up Roth's banner in Washington, DC, as chair of the Senate Permanent Subcommittee on Investigations. Levin held hearings and issued reports on private banking, tax evasion, and money laundering. In one hearing, Levin estimated that $70 billion in tax revenue was lost each year because it was hidden offshore. Levin noted wryly that if the IRS collected even half of that money, it could pay for a prescription drug benefit "without raising anyone's taxes or cutting anyone's budget." In another report, the subcommittee concluded that sixteen tax havens had licensed about four thousand offshore banks, which controlled an estimated $5 trillion in assets.

Levin filed a sweeping legislative fix for what his committee uncovered. The Money Laundering Abatement Act proposed forcing banks to change the way they had conducted business for two centuries. In the past, what customers did with their money was mostly their own concern. Financial institutions only had to report suspicious activities, large cash transactions, and cash purchases of negotiable instruments such as bearer bonds. Levin went farther by turning banks into agents of regulators and law enforcement. Under Levin's bill, U.S. banks needed to create due diligence procedures to constantly monitor private banking customer accounts. They had to identify foreigners who owned accounts in banks in the United States and respond within forty-eight hours to requests for anti-money-laundering information from federal banking regulators. For two years, antiregulatory Republicans stalled Levin's bill.

Then on September 11, 2001, hijackers piloted planes into the Twin Towers and the Pentagon. Fonseca was in Luxembourg at the time. After hearing the news, he looked out his hotel window. His face blanched. The room overlooked the headquarters of the European Atomic Energy Community, a prime terrorism target in his estimation. Little did he know that the fallout from the attacks would prove radioactive for his business.

Even though terrorist financing represented but a sliver of private banking and offshore activity, the federal government now desperately wanted more insight into how foreigners and offshore companies used the banking system. Levin's anti-money-laundering bill provided the template for what became Title III of the Patriot Act, which was passed a month after the attack. Among its requirements, it forced U.S. financial institutions to enact comprehensive anti-money-laundering procedures. Now, before a bank did business with a foreign financial institution, it needed to ascertain the identities of the owners. The law empowered the Treasury Department to issue further Know Your Customer rules for banks. And it promoted the kind of international cooperation that the George W. Bush administration had previously abhorred.

In March 2002, West's credit card data finally started to flow. IRS commissioner Charles Rossotti was now giddy with excitement over the project. "Simply put, the guarantee of secrecy associated with offshore banking is evaporating," he crowed to *Newsday*. "If people use these illegal offshore methods to hide their income, we will find out who they are."

West did not get to partake fully in the celebration. To participate in the offshore effort, he had temporarily left the international company division to work for the individual taxpayer part of the agency. His battles to push the project forward had not endeared him to many in its bureaucracy. One of his managers told him to run, not walk, back to his old division. Once he successfully launched the credit card project, he moved to a research division; the effort continued with West's colleagues, special trial attorney John McDougal and IRS revenue agent Dan Reeves, who had a background in data and money-laundering investigations.

Commissioner Rossotti ordered the agency to use the data to get 350 audits into the pipeline straightaway. But the hard work was only beginning. The IRS needed to look for patterns that pointed to individuals using the cards for noncommercial purposes. It then had to go to the merchants where the charges occurred to get names of possible tax evaders. This work was done by field agents whose main experience was checking boxes on audits. Their job experience did not include thinking creatively. Despite training sessions, working with this kind of data was new and threatening. Since Rossotti had prioritized volume and speed rather than quality, the first catches were duds, revealing mostly harmless foreign credit card users like exchange students. Field agents who had quotas to fill looked at the poor results and shied away from pursuing more.

Rossotti's claim of victory over offshore tax evasion proved premature. Nonetheless, publicity around the credit card project drove thousands of U.S. taxpayers to amend their returns or seek amnesty for offshore accounts. The mere threat of being caught was sufficient to dissuade those who were greedy but cautious. The joke around the agency was that West, McDougal, and Reeves had enriched many a tax lawyer hired to get their clients out of jeopardy over offshore holdings. The John Doe summons became an important IRS tool, eventually bringing billions in hidden tax revenue back to the United States.

However, West's career never quite recovered. The battles with the bureaucracy had worn him down. He retired young, proud of his accomplishments but embittered by the experience. Soon after leaving the IRS, West went into his backyard and made a pile of his redundant material from the credit card project. Laughing maniacally, he poured lighter fluid on the documents and lit the bonfire.

6

FULL SPEED

The March 2003 edition of Mossfon's company newsletter struck a triumphant note. The OECD had threatened "the financial privacy of our customers," but the offshore world forced it to retreat.

The OECD had demanded that tax havens eliminate low tax rates and provide international access to secret banking and corporate information. Panama led the resistance. It accused the OECD of imposing requirements on tax havens its own members refused to accept. An opportunity to highlight Western hypocrisy came when the European Union announced what it called a "savings directive," a treaty that required EU members to share information and collect taxes from the interest generated by foreign bank accounts held by EU citizens. Luxembourg, its economy based in part on financial secrecy, declined to participate but suffered no consequence for its defiance. Panama cried foul.

The tax havens had powerful ideological allies in Washington. Congressional Republicans and the Bush administration attacked the savings directive and refused to cooperate with the OECD. While the United States was happy to promote international cooperation to pursue terrorists, the administration didn't like forcing people to pay taxes. Well-funded think tanks lobbied Congress to eliminate the U.S.

contribution to the OECD—about 25 percent of its budget. The pressure forced the OECD to all but abandon its blacklist and tax reform efforts.

The victory, Mossfon's newsletter reported, ensured that "we have before us a very positive outlook."

Mossfon was entering the most profitable period of its existence. At the same time, new global standards increasingly required it to identify and jettison its worst customers. In the contest between growth and compliance, the profit motive proved the stronger. Mossfon continued to collect crooked clients and sidestep any scandals they brought.

In SEPTEMBER 2003, the partners sent Mossfon's chief operating officer, Christoph Zollinger, to Samoa to inquire about incorporating companies there. Jürgen Mossack and Ramón Fonseca had met Zollinger in Panama City six years earlier, at the local helicopter club. All three were pilots. The partners were quite taken with the handsome young Swiss lawyer's combination of boyish charm and technological know-how. After graduating law school in Switzerland, Zollinger had followed his future wife, Darlina, to Panama. Her father, a wealthy plastic surgeon, helped him secure a job with the country's first Internet provider. Mossack hired Zollinger as an assistant in 1997. He quickly made himself invaluable computerizing the firm's work flow. The two partners soon promoted Zollinger to COO and put him in charge of overseeing the technical work of the firm. After he successfully negotiated the license with Samoa, Mossack and Fonseca offered Zollinger a junior partnership in the firm, giving him a 10 percent stake in its profits.

Within weeks of his promotion, Zollinger faced one of his first ethical quandaries, courtesy of John Gordon's USA Corporate Services. In February 2004, Mossfon received a request from the Attorney General's Office of the Bahamas. Two officers from England's Merseyside Police Financial Investigation Unit were making inquiries into a Mossfon company called FRO Inc., which had connections to a drug trafficker sentenced to twenty-five years in prison. The police officers did not have a judicial order but the Bahamas wanted Mossfon's assistance anyway.

Mossfon had two women in charge of handling these kinds of requests, attorney Ana Escobar, a devout Christian described by one colleague as "tender but tough," and Sandra de Cornejo, who had a degree in marketing. Neither had a background in financial compliance.

Gordon had registered FRO Inc. while at Shorex in 1997. Escobar wrote to him asking for information. He responded that due to the age of FRO, whose registration had lapsed, any records had been long since destroyed.

"We have noticed that too many clients of yours have come to our attention due to investigations started by the authorities of several countries," responded Cornejo, who identified herself on the email chain as "Customer Care." She reminded Gordon that Mossfon Group, its clients, and its representatives needed to follow the Know Your Customer requirements of the jurisdictions in which they operated. It seemed that Gordon refused to heed instructions in this regard, she noted. For this reason, the firm was contemplating cutting off USA Corporate's access to future Mossfon companies.

The due diligence demands at the time varied by locale. Panama required Mossfon to do some basic checking on the professionals on whose behalf it registered companies but not the actual owners. Mossfon asked these professionals for a reference letter, a certified copy of a passport, and some details about their business. It advised the attorneys, accountants, and bankers to keep records on the end users of the companies. If Mossfon requested this information, it was supposed to be available. In return, Mossfon promised not to hand such information over to authorities without a government order forcing it to do so—a prohibition it was soon to disregard in the FRO Inc. case.

Gordon reacted to Cornejo's email with bewilderment. "I have read your message and find it very odd," he responded, adding that FRO had been formed before the current standards existed. USA Corporate Services now followed all the requirements Mossfon demanded, wrote Gordon. Perhaps recalling the Bahamas Software case, he continued: "It has become obvious to us, as well as to you, that lax standards are expensive in terms of legal fees and time lost rummaging through old files on behalf of unsavory clients." If Mossfon wanted to force USA Corporate to find another provider over mistakes that had occurred more than five years earlier, that was its prerogative, Gordon wrote.

His response circulated among the partners. Zollinger noted that USA Corporate had sixty-nine active companies with Mossfon, a significant number. If Gordon said USA Corporate was performing the necessary checks, that was good enough for Zollinger.

What concerned Cornejo were all the companies USA Corporate had created before it started reviewing its clients. She noted that USA Corporate had 494 inactive companies with Mossfon, in addition to the 69 active ones. Escobar rejoined the email chain to add that she, too, was worried about the dangers lurking in the old companies. Zollinger, telegraphing his impatience with exaggerated politeness, asked what "the esteemed lawyer" proposed. Escobar suggested that Mossfon request USA Corporate's due diligence on all its active clients. The partners agreed. Gordon assented but said it would have to wait for a staffer to return from maternity leave.

Most of the information never made it to Panama. "MF had a tendency to be demanding for stuff then drop it for quite a while, then suddenly be demanding again," remembers Gordon.

The implications of the USA Corporate discussion for Mossfon's company-creation factory were staggering. USA Corporate was only one of Mossfon's clients, and not nearly the biggest. There were hundreds of others. A 2004 list of all the clients and the companies they created ran 454 pages. How many banks, lawyers, accountants, and other intermediaries with whom Mossfon worked had created companies for criminals, money launderers, or even terrorists? What other scandals lurked in the tens of thousands of companies, active and inactive, the firm had registered? The partners did not seem particularly curious to find out. They reassured themselves that the intermediaries were doing the required reviews of their customers. Problems would be addressed as they emerged.

———

MEANWHILE, MOSSFON WAS moving forward at full speed. In 2002, the firm had incorporated more than seven thousand companies. Two years later, that number nearly doubled. The growth was attributable in part to the very action Panama had maligned, the European Savings Directive. The directive required European Union banks to monitor European account holders and, if they were not nationals of the country where the account existed, to collect taxes on savings interest, initially up to 15 percent. Europeans who secretly hoarded cash in foreign banks suddenly faced having to pay tax on it. However, the law—announced in 2003 but implemented in July 2005—had a significant loophole. It applied only to individuals, not companies.

By early 2004, many Mossfon clients, particularly banks, began to approach the firm to create companies so that their customers could escape the directive. It was a volume business. Ramsés Owens met with executives from the Denmark-based Jyske Bank, who told him the bank had created two thousand companies for customers as a result of the European Savings Directive, most in Panama or Gibraltar. HSBC marketed the strategy to its European customers hiding cash in its Swiss private bank. The Swedish-based Nordea Bank also helped customers circumvent the rule through Mossfon, as did many others.

Avoiding the savings directive was so easy, even the merely well-off took advantage. An HSBC banker described the attitude of one client, a Belgian cotton exporter. "We also discussed the impending ESD and despite the very modest benefit in saved tax, he has decided to form a company through Mossack and to transfer all assets across," wrote the banker in the client's file.

In the second week of August 2004, Mossfon hit a speed bump in this incorporation bonanza. The firm sent out a mass email to its clients and franchisees that its own personal tax haven, Niue, had decided to shutter its public registry. Mossfon had more than nine thousand companies registered on the island, about 4.5 companies per inhabitant, but the bad publicity had finally been too much for New Zealand. It agreed to pay Niue the amount Mossfon was contributing to the island's budget, in order for Niue to abandon the offshore business. Still, a small island has to survive. Even after it ceased creating companies, Niue maintained a lucrative trade in "900" sex telephone numbers. Meanwhile, those nine thousand companies had to find new homes in another friendly country.

The day after the Niue announcement, Mossfon lawyer Ana Escobar sent a note to the partners, informing them that the firm's due diligence procedures for its BVI office were out of date. The Road Town office lacked a compliance and money-laundering reporting officer and its anti-money-laundering compliance manual needed updating. She noted that the partners had been discussing some of these issues with Rosemarie Flax, the head of the BVI office, for several years, and Zollinger had assured the partners that he had spoken with Flax and that the BVI government was unconcerned.

Around the same time, the head of Mossfon's Luxembourg office emailed the partners describing a "really scary" phone conversation he had recently had with a client. The customer sent a follow-up fax, typing on the cover sheet, "Kindly treat this information with the utmost confidentiality, as the individuals involved are very dangerous and usually escorted by ex-Stasi [East German secret police] bodyguards."

The fax included a newspaper story about Francisco Paesa Sánchez, an infamous Spanish intelligence agent and world-class opportunist. Paesa did business with the dictator of the West African country of Equatorial Guinea. He sold missiles to Basque terrorists but installed secret tracking chips that enabled their capture—to win favor with Spanish officials. In 1994, Paesa helped the former director of Spain's national guard hide bribe money, siphoning millions of dollars for himself in the process. Then Paesa engineered his greatest feat of all by faking his own death. The obituaries reported he died of a heart attack in Thailand. The body was cremated. A forged death certificate helped dispel any doubts. Grieving relatives held a Catholic Mass in his honor.

In early 2004, a private detective working with a Spanish journalist discovered that Paesa was alive and living in Luxembourg. Paesa traveled on an Argentinian passport under the name Francisco Sánchez. Ever vain, the newspaper reported, Paesa had shaved fourteen years off his age through his new identity. In Luxembourg, Paesa worked with his niece creating offshore companies, and under his new name he served as a director of seven Mossfon companies. The newspaper article alleged that the Spaniard had incorporated companies for arms traffickers and Russian mafia. Paesa later blamed the death notice on an innocent mistake and denied any connection to organized crime.

"Investigate and Act. Urgently!!" Fonseca responded to the fax.

However, the compliance gears moved much more slowly at Mossfon than the company creation ones did. It took more than a year before Mossfon fully broke off the relationship with Paesa, citing fears that the notorious Spanish spy might tarnish its image. The fears were unfounded. Mossfon remained in the background.

ANA ESCOBAR TRIED yet again, in September 2005, to get the partners to focus on compliance. There had been still another scare. Once more the firm inadvertently discovered troubling details about an owner of several of its companies. This time the person fit a relatively new category of concern. The ultimate beneficial owner was a politically exposed person, or PEP. The phrase, shorthand for a government official or a relative of one, came into vogue in the late 1990s, after Nigeria tried to recover billions of dollars stolen by its former ruler Sani Abacha. Notoriously corrupt, Abacha had funneled some of his illicit money through Swiss banks and offshore companies. In order to fight this kind of high-level political corruption, the United Nations and the European Community demanded that banks and offshore providers review their customers to determine if they were PEPs. If the answer was yes, the banks and company providers needed to collect additional details about the source of the wealth.

Mossfon had yet to adopt these standards. Some months earlier, the firm received an inkling of its exposure to PEPs, when one of its companies requested an official signature from the firm to complete the purchase of a $13 million yacht for a BVI-based company, Mondeo Industries, that Mossfon had created at the behest of the Luxembourg office of the French bank Crédit Lyonnais.

Crédit Lyonnais had made a special request. Their customer didn't just want nominee directors for Mondeo, he also wanted a fake share-holder. Mossfon itself would appear to own the company but would actually be a trustee for a second anonymous company, SVG Invest-ments, which was the beneficiary of the trust and the owner of Mondeo. Behind SVG sat the real owner, three layers removed from his yacht. While this violated the central idea of a trust, which required the owner to relinquish control of the assets, Mossfon had readily agreed to serve as the company's fake owner.

The ultimate beneficial owner's London-based attorney contacted Mossfon Luxembourg. He needed Mossfon, as Mondeo's on-paper owner, to sign off on financing for the yacht—right away. The attor-ney asked if one of the lawyers at Mossfon's London franchisee could provide the signature. But the franchisee's lawyers immediately rec-ognized the risk. If there was something unsavory about the transac-tion and it landed in court, the signatory could be blacklisted or even prosecuted. This was not a low-level employee in Panama signing the documents as a director, this was a lawyer in London with a lot more to lose, who would be falsely claiming ownership of a company.

The London franchisee then did something Mossfon had failed to do: It investigated who was behind Mondeo. The internal paperwork indicated that the ultimate beneficial owner was Sergey Generalov. It didn't take long on the Internet to find Generalov. He was Russian, a red flag in and of itself, as the country was a cesspool of corruption. But it got worse. Generalov was, as they say in Russian, *ne nichtozhestvo*, "not a nobody." He had been vice president of the Russian oil giant Yukos, and subsequently he led the Fuel and Energy Ministry. He then won a seat in the Duma, the Russian parliament, and another on the National Council on Corporate Governance. In other words, Generalov was the epitome of a PEP.

"Think of the potential scandal," wrote the head of Mossfon's exclusive London franchisee to the partners in Panama. "Since 2003 [Generalov] has been dealing with corporate governance in Russia!!!"

Emails flew between London, Panama, Luxembourg, and the BVI. A Mossfon lawyer in Panama sheepishly admitted he didn't know about Yukos and wasn't really up on matters of Russian politics. Mossfon decided not to sign the document. The next month, Generalov dumped the firm as its registered agent.

Ana Escobar and Sandra de Cornejo urged the partners to improve Mossfon's due diligence practices. "I'd like to take advantage [of the Mondeo situation] to note again suggestions I have made in the past but for one reason or another have not crystallized (I don't remember if someone said that it would be too complex)," Escobar wrote to the partners.

Mossfon subscribed to a Google-like paid search service called World-Check to help identify PEPs and criminals. It also, not for the first time, sent a letter to its professional clients requesting that they conduct a customer review. There was little follow-up. It was a question of incentives. When scandals sporadically came to light, they always seemed to resolve themselves without undue harm to the firm. Meanwhile, business was booming. In 2005, the firm tripled the number of shell companies it created on behalf of banks. By the end of the year, Mossfon had more than seventy thousand active companies. To do the necessary due diligence on all of them would have been prohibitively expensive, and sometimes impossible. In a business predicated on secrecy, no one wanted to produce the information.

"In many cases, existing customers would just ignore our requests," says John Gordon of USA Corporate. "Since we were not the registered agent [which was Mossfon] there was not much we could do to them as a credible threat."

Around this time Mossfon discovered another challenge its accelerated growth presented. Vianca Scott, age thirty-six, mother, wife, Mossfon employee, and devoted member of the firm's baseball team, died in a car accident late on the night of September 2, 2005. The firm's "special projects department" employed Scott to act as a nominee director for Mossfon companies. At the time of her death, she was an officer in nearly eight thousand companies. Despite Scott's never leaving her Panama City office, her financial activities spanned the globe, from the BVI to the Seychelles to Hong Kong.

The company-wide memo announcing her death voiced what many must have wondered. "For those who this will concern," it concluded, "we are at this moment considering how to make the changes of directors in the companies where Vianca appears as director."

The Geneva office led the discussion. Of all the Mossfon offices, it used nominee directors the most. Everybody concerned wanted to ensure that replacements existed for Scott, to avoid a business slow-down. Mossfon Panama suggested three possibilities from among its staff. Their last names were Allen, Wilson, and Wong. Each was young but also offered another important selling point. As Zollinger pointed out, they had names that sounded good internationally, their very blandness another layer of anonymity that could be commoditized.

Mossfon prepared forms authorizing Scott's replacement with another director, which they placed in the files of the active companies. When it was time for the nominee directors to perform an official act for the company—open a bank account or approve a contract, for example—the newly appointed director performed the act. Nonethe-less, ten years after her fatal car crash, Scott still remained the direc-tor for many Mossfon companies—those that had not required their director to perform an official act. A life tragically cut short lived on as an instrument of secrecy.

EVEN THOUGH MOSSFON proved adept at avoiding serious harm to itself over the activities of its companies, others were less fortunate. Toward the end of 2005, the firm began to receive emails from pan-icked investors in Argentina. They had placed their money in a sure-fire fund run by Eugenio Curatola, a charismatic former insurance agent. For years, they had received returns of up to 45 percent, with-drawing money without difficulty.

Curatola had told his customers that he had invested their savings in the foreign exchange market through a Panamanian company called Forexvan, which kept a bank account in Bermuda. A password allowed investors to access Forexvan's website and follow the upward march of their account value. At some point in 2004, Curatola froze the accounts. Phone numbers for Forexvan didn't work. Investors received emails saying Forexvan was under audit. When reached, Curatola insisted he had no control over Forexvan, he just did business with it. Still, on Forexvan's Web page, the value of the accounts continued to climb.

Vanderbelt Management Group Limited, a BVI company, owned Forexvan, according to the website. Investors contacted the financial services commission of the BVI to find out what was happening. BVI officials directed them to Vanderbelt's registered agent, Mossack Fonseca.

Mossfon's research revealed that despite Curatola's public denials, USA Corporate Services had sold Vanderbelt to him. In the process, it had provided the tools for the biggest Ponzi scheme in Argentinian history. Collectively more than four hundred people lost $90 million. The local media dubbed Curatola "the Argentinian Madoff."

Escobar wrote to New York, asking USA Corporate, which had created the company, for its due diligence. This was the first that USA Corporate had heard of the Ponzi scheme. Mossfon resigned as registered agent, grateful that Curatola hadn't requested the firm's nominee directors for his company. Argentinian authorities sentenced Curatola to five years in prison but paroled him after two.

While the firm disentangled itself from Curatola, Mossfon's Luxembourg office posed a question to the firm's lawyers that indicated just how far Mossfon would go—for the right price. In March 2006, a company created by an Icelandic bank asked to backdate a loan agreement for £500,000. The new date was December 2004, fifteen months earlier, a change that would yield a gain in dollars of about $92,000. Backdating official loan documents to play with currency changes could facilitate money laundering or serve as a vehicle for shady payments.

This was not the first time Mossfon had backdated official documents for clients. In fact, the practice was starting to occur with such regularity that the firm wanted to charge for it, particularly because its nominee directors were going to sign the agreement on behalf of the company. "Retroactively signatures are not within the 'free of charge' policy applied to our representative offices," an assistant to the partners emailed the Luxembourg office.

Emboldened by the profits pouring in, the partners took more risks by agreeing to handle money rather than simply create companies for others. They joined with two former Dresdner Bank executives to create an asset management business. Ramsés Owens also started an escrow fund, creating a holding account to allow for the clandestine movement of cash. At first he tried to get HSBC interested in hosting the fund. He explained to the bank in an email that Panama's reputation as a tax haven made it difficult for clients to send money to the country. "Penalties/fines are charged in many countries for outgoing money sent to tax heavens [sic]," Owens wrote. "If the money can be sent to Switzerland in Escrow, we can re-deliver the money to Panama afterwards."

HSBC declined to participate. Owens eventually found a home for his escrow account with Winterbotham Trust, a bank in the Bahamas.

On December 31, 2006, Niue officially shut down Mossfon's public registry. In anticipation of that event, Zollinger returned to Samoa and negotiated a deal with its government to waive the transfer fee for the first one thousand Mossfon companies that moved from Niue. The following month, Mossfon agreed to reactivate three Niue companies via the magic of backdating so that they could be transferred to another locale. A few months after that, the Luxembourg office devised a fee schedule for backdating loan documents. Each loan agreement backdated six months or earlier cost $105. Anything backdated beyond six months was an additional $8.75 per month. If the loan had a value in excess of $10 million, the firm tacked on an extra $20 charge per each additional million above that amount.

If there was any doubt that during this period Mossfon did not look closely at who bought its companies, a British customer named John Knight dispelled it. Knight purchased BVI-based Endeavour Resources Limited in 2005. It's not clear if Mossfon initially knew that Knight was the end user. At some point, Knight provided the Cyprus firm creating the company an empty bank account statement from 2002 and a passport scan as part of his due diligence. Unmentioned, apparently, went his decades-long business as an arms dealer.

The year before Knight incorporated his company in the BVI, Amnesty International included Endeavour Resources, then based in the UK, in a report on the weapons trade. Knight had tried to sell a huge cache of Soviet-era weapons to the Sudanese government, while it was in the midst of slaughtering hundreds of thousands of civilians in Darfur. The deal, financed by Iranians and Russians, included battle tanks, rocket launchers, cruise missiles, and five thousand semi-automatic pistols. When the United Kingdom forbade its citizens from trafficking in certain military equipment, Knight settled for providing Sudan "nonmilitary" equipment such as "crop-spraying airplanes" that the government retrofitted for carpet bombing.

A reporter for the *Scotsman* newspaper asked Knight why he had agreed to sell weapons to a regime as disreputable as Sudan. In his response, the arms dealer made a case for profit-seeking amorality. As long as there was a need, someone would fill it, no matter how distasteful the regime. Knight even mentioned Hitler as an example: "People were supplying him with stuff. He was the biggest tyrant of the lot. Saddam Hussein was being supplied by the British government and he was killing his own people."

In 2006, the BVI Endeavour Resources asked for a license from the British government to sell German-made machine guns to the Kuwaiti Interior Ministry. British authorities suspected Kuwait was not the final destination for the guns and declined to license the transaction. Knight then created a fake paper trail to make it appear as if he had canceled the deal himself. Instead, he bought similar machine guns from Iran. When they arrived in Kuwait, customs officials intercepted them and tipped off the British.

British government investigators descended on Knight's $3 million country estate in Kent, alarming the neighbors, who were unaware that an arms dealer lived among them. But all they found was a pile of shredded documents. Over the ensuing months they painstakingly pieced the shredded pages back together. In 2007, Knight was sentenced to four years in prison for arms trafficking.

7

THE NORTH STAR

Vladimir Putin haunts the Mossfon files. The Russian leader manages to be both present and invisible at the same time. No documents exist with his signature. No company form carries his name. He is not officially the director or owner of anything. Nevertheless, he is the North Star in a vast constellation of offshore companies.

Putin's authoritarian regime exists to enrich a minority at the expense of the majority. Russia has some of the highest income inequality in the world, with the top 10 percent of wealth holders owning 85 percent of all household wealth. Oil revenue, media monopolies, rigged courts, baton-carrying policemen, high-profile assassinations, and nationalism keep Putin's ship of state afloat. Charting its course toward illicit riches for the chosen few requires the secrecy world.

Putin's pals used structures built by Mossfon to covertly move billions of dollars, often from state-run banks or enterprises, into private pockets. These deals, from simple payouts to intricately planned takeovers of major industries, could have thrived only with Putin's approval. His cronies did not need a piece of paper signed by Putin to spell out his involvement. In Russia, Putin is the law. Businessmen covet his protection. What Putin receives in return is understood by the parties involved, a written contract superfluous.

The Russian leader has long been rumored to be one of the planet's wealthiest people. The income he declares, about $110,000 a year, is not an accurate representation of his wealth, according to U.S. government officials. If Putin indeed sits atop a fortune of tens of billions of dollars, as many claim, much of his treasure has passed through the secrecy world first, where intermediaries have transformed it into company shares, palaces, and yachts under straw men owners. But what belongs to Putin directly, and what is at his disposal, may in the end be a distinction without a difference.

How to manipulate the offshore system is second nature to Putin and the men around him, many of whom have intelligence backgrounds. Like the United States, the Soviet Union used tax havens and bank secrecy to fund covert activities during the Cold War, with the KGB maintaining the Politburo's secret foreign bank accounts. Whether funneling money to Communist parties in Europe, providing guns to third world insurgencies, or running spy rings, senior KGB officials learned to manipulate offshore banks and companies as part of their tradecraft.

As a youth, Putin's ambition was to be a member of the KGB. He achieved his goal in 1975, when he joined Russia's spy agency in his early twenties. During the next fifteen years, he rose in the ranks from lieutenant to major to colonel. At each step, his training grew in sophistication. A final stint at the Red Banner Institute, the KGB's most elite foreign intelligence instruction facility, was a graduate school of sorts. From there, the KGB posted him to East Germany, where as a lieutenant colonel Putin watched the Soviet empire crumble before him. He returned to Leningrad and took a job with the municipal administration, becoming head of a committee to promote investment in the city rechristened Saint Petersburg.

The friendships Putin formed in his younger days are key to understanding the movements that swirl around him in the Mossfon files. Autocrats who squirrel away hidden fortunes face a common thieves' dilemma, times ten. Millions of people desire their downfall. Whom can they trust? Only their nearest and dearest. Fear may be an effective motivator, but it is not as durable as love. Putin's relatives and oldest friends revealed their worth to him over decades. They demonstrated their loyalty long before power and riches entered the equation.

The Mossfon files contain the names of Putin's friends like Sergei Roldugin, a classical cellist who was like a brother to the budding intelligence agent. In their twenties, the two cruised the streets of nighttime Leningrad in Roldugin's boxy Lada, talking, drinking, and occasionally getting into fights. Roldugin orchestrated the double date where Putin met his future wife and served as the godfather of the couple's first child. He was also the owner of multiple Mossfon companies. The Rotenberg brothers, Arkady and Boris, also used Mossfon. They sparred with their childhood friend Putin in the same martial arts club. State contracts, including construction projects for the Sochi Olympic Games, made the brothers billionaires. Their Mossfon companies funneled millions of dollars in secret payouts.

From his time in Germany and as a government official in Saint Petersburg, Putin collected additional collaborators. Mossfon was not their only offshore provider. Dmitry Medvedev, Putin's prime minister and successor as president, worked alongside the future Russian leader in the same municipal office in Saint Petersburg in the 1990s. Medvedev has different offshore providers and his own network of school chums who serve as apparent proxy owners of foundations and anonymous companies. These confidants and their structures in turn hold palaces, yachts, and vineyards allegedly on Medvedev's behalf.

THE SAINT PETERSBURG–based Bank Rossiya, described by the U.S. Treasury as "the personal bank for senior officials of the Russian Federation," sits at the center of these Putin-related Mossfon companies. Bank Rossiya executives methodically created a web of offshore companies with Mossfon during Putin's second term as president, from 2004 to 2008. The activities of these companies crisscrossed the globe, with home bases in places like the BVI and Cyprus and bank accounts held in Switzerland and Luxembourg.

Putin's relationship with Bank Rossiya dates to July 1991, when, in his first week running the newly formed Committee for Foreign

Liaison, he directed the Leningrad municipal government to enter into a joint venture with the bank. The bank was owned by the local Communist Party at the time, but that was about to change. By the end of the year, the Soviet Union had collapsed, and Russia ceased to be ruled by the Communist Party.

Yuri Shvets, a former KGB officer, testified before Congress about the scramble for riches that ensued. For KGB officers, the number one priority was to establish new businesses or penetrate existing ones, including banks, he said. Soviet accounts held overseas disappeared, only to reemerge as personal fortunes. "Wide-scale infiltration of the Western financial system by Russian organized crime started right on the eve of the collapse of the Soviet Union," he testified. "The main players of the game were high ranking officials of the Soviet Communist Party, top KGB leadership and top bosses of the criminal world. The primary objective of this brotherhood was to accumulate maximum personal wealth and build safe havens abroad before Russia plummeted into financial chaos."

The bulk of the Communist Party's shares of Bank Rossiya were transferred to a group of Saint Petersburg businessmen, among them Yury Kovalchuk, a physicist-turned-banker, and Nikolai Shamalov, a representative for the German-based multinational firm Siemens, who had originally trained to be a dentist. Using his government position, Putin helped legalize the transfer from state asset to private hands.

The Rossiya shareholders and Putin, their government benefactor, maintained dachas together in a gated community on the eastern shore of Lake Komsomolskoye, outside Saint Petersburg. How Putin managed to afford the summer house on a municipal salary is a mystery. The men formed a cooperative society for the compound's occupants, which they called Ozero (the Lake). The cooperative kept a communal bank account into which any of the members could deposit or withdraw money, a possible model for the activity found decades later in the Mossfon files, where the same men are connected to companies that serve multiple interests and masters.

Another early investor in Rossiya was Gennady Petrov. Law enforcement sources now identify him as a leader of the Tambovskaya, a Saint Petersburg–based criminal gang. In 1995, Mossfon created a company on behalf of USA Corporate Services with a director of the same name. It's unclear if the owner was the crime boss or what the company did before it disappeared three years later. The Organized Crime and Corruption Reporting Project has linked Ivan Malyushin, a Putin ally and the Kremlin's former head of the Department of Presidential Affairs, as a business partner of Petrov dating to those early Saint Petersburg days. Malyushin himself had a company with Mossfon. Petrov has additional links to Putin's inner circle, as the Russian intelligence service has a long history of working in cooperation with the Russian mafia for help in extralegal activities. Similar activities continue today with cybercriminals.

Petrov is not the only Russian mafia figure with links to the Mossfon files. Associates of Semion Mogilevich, known at one point as "the boss of bosses" for his criminal reach, have multiple companies with the Panamanian firm. U.S. prosecutors believed that one of the Mossfon companies, Rosebud Consultants, was paying $20,000 a month to the crime boss for reasons unknown. There are also links in the files to the Brothers' Circle, a transnational gang with Russian roots that the U.S. Treasury believes acts as a coordinating body for multiple criminal networks.

While the Bank Rossiya shareholders and Putin supported each other in the 1990s, greater riches awaited once Putin vaulted to power. In 1996, Putin's boss, the mayor of Saint Petersburg, lost his election. What seemed like a setback became an opportunity. Pavel Borodin, who ran the Kremlin's Presidential Property Management Directorate, tapped Putin to be his deputy. Under President Boris Yeltsin, Russia was a smorgasbord of corruption, but it still had a freewheeling media, and commentators called the directorate "the Ministry of Privileges" for its role in Yeltsin's patronage network.

Borodin's subsequent troubles earned him a mention in the Mossfon files. Around the time Putin moved to Moscow and started work, Borodin signed a contract with a Swiss construction company to renovate the Grand Kremlin Palace. More contracts with sister companies followed. The rash of projects generated about $30 million in kickbacks for Borodin to distribute, according to a calculation by Swiss authorities. The money flowed through well-trodden routes: a Cyprus shell company, bank accounts in Geneva and Lugano, and founda- tions in Liechtenstein and Panama. Borodin made sure Yeltsin received a taste. The Swiss company paid credit card bills for the Russian pres- ident, his wife, and two daughters.

An independent prosecutor, Yury Skuratov, investigated. Despite the release of a sex tape featuring someone who looked a bit like him, Skuratov refused to get the message and back down, so Yeltsin dis- missed him. Yeltsin had named Putin to head the Federal Security Service, the successor to the KGB, a year earlier, in 1998. Putin's loyalty to Yeltsin then won him the post of prime minister. Yeltsin resigned on December 31, 1999, right before the Swiss issued an arrest warrant for Borodin, and Putin became acting president. Among Putin's first acts was to pardon Yeltsin and name Borodin the state secretary of the Union of Russia and Belarus, a position that came with diplomatic immunity. Mossfon first became aware of Borodin in 2009, nearly ten years later, when the firm discovered that one of Borodin's bankers—a Mossfon client—had been indicted in a Swiss court on charges of money laundering in the Borodin case. The banker pro- tested his innocence. Mossfon resigned from his companies anyway.

Jürgen Mossack maintained a healthy fear of doing business directly with the Russians. "After the collapse of the Soviet Union, assistant managers of factories were becoming oligarchs," he explains. "It was not normal—anybody could see that."

John Gordon of USA Corporate Services teased Mossack that he should lighten up, the Cold War was over. Regardless of Mossack's apprehension, the vast amounts of Russian money flowing into Cyprus and Switzerland via tax haven–based offshore companies, founda- tions, and trusts made it all but impossible to avoid. Russians obtained Mossfon companies through their lawyers and bankers in the hundreds, if not thousands. The Bank Rossiya network itself came to Mossfon through Swiss attorneys who had a prior relationship with the Pana- manian law firm.

IN A COUNTRY without a functioning legal system and a lurching economy, Russians who had the opportunity to safeguard their money did so. Russia experienced a total net capital outflow of about $550 billion between 1999 and 2015, according to the Russian government, although some suspect it could actually be higher than $1 trillion. Offshore companies were common vehicles to spirit cash out of Russia.

Sometimes, though, even these precautions were insufficient, as Mossfon discovered when someone illegally tried to tamper with one of its Panamanian registered companies. The beneficial owner was a Russian spice importer. The culprits had enlisted a local lawyer and translator to gain control over the company by illegally changing its directors. When Mossfon discovered what was happening, it put a stop to the scheme. A lawyer in Austria who dealt with Mossfon on behalf of the Russian importer was unsurprised. "This kind of taking over companies is now in fashion, practiced in Russia every day," he told the firm in an email. "You can lose your company over night."

For those favored by Putin, state spoils could be obtained legally. Gennady Timchenko was part of Putin's network back in Saint Petersburg. He was also a shareholder of Bank Rossiya. Timchenko earned billions through an oil-trading firm called Gunvor and through state-sponsored infrastructure projects. The U.S. government further asserted that Putin personally had a piece of Gunvor. Timchenko sold his shares in Gunvor the day before the United States announced sanctions against him.

According to the U.S. Treasury Department, Timchenko was linked to a Mossfon company registered in the BVI named Southport Management Services Limited. It was created by a Liechtenstein-based firm, Sequoia Treuhand Trust, which had an exclusive Eastern European clientele and a close and profitable working relationship with Mossfon. Sequoia masterfully layered companies and foundations together to guarantee its clients total anonymity. It created at least 222 companies with Mossfon, but the Panamanians had no idea to whom most of them belonged. Despite Mossfon's requirement that all clients make such information available, Sequoia stubbornly resisted imparting pertinent information on who owned its companies. Sequoia even declined to sign the agreement Mossfon sent to clients, according to meeting notes found in the files. "They do not want to disclose details of beneficial owners/end users to us," the notes stated.

Unlike Sequoia's black-box operation, the Bank Rossiya network of companies is laid bare in the Mossfon files. An executive with Bank Rossiya contacted the Swiss law firm Dietrich, Baumgartner, to create a shell company. The firm enlisted Mossfon, and in March 2006 the Panamanians registered Sandalwood Continental in the BVI. Over the next seven years, as much as $2 billion flowed through the shell company. Sandalwood sucked money from the Russian Commercial Bank of Cyprus (RCB)—which was partially owned by Russian state bank VTB—engaged in questionable loan arrangements, and consistently benefited from curiously advantageous share deals. There are approximately a hundred separate transactions involving Sandalwood and four additional companies created as part of the Bank Rossiya network. Altogether, they chronicle a Candyland trail of secret interests, payoffs, and preferential loans.

In order to hide its dealings, the Bank Rossiya executive who set up the network requested Mossfon's nominee directors for Sandalwood and the other companies. The names of Sandalwood's directors—Allen, Alexander, Wong—are on dozens of loans and share deal documents, offering another layer of concealment—at least in theory. Every official company record that required signatures of the nominee directors had to pass through Mossfon's Panama office, where they were filed away in the firm's archives.

On paper, Oleg Gordin, the designated owner of Sandalwood Continental, was a small-time businessman who described himself on an account-opening form with RCB as having a background in "law enforcement agencies." The Bank Rossiya executive who created Sandalwood and directed its activities would have been hard pressed to find someone more innocuous than Gordin. Yet for someone with such a low profile, he had access to a staggering amount of capital. Between 2009 and 2012, RCB offered Sandalwood lines of credit up to $800 million. The bank made this money available to a man with no track record and a company with no discernible business model.

Even the partners in Panama noticed that something was off about Sandalwood's relationship with RCB. One of RCB's first loans to Sandalwood was for $103 million. The size of the loan and the unanswered questions surrounding it raised red flags for the Panamanians. There was nothing in the loan document that detailed what rate of interest would be charged, when the loan would be paid back, or the purpose of the outlay.

"I believe this is delicate," wrote Jürgen Mossack in Spanish in an email to the partners. Mossack often employed the word *delicado* when confronted with suspicious activity. The word functioned as a linguistic yellow traffic light—an opportunity to pause and recalculate the amount Mossfon charged to ensure the sum was commensurate with the risk to which the firm was exposed.

Mossack explained that if Mossfon's nominee directors signed for such a large loan without the requisite detail, the firm "could be in the presence of payments of a doubtful origin and a doubtful destination." It didn't want to be held culpable later if the loan turned out to be improper. Christoph Zollinger concurred, responding that the firm shouldn't sign without first obtaining a letter of indemnity, releasing it from responsibility.

With prodding, the Bank Rossiya executive who was shepherding the loan provided a bit more detail. The loan appeared to exist to buy tanker ships. The executive tacked on a repayment schedule and added the requested letter of indemnity. The loan went forward. It wasn't the first loan the Bank Rossiya network shepherded through Mossfon, nor, as the partners knew, was it likely to be the last. On this one deal, Mossfon earned more than $2,000 simply to provide a few signatures. The specter of future profits likely weighed heavily in the firm's calculations. The partners gave a green light to future transactions, allowing the Mossfon nominees to approve the transfer of hundreds of millions of dollars from the state-owned bank to the anonymous company.

In the Bank Rossiya network of companies, Sandalwood acted as a clearinghouse for loans and as a credit card for miscellaneous expenses. It was reminiscent of the Ozero cooperative bank account, writ large, a vessel into which communal money flowed. The Mossfon files show that Sandalwood loaned out about $600 million in 2009, and at least $350 million in 2010. Most of the money went to companies created by company providers other than Mossfon.

Sandalwood lent around $737,000 to a company that owned land and a hotel complex in the city of Sortavala, on the northern tip of scenic Lake Ladoga. The Organized Crime and Corruption Reporting Project reported that local blogs had identified the location as a possible holiday house for Putin. Over several years, Sandalwood lent $11.3 million to the Russian company Ozon, at an interest rate of 1 percent. Repayment terms on the loans sometimes stretched for as long as twenty years. The loan terms also changed currencies, further depreciating how much Ozon needed to repay. Sandalwood lent another $590,000 on similar terms to a second company that shared an address with Ozon, to build a yacht club on Lake Ladoga.

Bank Rossiya's Yury Kovalchuk was a co-owner of Ozon at the time it received the Sandalwood money. By this time, Kovalchuk was the bank's CEO and its largest shareholder. A few years later, the U.S. government would identify Kovalchuk as one of "Putin's cashiers."

A year after Sandalwood started loaning money to Ozon, Kovalchuk's company acquired an extensive mountain property not far from the Ozero cooperative's compound. Ozon built the Igora ski resort on the site, reportedly now one of Putin's favorite places to ski. There is a dacha on the grounds that locals claim exists for the Russian leader's exclusive use. In 2013, under tight security, the resort played host to the wedding of Putin's younger daughter, Katerina Tikhonova, to Kirill Shamalov, the son of Nikolai Shamalov, the former Siemens representative who was a major Bank Rossiya shareholder and Ozero cooperative member.

In 2007, a year after creating Sandalwood, Bank Rossiya executives started another company, Sonnette Overseas. It had an even more improbable owner than Oleg Gordin. On paper, the company belonged to Putin's dear friend, Sergei Roldugin, the cellist. Broad-faced and often sporting a pageboy haircut, Roldugin has served as a gracious interlocutor for Putin, humanizing the Russian leader in interviews. A year after creating Sonnette, Bank Rossiya formed another company, International Media Overseas. Roldugin ostensibly owned this company, too. For a self-described musician with no business experience, Roldugin's companies demonstrated an uncanny ability to earn profits and navigate complex corporate transactions.

Mysterious payments flowed to Roldugin's companies through multiple avenues, including stock deals. In 2010, International Media agreed to buy shares of the Russian technology company Rosneft. Another anonymous Panamanian company, unaffiliated with Mossfon, was on the other end of the deal. The transaction details included a provision that if the deal failed to go through, Roldugin's company was to earn almost $750,000 in a penalty payment. Two deal documents went out on the same day. The first executed the sale. The second canceled it, triggering the failure provision and guaranteeing the bonanza for Roldugin's company. In this way, an unexplainable payment was made to look legitimate.

Another arrangement, with an anonymous Cayman Islands company, involved swapping identical share amounts of the Russian military corporation Rostec. No actual Rostec shares exchanged hands since the amounts offset each other. The agreement was then backdated. The value of the Cayman company's shares was lower on the older date. It now had to pay International Media the difference. In 2011, a series of these deals netted International Media Overseas $463,800. Questionable payments were made legal. Sandalwood Continental entered into similar transactions, earning at least $4 million from them between 2008 and 2011.

Roldugin's company Sonnette Overseas was even more ambitious. It joined a consortium in a secret and convoluted plan to take control of Russia's largest truck manufacturer, Kamaz. Several agreements in the Mossfon files show exchanges of company percentages and responsibilities. If the deal prospered, the cellist would win a say in the business plan, budget, and role of foreign investors in Kamaz. Derailed by the 2008 financial crisis, the deal never came to pass.

Despite the sophistication of his companies, Roldugin exhibited a remarkably laissez-faire attitude toward his business interests. "It's difficult for us sometimes to get ahold of the [beneficial owner] of International Media and other companies to get his signature," the

Bank Rossiya executive complained in an email to Mossfon. He suggested an end run around this problem. The executive would appoint an authorized person to sign documents; that way, he would not have to bother the musician.

In 2008, Putin stepped down from the presidency. The Russian constitution did not allow more than two consecutive presidential terms, so he swapped places with his prime minister, Dmitry Medvedev. The change in title did little to diminish Putin's authority. During Putin's time as prime minister, from 2008 to 2012, Bank Rossiya's balance sheet more than doubled in size from $4 billion to over $8 billion. The offshore network established with Mossfon also went into high gear.

Prior to Putin switching titles, Bank Rossiya had aggressively moved into media ownership. It purchased a stake in a television network, which Putin then made a national broadcaster. The bank also grabbed Ren TV, whose reputation for crusading journalism ended under its new ownership. Publicly, Bank Rossiya also owned 16 percent of Video International, one of Russia's biggest advertising wholesalers. International Media Overseas also held a 12.5 percent stake in the company, worth about $10 million a year in dividends to Roldugin, according to a bank account form found in the Mossfon files.

Cyprus was a focal point for much of the Bank Rossiya network's offshore activity. The country, a doorway into the European Union, was so corrupt, one could buy shell companies that came with an open bank account already attached, no questions asked. Russians with money had flocked to the island's banks for years. It was also where Sandalwood's piggy bank, RCB, was located. But in 2012 Cyprus began to slip into financial crisis. As the island's overleveraged financial institutions tumbled into default, the Bank Rossiya executives began to move their companies to other jurisdictions and providers. They were not alone. Direct investment by Russians in the BVI during this period increased eightfold as their compatriots fled Cyprus.

In a series of loan assignments, Sandalwood Continental transferred the rights to hundreds of millions of dollars to another BVI-based company, OVE Financial. The new owner often received the right to these loans for $1. OVE Financial was registered to Mossfon's Panamanian competitor, the law firm Morgan and Morgan. Rather than work out of Cyprus, OVE Financial did business in the more stable tax haven of Luxembourg.

Around the same time, three shell companies made huge payments into Sunbarn Limited, another Mossfon-Rossiya creation. Arkady Rotenberg, Putin's childhood martial arts friend, appears to have controlled the companies doing the paying, perhaps in response to government contracts to build a proposed $40 billion natural gas pipeline between Russia and Europe. The pipeline deal failed to materialize. Still, when the U.S. Treasury Department sanctioned the brothers to penalize Putin for his invasion of Ukraine in 2014, the Russian leader opened the spigot to more contracts for the Rotenbergs. For those in Putin's inner circle, the Russian leader rewards loyalty with protection and opportunity. In 2016, Arkady Rotenberg placed first on the *Forbes* list of Russian state contractors with a haul of $8.2 billion's worth of projects.

The files show that the men around Putin have started to move some of their wealth to their children. Arkady Rotenberg, for example, has transferred ownership of a number of his secret offshore companies to his son Igor. A Reuters report indicated that the Russian leader himself was setting the example. Not long after Putin's daughter married Shamalov's son at the Igora ski resort, the younger Shamalov, barely thirty, managed to borrow about $1.3 billion from state-controlled Gazprombank. He used the money to acquire a 21 percent stake in one of Russia's largest petrochemical companies. Within a year, the stake had grown in value to at least $2 billion.

As PUTIN AND his cronies transfer billions of dollars to their children, ordinary Russians struggle to survive. In a country rich in natural resources, Russia has a GDP per capita of about $9,000. The economic situation has forced many Russians to seek work abroad, people like Vladimir Kraevoy, a sixty-three-year-old machinist. In 2011, Kraevoy joined the crew of the Russian cargo ship SS *Ross*. He signed a six-month contract that paid him $3,000 a month—a small fortune for most Russians.

The *Ross* was owned by the Damelo Group, a BVI company created by Mossfon in 2004, through an intermediary in the United Arab Emirates. According to Mossfon's files, through this offshore company and others, four Russians owned the *Ross* and several other ships. They added an additional layer of secrecy by shuffling the registration of their ships among small Pacific island nations like Tuvalu and Kiribati, which required little information or regulation for the ships that flew their flags.

Instead of economic opportunity, Kraevoy found himself a prisoner aboard a slave ship. The captain of the *Ross* stripped Kraevoy and the other crewmen of their identification documents. The ship itself had no air-conditioning. The sailors baked as it sailed through the Persian Gulf. Vermin infested the cabins. Food and water were scarce, soap nonexistent. The captain physically abused sailors who complained and refused to pay them.

At 423 feet, the *Ross* was compact, with two large cranes in the middle and three enormous cargo holds belowdecks. While working on a diesel engine in the stern, Kraevoy took a bad fall. Despite docking at several different ports, the captain denied his request to seek medical care. Instead, he forced Kraevoy to fulfill his duties, including turns at night watch. Within a month, the machinist was dead. Another crewmate, Edward Bordachenko, went missing from the ship after complaining to the Russian Seafarers' Union about the conditions aboard the *Ross*. His body was never discovered. Bordachenko's wife is convinced her husband was thrown overboard. When the captain refused to pay the rest of the sailors, they managed to escape and sought refuge at the Russian embassy in Kuala Lumpur.

Russian police issued an arrest warrant for the ship, but the owners simply changed its name to MV *Nerei* and continued sailing. The men also owned, through a separate Mossfon company, the SS *Veles*. This ship they abandoned in the Philippines, stranding a crew that included twelve Russians, eight Indians, and one Ukrainian, without paying them for their work. The owners declared bankruptcy and walked away from the company.

In May 2012, Russian prosecutors filed charges against two of the owners, Vladimir Bobrov and Gleb Klokov, for "use of slave labor with the threat of violence" and "slave labor, which entailed the death of a person." The men were detained but to date have avoided trial or prison.

8

THE ART OF SECRECY

Just as Switzerland excelled at stashing the money of foreigners in its banks, the alpine nation performs a similar service for art. The art trade in Switzerland is a multibillion-dollar business. At its center is the Geneva Freeport, more than 600,000 square feet of storage space in an industrial area west of the city. There, in the main complex, behind security fencing, stands a row of multistory gray-red warehouses. They contain approximately 1.2 million pieces of art, everything from Roman antiquities to an estimated one thousand Picassos. Together the goods inside the Geneva Freeport are conservatively valued at more than $100 billion. Unlike a museum, nobody ever sees all these treasures together. They are locked away in vaults, the contents of which, in many cases, are known only to their owners.

For another layer of anonymity, one can, as many Freeport customers do, create an offshore company based in the BVI or a similar secrecy jurisdiction, and rent a vault under the company name. In Switzerland, there is no obligation to disclose the beneficial owner of an offshore company. The Freeport will not ask for the identity of the owner behind the company. Yet it is the financial benefits of the Freeport, even more than the secrecy, that draw people to this drab, visually unappealing setting. As long as the art resides within the

Freeport, it is tax free. One can buy a painting at auction in New York, ship it to the Geneva Freeport, and no government will collect a cent until it leaves the confines of this concrete tax haven.

While the Geneva repository is the oldest, other freeports specializing in art can be found in Luxembourg, Monaco, Singapore, Beijing, and Delaware. They are popular with the wealthy and the unscrupulous. In 2016, Italian police pried open crates in the Geneva Freeport that had sat for fifteen years in a vault rented by an offshore company. Inside they found a priceless collection of looted Roman and Etruscan artifacts stockpiled by a bankrupt English art dealer sentenced to jail for lying about his assets in court. Authorities fear there are more such cases waiting to be revealed. There is no way to know for sure, as inventory is not consistently tracked.

The freeports do not stop at merely storing art. Sales are conducted within their walls as well. Sometimes, the art simply shifts from a seller's vault to a buyer's and cash is transferred between the bank accounts of shell companies. The art itself never leaves the premises.

Government officials around the world fear this may allow for money laundering. Conceivably money launderers could create fictitious sales between separate offshore companies with the same owner. The companies would then buy and sell items within the freeport at an inflated cost to give the extra cash a clean provenance. Transactions could even involve items that do not actually exist, with the freeport providing a patina of legitimacy to the arrangement. Whether these practices occur and with what frequency is unknown.

For actual art transfers, an entire business has developed to allow participants to remain anonymous and minimize fraud. Firms that operate within the freeports hold the purchase price in escrow and act as custodians of the work of art. At the right moment, they oversee the exchange, ensuring that neither party gets burned. Some companies even have laboratories within the freeport where they will test the authenticity of a painting or perform restorations.

The freeports are only one example of the secrecy upon which the art business thrives. Worldwide the art trade is valued at $30 billion annually, and more than half of all art sales are private. Every participant in the business finds the secrecy world useful. Anonymous companies help art dealers, who connect buyers and sellers, to avoid red tape and paperwork. Dealers trade in nonpublic knowledge as much as the art itself—what is for sale, who wants to buy, and for how much. Hiding ownership allows the middlemen to control that information. Auction houses such as Christie's and Sotheby's benefit from secrecy as well, obscuring the identity of those behind sales to increase bids or guarantee prices. Finally, the buyers and sellers themselves employ offshore companies to hide their activities from everyone from the taxman to relatives to business associates.

Beyond secrecy, there are multiple ways tax havens, freeports, and anonymous companies are useful to the art business. Basing operations in a tax haven makes financial and logistical sense because a single painting can transit multiple countries from purchase to destination. It also provides a degree of protection in case of litigation. Freeports offer climate-controlled state-of-the-art secure storage and minimize insurance premiums. An expensive painting hanging at home costs more to insure.

Mossfon's files contain some of the biggest names in the art business, customers who used the firm's companies to buy and sell art, often to move it to freeports. The amount of identifiable art activity in the files is likely only a fraction of what actually took place. The vast majority of companies Mossfon sold had little contact with the firm afterward. Since no public registries exist of freeport owners, it is difficult to know how many Mossfon companies kept valuables there or were otherwise involved in the art business.

Art has always been a convenient way to store and transport value. When banks fail and blood runs in the street, people grab their art and jewelry before they flee. A small painting worth millions can fit in a suitcase. Art is also a storehouse of emotion in a way that cold cash can never be. More so than yacht purchases or real estate acquisitions, many of the art deals found in the Mossfon files come freighted with messy family dramas and the burden of a tumultuous personal history.

The freeport concept itself dates to the nineteenth century, when so-called bonded areas were utilized for temporary storage of commodities such as grain, tobacco, and industrial goods. They gradually transformed into tax-free treasure troves to house art, antiques, jewelry, watches, and vintage wine for the uberwealthy. Today more than 65 percent of the articles stored in the Geneva Freeport are art and antiques.

The switch from dry goods to luxury items parallels a behavioral shift in art collecting that accelerated with the emergence of an empowered and mobile global elite. In the past, art patrons donated their collections to museums in the places where they lived. National tax systems provided incentives for such donations—for example, through charitable tax deductions. Today, the wealthy are less tied to a single location or tax regime. In 2014, 76 percent of collectors purchased art as part of an investment strategy. Works of art that once decorated mansion walls as showy status symbols or as the joyful passions of knowledgeable collectors serve instead as investments to be hoarded, often in secret, while their value increases. This change in the art business is revealed in the Mossfon files.

THE LARGEST SINGLE collection of Picassos in private hands, outside of the Picasso family, is believed to reside in the Geneva Freeport. The paintings belong to the Nahmad family, Syrian Jews who pioneered the commodification of fine art, buying paintings and holding them in the Geneva Freeport until they reached an attractive sales price. The family was also a longtime Mossfon customer, dating back to the days of Antoni Guerrero's Geneva office in the early 1990s.

The Nahmads made their first fortune speculating on currencies. Their conversion into art entrepreneurs began in the 1950s, led by Giuseppe Nahmad, the oldest of three brothers. Giuseppe, known as Joe, owned apartments in Rome, Milan, Portofino, and London, the walls of which he filled with fine art. It was part of an extravagant and acquisitive lifestyle that prompted his friends to nickname him "Farouk," after an ostentatiously wealthy Egyptian ruler whose collection of everything from rare coins to luxury cars was legendary.

Joe Nahmad was willing, on occasion, to push the limits of the law in pursuit of his business interests. He was arrested, briefly imprisoned, and fined in Italy in 1957 for possession of $70,000 worth of stolen British pounds. Four years later, tax officials investigated him for failing to pay taxes on $92 million in stock market trades. Experiencing a cash crunch in the early 1960s, Joe had his younger teenage brothers, Ezra and David, sell some of his art. The two were so successful, they started buying paintings cheaply in Paris and flipping them in Milan, where they fetched higher prices. It was the launch of a business model.

In the ensuing years, the three brothers gained a reputation for sharp elbows and creative financing. In the process, they put together a billion-dollar collection and became pillars of the global art market. Auction houses approached them for paintings to help fill out their sales. When the market dipped, the Nahmads would buy, keeping prices stable. Aside from a sexual harassment complaint and a grandson's involvement in an illegal Russian gambling ring run out of New York's Trump Tower, the family largely avoided controversy—that is, until accusations over a painting stolen by the Nazis dragged them into court, and the Panama Papers exposed their secret business activities to a global audience.

The brothers registered their first Mossfon company, Swinton International, in 1992, but they were likely using the offshore world well before then. Swinton was followed by International Art Center three years later, though this company may have existed previously in another jurisdiction. A document in the Mossfon files mentions a company with the same name purchasing the pastel *Danseuses* by Edgar Degas in October 1989.

Initially, the brothers owned International Art Center through bearer shares, but in 2001 a resolution signed by Mossfon's nominee directors issued one hundred shares in the company and granted them to Joe. However, both companies operated jointly, with all three brothers participating. At different times David and Ezra had power of attorney over the companies' bank accounts at the Swiss bank UBS and at Citibank. In 1995, Swinton International authorized David to sell five paintings, including a Matisse and a Picasso. Several of the paintings subsequently went to auction at Sotheby's, with the catalog identifying them as from a private collection.

The following year, the Nahmads, through International Art

Center, purchased an oil painting at auction at Christie's for $3.2 million. The 1918 painting by Amedeo Modigliani, known as *Seated Man with a Cane*, is a portrait of a dapper gentleman with a thin mustache, sporting a stylish hat. The man appears to be Georges Ménier, the scion of a dynasty of Belgian chocolatiers, who was chummy with the artistic elite of the day. As with many of the particulars involving the painting's past, even this fact is in dispute.

The Christie's catalog entry detailing the provenance of the painting was sketchy and should have raised a red flag. It began with an anonymous sale sometime between 1940 and 1944. During this period, the Nazis and their collaborators, particularly in France, were busily despoiling Jews of their art collections. Jews like Oscar Stettiner, an art dealer who fled Paris to escape the German invasion. The collection he left behind was seized and sold for the benefit of the Nazis. Among the paintings appears to have been *Seated Man with a Cane*.

Immediately after the war, Stettiner filed a claim to begin the process of recovering the painting, only to die a few years later with the petition still pending. In the meantime, the work had been purchased by an unscrupulous gallery owner. Christie's provenance didn't have that part of the story. Instead, the auction house claimed that the portrait went to a J. Livengood. He passed it down to his descendants, who finally offered it for sale in 1996 through Christie's. In fact, Livengood was the husband of the gallery owner's daughter and was too young to have purchased the painting as claimed by Christie's.

After buying the work, the Nahmads tucked the Modigliani away in the Geneva Freeport to appreciate in value. The painting only left their vault twice to be exhibited and once in 2008 for an aborted auction where it failed to fetch the baseline price set by the Nahmads. Years after the brothers bought the painting, Mondex Corporation, a Canadian-based art recovery outfit, stumbled upon the backstory of *Seated Man with a Cane* while researching another work of art.

James Palmer, a self-styled "art detective," is Mondex's founder. Palmer finds potential cases of looted art and then hunts down relatives who may have a claim. Mondex handles the litigation in exchange for costs and a sizable cut of any proceeds. In the art world, opinions on Palmer vary. He has been portrayed as a shakedown artist, "an art world ambulance chaser" who manipulates the media with faulty research to call attention to cases that ultimately benefit his company more than the families of the original victims. Others see Palmer as a driven advocate who plays an important role in righting past wrongs.

For Palmer and the Nahmads, there was much at stake. Modigliani's paintings have been known to fetch as much as $170 million. The portrait of the little man with a cane could be worth $25 million.

Palmer found a living heir, Oscar Stettiner's reclusive and ailing French grandson. He and his team of lawyers then filed a case in federal court in New York in 2011. It was withdrawn for improper venue. They filed again. The case moved to New York State supreme court, where the Nahmads challenged it on procedural grounds. Location was key. Unlike many places in the world, the U.S. judicial system allows plaintiffs discovery. If the plaintiffs can convince a judge that their complaint has merit, they are allowed to request evidence from the other side. The Nahmads challenged the case on venue and argued they were not even the right defendant. They claimed they didn't own the painting; International Art Center, a Panamanian company, did.

The Mossfon files indicated that the Nahmads had actively controlled International Art Center for more than twenty years. In 2008, Joe transferred the hundred shares in the company to Ezra and David. After Joe died four years later, *Forbes* estimated the surviving brothers were worth a combined $3.3 billion. Despite Ezra being the older of the two, David, who is also a championship backgammon player, took control of the business. In 2014, David became the exclusive shareholder of International Art Center.

Palmer and the New York court were not aware of these details.

The Nahmads succeeded in dragging out the case on procedural grounds for more than three years. In April 2017, Judge Eileen Bransten ruled that International Art Center did not insulate the Nahmads from liability over the painting. With the publication of the Panama Papers, Mondex could prove the company and the Nahmads were one and the same. The case could continue.

"IAC did not have a corporate identity independent of its individual owner," Judge Bransten ruled.

BY THE TIME the final gavel fell at Christie's on November 10, 1997, the modern art business had changed forever. The Ganz Collection, painstakingly assembled over a lifetime of judicious purchases, had fetched record sums in one blowout sale. After that high-wattage night in New York, prices in the art world soared as the megawealthy embraced a newly lucrative investment. Hidden in the background, making it all possible, was a Mossfon company.

Victor and Sally Ganz, a husband and wife who owned a costume jewelry business, had been collecting paintings for fifty years. The couple were passionate art lovers of the old school. The paintings they bought became cherished family members, hanging on the walls of their home. They championed Frank Stella and were patrons and friends of Jasper Johns, Robert Rauschenberg, and Eva Hesse. When they had a little extra money to spare, they splurged and bought a Picasso. Over five decades, they spent roughly $2 million assembling their collection.

After the couple died, their children, faced with a hefty inheritance tax, opted to sell. The prospect of the auction generated excitement for months, starting with the auction houses eager to get the commission. Competition for the Ganz Collection was fierce but Christie's prevailed. Art insiders assumed that Christie's had set a sales price for the Ganz children, a base amount they were guaranteed to earn regardless of the auction's outcome. What Christie's had offered and how it was done remained a mystery, obscured by Mossfon and the secrecy world.

The real story began with a Mossfon company, Simsbury International Corp., incorporated in Niue in April 1997, less than three months after Sally Ganz died. The company's purpose and activities were well insulated. Simsbury was owned through bearer shares. Mossfon's nominees served as directors.

A few weeks after its creation, in a private transaction, Simsbury purchased the most valuable of the Ganz paintings from Spink and

Son, a London auction house then owned by Christie's. Simsbury paid the staggering sum of $168 million, a huge gamble, but not by the auction house. The money appears to have been fronted by Christie's largest shareholder at the time, Joseph Charles Lewis, a billionaire British currency trader. Lewis had power of attorney over Simsbury's bank account, which was held in Safra's Republic National Bank of New York. Presumably the money made it to the Ganz heirs.

Notoriously publicity shy, Lewis owns more than two hundred companies in fifteen countries. His business interests have included, at one time or another, football clubs, restaurant chains, and oil companies. He held multiple companies through Mossfon, including the Bahamas-registered Aviva Holdings Limited, which shares the name of his gigantic yacht, on which he sails the world conducting business surrounded by a collection of paintings by the likes of Picasso, Paul Cézanne, and Gustav Klimt.

The auction documents found in the Mossfon files indicate that if the listed Ganz paintings sold for more than $168 million, Simsbury and Spink would split the difference. It was a calculated risk by Lewis but one that could pay off in multiple ways. In addition to earning money if the sales price was higher, the much-sought-after auction would raise Christie's share price. Under the terms of the deal, Lewis was forbidden from bidding on the paintings himself, although that provision was largely unenforceable, since a buyer could hide behind a proxy and an anonymous offshore company.

In the weeks before the auction, twenty-five thousand spectators filed through Christie's for a once-in-a-lifetime glimpse of the masterpieces on offer. Among the paintings for sale were four of a series of fifteen paintings by Picasso called Women of Algiers. A high-powered subsection of cultural New York, including the cosmetics tycoon Leonard Lauder, the developer Mortimer Zuckerman, and the father of Microsoft, founder Bill Gates, braved a cold Monday to attend. The Nahmads were also present, of course.

Those who closely read the finely bound Ganz auction catalog might have seen an innocuous statement buried among the fine print. It read: "Christie's has a direct financial interest in all property in this sale."

The statement raised more questions than it answered. The nature of that interest was not revealed. It is impossible to say whether the knowledge that Lewis already owned the paintings, and not the Ganz family, would have dampened enthusiasm for the auction.

When it came time for the bidding on the most magnificent of the Women of Algiers series, Version O, the crowd audibly gasped as the numbers soared. When the final hammer dropped, the painting had sold for a record $31.9 million. The buyer was a London dealer, reportedly acting on behalf of a wealthy Middle Eastern client. When Victor and Sally Ganz had purchased the painting forty years earlier, they had paid $7,000.

That night David Nahmad bought Version H of the Women of Algiers series.

Total sales from the auction topped $206.5 million.

IN 2004, AGENTS acting on behalf of a New York art dealer contracted with Mossfon to perform an "urgent" corporate search in Panama's public registry on Wilton Trading S.A., a company not registered by the firm. They asked for a complete history, particularly for the period between 1985 and 1993. Mossfon did the work in a day and charged $110. The firm never concerned itself with the actual name of the requestor, Ezra Chowaiki, or why he wanted the information.

Chowaiki was trying to get to the bottom of how eighty-three paintings worth around $3 billion had gone missing. He had a financial stake in their recovery. What Chowaiki did not know when his agents approached the Panamanians was that some of the answers he sought existed in the company files of another Mossfon customer.

According to the information Mossfon uncovered for Chowaiki, Wilton Trading was created in 1981 but did not have directors until sixteen years later. Its most momentous act occurred without directors, four years after its creation. This part was not in the Panamanian registry. In 1985, the Greek shipping tycoon Basil Goulandris allegedly sold his entire collection of eighty-three masterpieces—which included works by Renoir, Van Gogh, Matisse, and Picasso—to Wilton for the ridiculously low sum of $31.7 million. The magnate's nephew, Peter J.

Goulandris, says his uncle sold the works because he was experiencing a cash crunch. The owner of Wilton was Peter's mother, Maria Goulandris, Basil's sister-in-law, now deceased.

The reason for the sale makes little sense since just a few of the paintings, rather than all eighty-three, could have conceivably fetched a similar sum. There has never been any proof offered that money changed hands. Chowaiki questioned whether in fact the sale ever occurred.

Despite the alleged transaction, Basil and his wife, Elise, kept the artwork in their possession, even lending works to museums and selling a few paintings to dealers with the provenance listed as if each one still belonged to them. After Basil's death in 1994, Elise was told about the sale to Wilton and was convinced to go along with it in exchange for a portion of the paintings. She died in 2000 without any offspring. A year later, her niece Aspasia Zaimis sued the executor of Elise's will for a share of the eighty-three paintings. Chowaiki decided to give financial backing to the legal effort a few years later in exchange for first crack at buying any of the recovered paintings Zaimis chose to sell, according to the *Wall Street Journal*.

One of Chowaiki's biggest questions was: Where are the paintings today? He suspected they might be locked away in a freeport somewhere.

Around the same time that his team urgently began investigating Wilton Trading, some of the paintings started to appear for sale. The owner was always listed as an anonymous Mossfon company, usually based in the BVI. Tricornio Holdings sold Pierre Bonnard's *Dans le cabinet de toilette* in a Sotheby's auction in London. Heredia Holdings agreed to sell Marc Chagall's *Les comédiens* through Sotheby's as well. Talara Holdings also put up a Chagall, *Le violoniste bleu*, for auction. A private sale by Jacob Portfolio Incorporated sent an 1888 depiction of a basket of oranges by Vincent van Gogh to a California direct marketing tycoon for $20 million.

Chowaiki could see the sales. He knew the paintings had belonged to Basil and Elise. He just did not know who was selling them. The Mossfon files identify the owner of all these companies as the Greek socialite Marie "Doda" Voridis, the sister of Basil Goulandris. It would

take publication of the Panama Papers before Chowaiki could prove
the family connection.

PAUL GAUGUIN PAINTED *Mata Mua*, which means "olden times" in
Maori, in 1892. The lushly colored oil-on-canvas depicts a landscape
enclosed by mountains, where bare-shouldered brown women dance
around an enormous blue idol depicting the goddess of the moon. It
is "an elegy for a lost Golden Age," according to the description from
Madrid's Thyssen-Bornemisza Museum, where *Mata Mua* hangs.

The painting is on loan to the museum from Carmen "Tita"
Thyssen-Bornemisza, a Spanish heiress and former beauty queen,
whose private art collection contains about seven hundred paintings
worth more than half a billion dollars. Her now-deceased husband,
Baron Hans Heinrich von Thyssen-Bornemisza, amassed one of the
world's great art collections. He also took advantage of a golden age of
tax avoidance and offshore secrecy, a legacy his widow struggled to
maintain in a time of leaks and tightening restrictions.

The baron was Dutch-born but from German stock and fortune.
His title was Hungarian. He claimed Swiss citizenship but lived in
Monaco for tax reasons. While alive, his heart resided in Lugano,
where he owned Villa Favorita, an eighteenth-century mansion that
housed more than a thousand paintings. Until they were transferred
to a family foundation, the baron's artworks were divided among
thirty to forty companies, his wife's lawyer told the Spanish newspaper *El Confidencial*.

The offshore structures allowed the baron and his wife to avoid
millions of dollars in taxes.

In 1993, after Spain built a museum to house the artwork, the baron
sold 775 paintings to the Spanish government, about half his collection. Initially, he dangled the idea of a gift but then charged Spain
$350 million for the works, still significantly below market value. The
following year, the baroness started collecting herself, masking her
purchases through offshore companies as her husband did.

A year after the sale to Spain, the baroness created Nautilus Trustees Limited and Sargasso Trustees Limited. Both were based in the

Cook Islands, a remote tax haven in the South Pacific. The companies were owned via bearer shares. Over the next seven years, they bought paintings from Sotheby's and Christie's, among others, moving the art all over the world. The corporate structures were deliberately complicated and opaque to shield the paintings from the baron's quarrelsome family, according to her lawyer. The baron had four children from as many marriages. He also adopted Tita's illegitimate son, Borja.

In 2002, the baron died. The probate was messy and secret. A year later, the Cook Islands mandated that all bearer shares needed to be held by a registered agent. The lawyers for the baroness searched, but the shares could not be found. In the end, new ones had to be issued. Under the new shareholder arrangement, she split the company with Borja, an arrangement that grew complicated when he announced that his longtime girlfriend was pregnant and the baroness cut off contact with him.

At least one of the baron's companies, Cornelia Company, was registered with Mossfon. In the early 1990s, Cornelia had taken out a short-term loan from Berliner Handels- und Frankfurter, a German private bank, with *Mata Mua* and *The Lock*, a painting by the English artist John Constable, as collateral. The loan was released in 1993. After the trust agent who operated the company on behalf of the baron changed registered agents, the company moved away from Mossfon.

Despite being ranked by a Swiss magazine as the seventh-richest woman in Switzerland, with a fortune worth more than a billion dollars, the baroness has complained that all her liquidity is tied up in paintings. In 2012, she decided to sell *The Lock*. It's doubtful she would have ever parted with *Mata Mua*, as it's one of her favorites and the name of one of her yachts.

The Constable painting fetched $34 million, making it one of the most expensive sales for a painting of its type. It was sold through Omicron Collections Limited, an offshore company in the Cayman Islands controlled by the baroness. Later, her son, Borja, tried to pierce the company's corporate shell, claiming the baron had given him a Goya and Giaquinto with an estimated value of $9 million, owned by Omicron. Borja lost that battle. The offshore art fortress constructed by the baroness remained intact.

9

THE VIKINGS LOSE THEIR FERRARIS

In March 2009, an Icelandic Sunday talk show invited a French former judge and anticorruption crusader, Eva Joly, on air to discuss the country's perilous situation. Iceland's economy had imploded four months earlier, one of the first casualties of the 2008 financial crisis. The nation's three leading banks had ballooned to ten times the country's gross domestic product and then popped. The national debt amounted to $403,000 per man, woman, and child in the small island nation. Liquidity dried up. The value of Iceland's currency, the krona, plummeted. Overnight, Icelanders couldn't repay their loans. The cost of imports, an island necessity, soared out of reach. Impoverished, bewildered, and angry, Icelanders took to the streets of downtown Reykjavík, looking for someone to blame.

Joly, a Norwegian by birth, had long admired the hardy Icelanders. Despite centuries battling the harsh elements as poor fishermen, they did a far better job of keeping their Viking culture alive than her fellow Norwegians. Joly had returned to Norway herself, having left France after six years of investigating the Elf oil company, which had been at the center of a web of corruption, bribery, and money laundering. After years of trials and investigations, the French public had grown weary of the scandal and the crusading judge presiding over the cases. Leaving the death threats and bodyguards behind, Joly had taken a job with the Norwegian Agency for International Development as a counselor to its campaign against global corruption.

Joly accepted the invitation, using the program to denounce the illegal activity she assumed had led to Iceland's financial collapse. Within hours of her interview, hundreds liked a Facebook post asking her to join a government investigation of the crisis. Iceland's justice minister pulled Joly aside the day after her television appearance and begged for her assistance. Iceland was small enough where one could discover the real truth of what occurred, Joly thought to herself. She agreed to help.

After the attorney general recused himself because his son was a top bank executive, the Icelandic parliament created an office of special prosecutor to hunt for wrongdoing. When the government advertised the prosecutor position, only one person in the entire country of 320,000 stepped forward.

Square-jawed, plainspoken, and stoutly built like an oak, Ólafur Hauksson had served for a decade as the district commissioner of Akranes, a small port town on the country's west coast, about twelve miles north of Reykjavík. The district commissioner was police chief, customs officer, and tax collector all rolled into one. Even with these responsibilities, Hauksson still found time to fish. He agreed to take the special prosecutor job because the scale of the crisis screamed for a response, he says. Hauksson didn't know what to expect but figured he'd be back in his old job in about two years.

Eight years later, Hauksson was still special prosecutor. In addition to offering guidance, Joly successfully fought to fund the effort. Hauksson began work in an empty office with a team of four: a law professor, two police investigators, and a lawyer from the Ministry of Justice. At its apex, the staff expanded to include 110 employees and ten contractors. As Joly suspected, the team found widespread wrongdoing by a select group of banking insiders, particularly in the leadup to the collapse. The special prosecutor investigated two hundred separate cases, bringing thirty to court. In their inquiry, Hauksson and his team searched deep into the secret back alleys of global finance, from Iceland to Luxembourg and beyond. Throughout it all, one company name kept reappearing—Mossack Fonseca.

Hauksson never targeted the Panamanians—he was laser-focused on Icelandic wrongdoing. Still, he noticed that the "Viking raiders"—as the media dubbed Iceland's modern-day robber barons—had created hundreds of anonymous companies with Mossfon. The companies were an essential ingredient in the self-dealing and market manipulation Hauksson unearthed. Each company represented another layer of secrecy to deconstruct.

Mossfon "was a well-oiled machine," says Hauksson with grudging respect.

THE ICELANDIC ELITE could scarcely imagine their ruinous fate when they started privatizing the country's banks in the late 1990s. Iceland's finance minister, Geir Haarde, took the occasion of the 2002 sale of Landsbanki, a leading Icelandic bank, to offer a toast. Thoroughly indoctrinated in the cult of market efficiency, Haarde quoted Ronald Reagan: "The government is not the solution to our problems, the government is the problem." He then delivered Landsbanki, which held the deposits of one in three Icelanders, into private hands.

With the krona strong and investment capital widely available, cheap money flooded Iceland in the early 2000s. The U.S. stock market doubled between 2003 and 2004, but in Iceland stocks grew by a factor of nine. Icelandic bank shares were particularly popular. The sleepy island of fishermen embraced living beyond their means. Icelanders took out loans to fund a nationwide buying binge, snapping up everything from fishing boats to cars to houses. A banker at the Luxembourg subsidiary of Iceland's largest bank, Kaupthing, traces the onset of the mania to the summer of 2003, when he first noticed Icelanders arriving at the bank in new Ferrari sports cars.

Luxembourg was Iceland's portal to the world. The newly privatized banks all had subsidiaries operating there. The Luxembourg subsidiaries helped their shareholders create offshore companies to buy and sell assets and bank shares. Once offshore, these transactions were hidden from Icelandic tax and banking authorities.

Not coincidentally, Luxembourg was the site of one of Mossfon's busiest offices, run by the husband-and-wife team of Jost and Anabella

Dex. Jost, tall, handsome, and German, had a background in physical education. His Panamanian wife, Anabella Ines Saez de Dex, petite, pretty, and wiser, was more experienced in financial services, having worked for Merrill Lynch as a stockbroker. She knew Ramón Fonseca from their school days and was close friends with one of his ex-wives. In 1996, the couple convinced Mossack and Fonseca to sell them the Luxembourg franchise, which had largely been an afterthought. The existing Mossfon franchisee had stopped recruiting clients. With nothing to lose, the partners agreed to sell five hundred shares of Mossack Fonseca & Co. Luxembourg to the couple for $1 a share, on the condition that they could only sell the company back to Mossfon.

Jost and Anabella divided their labor. He focused on the service side, employing a heavy dose of old-world charm to drum up business and keep customers happy. As the tougher, more street-smart of the two, Anabella kept the back office running and handled collections. Compared to her husband, Anabella's name seldom appeared on correspondence or documents, but together they transformed the Luxembourg office into one of the firm's biggest moneymakers, much of it built on the Icelandic business.

By 2004, Landsbanki alone was incorporating more than one hundred companies a year with Mossfon Luxembourg. A father-and-son team, Björgólfur Guðmundsson and Björgólfur Thor Björgólfsson, had purchased a majority of the bank. Thor, the son, made his first fortune in the 1990s, with a brewery in Saint Petersburg, Russia. It was in Saint Petersburg that he realized that a little capital and a lot of debt could multiply one's initial wealth many times over. Thor turned the hammer wielded by his namesake, the Norse god of thunder and lightning, into the Björgólfur corporate symbol, but what he and his father really worshipped was the god of leverage. The two men were typical of the Icelanders running amok in global finance at the time—brashly overconfident and out of their depth.

In September 2004, Landsbanki Luxembourg came to Jost Dex with a remarkable request. The bank typically purchased the services of Mossfon's nominee directors for the Panama and BVI shell companies it acquired. The paper officers granted power of attorney to the Landsbanki clients or provided signatures to finalize loan and pledge agreements. These transactions often involved tens of millions of dollars. Mossfon usually demanded a letter of indemnity for the directors so they would be held harmless if the deals misfired. In this way, the partners hoped to avoid liability for problems arising from the directors' consent.

Landsbanki was doing so much business, it wanted to streamline the process. The bank asked Dex if it could sign a blanket letter of indemnity—"a smoother solution"—to cover all future transactions and companies created with Mossfon. "Like this we could provide our services much faster and would not have to keep cases open for weeks or months just waiting for letters to be signed and sent to you," Dex wrote the partners in Panama when relaying the request. "It's not that they are not willing to send us all these letters, but each time they have to get the client's approval or even signature, and this is what bothers them and all of us."

Dex reassured the firm that Landsbanki had in its records the complete due diligence of all the beneficial owners. He also noted that the Luxembourg banking regulator supervised the bank. Under this arrangement, Mossfon would forfeit an opportunity to exercise oversight into what its directors authorized. Still, the partners agreed in principle to the proposal. They were happy to off-load due diligence onto someone else, particularly a bank, providing it didn't put the firm at risk.

Mossfon sent Landsbanki a draft indemnity letter to review. The bank removed a section vouching for the trustworthiness and creditworthiness of its clients. It also added language exempting the beneficial owners from actions taken under the power-of-attorney authorizations granted by Mossfon directors. In other words, once the company was operational, Landsbanki wanted any trouble the beneficial owner created to rest with Mossfon's shell companies and nominee directors rather than the bank. This, of course, negated the entire purpose of the letter of indemnity.

When a lower-level Mossfon lawyer received the changes, she rejected them. Fonseca instructed her to figure it out with Dex and Landsbanki. The two sides went back and forth for almost two years before reaching an accord. In March 2006, Landsbanki finally accepted

Mossfon's initial draft. Both sides agreed to handle any disputes arising from the indemnity issue through international arbitration.

By that point, the bank may have been eager to resolve the matter. A month earlier, in February 2006, the rating agency Fitch issued a negative grade for Iceland's economy, calling it "unsustainable." Fitch stressed all the reasons that would eventually sink the island's financial sector—excessive credit growth, huge deficits, too much debt. Yet despite Fitch's forecast, Iceland's profligate ways continued for two more years. The rating agency could not foresee that Iceland's top banks would engage in a criminal conspiracy to keep the money machine chugging. As Mossfon companies were a key ingredient to this conspiracy, it was better for Landsbanki to avoid returning to the firm for new letters of indemnity for each and every questionable deal.

Ólafur Hauksson relates a colorful anecdote from this period that encapsulates the game the major Icelandic banks played. A junior banker at Kaupthing had a simple job in 2006. He awoke early each morning and bought the bank's shares on the Swedish stock exchange. Kaupthing's purchases of its own stock kept the share price artificially high, allowing the money machine to roll on. Shareholders stayed rich. Bankers reaped fees from continued lending. Until, one day, the junior banker overslept. Without his timely purchases, the stock tumbled 4 percent in a matter of hours while the market struggled to find its proper level.

In the year leading up to the financial crisis, Landsbanki created more than eighty companies with Mossfon. Bank shareholders and executives used many of these companies to enrich themselves through deals that gave the outward appearance that the bank was thriving. During the first six months of 2008 alone, Landsbanki lent its own board members 40 billion kronur (about $562 million). From the outside, all the public could see were companies in places like the BVI and Panama receiving loans and buying and selling shares and assets. To all the world it appeared to be perfectly legitimate market activity.

In one example, the widow of a pharmacist, along with her two sons, owned substantial shares in a pharmaceutical company that

Björgólfur and Thor had purchased. The family created eight Moss-fon offshore companies through Landsbanki Luxembourg. These companies in turn borrowed millions of dollars from Landsbanki. The family then used the borrowed money to purchase shares in other assets owned by Thor and his father. While this kind of insider deal-ing could be construed as dangerously foolish banking because it con-centrated risk in the same family of companies, it was not necessarily criminal. The same couldn't be said for a scheme hatched by Lands-banki's CEO, Sigurjón Árnason. In 2007, two Panamanian companies created by Landsbanki, one of which was registered by Mossfon, received tens of millions of dollars in loans from the bank. Árnason orchestrated these loans so that the companies could buy Landsbanki stock, thus fraudulently boosting the bank's share price.

Kaupthing did the same but on a larger scale. In September 2008, a month before Iceland's financial collapse, Kaupthing made a major announcement. Sheikh Mohammed bin Khalifa al-Thani, an inves-tor from Qatar, was buying 5.1 percent of the bank. At a time when international lending was severely constricted, it was a remarkable show of confidence in a financial institution whose solvency was under question. The percentage was no coincidence. Any amount over 5 percent had to be publicly declared. The purchase made al-Thani, a friend of Kaupthing's CEO, Hreiðar Már Sigurðsson, the bank's third-largest shareholder. Sigurðsson and the bank's second-largest share-holder took to the airwaves, proclaiming the investment a sure sign that the bank was healthy and growing. The al-Thani stock purchases were proof.

Behind the scenes, a tangle of Mossfon companies created through its Luxembourg office told a different story. In July 2008, Jost Dex sold a BVI company, Brooks Trading, to another intermediary working on behalf of Kaupthing. Brooks Trading quickly opened a bank account with Kaupthing. The hidden owner of Brooks was another Mossfon company, which in turn was held by Al-Thani. On September 19, 2008, Kaupthing put $50 million into the Brooks account. The loan carried no guarantee or collateral and would have raised alarms in any prop-erly run bank. Ten days later, Kaupthing issued more loans, worth a combined $125 million, to two additional Mossfon BVI companies controlled by Al-Thani. The money found its way to a Cyprus company, which then purchased the sheikh's 5.1 percent of Kaupthing. What appeared from the outside to be a stunning show of confidence was in fact a fraud perpetrated by Kaupthing to disguise the purchase of its own shares.

THE U.S. FINANCIAL crisis sent Iceland's banks into meltdown. On September 15, Lehman Brothers declared bankruptcy. The global financial system seized up. Within three weeks, the Icelandic government nationalized its three largest banks, Glitnir, Landsbanki, and Kaupthing. When Eva Joly arrived to help Hauksson in early 2009, there were still only inklings of the extent of the criminal conspiracy.

"They went off the cliff but there were no skid marks," says Hauksson, noting the absence of the gradual decline one might expect to see. The banks were healthy one day and bankrupt the next—a financial illusion achieved with the aid of Mossfon and the Dexes.

While the machinations leading up to the financial crisis could be kept secret, the aftermath was inevitably public and bloody. The global financial crisis bit deep into Mossfon's profits. The firm's incorporations in the BVI, its most popular jurisdiction, dropped by 35 percent. In early 2009, Fonseca informed Jost Dex that Mossfon was raising its annual fee on offshore companies by $18. Dex protested. The financial crisis was the worst time to raise fees, he argued. He and his wife refused to comply; in a letter to the partners, they characterized the unilateral action as a breach of their contract. Instead they kept the prices the same for their 6,658 active companies, deducting $18 from each invoice Mossfon sent, before forwarding the money on to the firm. That translated into an annual shortfall of nearly $120,000.

In February, the couple offered to sell the Luxembourg franchise back to Mossfon for 10 million euros, a proposal the partners rejected as too expensive. Rather than provide a counteroffer, they forced the couple into an arbitration proceeding in Panama. The arbiter ruled against the Dexes, who appealed. Mossfon next sent letters to all the Luxembourg clients notifying them that the Dexes no longer had the right to sell the firm's companies. The Dexes countersued, accusing

Mossfon of fraud and tax evasion in both Luxembourg and Panama. The cases dragged on for years, transforming the former business associates into implacable enemies.

The Dexes weren't the only ones skirmishing as a result of the crisis. In downtown Reykjavík, daily demonstrations called for the resignation of the government. More than fifty thousand Icelanders had lost their savings. Unemployment jumped from 2 percent to 10 percent in six months. Protesters banged on pots and pans and pelted official buildings with splattering foods. Throughout the world, governments drastically cut back on services in response to the economic crisis. The austerity fed a popular movement focused increasingly on the role tax havens played in stripping public treasuries of needed revenue.

For years, a committed group of activists, Eva Joly among them, had campaigned against the political corruption and tax evasion enabled by the offshore system. The Norwegian government gathered these activists together behind the idea that chasing down money stolen by elites could help eradicate poverty. It invited them to Oslo to tackle the problem. Among those who took part in the initial meeting of what was called the Task Force on the Development Impact of Illicit Financial Flows was John Christensen, the former economic adviser from Jersey.

Christensen's interest in the topic of tax havens predated his pariah status as a whistle-blower. Born into a well-to-do Jersey family and educated at Oxford University and the London School of Economics, Christensen was by all appearances a pillar of the British establishment when he returned to the island in the mid-1980s. In reality, he harbored a secret. He took a job at a Jersey trust management company with the goal of researching the industry from the inside to expose its flaws.

Jersey was growing as an offshore destination, warping the political culture and crowding out other businesses. At his new job, Christensen learned how to layer trusts, companies, and foundations together to hide a client's money. Etiquette required that he never directly ask what his customers were doing but "you would have to be a moron to not realize that the vast majority were about tax evasion," he says. As part of his job, he became acquainted with other intermediaries, including Mossfon. He remembers the Panamanians as competent, fast, and cheap.

Christensen left the trust company to take the powerful post of economic adviser to the island's government. It was in this position that he received a call late one evening from a *Wall Street Journal* reporter who told him about allegations of governmental corruption in Jersey. With Christensen's help, the *Journal* published a front-page story labeling Jersey an "offshore hazard."

"That was the end of road," Christensen says. "I could no longer pretend."

He spirited his files off the island to a safe-deposit box in London. Facing animosity from his former colleagues, he and his family followed the files into a self-imposed exile in 1998. Christensen opened a small publishing house and helped Oxfam write a report on how tax havens affected international development. Four years after leaving Jersey, he was contacted by a special-needs teacher working in Jersey's only prison. She visited Christensen in London for tea, bringing along two retirees, a merchant seaman and a nun. The group hoped to fight against what they saw as the harmful impact of the industry.

From this small beginning, in 2003 Christensen launched the Tax Justice Network. It spread across the world from Washington, DC, to Africa. Christensen developed a presentation that revealed how Jersey trust companies enabled bribery, embezzlement, and fraud. The network's organizing and educational work kicked into high gear after the financial crisis. In 2009, it also unveiled an index that evaluated laws, regulations, and practices of different jurisdictions to reveal the most prolific purveyors of financial secrecy. The release of the first index created a stir. Topping the list was not the BVI, the Cayman Islands, or some other sunny tax haven island, but Delaware and the United States. Second was Luxembourg.

This growing opposition to tax haven abuses was met with an equally committed and largely American-backed movement hostile to the very idea of taxation. With names like the Center for Freedom and Prosperity, the Coalition to Protect Free Markets, and Citizens for Limited Taxation, a coalition of well-funded advocacy groups solicited money from Mossfon and other offshore providers for their campaigns. They portrayed tax havens as beleaguered bastions of freedom. The secrecy world was all that was preventing Western governments from violating the privacy of their citizens in a relentless pursuit to confiscate taxable wealth.

One group that served as a particularly effective conduit between American libertarians, wealthy business interests, and the offshore world was the Florida-based Sovereign Society. Ostensibly a publishing outfit, it hosted conferences that connected Americans with offshore providers like Mossfon. The objective, according to its own website, was to prevent "the plunder of onerous taxation and frivolous lawsuits." Mossfon kicked in a 10 percent commission to the Sovereign Society for any new business it brought to the firm. According to the law firm's files, the Sovereign Society was responsible for at least sixty-nine Mossfon companies.

Mossfon's Ramsés Owens was a frequent guest speaker at the Sovereign Society's gatherings. A 2008 brochure for a conference in Panama City announced a talk by Owens on the wonders of Panamanian companies: "Secure your wealth with an 82-year-old, proven, virtually 100% courtroom-proof structure. This fascinating structure has managed to evade the slickest attorneys' tricks and protect the wealth of individuals worldwide for the last eight decades. Find out how this surprisingly affordable and accessible structure can save you from embarrassing, life-changing lawsuits—and protect your family's life savings."

The following year, the Sovereign Society held a four-day conference at a swank resort in Bermuda. The location raised concerns at MAMSA, Mossfon's asset management company. Its staffers wanted to bring pamphlets to the conference advertising its services, which happened to include illegally hiding money from the U.S. Internal Revenue Service. A MAMSA staffer contacted Owens for advice. If the vast majority of those attending came from the United States, would it be illegal to bring the pamphlets? she asked.

Owens assured her that there were usually at least three European banks doing the same.

"But beware!!!" he cautioned. "We have to travel via the USA."

If U.S. Customs discovered printed material describing how to break U.S. law, it could be problematic for the traveler carrying such documents. Owens explained that the trick was to send it to the Bermuda hotel in advance of the conference rather than carry it through U.S. Customs.

Owens himself was not always so careful. An American real estate tycoon who was a Mossfon client complained about having been contacted by U.S. authorities after names and addresses were found in Owens's carry-on luggage. A team of Mossfon lawyers assured the secretive American that the firm's policy was not to carry documents while traveling lest they put confidential information about clients in jeopardy.

The Sovereign Society's referrals included those who wanted into the secrecy world for purposes beyond tax avoidance or civil lawsuit protection. One such person was the Alaskan real estate agent and investor Lance Lockard, whom the group recommended to Mossfon in 2006. Lockard asked the Panamanians for a full complement of secrecy. A Mossfon staffer wrote in client notes that Lockard's "main concern is confidentiality." The firm set Lockard up with a company registered in the Seychelles, which acted as "a consultant" to a Panamanian foundation he controlled. It also created a secure email drop and recommended a bank, for an additional fee.

In a 2007 email, Lockard notified the firm that he expected to be making as many as fifty money transfers a year to Switzerland, Australia, and the United States. The transfers could be as high as $500,000 each. The money was from investment proceeds and would be used for currency trading. In actuality, some of Lockard's money derived from the largest case of mortgage fraud in Alaska's history.

In December of that year, federal prosecutors indicted Lockard for bank fraud and conspiracy. Prosecutors charged that he and his coconspirators had falsified documents, inflated appraisals, faked down payments, and fabricated nominee borrowers and purchasers in a scheme that had gone on for nearly five years. In all, the group had defrauded thirteen Alaskan mortgage lenders of more than $2.5 million, according to the indictment.

After his arrest, Lockard's lawyer contacted Mossfon. He asked the firm to certify that it had never helped open a Panamanian bank account for him. The request immediately went to the partners. "I want to know the entire history of this client," wrote Jürgen Mossack. "How is it possible that nobody but nobody in compliance couldn't smell something rotten the moment they interviewed the client?"

Mossfon compliance reviewed the case. After the Sovereign Society referral, Lockard had sent the standard documentation of a passport, utility bill, and bank account statement. No in-person interview had occurred. Lockard had seemed legitimate until the onset of the financial crisis flushed him out. In response, Mossfon resigned from the company and foundation it had set up for Lockard. The firm then sent a letter to Lockard's lawyer. To the best of its knowledge, Mossfon stated, Lockard had no bank accounts in Panama, although he did have accounts in Switzerland. It also asked for back fees of $14,354, which included a charge for the bank account information search.

Lockard pleaded guilty and was sentenced to six years in prison. Prosecutors recovered only $116,000 of his illicit money. Owens suggested to the partners that they not worry about recouping its own fees. "Even if we don't receive a single cent for the due diligence, it's worth it to save our reputation," he emailed.

IN REYKJAVÍK, THE boisterous crowds gathering in the small square in front of the Icelandic parliament sprayed the building with catsup and yogurt. Geir Haarde, the Reagan-quoting finance minister who had overseen the bank privatization a decade earlier, had risen to prime minister when the financial crisis hit. With demonstrators demanding his head and minority parties calling for early elections, Haarde resigned, citing health concerns.

Sigmundur Gunnlaugsson, a young television journalist turned politician, seized the moment to begin his own ascent to power. Gunnlaugsson led opposition to a proposal that Iceland bail out the international creditors who had lost billions of dollars to its banks. He excoriated the vultures who were buying Icelandic debt in the hopes of a quick score, playing to the island's nationalism. Icelandic voters listened. They rejected the foreign creditor bailout. As leader of the

Progressive Party, Gunnlaugsson threw his weight behind the winning electoral coalition that assumed power from Haarde.

Gunnlaugsson entered parliament triumphant. Unbeknownst to his fellow Icelanders, he had millions of dollars shielded offshore from public view. In December 2007, Landsbanki Luxembourg had sold Gunnlaugsson and his wealthy heiress wife, Anna Sigurlaug Pálsdóttir, a Mossfon company called Wintris Inc. Its address was that temple of secrecy in the British Virgin Islands, the sky blue Akara Building. The couple used Wintris to invest Pálsdóttir's inheritance in, among other things, Icelandic bank bonds. After the financial crisis, it sold the bonds to the same vultures Gunnlaugsson had criticized.

A charismatic populist, Gunnlaugsson yearned to be more than a member of parliament. He coveted the office of prime minister. Despite the anonymity afforded by the Akara Building, Gunnlaugsson put even more distance between himself and Wintris. On the last day of 2009, he sold his half of the company to his wife for one dollar.

10

COMBING THE MONSTER

In 2009, the U.S. government punched a hole in Switzerland's tradition of bank secrecy. The Swiss bank UBS was the battering ram. Tax authorities and prosecutors from around the world rushed through the breach looking for the hidden assets of crooked politicians and tax dodgers. Since secret bank accounts are often paired with anonymous companies, the scrutiny on tax havens also increased. In response, Swiss bankers scrambled to distance themselves from their offshore business, and Western governments upped their demands for information from intermediaries like Mossfon.

For Ramón Fonseca, the UBS scandal was the moment Mossfon's business changed. "That's where the real pressure began, with the exchange of information," he says. "We had created a monster and then we were handed a comb and told to brush it."

A former employee named Bradley Birkenfeld was the key to the UBS case. Birkenfeld worked at the UBS Swiss private bank in Geneva for almost five years in the early 2000s, but he became disenchanted after he realized that UBS was setting up its bankers to take the fall for its own illegal activities. Birkenfeld found a compliance document hidden on the bank's server that explicitly forbade the very practices his bosses encouraged. When he brought the document to the attention of UBS executives, he was told to ignore it. Instead, he quit. A year after leaving the bank, Birkenfeld approached the U.S. Department of Justice, seeking immunity in exchange for information. He claimed that roughly nineteen thousand high-end American customers had hidden almost $20 billion with UBS.

The UBS Swiss private bank called its American business "toxic waste," in a nod to its danger. The nickname became self-fulfilling. Its bankers were not licensed to operate in the United States, but Birkenfeld and his colleagues had often traveled to America to meet with account holders and troll high-dollar events for new customers. In 2004 alone, UBS bankers visited around thirty-eight hundred American clients. The bankers kept account information encrypted on laptops. They even smuggled assets. Birkenfeld himself transported diamonds for a customer in a tube of toothpaste.

The IRS attorney John McDougal, who worked with Joe West on the credit card project, was among the federal officials who interviewed Birkenfeld. The Swiss private bankers were already on the radar of U.S. authorities, but Birkenfeld provided the kind of hard facts needed to convince a judge to allow them to pursue the case. Unlike other Swiss banks, UBS was particularly vulnerable to American justice, as it conducted its business through American branches rather than a subsidiary. This meant the IRS could serve a subpoena for information in the United States for material held by the private bank in Geneva. McDougal recognized that the John Doe summonses pioneered by West offered the legal means to pry out the bank's American account holders.

Swiss finance minister Hans-Rudolf Merz had defiantly stood before the Swiss parliament and declared to "everyone who is attacking Swiss bank secrecy, I can tell them on this bank secrecy, you will break your teeth." The IRS filed a John Doe summons anyway. A federal judge approved it. Then the IRS waited for the Justice Department to do its work. In February 2009, the Swiss government, fearful that its leading bank could be criminally indicted, allowed UBS to settle with the U.S. government for a then record $780 million. Soon after, Merz suffered a severe heart attack, which he attributed to the stress of dealing with the UBS issue. UBS also broke with tradition by giving up the names of 280 American account holders. The Swiss government rationalized the disclosure as falling within an exception to its bank secrecy law for fraud and other illicit activities, even though tax evasion was not a criminal offense in Switzerland. (In 2016, the Swiss changed their law to create a "serious tax offense," one involving more than $300,000, a predicate for a charge of money laundering.)

The day after the settlement was announced, the IRS asked a federal district judge in Miami to enforce the John Doe summons. The Swiss resisted at first but changed course upon realizing that UBS might lose its license to operate in the United States. Without the license, the bank would be incapable of conducting international business, because most major dollar transactions are routed through New York. In August 2009, UBS turned over an additional 4,450 names to the IRS. The age of absolute Swiss bank secrecy had come to an end—an achievement initiated by a stubborn Japanese African American IRS agent named Joe West.

BOWING TO INTERNATIONAL pressure, the BVI toughened its anti-money-laundering laws in 2008, adding new record-keeping and Know Your Customer requirements for offshore providers like Mossfon. But having laws on the books and enforcing them were separate matters. For the first few years, Mossfon slow-walked its compliance, to minimal protest from the BVI.

What the firm could not flout was a change in the BVI's approach to bearer shares. These certificates of ownership acted as a constant point of tension between tax havens and Western governments. Once the shares were issued, it was almost impossible to determine who owned the company, since it depended on whoever held the paper. Bearer shares made tracking assets a nightmare for taxation agencies or prosecutors. To those who wanted secrecy, for legitimate reasons of privacy or to engage in illicit activities, there was no better instrument than bearer shares. Their use was widespread.

Vladimir Putin's billionaire pal Gennady Timchenko had bearer shares for his companies. The Belgian diamond fugitive Mozes Victor

Konig did as well. Jeffrey Tesler's companies started with bearer shares before switching to foundations, as did the South Africans behind the Fidentia fraud. In 2009, the U.S. Treasury Department sanctioned another Mossfon customer, Kassim Tajideen, for being a financial contributor to Hizballah. Tajideen held ownership of his companies through bearer shares.

Ian Cameron, the father of the future British prime minister David Cameron, ran his investment fund via a Panama-based Mossfon company, Blairmore Holdings, which was owned through bearer shares. Hundreds of investors in the fund received these share certificates, but Cameron opted to keep the certificates together, locked away in an office in the Bahamas, where the fund was based. Each year, Cameron and his associates laboriously counted them to ensure they were all present. The secrecy was apparently worth it. Through its adroit use of tax havens, the fund paid no UK taxes during thirty years of operation, despite being top-heavy with British investors.

In 2000, the Bahamas outlawed bearer shares. Blairmore was unaffected because the company was registered in Panama, which continued to allow the certificates. But Mossfon saw an immediate and dramatic drop in its Bahamas business. Mossfon incorporated 1,217 companies in the Bahamas in 2000. One year later, Mossfon's production had fallen by 82 percent.

When the BVI contemplated taking similar action in 2002, Jürgen Mossack wrote to the country's Financial Services Commission beseeching it to reconsider. Mossack detailed what had occurred in the Bahamas. "The decline in the offshore industry seriously weakened The Bahamas economy," he wrote. He also noted that at least the Bahamas had other industries to fall back on. This was not the case in the BVI. "If BVI were to suddenly lose 50% or more of the income produced by the Registry (as happened in the Bahamas), what would replace it?" he asked.

The BVI was not contemplating outlawing bearer shares outright. Rather, it proposed doing what Ian Cameron did, forcing fiduciaries or registered agents like Mossfon to be custodians of the shares. Mossack tried to talk the BVI commission out of the idea. "We feel that many clients will believe, as we do, that restricting/controlling their bearer shares is effectively the same as eliminating them," he wrote. And he was forthright in detailing the value of bearer shares, not only to the BVI economy but also to users and registered agents: "Confidentiality is a client magnet and bearer shares provide much desired confidentiality."

Mossack's pleas failed to sway the BVI, which passed the law two years later. As of January 1, 2005, it forbade the free movement of bearer shares for the companies registered there. The BVI Financial Services Commission gave the tens of thousands of companies that already had bearer shares until the end of 2009 to convert them into registered shares or put them under the control of custodians.

Mossfon's BVI company incorporations decreased 35 percent between 2007 and 2009. While the financial crisis and new regulations had much to do with the drop, the restrictions on bearer shares were likely a factor as well. As Mossack predicted, those who wanted bearer shares went elsewhere. The biggest beneficiary was Panama, which continued to allow them. The firm saw the number of Panamanian companies requesting bearer shares increase by more than ten times in just a few years. Another winner was the Seychelles, which also offered bearer shares.

Meanwhile, Mossfon needed to deal with all of the BVI bearer share companies it had released into the world: 3,417 active companies created on behalf of 760 different clients. By June 2008, the firm reminded the clients who hadn't already converted their bearer shares that they needed to comply with the change in the law. The firm would goad clients for information about their bearer share companies for the next several years, with mixed success.

Some of the biggest holdouts were the banks. Société Générale switched the shareholders of the companies it had created for bearer share clients to Panamanian foundations in a bid to maintain a similar level of secrecy. Other clients simply resisted turning over information. In April 2010, in a bid to convince HSBC to provide information on its clients who had bearer shares with BVI companies, Mossfon promised it wasn't asking who actually owned the company, "we just need to know names and addresses of the holders of the bearer shares (and not the name of the ultimate beneficial owner)."

By the beginning of 2010, the BVI had begun to implement fully the new anti-money-laundering law. The Financial Services Commission informed Mossfon that it planned to audit the firm. After a review of its files, Mossfon realized that some of the information the commission expected to see was missing. The firm sent a request to its intermediaries asking for basic details about the companies they had created for their customers: the names of directors and shareholders, and some kind of acknowledgment that someone knew the identity of the beneficial owner.

Mossfon had long operated under the assumption that the intermediaries with which it did business maintained basic information such as who actually owned the company. For years, it was a convenient fiction that allowed Mossfon to avoid responsibility for the companies it sold. Now the firm could no longer pretend. What Mossfon learned as it tried to collect the necessary information was that when it came to the relationship between itself and its clients, the power lay with the clients.

In September 2010, the head of global wealth management and business for UBS asked for a meeting with Dieter Buchholz, Mossfon's Zurich representative. Buchholz expected another awkward discussion about bearer shares. (At least twenty-two BVI companies created by UBS for its account holders still had outstanding bearer shares.) Buchholz and Christoph Zollinger had already met with UBS executives in April over the bearer shares issue. At that meeting, the UBS executives seemed to be looking for a way around the new rule. They asked Zollinger and Buchholz for the legal basis of the BVI's threat to fine companies $20,000 for not complying with the law.

After arriving at UBS, Buchholz quickly learned this new meeting was not about bearer shares. Instead, the bank executive was furious over Mossfon's request for information about its BVI companies. He insisted that Mossfon should be asking the beneficial owners of the companies directly for the material, rather than UBS. The conversation, as described by Buchholz to the partners in an email, quickly took on an Abbott-and-Costello upside-down feel.

The UBS executive claimed that the bank had never been a contracting partner with Mossfon. This was a surprising statement since

Buchholz and Zollinger had met with UBS only a few months earlier to discuss its bearer share companies. Altogether, the bank's various branches and subsidiaries had created more than one thousand companies through Mossfon. Buchholz explained to the UBS executive that he was misinformed. In many cases, Mossfon didn't even know who actually owned the companies the bank commissioned, Buchholz said.

The UBS executive professed to be shocked by this revelation. He responded that he might have to inform authorities about the firm's violation of the Swiss money-laundering code. Buchholz noted that in the past Mossfon had specifically demanded that UBS and other banks supply the identities of the owners of the companies but that the banks had not been forthcoming. The executive hotly denied this.

Recognizing that the conversation was going nowhere, Buchholz argued that UBS and Mossfon had cooperated successfully for years. In the face of new legal changes in most jurisdictions, they should work together to solve these new challenges. This seemed to calm the situation somewhat.

The executive agreed to provide information—although he said that if Mossfon's nominees were directors of the company, the firm would have to contact the beneficial owner directly. He also insisted that if any companies were in arrears, the bank expected Mossfon to absorb the loss. When Buchholz relayed the message to the partners, Zollinger noted that the bank was trying to "push their responsibility away" and suggested that if UBS wanted to stick Mossfon with the tab for the companies, perhaps the firm should resign from the directorships of all UBS companies.

Adrian Simon in the Geneva office chimed in. "UBS has totally changed and because of the problems they had to face they are now reacting in an outrageous way," he wrote, noting that through the years UBS had substantially marked up the Mossfon companies it helped clients create.

Zollinger replied: "This is actually a VERY GOOD POINT!!! They have SOLD the companies for a much higher price to the clients and THEY have paid our invoices to us, NOT their final clients . . . UNBELIEVABLE!"

Mossfon and UBS devised a strategy to deal with the problem. Mossfon called it "due diligence light." The firm agreed to take on the UBS companies as private clients, but it would continue to rely on the bank to review the clients. The company owner had to submit a copy of a valid passport with every page certified by the bank. Mossfon also asked UBS to provide a reference letter. This way, the account holder quickly got an offshore company but the bank itself could pretend it was not directly responsible. Later, Credit Suisse and HSBC received similar treatment.

HSBC had been even more active in trying to distance itself from its offshore business. The move coincided with the arrival of Alexandre Zeller in 2008 as the new CEO of the Swiss private bank. Zeller had come from a state-owned cantonal bank, and he was shocked by what he found when he arrived at HSBC. The individual desks acted like independent fiefdoms. There was next to no review of clients. Bankers were not only creating offshore companies for customers, they were serving as directors for them. The files for the highest-level clients, such as Middle Eastern royalty, were not in the system but were kept in a safe in the CEO's office.

Even though HSBC was supposed to cater to private individuals, it had also opened accounts belonging to Venezuela's central bank—accounts that held almost $700 million at one point. A secret Swiss bank account could have had any number of uses for a regime that supported an embargoed Cuba and a military insurgency in Colombia and had repeatedly failed to live up to its obligations under international narcotics control agreements, according to the George W. Bush administration. Government officials from Venezuela were quite conversant with Swiss banks and the offshore world; some of them had offshore companies with Mossfon, including President Hugo Chávez's chief bodyguard and his wife, the country's former treasurer.

In response to Mossfon's request for information, HSBC informed the firm that the relationship managers who had created many of the companies would now act "independently" of the bank. They would continue as the contact person for the companies, but Mossfon should change its records to reflect the fact that HSBC Swiss Private

Bank was no longer the administrator. The CEO of HSBC Luxembourg clarified the situation somewhat in a meeting. The bank was no longer actively promoting offshore services as it had in the past, he said, but if a client asked for a structure, it would connect them with the appropriate intermediary.

Zeller received limited support from HSBC headquarters in London. He also appears not to have fully been aware of how bad the situation truly was. One of the desks in his bank was actively managing a major drug money-laundering operation. At its center were the brothers of Judah Elmaleh, the head of HSBC's Mediterranean, Europe, and Israel (MEDIS) desk, which it had inherited from Edmond Safra's Republic Bank.

The chain began with marijuana grown in Morocco. The product initially was shipped to Spain. From there, convoys of "go-fast" cars drove it to Paris at speeds too fast for the police to safely interdict. Parisian gangs sold the drugs, generating huge amounts of currency. Dealing with the money was where the Elmalehs entered.

Judah Elmaleh's brother Meyer, who operated a small asset management company in Geneva, would later claim that the scheme had begun when a friend asked, "I have clients who have cash, do you have customers who need cash?"

The cash was transported in heavy plastic bags to Mardoche Elmaleh, another of Judah's brothers. He counted the money and informed Meyer, who then communicated the amount to yet another brother, Nessim, who worked alongside Judah on the MEDIS desk inside HSBC. Nessim identified French clients of the bank who had secret accounts in Switzerland. The account holders wanted to access their money, but if they transferred it legally, they would have to pay taxes.

One such customer was Florence Lamblin, the Green Party deputy mayor of the thirteenth arrondissement in Paris, who had a century-old inheritance stashed at HSBC in Switzerland. Mardoche Elmaleh met Lamblin in her office and handed over a garish red bag with "Paris" written across it in large letters stuffed with €355,000 in 20-, 50-, and 100-euro notes. The scene was repeated multiple times with other wealthy Parisians. Nessim Elmaleh then withdrew the same amount that was delivered in cash from the recipient's secret HSBC account. This way, the account holder received his or her money without having to declare it.

The Elmalehs took the money deducted from the secret HSBC accounts and ran it through two shell companies based in London, Yewdale Limited and Globalised Limited. From these companies, the money was sent to one of more than four hundred Panamanian trusts the brothers created. These trust accounts in turn were used to buy real estate in North Africa and the Middle East. The Elmalehs received an 8 percent cut for their work and may have laundered as much as €100 million a year. The brothers had so much money coming in, they complained that their safe-deposit boxes could not fit it all. They solved the problem by converting the cash to gold.

The brothers were adroit manipulators of the secrecy world. Meyer Elmaleh was a director of at least thirty-five of Mossfon's Panamanian companies and four in the BVI. Nessim and Judah controlled companies with Mossfon as well. Judah held his through bearer shares. Yewdale, one of the two London shell companies used to launder the drug money, while not a Mossfon company itself, was mentioned more than one hundred times in the Panama Papers.

IN WASHINGTON, DC, Laura Stuber, a young lawyer working for Senator Carl Levin's Permanent Subcommittee on Investigations, noticed that its investigations kept bumping into HSBC. The bank made an appearance in a 2004 inquiry into Riggs Bank, which hid the money of despots such as the former Chilean dictator Augusto Pinochet and the president of Equatorial Guinea through secret bank accounts and offshore companies. When Riggs tried to get information on one of the Central African Republic's accounts held by the bank, HSBC, citing secrecy restrictions in Luxembourg, declined to reveal the identity of the owner. In the following years, there were other instances, including when the committee looked into the family of the president of Gabon, who used HSBC among other banks to funnel illicit cash to his daughter.

In late 2010, Stuber got Levin's permission to start looking into

HSBC's activities. It took a year and a half, but the end result was a blockbuster report, followed by a dramatic Senate hearing in which HSBC's head of compliance publicly tendered his resignation while testifying before the subcommittee. The report's most explosive finding detailed how HSBC purchased a Mexican bank that became a go-to financial institution for drug cartels. There were also allegations that HSBC laundered as much as 60 to 70 percent of the illicit money in Mexico. An estimated 15 percent of the Cayman Islands accounts operated by the Mexican bank—through which passed as much as $2.1 billion—had no information on the customers who held them. Stuber and Levin's committee did not just focus on the Mexican operation. The inquiry also touched on matters closer to home, although the committee did not have the time or resources to look at HSBC's Swiss operation in detail. It would only be apparent later that several of the cases the committee investigated involved Mossfon.

The committee's report described how HSBC's U.S. operation had opened more than two thousand accounts in the name of anonymous bearer share corporations. The vast majority of these accounts had come through the bank's Miami office, where bearer share accounts held assets totaling an estimated $2.6 billion, generating annual revenue of $26 million for HSBC. One of the examples the committee used to highlight the risks from these certificates centered on Mauricio Cohen Assor and Leon Cohen-Levy, father and son, two Miami Beach hotel developers who had been sentenced to ten years in prison for tax fraud a few years earlier. They were also longtime Mossfon customers.

The Cohens had at least thirteen offshore companies with Mossfon, companies that had been created with the help of the Swiss lawyer André Zolty, who had extensive dealings with Mossfon and HSBC. His firm specialized in helping an international clientele avoid paying taxes and had as many as 895 companies with Mossfon. Zolty was one of the clients Mossfon inherited when it took over the Geneva office from Antoni Guerrero in 1998.

The Senate report highlighted two of the Cohens' Mossfon companies, which held HSBC accounts through bearer shares: Blue Ocean Finance Limited and Whitebury Shipping Time-Sharing Limited, registered in Panama and the BVI, respectively. The companies helped hide $150 million in assets and $49 million in income, according to the Senate report. They also attempted to shield an opulent lifestyle that father and son enjoyed quite publicly.

The companies' real estate holdings included a $10 million apartment at Trump World Tower in New York, a $26 million Miami Beach mansion, and a $10 million condo on ritzy Fisher Island. The inventory of cars the Cohens collected included a Rolls-Royce Phantom, a Porsche Carrera GT, a Bentley, a Ferrari Testarossa, and a limousine. And of course, to rise above Miami's brutal traffic, they owned a $1.2 million helicopter.

Senate investigators obtained transcripts of phone conversations between Mauricio Cohen and his HSBC banker from 2007, in which the banker unsuccessfully tried to convince his client to register his bearer shares. Cohen threatened to take his business elsewhere. He said: "But, I can't put that, otherwise I have to declare them in the United States? I can't do that, I don't want to declare . . . otherwise, I have to close the accounts with you and go to Geneva."

Cohen implored the HSBC relationship manager to take his name off the Whitebury Shipping account. He also wanted the banker to explore whether he could transfer the company to Panama, where bearer shares were still allowed. It does not appear the company was moved, although Mossfon's files show that shortly after the conversation Cohen changed who held power of attorney over Whitebury.

The Cohens were accused of opening bank accounts in the name of nominees, among them their secretary and their limousine driver. Father and son were convicted of filing false tax returns, and the court ordered them to pay back taxes, interest, and penalties of more than $17 million—in addition to their ten-year prison sentences.

More troubling still was what the Senate committee discovered about HSBC's cavalier attitude toward its customers who were under sanction by the U.S. government. In February 2008, the U.S. Treasury Department froze the assets of Syrian businessman Rami Makhlouf, having charged him with manipulating the Syrian judicial system and using its intelligence officials to intimidate business rivals to gain control over profitable commodities contracts, lucrative oil exploration, and power plant projects. Makhlouf could do this because he was the cousin of President Bashar al-Assad and because his brother, Hafez, was the bloodthirsty head of Syria's feared civilian intelligence agency, the Mukhabarat. The sanctions also prohibited U.S. persons from engaging in business with Makhlouf. A week after the sanctions were announced, according to the Senate report, a compliance officer in the Cayman Islands branch of HSBC informed colleagues in New York that HSBC's Swiss private bank administered a trust for Makhlouf. The compliance officer was told that David Ford, HSBC's anti-money-laundering officer, had assured them that the Makhlouf relationship had been reviewed at the highest levels of the bank. HSBC had decided to continue with the customer.

Mossfon would not realize until a compliance check in 2011 that seven of the BVI companies it administered for the HSBC Swiss private bank had either Rami Makhlouf or another brother, Ehab Makhlouf, acting as directors. Adrian Simon, the head of Mossfon's Geneva office, contacted the HSBC relationship manager in charge of the account for explanation. The relationship manager told Simon that HSBC was aware that Makhlouf was the cousin of the Syrian president, but the bank "was comfortable with him." He said that if Mossfon chose to resign from the companies, HSBC would move them to a competitor, the law firm Alemán, Cordero, Galindo & Lee.

The compliance officer at Mossfon's BVI office was not comforted by the response. In an email, she described the situation as "high risk" and urged the firm to disassociate itself from the Makhloufs. Christoph Zollinger disagreed. He wrote: "From my part—if HSBC headquarters in England—do not have an issue with the client, then I think we can accept him. As far as I can see, there are allegations (rumors), but not any facts or pending investigations or indictments against these persons."

A few months after Mossfon's discovery, the European Union sanctioned Rami and Hafez Makhlouf, the latter having been implicated in violently disrupting demonstrations against the regime. Even Switzerland followed suit and put the brothers on its blacklist. After that, both HSBC and Mossfon finally terminated the accounts.

By this point, morale in Mossfon's Geneva office was low. Swiss banks were shedding foreign clients who didn't have enough money in their accounts to make the risk worthwhile. Customers were transferring their funds into hard assets: diamonds, gold, antique watches. Bankers insisted on meeting Mossfon employees outside their offices. Where Swiss clients once asked for ten companies, they only requested two or three. There was a palpable sense in Geneva that a golden age of secrecy had ended.

Even Adrian Simon was ready to move on. The year before, a former employee at the Geneva office who had moved to HSBC to administer its offshore company accounts left the bank to join Alemán, Cordero, Galindo & Lee. Before leaving, he convinced HSBC to move many of the companies Mossfon administered to the rival firm. "We have lost HSBC Geneva," Simon wrote to his superiors in Panama City. "I do not see a reason not to resign."

While Mossfon resigned from the Makhlouf companies a few months later, it continued to do business with HSBC.

In early 2012, Alexandre Zeller parted amicably with HSBC and stepped down as CEO of the Swiss bank. A few months later, French police arrested the Elmaleh brothers. Using wiretaps and other forms of surveillance, they had watched the ring at work, including the cash delivery to Florence Lamblin. The police dubbed it Operation Virus. In a six a.m. raid in Geneva, Swiss police and prosecutors took Meyer Elmaleh into custody and seized €800,000 in cash and 160 luxury watches in a hidden safe in his closet. He was sentenced to three years in prison but only served six months. Judah fled the country. His brother and fellow banker Nessim pleaded guilty and received a two-year suspended sentence. Mossfon learned of the arrests a year later but continued to do business with some of the brothers, including Nessim.

Around the time that police were rounding up the Elmalehs, the BVI Financial Services Commission fined Mossfon $20,500 for deficiencies uncovered during its audit.

Levin's Senate report and hearing made headlines across the world. The Obama administration's Department of Justice opted not to prosecute HSBC despite the bank's "blatant" criminal activity. Instead, HSBC paid a record $1.9 billion in fines. Stuber, the committee lawyer who started its investigation of HSBC, hoped exposing the bank would lead to greater reforms. "I don't think HSBC was an anomaly, it was just where we looked," she says today.

11

JOURNALISTIC FIREPOWER

The first cross-border journalistic leak investigation into the secrecy world unfolded as a series of disasters. It began when a dozen or so reporters and editors met in Washington, DC, at the offices of the International Consortium of Investigative Journalists (ICIJ) in January 2012. They came from the United States, Latin America, Canada, Europe, Russia, and New Zealand. Gerard Ryle, ICIJ's newly hired director, an Australian by way of Ireland, briefed the group. He had obtained databases from two unrelated offshore companies, Singapore-based Portcullis TrustNet and BVI-based Commonwealth Trust Limited. The combined data set offered the most comprehensive view into the secrecy world ever afforded journalists.

In the past, media exposés of the offshore system tended to be localized, dependent on a small number of internal documents, the testimony of whistle-blowers, hidden camera interviews, or legal filings. An inability to look at the system comprehensively made reporting difficult, if not perilous. Secrecy laws and incomplete information hog-tied journalists who tried to expose offshore wrongdoing. Lawsuits and public ridicule frequently followed publication. A partial picture allowed critics to dismiss findings as anomalies rather than patterns.

Ryle's documents told a broader story, an unprecedented macro view of a hidden world. The data consisted of approximately two and a half million files. In size, it was 260 gigabytes, more than 160 times larger than the cache of U.S. State Department documents WikiLeaks obtained two years earlier. The data contained beneficial owner information, money transfers, incorporation dates, and criminal behavior by the rich and powerful. It provided insights into scandals touching Russia, the United States, Africa, and the Philippines, among other places.

In Washington, Roman Shleynov, a Moscow-based investigative reporter, was unimpressed. It's common knowledge in my country that Russians have offshore companies, he said. What's the big deal?

Ryle groaned inwardly. Since joining ICIJ the previous September, nothing had gone according to plan. Even for someone accustomed to adversity, ICIJ was proving an exceptionally hard road.

Ryle was raised in Ireland, in a working-class family, the third child of nine. His great-grandfather had been a prominent newspaper editor, but Ryle's parents looked down on the profession. They wanted their son to be a doctor or an engineer. Unfortunately for them, he was an inattentive student. Journalism was about all he was qualified to do, he jokes.

Lacking connections or an exclusive school on his résumé, he struggled to break into the elitist Irish newspaper industry. Ryle worked at the first of a series of small Irish newspapers for free, while living on the dole. A few years later, when a colleague returned from Australia with stories of sunny skies and beautiful beaches, Ryle decided to give it a try. He wrote to three Australian newspapers and received three rejection letters. He went anyway.

Ryle arrived in Melbourne, where he had a cousin, and telephoned the *Age*, one of the newspapers that had rejected him. He told the editor's secretary that her boss had sent a note summoning him. Fortunately for Ryle, the secretary was Irish. Seeing through the lie but charmed by the bravado, she laughed and told him to come around. The editor tried his best to get rid of the eager young reporter, but Ryle wouldn't leave.

Over the next twenty-five years, he transformed himself into one of Australia's top journalists, married a local multimedia editor, and bought a condo near the beach in Sydney. Thin and rangy, Ryle had a twinkle in his eye and a soft Irish lilt that contrasted with the careworn expression he often wore. In his adopted country, Ryle built a reputation for hard-hitting investigations. His subjects included police corruption, crooked land deals, and questionable medical experiments. He was a twelve-time finalist for the Walkley Awards, Australia's top honor for journalists, and won four of them.

While working for the *Sydney Morning Herald*, Ryle broke a story about Firepower, a Perth-based fuel technology company that was in fact an elaborate financial fraud. The company claimed to have invented a pill to improve fuel efficiency and reduce pollution. In reality, it was a multimillion-dollar hoax to bilk investors and win government contracts. Ryle spent three years digging into the scandal, later writing a book on the scheme called *Firepower: The Most Spectacular Fraud in Australian History*.

Ryle's work on Firepower caught the attention of an anonymous source who contacted him, asking for the best way to deliver documents connected to the case. Ryle gave his address at the newspaper. In the summer of 2011, a bulky hard drive arrived by mail, containing millions of leaked offshore files.

Ryle would subsequently learn that tax authorities in the United States, Australia, and the United Kingdom also possessed the data but had not done anything with it. This was understandable. The files were jumbled together in various formats and needed to be reconstructed in order to understand fully what they contained. Despite the help of the IT staff at his newspaper, searching through a single company could take all night. Ryle did not know precisely how to make the data accessible, but what he saw suggested it was worth the effort.

Around this time, ICIJ advertised for a new director. Ryle had recently finished a yearlong journalism fellowship at the University of Michigan. A friend at the program, an ICIJ board member, urged Ryle to apply. When Ryle interviewed for the job, he did not volunteer that he had a hard drive crammed with offshore documents. Instead, he suggested that the offshore world might be a fruitful area for cross-border collaborative journalism, which was ICIJ's mission. He was hired. America, the land of opportunity, beckoned.

In his eagerness for the challenge, Ryle failed to do basic due diligence on his new employer.

"Some investigative journalist I am," he says in retrospect. "I didn't want to know."

ICIJ WAS A creation of the Center for Public Integrity (CPI), one of the pioneers in nonprofit investigative journalism. The center was founded in 1989 by Charles Lewis, a hard-charging former *60 Minutes* producer who quit CBS after his superiors pressured him to censor a segment. Lewis's favorite saying was, "Don't ever let the bastards get you down or intimidate you." The center put it on its mousepads. Under his direction, CPI became a journalistic force, breaking stories on the Clinton and George W. Bush administrations, including the high-dollar donor sleepovers in the Lincoln Bedroom and Halliburton's no-bid wartime contracts.

In 1992, at an international journalism conference in Moscow, Lewis had an epiphany. The subjects that CPI tackled, from political corruption and environmental devastation to human rights violations and financial fraud, did not respect national boundaries. Great reporters from around the world investigated these subjects alone. Lewis envisioned a network where the best investigative reporters from multiple countries could collaborate on stories of global concern. It took him five years to raise the money to create ICIJ. In 1997, CPI flew some of the world's top reporters to the United States for a kick-off conference at Harvard University. Lewis told them he wasn't asking for anything; he wanted to help.

Underneath the collegiality, some detected a certain degree of paternalism, although not from Lewis directly. Others questioned whether ICIJ should be a stand-alone organization rather than an appendage of an American nonprofit whose initials sound like a U.S. intelligence agency.

"There was this thing in the air that they were going to bring American standards of journalism to the poor benighted denizens of the developing world," acknowledges the *Guardian*'s David Leigh, who was one of the original ICIJ members.

Jürgen Mossack, the German-Panamanian attorney and cofounder of the Mossack Fonseca law firm.
[Photo by Mossack Fonseca & Co.]

Ramón Fonseca Mora: lawyer, author, politician, and cofounder of Mossack Fonseca.
[Photo by Mossack Fonseca & Co.]

At its height, the innocuous-looking Akara Building in the British Virgin Islands housed more than 45,000 active Mossack Fonseca companies. [Photo by author]

Ramsés Owens, a talented lawyer at Mossack Fonseca, never made partner but left his mark on the firm.

[Photo by Owens & Owens]

Mossack Fonseca partner Christoph Zollinger returned to his native Switzerland in an unsuccessful bid to become an Olympic bobsledder.

[Giancarlo Cattaneo/fotoSwiss. com]

John Gordon was Mossack Fonseca's exclusive representative in the United States.
[Photo courtesy of John Gordon]

HSBC Private Bank in Switzerland enjoyed a longstanding relationship with Mossack Fonseca. [Photo courtesy of Titus Plattner]

In the 1990s, Mossack Fonseca began to advertise a new product, companies based in Niue, its exclusive tax haven located on a remote island in the South Pacific.
[Advertisement found in the Panama Papers]

Sergei Roldugin, a celebrated Russian classical cellist, old friend of Vladimir Putin, and key player in a network of Mossack Fonseca shell companies.

The goods tucked away in the drab Geneva Freeport are conservatively valued at more than $100 billion and include some of the world's great artistic treasures.

Gerard Ryle, the director of the International Consortium of Investigative Journalists, oversaw multiple challenging investigations of hidden money, culminating in the Panama Papers, for which the organization was awarded the Pulitzer Prize. [PHOTO BY AUTHOR]

Left to right: Marina Walker Guevara, ICIJ's deputy director; researcher Emilia Díaz-Struck; and Mar Cabra, the head of data and research. [PHOTO BY AUTHOR]

Giannina Segnini and Rigoberto Carvajal, the Costa Ricans at the forefront of ICIJ's data success.

[PHOTO BY AUTHOR]

Edouard Perrin, French documentarian, at the ICIJ-sponsored meeting in Brussels for Lux Leaks.
[Photo by Mar Cabra, courtesy of ICIJ]

Süddeutsche Zeitung reporters Bastian Obermayer (left) and Frederik Obermaier.
[Photo by author]

Ólafur Hauksson, Iceland's special prosecutor, investigated the role of Mossack Fonseca companies in his nation's banking crisis.
[Photo by Jóhannes Kr. Kristjánsson]

Icelandic journalist Jóhannes Kristjánsson in front of Mossack Fonseca's building in Panama, December 2016.
[PHOTO BY AUTHOR]

Prime Minister Sigmundur Gunnlaugsson of Iceland refused to answer questions from Jóhannes Kristjánsson and walked off in the middle of an interview.
[PHOTO COURTESY OF REYKJAVIK MEDIA/SVT]

Rita Vásquez and Scott Bronstein, journalists with the Panamanian daily *La Prensa*. [COURTESY J. SCOTT BRONSTEIN AND RITA VÁSQUEZ]

Donald and Ivanka Trump at the opening of the Trump International Hotel & Tower Toronto. [CNW GROUP/TRUMP INTERNATIONAL HOTEL & TOWER TORONTO]

Leigh, along with another founding member, Duncan Campbell, helped the network score its first major success. They made eleven thousand internal company documents from British American Tobacco (which were public but largely inaccessible) widely available to partners in multiple countries for a cross-border investigation into how Big Tobacco circumvented health laws and laundered money. It was a steam-powered version of the leak investigations to come, relying on the knowledge of local reporters and the sharing of documents, albeit hard copies. The initial story, published in January 2000, made the front page of the *Guardian*, which gave the consortium some much-needed credibility. Other projects followed, covering topics such as military contracting, U.S. support for death squads, and water privatization.

Lewis stepped down as CPI's executive editor in 2005. Deprived of his vision and force of personality, ICIJ withered. Officially there were dozens of ICIJ members around the world, but the network itself accomplished little. Members had little direct input in its operation. CPI also struggled. Lewis had originally created a board for CPI entirely of journalists. It gradually morphed to one selected for fundraising rather than journalism. The center was slow to adapt to the digital age and to increased competition for scarce dollars by a growing cadre of nonprofit journalism organizations.

In 2010, CPI fell victim to John Solomon, a smooth-talking and energetic journalistic entrepreneur. Solomon vowed to bring innovation and funding to the center. His proposals were ludicrous on their face, including publishing between ten and twenty original investigative stories daily and selling fifty thousand annual Web subscriptions at $50 a pop. At the time, the center would have been lucky to muster ten thousand Facebook likes; nonetheless, CPI's head Bill Buzenberg and the center's board embraced the fantasy and appointed Solomon executive editor.

One person who saw through Solomon's promises was David Kaplan, the director of ICIJ. Conflict between the two was inevitable. Matters came to a head when ICIJ published a major investigation into the multibillion-dollar black market for bluefin tuna. Overfishing was decimating tuna, a keystone species, and the multinational regulatory system designed to prevent overfishing was not working. The ICIJ team gained access to a multinational regulatory database that tracked tuna catches. The team's investigation exposed the database as woefully incomplete.

Solomon then attacked Kaplan and the international team of journalists, accusing them of illegally accessing the database and paying a consultant quoted in the story. Solomon took his complaints to the CPI board, which hired a law firm to investigate. The investigation cleared ICIJ of any wrongdoing. Board member and Columbia journalism professor Sheila Coronel insisted upon a public exoneration, but Kaplan eventually decided to quit rather than continue to report to Solomon. Four months later, in May 2011, Solomon resigned as well, leaving CPI's morale shaken and its finances precarious. Buzenberg spent the next three years pulling the organization back from the brink.

Ryle arrived in Washington that September, largely clueless of the controversy over the fishing project and the wreckage Solomon had left behind. Buzenberg had helped Ryle coax his wife, Kimberley Porteous, to America with a job as the center's chief digital officer. The couple arrived for a new life in America on a stormy Labor Day weekend. They spent the first days in an unsuccessful search for a home in Washington's tight housing market. On Labor Day, Ryle went into CPI and ICIJ's empty suite of offices to meet with his new boss.

Buzenberg informed Ryle that he had given Porteous's job to someone else. The numbers for ICIJ's budget and staff were also different, Ryle discovered. The budget was less than half of the $1.5 million he had been promised, and the actual staff was six employees rather than seven, whom budget cuts reduced to four shortly after his arrival. Ryle returned to his hotel disconsolate. Porteous had been shopping. A new outfit for her first day at work hung in the closet. Ryle struggled to break the news. The job he had left behind as deputy editor of the *Canberra Times* was already filled. There was no turning back.

A few weeks later, Ryle, racked with guilt, left Porteous in a house with no furniture in Washington and flew to Kiev for the Global Investigative Journalism Conference. In addition to sharing skills and stories, the conference and other multinational journalism gatherings offer a place for international journalists to mingle and drink together after hours. They became essential in forging the relationships that would make ICIJ's future collaborations function.

At Ryle's side was the ICIJ deputy director he inherited, Marina Walker Guevara, an Argentinian journalist who had worked with Kaplan. An investigative reporter in her native Argentina, Walker had come to America in 2002 for a six-month fellowship at the *Philadelphia Inquirer*, when the paper was still a journalistic standout. Argentina was in the midst of its economic crisis, and in order to support her mother, she stayed, juggling school with various journalism jobs before landing at ICIJ. Walker's familiarity with the developing world was matched by a Swiss-like ability to organize. She was friendly and engaging but could also be steely and demanding when called upon. Above all, she had credibility with the international members, many of whom were still angry about the bluefin tuna imbroglio and what they saw as the excessive U.S. orientation of the organization.

"Marina is not a bigoted American," says Fredrik Laurin, a tart-tongued Swedish television journalist and early ICIJ member. "She really understands what this is all about, that the world is bigger than the United States."

The group that came to Washington in January 2012, which included Laurin and the *Guardian*'s David Leigh, had been recruited in Kiev, where Ryle had introduced himself to many of ICIJ's members. Ryle desperately wanted the *Guardian*'s participation, which would add needed credibility to the project. Each partner committed to some basic precepts necessary to make the collaboration work. They agreed to publish together at the same time. No one would leak the data. They would uphold journalistic standards.

Soon after the journalists returned home, large hard drives encased in rubber and full of Ryle's data arrived at their offices via FedEx. At the time, ICIJ was not particularly security-conscious. None of the data was encrypted, although Ryle opted not to send a hard drive to Russia.

Possessing the data and making sense of it were separate matters. In addition to multiple formats, including ancient email systems long since abandoned and document scans, the names and companies found in the data were in separate spreadsheets that needed to be matched somehow. Several in the group also received a copy of a powerful indexing software that could search the data. Ryle had convinced Nuix, an Australian company, to donate its forensic investigation software with the vague promise that a future project, if successful, might bring it good publicity. Simply to run the program, the *Guardian* and ICIJ had to buy more powerful computers. In total, Nuix provided ten licenses, a mere fraction of the number needed.

Initially, Ryle and Walker thought that partners would travel to hubs, such as Washington or Bucharest, where they could explore the data. Few took the offer. To attract the interest of more journalists, spreadsheets were distributed to individual partners with local addresses and the names of their country's citizens found in the data. If the partners wanted to research further, they were to contact ICIJ, which would help pull the documents together. This, too, proved untenable. Almost a year into the project, Duncan Campbell, with the help of a developer, created a searchable and secure website that the partners could use to explore the documents on their own. Campbell, an investigative reporter who doubled as a forensic expert on data and communications, had helped expose the Echelon global government surveillance program in 1988. He was justifiably famous in investigative journalism circles.

The group agreed to publish in September 2012.

Ryle then went looking for top media partners around the world. In contrast to CPI's Lewis, who had targeted specific journalists, Ryle felt that only big media organizations would bring the impact he desired. One of his first stops was the *New York Times*. Bill Kovach, a CPI board member (and a former *Times* reporter and editor), set up a meeting with Richard Berke, a senior editor at the newspaper. Ryle took a copy of the data with him. When he was shown into the meeting, Berke appeared to have no idea why he was there. Ryle revealed some of ICIJ's initial findings. Berke was intrigued. He gathered some of the top editors together. Ryle went through his presentation again. The high-powered audience was more skeptical. While Ryle had a serious reputation in Australia, it meant little to the Americans.

They agreed to discuss the matter further. Negotiations dragged on for months. The *Times* wanted Ryle to hand over the material and reveal his sources. In return, it would credit ICIJ in its stories. The paper also refused to collaborate with multiple partners or share bylines on stories with journalists outside the *Times*. Talks broke down and Ryle abandoned his pursuit.

It was a similar story elsewhere. Major European media outlets like Spain's *El País* and Germany's leading newsmagazine, *Der Spiegel*, rejected Ryle's overtures. The offshore system was disregarded, if acknowledged at all. And a journalistic collaboration of this ambition had never been attempted.

Ryle went to Paris to meet with someone at *Le Monde* to see if the French newspaper would participate. He arrived at the paper's new glass-encased office building on time but his contact had forgotten the meeting. As Ryle waited in the lobby, he watched a street person approach the building and begin to knock his head violently against the glass.

It felt like an apt metaphor.

As HE ORGANIZED the collaboration, Ryle remained in contact with the leakers. It had been almost a year since he received the hard drive, and they were growing impatient. Ryle didn't blame them. He wasn't entirely positive he could pull the project off himself.

The September deadline was looking increasingly unrealistic. Making the data accessible for the partners had turned into a complicated slog. Many of the documents consisted of photos or PDFs. Each one had to be put through optical character recognition software in order to be keyword searchable, a slow and laborious process.

Ryle set up a special dedicated computer at ICIJ to give the leakers remote access to the material. The idea was that they would help reconstruct the data and add their insights. One day while on the computer, Ryle discovered a communication he wasn't supposed to see. The leakers had forgotten to delete a message they had shared with one another: they had lost confidence in him. The message detailed a plan to stealthily delete the data and scuttle the project. Ryle acted quickly. He cut off their access to the computer and pretended to go off-line temporarily. When he resumed contact, Ryle acted as if the incident had never occurred.

ICIJ had come too far to turn back. Project members identified a number of compelling stories. Each day added more. They discovered links to the families of the deposed Philippine dictator Ferdinand Marcos and the president of Azerbaijan. There were government officials from Venezuela, Thailand, and Mongolia in the data, along with some of the richest citizens of Jordan, Saudi Arabia, Indonesia, and Spain. They even found celebrities. Australia's Paul Hogan, of *Crocodile Dundee* fame, had trusted the wrong asset manager, who stashed some of his fortune offshore.

The data revealed the secret holdings of Denise Rich, whose billionaire ex-husband had been at the center of one of the worst scandals of the Clinton administration. Marc Rich's commodity trading business, called Glencore today, profited from selling embargoed oil. He hid out in Switzerland after Rudolph Giuliani, then a federal prosecutor in New York, indicted Rich for tax evasion and racketeering. Millions of dollars in donations to Democratic politicians and the intercession of his wife won him a pardon from Bill Clinton on the president's last day in office. The files showed that Denise Rich had a trust in the Cook Islands that held $144 million and a yacht called the *Lady Joy*.

The secret assets and privacy concerns of Tony Merchant, Canada's "class action king," were also in the data. Merchant, a colorful plaintiff's attorney in Saskatchewan, had waged a bitter battle with the Canada Revenue Agency over back taxes. Apparently unbeknownst to the Canadian government, he, too, had a trust in the Cook Islands, where he kept at least $1.1 million. Merchant insisted on paying for his trust by mailing untraceable cash to the other side of the world. His offshore service provider joked that if they sent him a fax with his name on it, he would have a stroke. Merchant was one of more than four hundred Canadians found in the material.

As Roman Shleynov had suspected at the initial meeting in January, there were plenty of Russians, including politicians and business leaders. He decided to contrast the findings with Putin's repeated calls for Russians to forsake the offshore system. The hypocrisy made it newsworthy.

Among its stories, ICIJ staffers highlighted ties to the so-called Magnitsky affair. The BVI-based firm Commonwealth Trust Limited had created at least twenty-three companies that were used in the theft of Russian businesses owned by an American hedge fund, Hermitage Capital Management Limited. The hedge fund's Russian lawyer, Sergei Magnitsky, protested and was imprisoned. Magnitsky died from mistreatment while in custody. Commonwealth appeared not to have known about the activities of its companies until it was contacted by Hermitage.

Good news arrived from Germany, when Ryle's second choice, the Munich-based newspaper *Süddeutsche Zeitung*, accepted his invitation to join the effort. The paper assigned a young reporter, Bastian Obermayer, to the project. Obermayer had originally been a feature writer. It was a sign of how little his bosses thought of the project that they picked a reporter with scant investigative experience to work on it.

Since so much of the offshore data ran through Switzerland, Ryle and Walker also looked for a Swiss partner. It was a difficult proposition. Switzerland was built on a bedrock of bank secrecy; it acted as a launching pad into the offshore world. A French colleague at *Le Monde* suggested Tamedia, a media company with newspapers in both the French and German parts of Switzerland. Tamedia had recently formed an investigative unit and put Oliver Zihlmann, a former Berlin correspondent and news editor, in charge. Little did ICIJ know that the owner of Tamedia, Pietro Supino, was an offshore lawyer himself. To his credit, Supino was also a zealous advocate for journalists. He declined to interfere with the project despite the fact that it implicated his own colleagues.

Zihlmann paired one of his top reporters, Titus Plattner, with Obermayer to investigate Gunter Sachs, a flamboyant millionaire German-Swiss photographer who had once been married to Brigitte Bardot. It was a difficult story. For starters, Sachs was dead. The reporters struggled to determine if he had broken the law. When they mapped out the welter of trusts, companies, and foundations connected to the Swiss law firm that serviced Sachs, the dozens of crisscrossing lines looked like a schooner's rigging.

It was the *Guardian* in Britain that was furthest along in writing and reporting. The paper planned a package of nine stories detailing everything from nominee directors to who was using anonymous companies to buy property in London. David Leigh even had a story about a controversial plastic surgeon in London who appeared to be using offshore structures to avoid liability.

By the summer, Ryle had conceded the obvious. They were way behind schedule. Collaboration only functions if everyone is working, but the effort from partners was not there. The topic was new. The data was confusing and still largely inaccessible. The media organizations participating had not bought into the project. Ryle pushed the publication date back to early March 2013.

The *Guardian* balked. It refused to wait until March. Leigh told Ryle the paper planned to publish in November.

There was nothing Ryle could do. The *Guardian* was the biggest media player in the project. It was coming off a string of high-profile investigations including the WikiLeaks cables and a newspaper phone-hacking scandal. Most important, it physically had the data. Ryle had no leverage. The *Guardian* didn't need ICIJ. It was of small consequence to the paper that the other partners in the collaboration had all convinced their bosses to support the project with the promise that no one would scoop the others.

THERE WERE DAYS during the project so full of disaster and discord that Ryle and Walker would look at each other and say, "This will surely kill us." They dubbed them "cancer days."

The *Guardian*'s decision to break the embargo was a cancer day. Nonetheless, Ryle deftly managed to downgrade its seriousness from life threatening to temporarily debilitating. He negotiated with the *Guardian*'s editors not to mention the names of the two offshore companies involved or the fact that the information was the result of a leak. And in the end, the newspaper's muddy coverage failed to attract broad public attention.

Ryle and Walker worked overtime to mollify the other collaborators. Ironically, the *Guardian*'s publication of the stories provided tangible proof that the data was legitimate and the stories worthwhile. Skeptical European partners, which held the *Guardian* in high esteem, suddenly embraced the project enthusiastically.

"The *Guardian* says, 'Shit tastes great' and then editors say, 'Great, let's try some shit,'" Mar Cabra, ICIJ's research editor at the time, recalls with a laugh.

Cabra, a vivacious and diminutive Spaniard who had trained as an actor before turning to journalism, was another holdover from the pre-Ryle days of ICIJ. After burning out as a news reader on Spanish television, she talked her way into Sheila Coronel's journalism program at Columbia University. As a student journalist, Cabra collaborated on a documentary program on the overmedication of foster children that was aired nationwide on PBS. After a stint at the *Miami Herald*, she returned to Spain, where she worked on ICIJ's fishing project.

Cabra's job was to make the project's research hubs work. She quickly realized it would be impossible to provide all the documents needed. The reporters in each country had to be able to explore the material themselves. Unfortunately, the information processing was still ongoing. Data journalism was in its infancy. Cabra was one of the only practitioners in Spain. ICIJ was depending on freelance data journalists over whom it had little control.

Cabra suggested bringing in Giannina Segnini, a data journalism pioneer employed by *La Nación* in Costa Rica. Segnini had started working with large data sets in the early 1990s, before the Internet. She investigated a Costa Rican government program to provide subsidies for the homeless, which was allegedly helping around two hundred thousand people. She had never seen that many homeless people in Costa Rica and went to court to get access to the database. Segnini discovered "homeless people" receiving subsidies who had cars, salaries, and beach houses. She was hooked, rejecting a promotion so that she could create and oversee a data team to do similar stories.

One of her early hires was Rigoberto Carvajal, a soft-spoken genius-level twenty-four-year-old software engineer who had grown up in humble circumstances in the remote Costa Rican province of Guanacaste. Together Carvajal and Segnini scraped every major government database in the country to create a single searchable master. It took them about two years.

A hard drive with the data, still unencrypted, was shipped to the Costa Ricans. Segnini waited for the files to arrive, eager to get started. When the hard drive did not appear, she grew worried. Segnini did not want to be the person to tell Ryle that the precious files had vanished. Finally, she checked with Costa Rican customs. They had the package. It was being held up because the proper import duties had not been paid.

Duncan Campbell and the Costa Ricans had conflicts over the data wrangling. The experience was a lesson in the pitfalls of collaboration, and the importance of having data journalists on staff.

Meanwhile, it fell to ICIJ's editor Michael Hudson to coax articles from the foreign freelancers with whom ICIJ had contracted for the stories it published on its own Web page. Hudson was a veteran of the *Wall Street Journal* who had been one of the few journalists to report on problems in the subprime mortgage industry prior to the 2008 financial crisis. He had started at CPI but suffered under Solomon. Hudson was about to be laid off when Solomon departed and a position opened with ICIJ.

Hudson's unenviable task was to turn journalism from countries with different standards and practices into articles that met ICIJ's exacting requirements. Several of ICIJ's foreign freelancers for the project spoke English as a second language. Their writing styles often leaned heavily on conditionals, opinion, and passive voice. Nonetheless, Hudson recognized the danger of coming across as an overbearing American. He wrote a five-page memo that explained to the writers that editing would be a back-and-forth process and encouraged them to footnote their stories and attribute their facts.

"None of this reflects our trust in your work—it's a reflection of our need to protect everyone involved as we operate under various legal systems, to deal with the complexity of a tsunami of stories and information coming from a variety of places, and to reassure our funders and publishing partners that we're putting out the most rig-orously accurate investigative reporting we can," the memo read.

Ryle had finally signed on an American partner—the *Washington Post*. The partnership began on a discordant note when Ryle had to admit that he had already unsuccessfully approached the *New York Times*. Editorial skepticism and a lackadaisical effort at the *Post* hob-bled the collaboration. ICIJ and the paper collaborated on a short animated video that described how the secrecy world worked. The animation almost derailed their collaboration shortly before publi-cation when the *Post*'s lawyers and editors objected to the script for the video.

On February 11, outside events intervened: Pope Benedict XVI announced he would be stepping down at the end of the month. Ryle and Walker feared the project would be overshadowed by the pope's dramatic decision. They postponed the project's release yet again, this time to the beginning of April.

Less than a week before publication, ICIJ's luck finally turned. Months earlier they had discovered in the data the name of the dep-uty speaker of Mongolia's parliament, Bayartsogt Sangajav. Attempts to contact Sangajav in Mongolia were unsuccessful. In a last-ditch effort, Ryle reached out to the Mongolian embassy in Washington. It turned out that the deputy speaker was in DC for a conference. Apprised of the situation, Sangajav hurried over to the ICIJ office.

Ryle and Walker met with him in a conference room. Sangajav was distraught. If ICIJ published information about his secret offshore company, it would destroy his reputation and bring shame on his family, he said. Sangajav promised to return to Mongolia and resign if they kept the matter quiet. The company only had $1 million in its bank account, he told them as he started to cry. This was news to ICIJ. Ryle tried to be sympathetic with the distraught Mongolian. Walker, thinking of the long list of tasks that still remained, was brus-quer. Eventually, they convinced him to leave, without making any promises. ICIJ ultimately published his story, along with how much money the company had, adding a welcome human element to their data-intensive project.

A few days before publication, there was one final cancer scare. ICIJ had sent out an embargoed press release to the members of the network who had not participated in the collaboration so they could write stories once the leak investigation broke. A Brazilian member mistook the press release for the story itself. Excitedly, he tweeted news of the project. ICIJ caught the tweet before it went viral. Following an urgent call to Brazil, it was deleted.

THE PROJECT, which quickly became known as "Offshore Leaks," reverberated throughout the world when it was published on Wednesday, April 3, 2013. The website received more than six hundred thousand page views in a single day, a record for CPI. At ICIJ, the phones rang nonstop as media organizations begged for more details and the data itself. Ryle, Walker, Cabra, and Hudson fielded an endless stream of interview requests. The team had exposed an underground financial system that everyone knew existed but had never seen. In an age of austerity, it was now incontrovertible that many of the world's richest citizens were not paying their fair share. But it wasn't only the unprecedented look into the secrecy world that captivated attention. The collaboration itself became a story. It was the biggest cross-border investigative collaboration in journalism history, involving eighty-six investigative reporters from forty-six countries.

The *Washington Post* chose to publish its big story in the paper on Sunday, April 7, and online on Saturday, three days after everyone else, largely robbing it of the shared impact. In Switzerland, Oliver Zihlmann made a terrible miscalculation. He sent out a press release that Friday detailing plans to unveil the team's findings in Tamedia's Sunday edition. Instead, the dailies in the chain took stories from Germany's *Süddeutsche Zeitung*, among other outlets, and ran with them. Zihlmann had been scooped by his own newspaper chain. That weekend his team frantically produced a new story on Swiss banks found in the data.

Early in the project, the ICIJ team discussed publishing the material online. It eventually morphed into the idea of a searchable database of the company names, shareholders, and directors from the leak.

However, some on CPI's board resisted. They worried that a release of the raw data would unleash a flood of lawsuits. ICIJ's indefatigable libel lawyer, Michael Rothberg, calmed the fears. The biggest danger was a nuisance lawsuit from someone with a grudge and deep pockets. The information was clearly in the public interest. Fears of a frivolous lawsuit seemed a poor reason not to publish. To ensure that the material was not misunderstood, ICIJ added a disclaimer that stated that owning an offshore company was not illegal and that inclusion in the database was not evidence of a crime. They also agreed to withhold any information that clearly violated privacy, such as bank account details, passport information, or Social Security numbers.

A few days after publication, the IRS visited CPI. Bill Buzenberg remembers three beefy IRS agents in dark suits arriving at the office and threatening to issue a subpoena if the organization did not turn over the data. Ryle told CPI's lawyer that the IRS already possessed the material—they had it all along but had been slow to decipher it or apparently share it widely within the agency. A month later the IRS put out a face-saving press release announcing that it, along with Australia and the United Kingdom, had acquired a substantial amount of data.

In Panama, Mossfon received panicked emails from customers. "Our client is very concerned due to an offshore scandal around the BVI that there was some leak of information," one wrote in May. "Could you please advise if our client needs to be concerned as to the possibility of any leak of information that could link the company to our client since such information should be highly confidential."

Mossfon developed a standard response.

"Please rest assured that the Mossack Fonseca Group is consistently monitoring the situation regarding the alleged offshore leaks," it read. "Your confidential information is stored in our state-of-the-art data center, and any communication within our global network is handled through an encryption algorithm that complies with the highest world-class standards."

12

PROFITABLE PRINCELINGS

Mar Cabra, ICIJ's project research manager, gazed at the expectant faces gathered around the square table in the small conference room at the University of Hong Kong. It was July 2013, and she was about to deliver a crash course in digital security. Energetic and precocious, Cabra had learned the ins and outs of protecting data and emails only recently herself. ICIJ's days of sending unencrypted hard drives through the mail were coming to an end. Precautions had to be taken. Those at the table understood that what they were about to do was both historic and potentially dangerous.

The biggest chunk of the Offshore Leaks data consisted of nearly twenty-two thousand offshore clients with addresses in Hong Kong and mainland China. Ryle and Walker decided early in the project that they would husband the Greater China information for later. It was one of the best decisions the team made. They recognized that a worldwide collaboration would be challenging enough. Adding China to the mix would increase the level of difficulty by several orders of magnitude. Not only was it difficult to report inside China, but the country's offshore data was shrouded in layers of additional secrecy.

What was never in doubt was the need to focus on the Middle Kingdom. China played a central role in the secrecy world, not only for the companies found in the Offshore Leaks data but for Mossfon and other major providers as well. It is no accident that the biggest offshore provider in the world today, Offshore Incorporations, began in Hong Kong.

The Chinese government was neither prepared nor flexible enough to keep pace with the economic activity that Deng Xiaoping, China's paramount leader, had unleashed in the late 1980s. The sleeping giant's financial awakening was a boon to the offshore system. China needed a window to the world. If tax havens and anonymous companies hadn't already existed, the country's particular fusion of Communism and entrepreneurial capitalism would have created them. The government recognized the benefit of offshore companies and encouraged them.

Anonymous companies provided a way for China's economy to bloom, because even though they circumvented government restrictions and helped people avoid taxes, they also minimized economic turbulence and allowed for foreign investment. Tax haven–based companies provided the vehicle for foreigners to invest in Chinese subsidiaries without the difficulty of bringing money directly into the country. In order to buy equipment or make other purchases, Chinese businessmen found it easier to park money offshore, buy the material, and then import it.

Chinese entrepreneurs quickly learned that they could create offshore subsidiaries and then sell their goods to their own companies at low cost. The subsidiary company would then resell the product at a significant markup. This way, the Chinese-based firm reported low taxes in China and repatriated the profits from the resale by its subsidiary back to the country as nontaxable foreign investment. The process was known as "round-tripping."

Trillions of dollars left China, a fact easily ignored since an exponentially larger amount of foreign direct investment was flowing into the country.

The offshore system also provided a convenient way for the newly wealthy to hide their money and disguise the receipt of illegal payments. Many of the winners in China's new economy were connected to government officials. Among the most powerful were the so-called princelings, the children of China's Communist elite, part of what has become known as the "Red Nobility" for those connected by blood or marriage to the country's leadership, past and present. China does not require officials to disclose their assets publicly. Until journalists—first foreigners and then locals—started hammering away, the activities of the country's leaders were largely a mystery.

IN 2012, BLOOMBERG NEWS and the New York Times published a series of articles that revealed the hidden wealth of the families of China's top leaders, including then vice president Xi Jinping and then prime minister Wen Jiabao. The reporters cut through layers of partnerships and opaque investment vehicles to show how the politically connected gorged themselves on money from state-owned companies and cash from wealthy businessmen seeking favors. China's authoritarian regime quickly banned access to the two news organizations on the Chinese Internet, a censorship blockade known as "The Great Firewall." They also opted not to renew a visa for one of the reporters involved.

Now ICIJ was in possession of the hard data to build on these journalistic revelations. No one had ever seen the full breadth of Chinese offshore activities. Nor had local reporters ever taken the lead, in collaboration with foreign colleagues, to delve systematically into such a sensitive subject.

Journalists from the United States, Germany, Spain, Taiwan, Hong Kong, and mainland China crowded together on the second floor of Eliot Hall, a massive and majestic colonial-era building on the University of Hong Kong campus. The meeting was deliberately discreet. The woman in charge of bringing everyone together, Yuen-Ying Chan, a wizened Hong Kong–based journalism professor Cabra calls the "Yoda of ICIJ," did not tell her university colleagues it was taking place.

Chan was one of the original foreign journalists at the Harvard meeting where CPI's Charles Lewis had launched ICIJ in 1997. She was also one of the reporters behind its first major exposé on Big Tobacco in 2000. Born in Hong Kong, Chan had worked for twenty-three years for several U.S. media organizations, including the New York *Daily News*. Upon her return to Asia, she and a colleague exposed the Clinton administration's tawdry prospecting for campaign cash in Asia. A senior official in Taiwan's ruling party sued the reporters for libel. Her victory in the lawsuit set an important precedent for independent journalism in Asia, earning her the International Press Freedom Award from the Committee to Protect Journalists. In 1999, she founded the Journalism and Media Studies Centre at the University of Hong Kong, where she quietly helped train a generation of dedicated professional Asian journalists.

Chan enlisted the Hong Kong daily *Ming Pao* and Taiwan's *CommonWealth Magazine* for the project. Both publications were run by editors she knew and could trust. The biggest coup was the inclusion of *Caijing*, a Beijing-based investigative finance and economics magazine on the mainland known at the time for its independent reporting and elite readership. After the original project's publication, it had contacted ICIJ requesting to partner on Offshore Leaks.

Caijing actively pushed the boundaries of government censorship. One of its reporters, Luo Changping, had recently exposed the secret financial activities of a top economic planning official. While the magazine had not named the official, Luo did so on Weibo, China's version of Twitter. Months after the story was published, the official was dismissed.

Caijing demonstrated that if allowed, Chinese journalism could ferret out wrongdoing for the authorities to act upon. At the Hong Kong meeting, it was not clear if *Caijing* would publish stories—that would depend on what the team found—but it would help in the reporting. The government in Beijing had launched a widely publicized campaign against corruption, and those embarking on the project hoped that their reporting might dovetail with the crackdown.

The first day of the meeting Cabra focused on security. She taught the group how to use an email encryption program called PGP (Pretty Good Privacy) and virtual private networks to shroud the identity of Internet users and how to access the secret ICIJ website where the data could be searched. Code names were created for top officials the group suspected might be found in the data.

The second day focused on the data itself. The original plan was to do batch searching of high-profile names to look for matches, says Alexa Olesen, a China expert who led the ICIJ reporting team. Olesen had a degree in East Asian studies from the University of Chicago and a master's in Chinese literature from the School of Oriental and African Studies from the University of London. She had spent more than a decade in Asia, including eight years as an Associated Press reporter in Beijing.

"We didn't know what there would be in the data, maybe real estate, maybe corruption," she recalls. "It was new territory. The Chinese use of offshore hadn't been mapped this way before."

After the meeting concluded, the group gathered for dinner at a seafood restaurant, swapping a square table for a round one. Looking around the table, Olesen remembers feeling excitement. There was a palpable sense of shared purpose. The team had come from places whose political establishments had long been at odds with each other. Yet, here they were, working together, bonded by a common belief that journalism in the public interest could make the world a better place.

MOSSFON WAS ONE of the pioneers in selling anonymous companies in China. The firm opened a Hong Kong office in 1987, when the city was still a British territory. Panama and Liberia had long been the two most popular jurisdictions for Hong Kong's elite to hide their money, but when Panama's Manuel Noriega and Liberia's Samuel Doe trashed their respective countries, the appetite for offshore companies from these places diminished.

Mossfon set up shop in Hong Kong to promote a new jurisdiction, the British Virgin Islands, which did not have messy political problems. Ramón Fonseca spent a month living in a Hong Kong hotel. He would pick different buildings full of law offices and go door-to-door delivering Mossfon brochures and schmoozing with whoever would listen.

The firm's office was originally run by an Indian woman, but as the 1997 handover of Hong Kong from the British to the Chinese neared, it became clear the firm needed a native Mandarin speaker to head its efforts. In Panama, Mossfon had enlisted the services of Austin Zhang to help with its translation work. Born Zhang Xiaodong in Shaanxi in northwest China, Zhang had traveled the world, eventually landing in Panama, which has a sizable Chinese population. He was working for a local Chinese-language newspaper when Mossfon hired him as a translator. Zhang received a crash course in the offshore business while spending a year translating documents and brochures. He eventually wrote a booklet in Mandarin on how to set up an offshore company.

In 1997, Zhang moved to Hong Kong. His goal was to plant the Mossfon flag on the mainland. He was both bright and driven, and so the partners took a chance and gave him the go-ahead. Within three years, Mossfon had opened its first office in Beijing. Zhang became an acknowledged expert on offshore company creation, quoted widely in Chinese media and invited to speak at state-sponsored conferences on the subject. He was so successful, the firm opened satellite offices around China to market its wares.

China's economy was expanding rapidly, creating new wealth at an extraordinary pace. Zhang taught clients not only how to hide ownership through offshore companies but why such a service was valuable in the first place. His notes from meetings in the mid-2000s are almost breathless in their excitement over the possibilities.

Reporting back from northeastern China in 2005, Zhang described how there were many rich and well-operated companies. It was important to build ties of friendship, known as *guanxi*, with local officials. "North Eastern is an important strategic area for China in natural resources, heavy industries, oil, shipping and trade," he wrote. "The economy will develop fast. This will support our long-term development for providing offshore services and other commercial services to clients."

Around the same time, one of Zhang's Chinese colleagues at Mossfon spoke at a conference for exporters and importers. "To lower the political risks, we need to avoid showing the investment is from China," he told them. "We can 'filter' the origin by putting it in a transfer station (subsidiary), presenting it as if it's from Luxembourg, the Cayman Islands, etc."

In a meeting a year later with a potential customer who held trade-marks for his business in China, Zhang told the man a troubling story. He described the case of a large Chinese manufacturer of wood flooring. According to Zhang, a competitor had instigated a government investigation of the company, which found that its products contained "polluted elements." If the company had only had an offshore structure, with a trademark held outside China, it would never have been made public who owned it, Zhang explained. The implication was that the company could have dodged the investigation by changing its name and ownership. The potential customer suddenly understood the value of corporate anonymity.

"I could see from his face that he was really excited," Zhang wrote in his notes, "quite different from his way of talking to me at the beginning when he said there was nothing we could do in his trademark business."

Zhang and his Mossfon colleagues were in the business of providing solutions for a rapidly changing economic and political situation. For another client, who wanted to invest but was prohibited by government regulations, Zhang suggested the man make his daughter the owner of the company, since she had an American green card.

By far Zhang's most audacious solution was the creation of fake shareholders, known in the trade as nominee beneficial owners. This was an actual person paid to pretend to own the company. The fake beneficial owner allowed clients to achieve the kind of anonymity that had once existed with bearer shares before they were restricted. Using a fake shareholder or owner, the company could open bank accounts or evade government supervision without anyone but Mossfon knowing who the person really was.

In 2008, Zhang contacted Mossfon's main office for help in one such arrangement. His Chinese customer wanted a fake owner from Panama. In the requested scheme, the Panamanian nominee shareholder would own and be sole director of a Samoan company for three months. During that time, the Panamanian would register the company in China. After three months, the fake owner would transfer the Samoan company to the actual Chinese owner. For the purposes of the Chinese registry, though, the Panamanian would continue to be listed as the owner. The Chinese government and public would never know who actually owned the company.

The partners were leery of the arrangement. Mossfon had employed fake owners themselves, although rarely, and usually after a degree of due diligence or for particularly well-heeled clients. It was Ramsés Owens at Mossfon Trust who was often behind such machinations. Owens advised Zhang not to do it, even if his competitors did. He told him that Panama had explicitly outlawed such activity.

"Is competition offering NOMINEE BENEFICIAL OWNERSHIP services despite the fact it is a sensitive service?" Owens asked Zhang in his email. "Austin, be very careful."

(The files indicate that Owens did not take his own advice. A year later, he offered a similar service to Marianna Olszewski, a New York–based financial self-help author. Olszewski wanted to move $1 million she had in a bank account in Guernsey to another country but did not want to have to declare the transfer. Owens offered a "Natural Person Trustee." His assistant explained that it was "a very sensitive matter" and the "fees are quite high.")

Zhang affirmed that he had been offering this service for some time. When Mossfon suggested that he use a foundation instead, Zhang dismissed the idea. Local banks weren't familiar with the structure, he wrote. It would take too long for them to review it and gain approval. In the end, Zhang sent the customer elsewhere.

By that point, he could afford to be more selective. The firm had eight offices on the mainland. In time, Greater China would account for approximately a third of Mossfon's overall business. And the British Virgin Islands became so popular, it entered the lexicon. To have a "BVI" became shorthand in China for any offshore company, regardless of where in the world it was located.

ONCE THE ICIJ team discovered what appeared to be members of the Red Nobility in the leaked files, they had to verify that the names actually corresponded to these politically connected individuals. The data contained only basic information with perhaps a few identifying details. In each ICIJ leak investigation, the data was only the beginning of the reporting process. Names had to be checked. Companies researched to learn their activities. Stories filled out. Subjects contacted for comment.

In China, the task was even more arduous—and not only because available public information was limited. Most tax havens did not permit the use of Chinese characters for company, director, or shareholder names. Offshore providers employed Romanized spellings of Chinese names in documents and emails referencing their customers. This often led to confusion. For example, Austin Zhang's last name in Hong Kong was frequently spelled Cheung. Both names were common ones. In the same way, Wang might be spelled Wong or Ye as Yeh.

Alongside the name of the company owner, the documents often included an identification number specific to mainland China. This helped narrow the search somewhat. The eighteen-digit number, which all Chinese citizens are given, contains the date of birth, sex, and the region where the person was born. Addresses, news reports, public records, and known associates all helped winnow down the possibilities. Nonetheless, sometimes a name could not be confirmed and thus was omitted from the final article.

Portcullis TrustNet, one of the two companies whose files ICIJ's Gerard Ryle obtained for Offshore Leaks, had moved aggressively into China around the same time as Mossfon. TrustNet cultivated top accounting firms like PricewaterhouseCoopers, Deloitte & Touche, and KPMG. The firm also worked with Swiss banks including UBS, which created more than one thousand offshore structures for clients in Hong Kong, Taiwan, and mainland China.

In the data, the team found relatives of at least five current or former members of China's Politburo Standing Committee, which rules the country through its leadership of the Communist Party. Deng Xiaoping's son-in-law was present. So was the son of one of the Eight Great Eminent Officials, a group of elders who held sway in the Communist Party in the 1980s and '90s. Both the son and son-in-law of former premier Wen Jiabao had companies in the data. Wen's son Wen Yunsong created one BVI company with the help of Credit Suisse. The information further punctured the carefully crafted image of Wen

Jiabao, who stepped down in 2013, as a grandfatherly reformer concerned with the well-being of the poor.

Not surprisingly, the wealthiest and most connected used multiple incorporators. Deng Jiagui, a successful developer who was the brother-in-law of China's president, Xi Jinping, owned half of Excellence Effort Property Development, a BVI company registered by TrustNet. The other half was owned by a pair of real estate tycoons who benefited from winning government land auctions worth billions of dollars. Deng Jiagui also dealt with Mossfon. He acquired three companies from the Panamanians between 2004 and 2009.

Li Xiaolin, the daughter of Li Peng, China's former premier, had the distinction of appearing in nearly every leak investigation ICIJ conducted. Her father earned the nickname "the Butcher of Beijing," for overseeing the brutal repression of pro-democracy protesters in 1989. A senior engineer with a taste for luxury goods, Li Xiaolin is known as "the Power Queen," for her job leading a state-controlled energy company. Her interests have also strayed into other lucrative activities such as secretly helping a multinational insurance company break into the Chinese market. She was a director of two TrustNet companies, and her HSBC Swiss bank account held almost $2.5 million in 2006–2007. She also had a Mossfon company with her husband that exported industrial equipment from Europe to China.

Of all the Chinese elites with connections to ICIJ's leaked data, none was more notorious than Bo Xilai. His story neatly captures the combination of corruption and hypocrisy that is perhaps the greatest gift the secrecy world affords China's rulers. Bo was the son of Bo Yibo, an associate of Mao Zedong and one of the Eight Immortals of the Communist Party of China. Both father and son suffered cruelly during the Cultural Revolution. Deng Xiaoping rehabilitated the father and set Bo Xilai on a course that led him into government.

As mayor of Dalian in the 1990s, Bo Xilai transformed the port city into a prosperous metropolis that attracted foreign investment and tourists. In 2007, he was appointed party chief of Chongqing, a city-province with a population of thirty-three million known as "Fog City." From this position, he launched a vicious and high-profile anticorruption crusade dubbed "Smash the Black." His main henchman was the local police chief, Wang Lijun, the star of *Iron-Blooded Police Spirits*, a TV reality series.

Wang and his men persecuted officials and policemen suspected of corruption, torturing the guilty and the innocent alike. They administered electric shock treatment, forced people to stay awake upright for days in a metal "tiger chair," and stuffed wasabi into their noses and chili water down their throats. Bo trumpeted the campaign, appearing on television to declare that "Corruption is the Party's mortal wound." The anticorruption crusade was a big hit with the population, and China's leaders took notice. Bo Xilai was elevated to the Politburo and regarded as a strong candidate to join the inner circle, the Politburo Standing Committee, one day.

Meanwhile, secretly, he and his wife, Gu Kailai, had amassed a fortune in kickbacks. Estimates of their illicit wealth vary from $160 million to $1 billion. To get the money out of the country, Gu Kailai employed foreign middlemen known in China as "white gloves" because they allow one to keep clean hands. In 2000, Patrick Henri Devillers, a louche Frenchman, set up a shell company in the BVI called Russell Properties S.A. through the Saint Thomas–based provider Trident Trust. Xu Ming, a plastics billionaire, then paid Russell Properties $3.2 million to buy a steel shop overseas. The transaction was a farce. Xu received access to a land development deal. Gu Kailai pocketed the money and bought a six-bedroom mansion with a thirty-three-thousand-square-foot yard overlooking the French Riviera. The couple rented the estate to wealthy Russians to supplement their income.

In 2007, they enlisted another white glove, Neil Heywood, a Harrow-educated British expat who drove around China in a secondhand Jaguar S-Type with a Union Jack on the bumper. He worked part-time at an Aston Martin dealership and also as an investigator for a private intelligence firm. Heywood helped Bo and Gu get their son Bo Guagua, nicknamed "Little Rabbit" (mom was "Big Rabbit"), into his English alma mater. The school cost about £30,000 a year, while Bo's annual salary was at most the equivalent of £12,000.

In August 2011, the registration for Russell Properties was transferred by Trident to Mossfon. By this time, the relationship had soured between Heywood and Gu Kailai, who was herself a lawyer, the author of a popular book called *Winning a Lawsuit in the U.S.*, and the daughter of a famous People's Liberation Army general. Gu and Heywood had gone in together on a $200 million state-backed real estate deal that Bo had quashed because he was worried it might threaten his political career. Heywood had already spent the money in his head and demanded that Gu pay him $20 million in recompense. When she refused, he allegedly threatened to expose the couple and harm Little Rabbit.

On November 13, Gu lured Heywood to the Lucky Holiday Hotel in Chongqing. After getting drunk on Royal Salute whiskey, Heywood vomited and then asked for water. She served him up a glass mixed with rat poison and cyanide instead. She and an aide then sprinkled drugs around the room to make the death look like an overdose or drug-fueled heart attack. Chief Wang handled the investigation/cover-up. The body was quickly cremated without an autopsy. Wang reported the details to Gu the next day in a conversation he surreptitiously taped.

Two weeks later, Russell Properties was transferred to an address connected to Gu. When Chief Wang informed Bo of what his wife had done at the hotel, the party boss did not take the news well, demoting the police chief to vice mayor in charge of sports, sanitation, and education. Fearful that he would meet a similar fate to Heywood, Wang sought asylum at the American consulate in Chengdu in February 2012. The Americans handed him over to the Chinese authorities.

A month later, Bo Xilai was detained as he walked offstage in the Great Hall of the People after the closing ceremony of the National People's Congress. He was tried, convicted, and sentenced to life in prison for bribery, embezzlement, and abuse of power. Gu was sentenced to death, which was reduced to life in prison.

Shortly after Bo's arrest, the registration for Russell Properties was transferred to another Panamanian law firm. The Chinese government is believed to have sold the mansion on the Riviera.

THE ICIJ STAFF noticed that, despite Mar Cabra's instructions, the *Caijing* reporters were somewhat lax when it came to digital security. Sometimes they forgot to encrypt their emails. Yet they were doing good work, actively searching the database and contributing reporting to the project.

Then someone found Wang Boming, *Caijing*'s owner, in the data. He was the director of two companies and the shareholder of another. The group queried him about his holdings, trying to pin down their purpose. He responded to all the questions. There was no apparent impropriety. Despite the revelation, the project continued.

Two months before publication, *Caijing*'s deputy investigative editor, Luo Changping, the man who had defiantly published the corrupt official's name, was moved to another department. Not long afterward, the magazine's top editor sent an encrypted message to ICIJ's Marina Walker in Washington. The message explained that the magazine had been visited by state security. The government had told *Caijing* to cease participation in the collaboration. Someone had leaked information about the project. *Caijing* cut off communication with the partners. ICIJ blocked further access to the data, but any damage likely had already been done.

About a week before publication, staff from the Chinese embassy in Madrid requested a meeting with editors at *El País*, who had joined the collaboration after the first wave of stories. They told the editors that they knew about the project. They asked whether the *El País* China correspondent was involved and hinted his residency in the country might be in jeopardy. The lunch was tense and short. It was followed by a longer meal a few days later where the paper presented its findings and asked for comment. Despite the pressure, *El País* opted to publish anyway.

The stories went live on the afternoon of Tuesday, January 21, 2014. In addition to the princelings and other relatives of officials, the data revealed tidbits on China's richest woman, the founders of major Internet companies, the offshore activities of the country's oil industry, and its biggest industrialists. The stories presented an unparalleled view into the country's use of the offshore system.

ICIJ called it China Leaks.

In addition to Hong Kong's *Ming Pao* and Taiwan's *CommonWealth Magazine*, stories ran in *El País*, the *Guardian*, *Süddeutsche Zeitung*, and Switzerland's *Le Matin Dimanche*, among others. In the end, *Ming Pao*'s editors didn't fully embrace the project. Yuen-Ying Chan, the Hong Kong journalism professor who brought everyone together, speculates that in the end her hometown newspaper, focused on local news, did not fully recognize the value of the leak.

"Editors or even readers would say, 'We know this already,'" she says. "'The top guys are corrupt, what's the news?'"

The difference was that for the first time, everybody could see how the system operated and who was involved. To ensure wide distribution, ICIJ translated the stories into Mandarin.

The Chinese government recognized the danger almost instantly. Within hours of publication, Internet users in China were blocked from the ICIJ Web pages. The same happened to the *Guardian* and other partners in the project. The Great Firewall also removed mentions of the stories on Weibo.

There were ways to get around the censorship for the truly committed. They could use a VPN service to hide their Internet point of origin. Readers also passed around PDFs of the story. For the vast majority of Chinese, though, the revelations never happened.

13

FOLLOW THE LEAKS

Tax authorities and prosecutors around the world scrambled after the release of Offshore Leaks. Politicians whose names appeared in the data made excuses. Functionaries resigned. Governments promised more transparency. Luxembourg even announced that it would automatically share bank account information with U.S. tax authorities. Meanwhile offshore providers bemoaned a "crisis of confidence" gripping the industry as a result of the leak.

Offshore Leaks proved that investigative reporters from different countries and different cultures could collaborate. ICIJ had built a new kind of journalism machine, though the structure was still rickety. Reporters working together across borders formed the gears, but the power came from information—in this case, leaked data. Only high-grade data worked. The material had to be extensive and cover multiple countries. ICIJ's mandate required a strong public-interest rationale to publish—subject matter that involved the well-being of society. ICIJ director Gerard Ryle wanted stories that grabbed readers' attention and provided a worthy challenge for a crackerjack group of international investigative reporters. For these last two points, the secrecy world was made to order.

A chronic worrier, Ryle envisioned the momentum generated by

Offshore Leaks slipping away. A single successful collaboration was more proof of concept than a machine firing on all cylinders. Without a new project, the partners would inevitably disperse. He needed new fuel for the machine, and quickly.

Shortly after the publication of Offshore Leaks, Spain's *El País* printed a list of Spanish HSBC account holders suspected of tax evasion. The names came from data stolen from HSBC's Swiss private bank by a former employee, Hervé Falciani. The next day, ICIJ's data researcher Mar Cabra wrote a story in *El Confidencial* noting overlaps between people found on "Falciani's famous list" and Offshore Leaks.

The Falciani files had been the talk of Europe for several years. The public did not know what Falciani's data contained, but tax authorities around Europe were acting on it. The French had provided a handful of countries lists of their citizens who had Swiss accounts with HSBC. Some of those individual lists had leaked but no journalist had reviewed all the material. Cabra thought the HSBC files could be ICIJ's next project. After conferring with Ryle, she obtained Falciani's email address and sent him a note.

The pitch was simple: We have data. You have data. Let's put our data together.

HERVÉ FALCIANI'S PATH to government informant was a tortured one. Handsome, intelligent, and charming, as a youth he worked as a croupier at the Casino de Monte-Carlo while studying computer engineering. HSBC hired him in 2000. The Swiss private bank's IT operation was a disaster, its compliance systems inoperable, its transactions monitored manually. The maintenance of client data was carried out by French employees working from home on their laptops, according to one bank executive.

In 2006, Falciani was tapped to reorganize HSBC's client database and reinforce its security. Instead, working on weekends over a five-month period, he downloaded the data for himself. HSBC failed to notice.

Falciani covertly tried to sell the data in Beirut in 2008 with the help of his mistress, Georgina Mikhael, an attractive French-Lebanese computer scientist at the bank. He promised her that he would use the money to leave his wife and autistic daughter. He and Mikhael could not close the sale, but news of their trip eventually made it to the Swiss banking association, who alerted regulators.

Falciani also contacted Germany's foreign intelligence agency, the Bundesnachrichtendienst (BND), under a pseudonym. Earlier that year, the BND had purchased a DVD for almost €5 million containing the names of German citizens who used Liechtenstein's LGT Bank to avoid paying their taxes. It began a trend of German tax officials buying purloined tax data on their citizens from neighboring countries.

The subject line of Falciani's email to the BND read, "tax evasion." He wrote that he had a list of clients from one of the five largest private banks in the world, based in Switzerland, as well as access to its computer system. The Germans were interested. A meeting was arranged with a top official, who was multilingual and practiced at buying stolen data. At the last minute, though, the official broke his kneecap, and his replacement couldn't speak English or French. Falciani did not speak German. In the ensuing confusion, he lost an opportunity for a big payday.

Falciani also met with Inspector Jean-Patrick Martini of France's National Directorate of Tax Investigation. Colleagues nicknamed Martini "the apéritif" for his surname, but also because the downfall of fraudsters followed his presence like a meal after a cocktail. But the French wouldn't pay, and not even the persuasive Martini could dislodge the data from Falciani.

In December 2008, after learning that Falciani was cheating on her and that the Swiss police had her under surveillance, Mikhael gave him up to Swiss law enforcement, who took Falciani into custody. He was interrogated for several hours but convinced a Swiss prosecutor to release him so he could check on his wife and daughter, promising to return the following day. Instead, he and his family fled Switzerland that evening for France, with a laptop brimming with more than one hundred gigabytes of information on more than one hundred thousand HSBC clients. The files contained not only the evidence for tax evasion on a global scale but also the secret financial details of criminal activity by a broad swath of individuals, from corrupt politicians to arms traffickers.

Police in Nice soon arrested Falciani on a Swiss Interpol warrant. He called Martini, who arranged for his release from custody. The French refused to turn him over to the Swiss, and Martini took charge of the data. The French tax authorities dubbed it Operation Chocolate. Free on his own recognizance while he helped the French make sense of the information, Falciani traveled to Spain, where he was promptly arrested and held until he made a similar pact with the Spanish. Over the next few years, he would shuttle between both countries, offering his help to tax authorities sorting out the information.

In October 2013, on Mar Cabra's second try, Falciani answered her email. He was in Madrid, where Cabra lived, and agreed to meet her. The Spanish government had enveloped him in security by this point. Cabra received a call to meet at a public place, where she encountered a plainclothes policeman. He reviewed her identification documents and phoned to someone watching nearby. They then took her to meet Falciani.

Cabra was charmed, even smitten, with the fit and well-dressed Falciani. He demonstrated a deep knowledge of data technology as they discussed the tools of the trade. They met again three days later, and Falciani showed her a sample of the HSBC files. He proposed that ICIJ work in collaboration with the Spanish and French prosecutors. She was noncommittal on that point but suggested he meet with Ryle in Paris the following week.

In Paris, Falciani and Ryle took a long walk along the bank of the Seine. They forged an immediate connection, waxing rhapsodically over the power of public-interest journalism to change the world. Ryle left the meeting with Falciani as Cabra had, entranced and convinced that Falciani's data was the next ICIJ project.

During the following months, every chance they could, Ryle and Cabra met separately with Falciani to strengthen the relationship. In

March 2014, the three agreed to meet in Paris. In anticipation of receiving the data, ICIJ flew in Rigoberto Carvajal from Costa Rica.

The month before, Carvajal's boss, Giannina Segnini, had quit *La Nación*, the newspaper where she had worked for twenty years. She penned a farewell to readers that elided the real reason she had resigned. She and her team of data journalists had marshaled their expertise to create an app for the 2014 Costa Rican election that enabled voters to see each candidate's voting history, business interests, and even scanned court documents. They called the app "Don't Vote Blind." At the last minute, her bosses, fearful that a leftist party might win the presidency for the first time, tried to disable the app. Segnini's team followed her out the door and into the arms of ICIJ, which hired Carvajal and a Maltese software engineer named Matthew Caruana Galizia, who had left the *Financial Times* to work with the Costa Ricans. Segnini herself landed at Columbia University as a professor at the journalism school.

Ryle, Cabra, Carvajal, and Falciani met for dinner in Paris. Ryle had chosen a pizza place, earning him gentle ribbing from his colleagues. At dinner, they discussed Falciani's data and cybersecurity. It seemed that the transfer might have to occur through a third party, and Falciani told them he couldn't do anything without his lawyer. They arranged to meet again the following day at the law offices of William Bourdon, an internationally recognized white-collar defense attorney, who represented Falciani.

Falciani arrived at the meeting with an Italian journalist in tow. Ryle and Cabra looked at each other in confusion. This was a secret meeting to exchange the data and yet here was another reporter. Falciani launched into a proposal to start an international organization for whistle-blowers. The ICIJ team thought, *What is going on? We brought Carvajal all the way from Costa Rica for this?* Ryle then asked the Italian journalist to leave so they could speak privately with Falciani and Bourdon. The reporter reacted angrily. He let them know he was a good friend of Falciani's, with whom he had spent many an hour in deep conversation. It was like a horror movie where the plot comes into focus. Ryle suddenly realized he had been played. They had been

courting Falciani for five months. They weren't even the only journalists he had been stringing along.

Falciani and the other reporter left the room. Ryle explained to
Bourdon what had occurred. The lawyer said he understood. There
was another possibility, though. Someone else, he said, had the data
as well.

Bourdon said he would be in touch.

Cabra was crushed, and a little heartbroken. She, Ryle, and Carvajal met with Falciani later that day, explaining to him that theirs was
a small organization. Time was of the essence. The team was on
standby. A decision had to be made. Falciani would not budge.

Then Bourdon texted Ryle. A reporter at *Le Monde*, Gérard Davet,
had the data. This was perfect; *Le Monde* had been a partner on Offshore Leaks. Ryle excitedly texted Davet, telling him the team was
leaving Paris the next day but they would happily meet with him at
any time before then.

The response was curt and brutal. Davet was very busy and would
not be able to meet.

Ryle flew back to Washington the next day, crushed but with a fall-
back project in mind.

MEANWHILE, THE DEMANDS on Mossfon grew. The trend was clear.
Around the world, the countries where it based its companies wanted
more information. The firm fielded requests from government regulators while complying with new regulations that further constrained
its activities. When Mossfon's companies ran afoul of the rules, judgment came more swiftly and at a steeper price. The firm's low-cost
business model—provide cheap companies in volume, fast—buckled
under the onslaught.

In 2013, some of the last holdouts, Panama and the Seychelles, took
action. Panama restricted bearer shares, and the Seychelles outlawed
them. Among the few jurisdictions left that offered bearer shares
were the Marshall Islands and Liberia, whose public registries operated out of offices in Virginia and New York.

The following year, Hong Kong, one of the first foreign jurisdictions with which the firm did business, changed its company incorporation law. The new statute required that for new companies, at least one director had to be a human being, rather than a trust, a foundation, or another company. Mossfon contacted its clients in an arduous effort to get them to comply with the changing regulations. In the BVI, clients who did not meet due diligence requirements under its new anti-money-laundering law had to be approved personally by the firm's most senior compliance officer—in Mossfon's case, Jürgen Mossack.

In May, the BVI Financial Services Commission contacted Mossfon about Pan World Investments Inc., a company for which it had acted as registered agent for almost a decade. The company had come through the Credit Suisse private bank in Geneva and was owned by Alaa Mubarak, the eldest son of former Egyptian president Hosni Mubarak. Two years earlier, the Mubaraks (including another son, Gamal) were arrested on charges that they had taken public money destined for presidential palaces to build their own private residences.

Mossfon had accepted the Mubaraks with little screening, relying on Credit Suisse to vet the end users of the company. "You don't think when Mubarak walks through the door of a bank they don't know who he is?" explains Mossack.

After the Arab Spring, when as many as 846 people died in protests against Mubarak's rule, the BVI issued an order freezing the assets of officials tied to the Egyptian regime, including Alaa Mubarak. Still, Mossfon did not act until it received the letter from the BVI authorities. It then placed the company in a high-risk category.

As the firm discussed what to do about the BVI letter, it made a "most embarrassing" discovery, as one Mossfon lawyer termed it. The firm did not have a signed service provision agreement with Credit Suisse that spelled out vetting expectations for the bank. Without this document, the ultimate responsibility for due diligence could lie with the Panamanians. A Mossfon compliance officer acknowledged in an internal email that "our risk assessment formula is seriously flawed." This insight was not shared with the BVI. Instead, the firm's response to the Financial Services Commission's inquiry put the blame for the companies' irregularities on Credit Suisse.

For years, the commission had requested information from Mossfon, to little result. Between 2005 and 2008, the BVI asked the firm—in more than one hundred separate requests—for beneficial ownership information on various companies. Mossfon was able to provide the true owner's name for just five of those requests, according to an analysis by the *Guardian*. Times had changed. In November 2013, BVI's financial regulators fined Mossfon $37,500 for "failing to carry out the necessary enhanced customer due diligence measures of a high risk customer."

Mossfon then tried unsuccessfully to invoice Credit Suisse for the fine.

Sometimes controversy could be handled more quietly. In 2013, a compliance check on Malchus Irvin Boncamper, a Saint Kitts and Nevis–based accountant, with whom Mossfon had worked for more than a decade, revealed disturbing news. Boncamper was serving an eight-year prison sentence for money laundering and other crimes. He had been convicted two years earlier. This was a significant problem because Boncamper was currently serving as a director of about thirty of the firm's shell companies.

The tale attached to Boncamper had begun on a windless, sunny day in October 2005, when a group of mostly elderly tourists boarded the *Ethan Allen*, a thirty-eight-foot glass-enclosed fiberglass boat, for an hourlong fall foliage tour around New York's Lake George. Their average age was seventy-six.

The boat had been modified over the years, reducing its steadiness. The Coast Guard later determined it should have carried no more than fourteen passengers. There were forty-seven aboard.

It was already listing 2.2 degrees to port when it left the dock. Twenty-four minutes later, the captain noticed a two- to three-foot wake approaching the boat. He tried to steer into the wave but it was too late. Within seconds the boat had flipped, trapping passengers as the water flooded in. Twenty people drowned that day.

The survivors' nightmare was just beginning. It turned out the *Ethan Allen*'s insurance was worthless. The Quirk family, which owned the boat, thought they were buying legitimate protection. The insurance company was even reinsured by another firm, United Re-Insurance Group Limited, created by Boncamper, but it was all a scam.

The victims and their families settled with the family that owned the vessel for an undisclosed sum in 2008. James Quirk mortgaged his home and other assets to fund the settlement. The following year, Matthew Quirk, who worked with the boats for the family business, took one out onto the lake, tied an anchor to himself, and dove into the water. His body was found the next day.

When Mossfon learned about Boncamper's troubles, the firm's head of compliance, Sandra de Cornejo, ordered staffers to remove him as director from multiple companies and backdate the changes so it would appear that the removals had happened prior to his conviction.

IN THE SUMMER of 2011, the French television journalist Edouard Perrin struck gold. Antoine Deltour, a young auditor at the office of PricewaterhouseCoopers in Luxembourg, provided Perrin with hundreds of secret tax rulings that the accounting firm had obtained on behalf of multinational corporations. The Luxembourg rulings allowed some of the world's biggest companies legally to avoid paying hundreds of billions of dollars in taxes in the countries where they did business. It was yet another example of how the biggest exploiters of the secrecy world were multinational corporations. Perrin's only problem was that he couldn't immediately take advantage of the leak. The documents were so complex, they were all but gibberish to him.

Perrin had made a name for himself in France for covering complex subjects in interesting ways. He gravitated toward tax issues. Perrin believed the topic could be both informative and entertaining. In the wake of the 2008 financial crisis, European governments had imposed budget cuts that were bleeding their citizens. Viewers were anxious to know who was paying their fair share in taxes and who wasn't.

At a conference in October of that year, Perrin met with John Christensen of the Tax Justice Network and Richard Murphy, an accountant and cofounder of the organization. Perrin described the advice he needed. Christensen and Murphy sent him to Richard Brooks, a former investigator with the British tax revenue authority who was now a journalist. Brooks was skeptical of Perrin at first, especially since the Frenchman would provide few details over the phone. But when Brooks saw the data, he quickly recognized its value.

By December, the two were filming in Luxembourg. One of Perrin's goals was to capture footage of Marius Kohl. For more than three decades, Kohl had run Sociétés 6, the Luxembourg federal agency in charge of what the *Wall Street Journal* described as the country's most valuable export: tax relief. Sporting a beard and a ponytail, Kohl looked more like a biker than a tax official. He was known as "Monsieur Ruling," for the thousands of corporate tax deals he had sanctioned during his tenure.

There were hundreds of companies whose Luxembourg tax agreements were included in the leak. The agreements themselves were often quite complex, with diagrams in swirls of arrows and boxes that illustrated how money flowed between subsidiaries and countries. A tax deal for the Illinois-based pharmaceutical company Abbott Laboratories, for example, had seventy-nine steps to it. In another deal, PepsiCo used its Luxembourg subsidiary to reduce its tax bill on a $1.4 billion purchase of a controlling interest in Russia's largest juice maker by sending money to Bermuda and back. Luxembourg tax agreements enabled the Australian division of the Swedish furniture giant IKEA to pay little tax on an estimated $1 billion in profits earned in that country. FedEx used two Luxembourg affiliates to move earnings from Mexico, France, and Brazil to a subsidiary in Hong Kong. This allowed the company to significantly reduce its tax burden in the places where it actually earned the profits.

Marius Kohl had approved about 40 percent of the submitted tax agreements—which averaged between twenty and one hundred pages in length—on the very day they were submitted. On April 21, 2010, he had been exceptionally efficient, approving eight agreements that had been submitted that day, along with four that had come in earlier. Some of the submissions were incomplete, but it didn't matter.

Kohl himself did not provide written analysis of the deals; instead, he appended a ten-line form letter okaying each transaction.

What the majority of submissions had in common was that the corporation had no significant presence in Luxembourg. Many of these firms also took advantage of laws Luxembourg had passed to entice companies. For example, the country exempted tax on interest income, which is why many of the companies designed their businesses so that profits earned in other countries flowed into Luxembourg subsidiaries as interest. Luxembourg also exempted from taxation 80 percent of the income earned from intellectual property such as brand names, patents, and distribution rights.

Edouard Perrin never got to see Marius Kohl, but he did film the Sociétés 6 offices. His hourlong report for the program *Cash Investigations* aired on Friday, May 11, 2012, at 10:30 pm. Despite the late hour on the eve of a weekend, viewership was double the usual. The program incorporated reenactments, cartoons, old movie clips, animations, documents, and interviews. A week later, the BBC program *Panorama* followed with its own documentary. Brooks and Perrin had shared their data with the BBC journalists. Then a second source in Luxembourg, Raphael Halet, contacted Perrin with more tax agreements, this time featuring company documents from the likes of Amazon and Luxembourg steel manufacturer Arcelor Mittal. These documents provided the basis for a second film, aired a year later in prime time on a Tuesday; it earned record ratings for the program.

In November 2013, ICIJ received a copy of the Luxembourg data. It has never publicly disclosed its origin.

MEANWHILE, GERARD RYLE continued to pursue Falciani's HSBC files. He spoke with *Le Monde*'s editor in chief, Natalie Nougayrède, who listened to Ryle's pitch but told him *Le Monde* did not need ICIJ. The newspaper had correspondents all over the world. It would parcel out the specific country data from the files to its own staff; *Le Monde* reporters themselves could report and write the stories. Ryle returned to Washington dejected, yet again.

It did not take long for *Le Monde* to realize its plan would not work. Organizing the effort alone would be a logistical nightmare. Its correspondents were busy reporting other stories. They had no experience parsing this kind of data. Nor did they know the players in the different countries well enough to be able to identify who were the truly important people listed in the files. *Le Monde* contacted Ryle to ask for the collaboration.

In May 2014, Gérard Davet and Fabrice Lhomme, the two *Le Monde* reporters who had obtained the documents, along with a data specialist from the newspaper, traveled to Washington, DC, to meet with ICIJ. The HSBC files they brought to Washington—encrypted on a laptop—had been reconstructed by the French government from the data confiscated from Falciani. The French, perhaps feeling it was too explosive, had kept a tight hold on the information and selectively distributed smaller subsets. Davet and Lhomme have never revealed their source. Swiss authorities still wanted to prosecute Falciani over the theft. Despite the passage of six years, the mere existence of the HSBC files continued to create a commotion across the continent.

When the French journalists arrived, the ICIJ team gathered in a conference room at the Center for Public Integrity, ICIJ's parent organization. The meeting with the French was the culmination of a several-day team-building exercise. In the past two years, Ryle had tripled the number of ICIJ staff, including the addition of a three-person data team, and the organization had flown its entire reporting team to Washington to discuss the future and introduce themselves to the people at the CPI.

And now, after more than six months of pursuit by Ryle and Cabra, ICIJ would finally have the elusive HSBC data. *Le Monde*'s tech guru opened the laptop to decrypt the information. Decryption failed. He tried again. And then again. He couldn't access the files. It looked as if the three Frenchmen had traveled across the Atlantic for nothing. Then Davet spoke up. "I have the data on my own laptop," he volunteered. It had gone through U.S. Customs unencrypted. Nonetheless, everyone in the room was deeply relieved.

ICIJ was now working on two projects at the same time. Walker focused on Luxembourg. Ryle took the lead on HSBC. Mindful of the problems of Offshore Leaks, this time ICIJ would control who accessed the data and have a greater say in how the project was run.

The team struggled to turn the leaked Luxembourg tax agreements into a searchable database. At the start, there were roughly one thousand agreements. After review, a third turned out to be duplicates. Each agreement had to be scoured for relevant details such as company and subsidiary names, countries, and amounts. At the time, the main software that performed this kind of entity extraction belonged to the Reuters news agency. ICIJ did not want to send the data to a third party, so the process had to be done manually, one agreement at a time.

Once the data was extracted, it needed to be organized. Matthew Caruana Galizia, who had joined ICIJ from Giannina Segnini's team in Costa Rica, knew they could do better than the clunky search program that had been employed for Offshore Leaks. He wanted something that was open source so it could be widely available and improved by others. He chose Project Blacklight, an open-source software used by librarians to organize and share data. Rigoberto Carvajal then tweaked software called Oxwall, which operated like Facebook, allowing users to log in to a secure forum where they could post links, share files, and chat in real time. They had the components for a successful collaboration—a searchable database and a way to securely communicate findings. ICIJ would also be able to control access to the information.

A *Star Trek* fan, Carvajal christened the project "Enterprise."

In June, about twenty reporters from across the world gathered in a small room at the newspaper *Le Soir* in Brussels to discuss the Luxembourg data. ICIJ's deputy director, Marina Walker, had insisted on the group meeting. The data was too complicated. The collaborators needed to meet together or they would never understand it properly. ICIJ hired Richard Brooks to come from London and lecture for two hours on how the tax agreements functioned.

Edouard Perrin, whose early reporting had made the project possible, gave a talk at the outset. He was slightly intimidated by the international crowd of reporters, who appeared less than enthusiastic. After Offshore Leaks and now the beginnings of the HSBC project, the journalists arrayed before him looked tired and skeptical. The Luxembourg tax data was not only ridiculously complicated; it was also ostensibly legal. Where was the story?

Bastian Obermayer of *Süddeutsche Zeitung* wore a hangdog expression on his face. He was struggling to find a way into the material. The German team saw one angle they knew they could sell to their editors. It seemed likely that Luxembourg's longtime prime minister, Jean-Claude Juncker, might be elected in the fall to the presidency of the European Commission, which acts as the coordinating body for the European Union. If the journalists could release the information before Juncker's election, it might be a factor in the vote.

Mar Cabra and the ICIJ team knew there was no way a project of this complexity could be completed quickly. Walker suggested, with a smile, that the problem was that the Europeans took such long vacations. If the reporters were willing to sacrifice their summer holiday to work on the project, it might be possible to finish it sooner. Longtime Swedish ICIJ collaborator Fredrik Laurin rose to the bait. Europeans had been fighting for their rights as workers for too long, he said indignantly. No American was going to force a concession on this point. For the uninitiated, it was easy to miss the humor beneath the passionate sparring. Walker and Laurin had a long-standing friendship.

The group agreed to publish in early November and not time it to the election.

Still, Juncker's potential role in the EU focused the attention of the gathered reporters. The European Commission had avoided the issue of Luxembourg's tax avoidance business for years. The commission's tax committee, which logically would have handled the issue, was hobbled by a need for unanimity in its decision making. Luxembourg had an effective veto.

Around the same time the reporters gathered in Brussels, the EU's competition commissioner, Joaquín Alumnia, a Spaniard, decided to investigate Luxembourg's tax breaks for major companies like Starbucks, Apple, and Fiat Finance and Trade as a competitive violation between states. While the rulings that came out of Marius Kohl's office were legal, they were also secret. This gave the companies that availed themselves of this service a selective tax advantage against those who did not, Alumnia argued. An obvious point but one that potentially violated EU rules on competition.

Suddenly, Luxembourg's very success in the secrecy world threatened to be its undoing.

14

TROUBLE AHEAD, TROUBLE BEHIND

While ICIJ and its collaborators chased down leaks from Luxembourg and Switzerland, Mossfon found itself under siege by a new and powerful adversary. The firm became collateral damage in a high-stakes fight between the American hedge fund billionaire Paul Singer and Argentinean president Cristina Fernández de Kirchner. Played out in a federal courtroom in Las Vegas, their struggle would influence the trajectory of Mossfon, the secrecy world, and collaborative journalism.

The conflict dated to 2001, when Argentina, in the midst of an economic depression, defaulted on its sovereign debt. Singer's hedge fund, Elliott Management, had been buying Argentinean government bonds at a significant discount. Reasoning that something was better than nothing, most bondholders accepted steep reductions on their investments, absorbing losses of up to 70 percent. Elliott's business model was different. Singer held as much as $1.7 billion in Argentinean bonds; he wanted them repaid in full. The billionaire took his case all the way to the U.S. Supreme Court and won.

Elliott Management scoured the globe for Argentinean assets to repossess to satisfy the judgment and drive the Argentines to the bargaining table. The hedge fund froze $3 million's worth of equipment and warehouses in Maryland, temporarily grabbed a naval vessel in Ghana, and forced Fernández de Kirchner to ditch her official plane for fear it would be seized on a trip to the United States. The Argentinean president responded with intransigent nationalism. The vultures can take our boats, she declared haughtily, but they will never take our "freedom, sovereignty, or dignity."

While tossing around ideas for what to target next, Elliott personnel alighted upon a growing scandal in Argentina involving Fernández de Kirchner and her late husband, former president Néstor Kirchner, over allegations of money laundering. Jorge Lanata, an Argentinean television journalist known for mixing comedy with investigative reporting, broadcast a series of reports in April 2013 called "the K [for Kirchner] Money Trail" that centered around Lázaro Báez, a former bank teller turned millionaire businessman. In the early 1990s, Báez ingratiated himself with Néstor Kirchner, then a rising politician, by allegedly leaking confidential bank information about the couple's enemies.

A few weeks before Néstor Kirchner was elected to the Argentinean presidency in 2003, Báez created a construction firm that then won extensive public works contracts in Patagonia, in the south of the country. In exchange for these contracts, Báez allegedly funneled money back to the Kirchners through multiple channels, including a series of offshore companies. Lanata's broadcasts included video testimony of alleged associates of Báez explaining how they boarded his corporate jets with sacks full of cash. The illicit loot was destined for foreign bank accounts controlled by anonymous companies scattered throughout the world.

Exposés by Lanata and other Argentinean journalists led to a criminal investigation. Prosecutor José María Campagnoli issued his own report in December 2013, suggesting that Báez had laundered $65 million in embezzled state funds through 150 companies based either in Panama or Nevada. Campagnoli based his assumption in part on the companies' connection to Helvetic Services Group, a Swiss fund that served as a shareholder of some of the companies and was believed to be controlled by Báez. After washing the money through offshore companies, Báez allegedly sent it back to the Kirchners disguised as payments on permanently empty rooms in hotels the couple secretly owned. Reporters had a field day showing and describing empty hotel parking lots and quiet hallways. In response to the unproven allegations, Kirchner's general prosecutor attempted to fire Campagnoli, and ultimately succeeded in removing him from the investigation.

Nonetheless, the Campagnoli report provided enough evidence for Elliott Management, in its hunt for Argentinean government money, to file a subpoena on 123 companies based in Nevada allegedly belonging to Báez. The added value of embarrassing Kirchner compensated for what was admittedly, in this particular case, a near-impossible asset recovery mission. Even if the companies belonged to Báez and were used for illegal payoffs, the hedge fund could not prove anything until it broke through multiple layers of offshore secrecy. And if Elliott somehow managed to vault those hurdles, the money would likely have already moved elsewhere.

The alleged Báez companies all showed the same registered agent, M. F. Corporate Services (Nevada), Limited. When Elliott didn't get anywhere with the companies themselves, it turned to Mossfon's Nevada subsidiary, in what quickly became a frontal assault on the secrecy world.

Mossfon had opened its Nevada office in 2000. Nancy Broadhurst, who had discovered Niue as a tax haven for the firm, supervised the office's creation. The firm marketed the jurisdiction aggressively, particularly in South America. The degree of secrecy Nevada allowed put many tax havens to shame. As long as a foreigner made his money outside the United States, there was no requirement to report any financial activity. Nevada had no information-sharing agreement with the Internal Revenue Service. An economic boom in the state guaranteed first-world infrastructure. Most important, the firm told potential customers, Nevada did not have a reputation as an offshore center. Clients who located their companies there gained an extra degree of discretion because of this public misperception. By 2013, Mossfon was charging about $2,000 to register a Nevada company, and $1,775 each year afterward; it had almost 350 active companies.

In response to Elliott Management's subpoena for information on the activities of the supposed Báez-connected companies, Mossfon provided an affidavit signed by Leticia Montoya, who served as a director for all the companies. In fact, Montoya, who earned about $900 a month, was one of Mossfon's most prolific nominees, acting as a director for almost eleven thousand of its companies. Montoya's affidavit stated that none of the companies had responsive documents, nor did they do any business within one hundred miles of Las Vegas. Mossfon further claimed that M. F. Corporate Services was an independent contractor—a stand-alone entity—not controlled by the Panamanians. Paul Singer's team then sought to depose Patricia Amunategui, a Chilean-born former casino worker who had run Mossfon's Nevada office for more than a decade. The Singer/Elliott lawyers wanted to investigate how the Báez money moved and the exact relationship between Mossfon and M. F. Corporate Services. After a protracted court battle, the deposition was granted.

On September 11, 2014, Amunategui sat down with Dennis Hranitzky, a lawyer for Singer, for a seven-hour deposition. As the day progressed, it became increasingly clear that Amunategui was being evasive. Hranitzky deftly used her employment contract, obtained with the original subpoena, to highlight the absurdity of her claims. But it would take Hranitzky years to discover the true depth of her mendacity.

Amunategui insisted that she did not work for Mossack Fonseca. The Panamanians were simply clients of M. F. Corporate Services and did not direct her activities. She had never met the partners and could not say who handled the finances of her independent subsidiary. As Mossfon's internal communications show, this was not true.

Within a week of the deposition, Luis Martínez, Mossfon's IT manager, was on the phone with Amunategui discussing ways to build more distance between the two offices. The firm decided to separate the telephone and computer systems that linked the Nevada office to Mossfon Panama. The idea was to retroactively turn Amunategui's office into what she had claimed it to be in her deposition, a simple provider. They also tried to remotely clean the logs of her office computer so it would further hide the connections to Panama.

Still, Martínez came away from the call somewhat alarmed. He questioned whether Amunategui could pass a basic audit without leaving evidence. "I'm worried about Miss Patricia," he wrote to his colleagues. "She is forgetting things and she is very nervous. I think in this situation it could easily become clear that we are hiding something."

Mossfon then discussed moving the main responsibilities of the office to Panama, but it was too late. Even without any insight into the behind-the-scenes maneuvering of the Panamanians, Hranitzky's deposition of Amunategui had done its damage. A judge would rule that the Nevada operation was an "alter ego" of Mossfon and thus subject to the jurisdiction of American courts and, more dangerously, information subpoenas. Paul Singer and Elliott Management had demonstrated how to blow a hole through American offshore secrecy, yet few litigants followed their lead.

THE JUNE 2014 meeting in Brussels to discuss the Luxembourg leak was sufficiently productive that Gerard Ryle and Marina Walker replicated it for the HSBC investigation. This time, forty journalists attended, representing more than a dozen countries—about double the number of reporters as had gathered in Brussels for Lux Leaks. Television producers from *60 Minutes* rubbed elbows with journalists from NDR, Northern Germany's public television broadcaster. Japanese investigative reporters mixed with their counterparts from Peru, Argentina, and elsewhere.

Most of those present had signed an agreement with ICIJ, in which their news organizations committed to the collaboration. They promised to abide by the publishing embargo and not to share the data with others outside the project. Everyone would publish at a time determined by ICIJ. They also committed to share their findings with other participants in the project and to credit the source of the leak, in this case, *Le Monde* and ICIJ. The agreement carried no legal weight. It was more of a moral document, a symbolic code of conduct.

Walker had developed a profile of the kind of journalistic collaborator she sought. She wanted the antithesis of the macho, lone-wolf stereotype of the investigative reporter, the hard-bitten newsman jealously guarding his scoop. Usually before accepting someone into the project, she quietly researched the person to determine if the reporter met certain standards. She looked for the obvious professional abilities, people who were well regarded as top investigative reporters in their field and in their countries. Just as important, Walker wanted people with a high degree of emotional acuity. She was determined not to commit the same errors ICIJ had made in Offshore Leaks. Would the partner collaborate? Could he take direction? Did he eschew drama?

Ryle was interested in getting big names like *60 Minutes* or the *New York Times*. The bigger the platform, the greater the impact. Unfortunately, the larger news organizations did not always make the most congenial collaborators.

The HSBC meeting was held in early September in Paris, in *Le Monde*'s lofty executive conference room. The excitement was palpable, particularly among the Europeans. Everybody knew of the Falciani files. Many reporters had tried and failed to get hold of them. Corruption cases involving Swiss private banks filled their countries' newspapers on a seemingly daily basis. The foreign treasures stored in Swiss banks, licit and illicit, had captivated the literary fancies of writers from Ian Fleming to Robert Ludlum. Now, for the first time, reporters would have an actual look inside.

Rigoberto Carvajal code-named the project "Voyager."

Mar Cabra and ICIJ's data team had worked tirelessly throughout the summer to transform Falciani's files into something understandable and searchable. It was no easy task. Falciani had extracted the data from HSBC in segments. Then French tax authorities had broken the information into Excel spreadsheets by country to share with friendly governments. (By early 2015, approximately $1.36 billion in unpaid taxes had been recovered around the world as a result of the data.) ICIJ now tried to reconstitute the original database, putting the puzzle back together. The data spanned twenty years. It came in multiple pieces. Each name might be connected to one or several pieces. Each piece covered a different moment in history. There was client data that stretched from 1987 to 2007, which included names, addresses, and bank accounts. Then there were notes that HSBC's bankers had manually added to the files as part of the bank's client relationship management system. These covered only the year 2005. The data also featured bank account balances, but only for the maximum amount held from 2006 to 2007. The customers hailed from more than two hundred countries, collectively holding more than $100 billion, many through offshore companies located in tax havens.

In a normal data project, where the information came from a public source like a government agency, journalists could ask the provider questions to make sense of it all. In this case, the ICIJ reporters obviously could not go to HSBC and request help. Cabra likened it to reconstructing a deconstructed salad.

The group fell back on a software program that exposed relationships, automatically illustrating connections between names, companies, and addresses. The software came from a four-person start-up tech firm in France called Linkurious. The idea for Linkurious had originated years earlier as an aid for journalists to help them understand the interdependencies between banks to make sense of the 2008 financial crisis. Unfortunately, there was no money in journalism, so the team turned to business applications. After ICIJ released the Offshore Leaks database, Linkurious downloaded it to create a product demonstration for the company's blog. Linkurious then contacted ICIJ to see if it could help in future reporting projects. In this way, ICIJ became the firm's only pro bono customer. Oddly enough, Linkurious's cofounder Sébastien Heymann had recently met with Hervé Falciani, whom he had found elusive but enthusiastic. Heymann did not realize that the conversation, one of several, was actually an interview to see if Linkurious was an appropriate vendor for the French tax authorities, which then became a client.

In Paris, Cabra demonstrated how the data worked via Linkurious using as an example Emilio Botín, the executive chairman of one of the wealthiest European banks, Banco Santander. The Spanish government had already dunned the Botín family for €200 million in back taxes based on the Falciani list. Botín's company, North Star Overseas Enterprises Inc., created its first HSBC account in 2003 and was connected to five others. In the Linkurious graph, North Star sat in the middle of the screen with spokes fanning out to bank accounts, attorneys, and trusts. Clicking on each would potentially allow a reporter to explore the relationships in the data. Cabra knew her presentation had made an impression when, in the airport on the way home to Madrid, her phone lit up with messages from participants informing her that Botín had just died.

Among the journalists present in Paris were two friends, Titus Plattner and François Pilet, employed by competing Swiss newspapers. The two reporters had originally worked together on Offshore Leaks when they were with the Swiss media company Tamedia, but then Pilet left to join its rival Ringier. Since both journalists wanted to be part of the project, the competitors agreed to form an alliance and even share bylines on stories. Tamedia would publish in German, Ringier in French. It would be as if the *Washington Post* and the *New York Times* not only collaborated but allowed staffers to appear on the bylines of each other's respective newspapers—all for the greater good of the story.

Commentators and government officials in Switzerland had publicly castigated the Tamedia reporters after the publication of Offshore Leaks. Tax evasion formed part of the foundation of the Swiss financial system, and the creation of offshore companies was a key component of that system. Taking money from the rich and powerful, even from foreign government officials, was not seen as particularly scandalous in Switzerland. Other countries, deprived of the tax revenue, saw the matter differently. There were almost three thousand French citizens who banked with HSBC's Swiss private bank listed in Falciani's files. A French government investigation determined that only six of those three thousand had paid taxes on their Swiss bank accounts.

Oliver Zihlmann, Tamedia's head of investigations, saw an opportunity in the HSBC data. In addition to tax evaders, there were outright criminals named in the files, including drug traffickers, arms dealers, and others who profited from human misery. He hoped that if the team detailed the crimes and revealed the victims, it would be impossible for their fellow citizens to ignore Swiss complicity in a corrupt system.

Tamedia focused on HSBC customers like the Belgian diamond

dealer Emmanuel Shallop, whose HSBC bankers observed in 2005 that he "is under pressure from the Belgian tax authorities who are investigating his activities in the area of diamond tax fraud." Five years later, Shallop was found guilty in the Belgian Court of Appeals for facilitating the trade in conflict diamonds for the leaders of the Revolutionary United Front in Sierra Leone, which had tortured, mutilated, and murdered its way through the country for more than a decade. A UN-sponsored court convicted what was left of its leadership of crimes against humanity in 2009.

Tamedia's reporting also featured Arturo del Tiempo Marqués, a Spanish property developer in the Dominican Republic who at one point had nineteen HSBC accounts containing more than $3 million. In the space of a couple of years, del Tiempo had insinuated himself into the upper echelons of the Dominican Republic. He golfed with the chief of police, who made him an honorary colonel. He received a $12 million loan from the state bank to build a luxury condominium tower and had his photo taken with the president. The facade came crashing down when del Tiempo was arrested for smuggling 1.2 tons of cocaine into Spain hidden in a shipment of leftover marble from his construction site.

Del Tiempo also had multiple companies with Mossfon, including several that overlapped with his HSBC accounts. But a criminal conviction and a six-year prison sentence did not bring del Tiempo's travails to Mossfon's attention. It would take the publication of the HSBC files to stir the Panamanians to drop him as a customer.

WORKING ON TWO leak investigations simultaneously did not come without consequences. In September, ICIJ pushed back the publication date for what it was calling "Lux Leaks" until early November. The team was overworked and behind schedule. In the interim, as expected, Jean-Claude Juncker won the presidency of the EU. The ICIJ investigation had leaked out as partners approached the companies involved for comment. Several of ICIJ's collaborators tried to speak with "Monsieur Ruling" himself, Marius Kohl, but he turned down all their requests.

Then on October 21, a story appeared in the *Wall Street Journal* featuring an interview with Kohl, conducted in the now retired bureaucrat's kitchen in Luxembourg. The motive behind the interview was not clear. Did Kohl simply want to justify what he had done or was he telegraphing to Juncker and others that he would not take the fall for the tax avoidance shop he ran from Sociétés 6 all those years? Kohl told the *Journal* that none of his superiors in the finance ministry, including Juncker, who was its minister for two decades, ever disapproved of his activities.

"I never had any problems with Juncker," Kohl said.

While largely ignored in the United States, the Lux Leaks revelations, published on November 5, 2014, shook Europe. Thirty partners published at the same time. Europe's leaders professed to be shocked by what Luxembourg was doing. *Süddeutsche Zeitung*'s Bastian Obermayer even related an amusing, easy-to-understand story chronicling how he visited business addresses where hundreds, even thousands, of major companies were supposedly located, only to encounter the blank stares of lonely receptionists.

Juncker, just a few months into his EU presidency, went into hiding for a week after the publication of the first round of stories. While he was gone, Luxembourg was widely castigated as a tax parasite, prospering from the depletion of government coffers throughout the world. When Juncker finally emerged, he refused to talk much about his tenure as the head of a tax avoidance factory masquerading as a country. Instead, he promised that he would lead the charge to bring fairness to Europe's tax systems. Critics, not surprisingly, questioned his sincerity.

Shortly after publication, ICIJ received a semi-cryptic message through the tip form on its website. The writer claimed to have more tax rulings, "at my disposal if you want." After Walker checked on the source, she and Ryle accepted the offer. The new leak contained agreements from a number of American corporations including the Walt Disney Company and Koch Industries. The leak also showed how other U.S. accounting firms, including Ernst & Young, Deloitte, and KPMG were involved in the same activity as PricewaterhouseCoopers. The information spurred a new round of stories.

A special inquiry committee of the European Parliament was established to investigate Luxembourg's tax agreements. One of its vice chairs was Eva Joly, the former Elf prosecutor and consultant for Iceland, who had won a seat as a French member of the Green Party. The committee was scathing on the subject of Juncker's culpability but managed to do little more than embarrass him publicly. He easily beat back a no-confidence vote.

As Juncker defended himself over his activities in Luxembourg, the Mossfon partners were still fighting with Jost and Anabella Dex over the breakup of their business partnership there. The Dexes had fought the firm to a standstill. While Mossfon had won an arbitration case in Panama, the Dexes had blocked it in Luxembourg by filing a criminal case for fraud. Mossfon countersued. Over the next several years, lawsuits flew back and forth in both countries.

In one case in Luxembourg, Mossfon even managed to get a judge to freeze the company bank accounts belonging to the couple and put a lien on their house. The Dexes again offered to settle, this time for a lump-sum payment of €2.5 million. Once more the partners rejected the offer, instructing their lawyer to let the couple know they would get nothing. Fonseca and Mossack had succeeded in treating Jost and Anabella Dex like Mossfon employees who could be kicked to the curb rather than independent operators with equity in their franchise. The couple and the partners had thrived together in the good times. Now, as the firm was besieged on all sides, the acrimonious divorce and custody battle had left behind a pair of implacable foes.

In 2012, while this was going on, Mossfon hired a Panamanian business development company, Mercatrade S.A., to cleanse its online reputation and counter the growing perception that the firm was a conduit for criminal activity. Mercatrade promised to seek out and remove, whenever possible, negative references to Mossfon related to a dozen keywords in English and Spanish that included *tax evasion*, *scandal*, *money laundering*, and *arms trafficking*.

The service was insufficient for the amount of scrutiny Mossfon was attracting. The following year, the partners contracted with Burson-Marsteller, a U.S. public relations firm with a reputation for representing unsavory clients, including dictators and companies in deep trouble. One of its notable corporate clients was the military security contractor Blackwater, which required image cleansing after its security guards killed seventeen Iraqi civilians in September 2007. (As a result of the incident, Blackwater lost its State Department contract to its competitor Triple Canopy, which had Mossfon companies in the BVI.) Burson-Marsteller provided Mossfon with a crisis management handbook at the cost of $15,000. The Panamanians also agreed to pay Burson-Marsteller $5,500 a month for five months. With Paul Singer pounding away at the firm in Nevada, Mossfon renewed the contract in 2014.

In Luxembourg, the government struck back against the investigation that had exposed its activities. It indicted Antoine Deltour, the young PricewaterhouseCoopers employee who had leaked the tax agreements to Edouard Perrin, as well as the other leaker, Raphael Halet. Luxembourg also charged Perrin, although it took a while for the reporter to be notified of the legal peril he faced. His office in Paris was on the same floor as the weekly satirical newsmagazine *Charlie Hebdo*, for whom he and his wife had both worked. He was at his desk on January 7, 2015, when two brothers, masked and dressed in black, burst into the magazine office armed with Kalashnikov assault rifles and opened fire, killing twelve and injuring eleven. Perrin was one of the first on the blood-soaked scene after the killers departed. The letter from the Luxembourg judge notifying Perrin of his legal jeopardy was diverted after the massacre along with the mail to *Charlie Hebdo*; it would be weeks before the news reached him and years before he recovered from both experiences.

FOR THE QUICKENING HSBC investigation, ICIJ set a worldwide publication date of February 8, 2015. It called the project Swiss Leaks. David Leigh was running the *Guardian*'s end of the project. The *Guardian* had approached the account holders mentioned in its stories, who quickly notified HSBC, headquartered in London. The bank sent legal letters to the newspaper, threatening an injunction to prevent publication. Leigh and a *Guardian* lawyer met with HSBC and informed them that the investigation was being run by ICIJ, not the *Guardian*, and that some eighty journalists around the world were going to publish stories at the same time. If HSBC suppressed publication in Britain, all it would accomplish would be to make the story bigger elsewhere. The newspaper also promised to withhold the account information of anyone who wasn't implicated in some kind of wrong-doing. The bank backed off and provided a statement to the newspaper that framed its problems as belonging to a distant age with different standards.

HSBC then caught a lucky break when *60 Minutes* opted to focus its report on the colorful Hervé Falciani and his theft of the data rather than the contents of what he had stolen. This angle dovetailed with HSBC's narrative that it was the true victim of the story. American television audiences thus missed a full explanation of how HSBC had employed Swiss banking secrecy for decades to enable massive tax evasion and criminal activity around the world.

In Switzerland, readers who consumed their news in German received different information than those who read it in French. While Tamedia published the names of account holders mentioned in its stories, Ringier decided in some cases to use only initials. It depended on where you were in the country, for example, whether you learned that Li Xiaolin, the daughter of the butcher of Beijing, had a Swiss bank account with HSBC or simply someone identified as "Y."

Nonetheless, less than a week after publication, Geneva's lead prosecutor, Olivier Jornot, along with plainclothes investigators and vans to cart away evidence, paid a call to the Swiss private bank's headquarters. Switzerland's federal prosecutor, Michael Lauber, had declined to take action against HSBC. Lauber already had the Falciani files, having received them from the French, but declared that since the material was stolen, he could not act on it. But this didn't constrain the Geneva prosecutors, who were in the bank for several hours. On a cigarette break during the search, a deal was worked out, but it would take three months to announce the settlement. The bank would pay $43 million to the canton of Geneva to settle allegations of money laundering. While the sum was a mere rounding error for a bank the size of HSBC, it was the largest such fine in Swiss history.

The settlement allowed the bank to put the scandal behind it in

Switzerland. Prosecutors did not have to undertake the expense and uncertainty of a trial. It was a very Swiss solution. Practical. Efficient. And yet it was also revolutionary for the country. Not only was the fine unprecedented but so was the idea that the government could extract a penalty without proving illegality in court.

For the Swiss reporters, it felt like vindication.

15

FORTUNE FAVORS THE BOLD

On Tuesday, February 24, 2015, German government investigators, headed by financial authorities from the country's most populous state, North Rhine–Westphalia, launched a series of coordinated raids. They had planned the operation for months. The main target was Frankfurt-based Commerzbank, Germany's second-largest bank. Prosecutors and investigators also searched the homes of individuals, looking for evidence of a massive tax fraud scheme. Commerzbank insisted that the inquiry dealt with ancient history, old cases at least a decade or more in the past.

The German people read a more detailed version of events the following day, on the front page of *Süddeutsche Zeitung*. Investigators were pursuing as many as six hundred alleged German tax evaders and their enablers, with the raids focused on Commerzbank's Luxembourg subsidiary. At least three other major German financial institutions were implicated in the activity, which cycled through Luxembourg and Panama and involved offshore companies as vehicles for tax evasion. The damage to the German treasury could be as big as one billion euros, the paper reported. And contrary to the bank's assertions, the conduct was not a thing of the past.

"We are talking about a big fish here," North Rhine–Westphalia's finance minister, Norbert Walter-Borjans, told the newspaper.

That fish was about to attract the biggest leak in journalism history.

Norbert Walter-Borjans had made a name for himself buying tax data stolen from banks. Bankers from Luxembourg, Switzerland, and Liechtenstein would cross the border into Germany to sell compact discs to the government of North Rhine–Westphalia full of the names and account information of Germans who had stashed money abroad. A single disc could fetch more than a million dollars. The finance minister was adept at leveraging the media to make the most of these purchases. He would appear on television giving just enough information—the country or the bank involved—to strike fear into the hearts of German tax evaders. A stampede of Germans self-reporting to avoid criminal charges would then follow.

This case was no different. *Süddeutsche Zeitung* reported that the German tax authorities had purchased data that had come from the Luxembourg subsidiary of a Panamanian offshore incorporator named Mossack Fonseca Group, paying $1.14 million for the information. What the Germans had was only a fraction of what was available, the newspaper reported. It knew this because it had acquired a more complete set itself. The newspaper had received more than eighty gigabytes of customer and account data lifted from Mossack Fonseca by an unnamed source.

Süddeutsche Zeitung also reported that Germany was not the only customer for the data. Other European nations and the United States had also either purchased or expressed interest in acquiring information on their countrymen from the Mossack Fonseca Luxembourg data. The seller of the Luxembourg information stood to make millions of dollars peddling the material around the world.

The article acknowledged that the newspaper's reporters had yet to fully evaluate the material. Unstated was that the reporters had been occupied with the Swiss Leaks investigation, which had concluded only a few weeks earlier. The raid on Commerzbank convinced *Süddeutsche Zeitung* to publish its story ahead of schedule.

In Washington, ICIJ's Gerard Ryle was displeased. He knew that

Bastian Obermeyer had obtained the data and was hoping that ICIJ might have more time to review the information, to see if it could be used for a future collaboration. Why let the public know you had the data? On the positive side, the actions taken by Walter-Borjans had created a public-interest justification for journalists to publish stories about the information. (Nine months after the raid, Commerzbank paid a €17 million fine over the matter.)

What neither Ryle nor Obermayer knew was that *Süddeutsche Zeitung*'s timing was fortuitous in the extreme. In the weeks preceding the Commerzbank raid, a consequential conversation between another anonymous source and an investigative reporter from the *New York Times* had occurred. The source had provided the reporter with a small number of Mossfon documents, some of which related to Paul Singer's court case in Nevada. The source hoped for a story soon, within a few weeks, and hinted that much more information might be forthcoming. The reporter, who had written previously about shell companies, was skeptical. The Nevada case had already been well covered in the media. The reporter tried unsuccessfully to tease out the source's identity and his or her motivations. Eventually the reporter told the source that vacation plans made meeting the proposed publishing deadline impossible, but promised the information would be reviewed and discussed with editors.

A few days later, *Süddeutsche Zeitung* published its scoop on Mossfon's Luxembourg data. Soon after, the source who contacted the *New York Times* reached out to Obermayer. The initial approach was like something out of a spy novel.

"Hello. This is John Doe. Interested in data? I'm happy to share."

Obermayer wrote about what occurred next in a book he coauthored with fellow *Süddeutsche* reporter Frederik Obermaier (who was not related to him). In the book, the Germans altered details of the communication to protect their source. Obermayer immediately told John Doe that he was interested. The source explained how they would communicate over encrypted channels. The first sample of documents the source delivered was the Argentinean material that had failed to generate much interest at the *New York Times*. Obermayer quickly recognized that the information before him was extremely valuable and would be quite helpful to the case brought by Paul Singer in Nevada. He also saw that the data had come from Mossfon, a firm with which he was already familiar.

Obermayer inquired whether all the information involved the Argentineans. The answer was no. It was only the beginning.

The next day more documents arrived. These documents included bank transfer information for almost $500 million in gold. The transfers had gone through an offshore company owned by a Siemens executive, Hans-Joachim Kohlsdorf, who had been a subject in a far-reaching corporate bribery investigation. In Germany, Kohlsdorf had received a slap on the wrist. The documents seemed to suggest that the leniency may have been unwarranted. There were also documents relating to secret companies involving the Russian cellist Sergei Roldugin, including loan agreements in the hundreds of millions of dollars. Obermayer did some Internet research and discovered that Roldugin had never before been mentioned in conjunction with offshore companies but he was known as Vladimir Putin's closest friend.

Obermayer was now in a state of high alert. He asked the source why he was leaking the material. John Doe told him that the information needed to become public. Still, the source was worried. *Süddeutsche Zeitung* published in German and was not even Germany's biggest media outlet. The story might not get the exposure it deserved. The source suggested the Germans partner with a publication like the *New York Times*, even though the *Times* had been cool to the offer of the documents. Obermayer explained how the ICIJ worked and the worldwide collaborations the organization had accomplished. The promise of an ICIJ collaboration mollified the source's concerns.

They then discussed how to send larger amounts of material. Obermayer already had a sense of the scale of Mossfon's activities. In addition to the Luxembourg data, the ICIJ collaborators had encountered the firm's work in their research into Falciani's HSBC data for the Swiss Leaks investigation.

Obermayer asked how much information the source had.

"More than anything you have ever seen," came the reply.

As the data poured in and the Germans found additional cases of interest, Obermayer called Ryle, excitedly offering updates. Finally, the ICIJ director hopped on a plane to Munich to see for himself. He met with the German reporters and their editors over several days. Frederik Obermaier came into the office; he had been on paternity leave. Ryle discussed the idea of a collaboration with Wolfgang Krach, *Süddeutsche Zeitung*'s editor in chief.

By this point, the source had sent hundreds of thousands of documents. There was no way the Germans would be able to review all the material themselves. Furthermore, the companies and owners found in the data came from all over the world. There were no top German politicians but plenty of leaders from other countries. The source had helpfully flagged a few compelling cases, but only reporters native to the individual countries would be in a position to find all the connections and the most interesting names. A collaboration was the best way to achieve the biggest impact. Obermayer and Obermaier urged Krach to follow Ryle's lead. After several days of meetings, Krach agreed.

By late April, Ryle told Mar Cabra that he wanted her to meet with the Germans in Munich and figure out next steps. She suggested that Rigoberto Carvajal join her from Costa Rica. The goal of the trip was to make copies of the material and create an action plan.

Cabra realized once again that ICIJ would have to reconstruct connections from a deconstructed database. Still burned out after more than two years of leak investigations, she worried over what was to come. The nonstop high-pressure work had already taken a toll on her health. Soon after the publication of Lux Leaks the previous November, she had to have emergency surgery while on vacation in the Philippines, and in early 2015 she experienced a thyroid problem, another message to slow down.

There were two elements to the data: One comprised lists such as company names, shareholders, and directors. This information had likely been part of some central file. Cabra called this "the structured data." Unfortunately, since Mossfon had done a poor job tracking the actual beneficial owners of the companies, the identities of those behind the companies were largely absent from the structured data. In a typical company, the shareholders own the company. In the secrecy world revealed by the Mossfon data, many of the shareholders were either "bearer," which meant they were owned by anonymous bearer shares, or were controlled by a second company, foundation, or trust. The most revealing information—such as who actually owned the company—was buried inside the documents themselves. For example, power-of-attorney agreements often gave the actual owner control of the company. This would be inside a document. Financial transactions were in documents as well.

ICIJ would have to process the documents with optical character recognition software to make them searchable. It would be a mammoth undertaking. Then, once the documents were processed, teams of reporters would have to comb through the data to find their stories. Cabra knew they would need another data journalist. After she returned to Spain, ICIJ added a computer engineer, Miguel Fiandor, to the team to help with the reconstruction.

The German reporters said they wanted to publish in six months. Cabra told them it was impossible; there was too much to do. The Germans responded that they had already been investigating the leak for three months. Their bosses would not allow them to go beyond a November deadline. Besides, they already had enough great information to fill five separate front-page stories.

Cabra, who had just come off Swiss Leaks, where there was barely enough time to finish, called Ryle. This will be horrible, she told him, repeating the word *horrible* multiple times for emphasis.

"We cannot do this again," she told him. "There is no way ICIJ could meet the deadline."

Ryle agreed. "Leave it to me," he said.

When Cabra and Carvajal left Munich, they took with them one terabyte of data. The Germans expected to receive about half a terabyte more from John Doe. They were off by a factor of three.

After the Commerzbank raid and *Süddeutsche Zeitung*'s Mossfon Luxembourg scoop, the German-language Swiss newspaper *Tages-Anzeiger*, part of the Tamedia chain and an ICIJ partner, interviewed Switzerland's own Christoph Zollinger for a story. By the time Tamedia's Oliver Zihlmann learned about the article, he already knew that the Germans had more Mossfon data, but it was too late to halt the feature without arousing suspicion.

Zollinger had moved his family to Switzerland from Panama in 2011, to raise his young children in his native land. He had also become obsessed with bobsledding, hatching a plan to train a Panamanian team to compete in the 2014 Winter Olympics in Sochi, Russia. The bobsled idea—a track well grooved by Hollywood, which had chronicled the 1998 exploits of a similar Jamaican effort—received widespread backing in Panama, including a plug from the country's president. Zollinger even managed to wrangle diplomatic passports for himself and his wife. Despite procuring enough donations to train and produce a slick, albeit unintentionally comical, promotional video, the team's hopes were dashed when Zollinger injured his foot and the Panamanians failed to qualify at the Olympic trials.

Zollinger claimed to *Tages-Anzeiger* that he had never been a co-owner in the Mossack Fonseca firm. He said that he had withdrawn from the business to distance himself. "I do not want to be held accountable for the wrongdoing of third parties for which I am not to blame," he told the newspaper.

In truth, Zollinger had been a partner, with an ownership stake in the firm, for years. His technical and systems abilities had been a key ingredient in Mossfon's growth. All of the most controversial issues the firm faced, when elevated to the partners, went to him as well. And his work on behalf of the firm had continued from Switzerland. Nonetheless, his desire to distance himself from its activities was understandable. The business model had clearly changed. The Luxembourg leak was yet another example that keeping secrets was not as easy as it once was.

Zollinger's fellow partners, Jürgen Mossack and Ramón Fonseca, were also eyeing retirement.

In 2010, the partners brought in Rubén Hernández, a Salvadoran former chief financial officer of Heineken Panamá, as Mossfon's chief executive officer. The idea was that Hernández would gradually assume control of the firm so that Fonseca and Mossack could reduce their responsibility for the firm's day-to-day operations. However, neither partner envisioned future lives of idleness for themselves.

For Ramón Fonseca, retirement meant juggling three occupations instead of four or five. During his time at Mossfon, Fonseca had somehow managed to squeeze in a literary career, which in Panama was often more about prestige than profit. Between 1994 and 2000, Fonseca wrote three novels, one collection of short stories, and two books for young adults. All three novels won top prizes for literature in Panama.

Fonseca saw himself returning to books, putting pen to paper in a quiet writing cabin he planned to build on a mountaintop. In 2013, he purchased land for an orange plantation in Veraguas, where Father Héctor Gallego had worked. He gave away orange trees to local farmers in exchange for an agreement to sell the fruit to him for processing. He staked out the land for his cabin not far from the plantation.

Fonseca also entered politics, working to resuscitate his grandfather's Panamañista political party. In 2009, the Panamañistas forged an alliance with Ricardo Martinelli's Cambio Democratico Party. Martinelli and Fonseca were former classmates in grade school. It was yet another example of how in tiny Panama, childhood connections follow one through life. Martinelli won the presidency in 2009 and appointed Fonseca as counselor, a ministerial position. But two years later, relations had soured between the two old acquaintances. Fonseca went on television and called the president an autocrat. Martinelli fired Fonseca via Twitter.

Under Martinelli, corruption flourished. The former president spent most of 2017 in Miami fighting extradition to Panama, where he faces criminal charges over misuse of public money. Among the allegations is that he financed a vast surveillance effort that secretly monitored more than 150 Panamanian businessmen, journalists, and politicians. After Martinelli's term ended, Fonseca returned to government, when Juan Carlos Varela, a close personal friend and the head of the Panamañista Party, won the presidency. Varela appointed Fonseca a member of his kitchen cabinet and put him in charge of the party.

Meanwhile, Jürgen Mossack had found contentment with his third wife, with whom he started a new family. On weekends, the couple traveled to show jumping competitions in which their daughters participated. Mossack became an active participant in the local Rotary

Club and served on Panama's foreign relations council. He also bought land in Boquete and planned to spend time building retirement homes for wealthy foreigners.

In 2013, according to an insurance document, the firm had $42.6 million in income. After his hiring, Hernández had visited the various offices to try to understand the business and make it more profitable. He focused on ways to save money and increase fees. But when Luis Martínez, the head of IT in Panama, told him the firm should invest in computer security, Hernández expressed little interest. He was more intrigued by a new tool to track statistics.

Meanwhile, Mossfon struggled to fulfill the compliance obligations of a new era. In the Seychelles, the firm, concerned about a possible audit, asked a competitor who had recently experienced its own review what to expect. For direct customers, the government required the name and due diligence on the beneficial owner. For all companies that came through so-called eligible introducers, such as lawyers, accountants, and bankers, the government wanted full information on them. Mossfon reviewed its Seychelles companies. It had 14,086 of them. The firm knew the actual owners of only 204 companies. More than 12,000 of the companies were from clients who were not compliant with Seychelles regulations.

A week before Cabra and Carvajal came to Munich to collect the data, Hernández presided over a three-day corporate strategy meeting. The partners were not listed among the speakers on the schedule. On the first day, after a brief speech by Hernández, the executives discussed Mossfon's appearances in the media, covering the Nevada case, the Commerzbank story, and an unflattering piece in *Vice* titled "The Law Firm That Works with Oligarchs, Money Launderers, and Dictators." In one of the last sessions, on the final day of the meeting, Luis Martínez delivered his forty-minute presentation, according to the schedule. His subject was "Data Loss Protection."

JÓHANNES KR. KRISTJÁNSSON failed to make it home to his Reykjavík apartment in time for his scheduled Skype call with ICIJ's Marina Walker. He pulled into a gas station and parked near a car wash to take the call on his cell phone. It was May 28, 2015. The burly, bearded Icelander had no idea what Walker wanted.

Kristjánsson was one of Iceland's best-known investigative reporters, having already amassed enough triumphs and disappointments to fill several careers. Too curious and introspective for fishing trawler work, as a young man he gravitated to journalism, taking a job as a cub reporter for a weekly magazine in a Reykjavík suburb. He then found his way to the Icelandic television news Channel 2, quickly recognizing the power of television to bring a story to life. Not satisfied with the drudgery of a junior reporter, he pestered his bosses to allow him to investigate the growing influence of the Hells Angels in Iceland's drug trade. He was granted permission to work on the story on his own time. Kristjánsson produced five reports on the subject. Their quality convinced Channel 2 to launch a newsmagazine with Kristjánsson, which became *Kompás*, an award-winning program, which quickly made a name for itself with hard-hitting investigations. In its biggest scoop, the program exposed one of Iceland's most beloved and well-known Lutheran priests as a financially corrupt pedophile. The priest had run a rehab facility for teenagers with government funds. The stress over the story's publication contributed to the demise of Kristjánsson's first marriage.

In 2008, a few weeks after Iceland's first bank collapsed, *Kompás* aired a program focusing on tax havens and Luxembourg, asserting that Icelandic businessmen and bankers used them for tax evasion. The broadcast singled out Jón Ásgeir Jóhannesson, the owner of Channel 2, and his family. A furious Jóhannesson called Kristinn Hrafnsson, who hosted *Kompás*, and threatened to sue him over the program. Hrafnsson, with Kristjánsson listening in, pointed out to the owner that his contract specifically made the station liable for any legal damages. Jóhannesson would essentially be suing himself. The media mogul thought about this for a second and acknowledged that Hrafnsson had a point. But three months after the tax haven program aired, Jóhannesson canceled *Kompás*, citing its high cost. The station's CEO fired Kristjánsson and Hrafnsson by phone, telling them to gather their belongings and leave the building by day's end. Hrafnsson went on to serve as a spokesman for Julian Assange's

WikiLeaks. Kristjánsson, devastated over the loss of a program into which he'd poured his heart and soul, left journalism to paint buildings in downtown Reykjavík.

After a few months, he went back to work for a tabloid. On June 3, 2010, Kristjánsson's seventeen-year-old daughter died from an overdose of fentanyl, a powerful opioid. He tried to bury the pain in work, writing a book about a young Icelander imprisoned in Brazil for drug trafficking. But the project failed to exorcise the demons.

He found his daughter's letters and began to piece together the final year of her life, trying to find meaning in her death. Kristjánsson convinced the police to reopen an investigation into his daughter's boyfriend, who had injected her with the drugs and was too stoned himself to do more than watch her die.

Kristjánsson also proposed a news program for state television in which he would take his camera deep into the underground of teenage drug addiction. The two-part program featured graphic images of teenagers abusing drugs, the slurred 911 call from the boyfriend as Kristjánsson's daughter lay dying, and a reenactment of the ambulance ride to get to her. Kristjánsson personally rescued two girls from drug dens, taking them to rehab. It was powerful and disturbing television. Other Icelandic media outlets picked up the story, transforming it into a social phenomenon. The Icelandic health director investigated the prescription drug business. Several doctors who had overprescribed drugs had their licenses pulled.

After the program, Kristjánsson was hired by state television. He produced three influential investigative programs on the market manipulation by Icelandic banks in the lead-up to the financial crisis. The first one featured information leaked from the office of Ólafur Hauksson, the special prosecutor. Hauksson, who Kristjánsson says was not behind the leak, was attacked by defense lawyers for allegedly prosecuting his cases in the media. The next year, Kristjánsson was laid off due to budget cuts and instead put on a contract basis. When he took Marina Walker's call, his contract had just run out.

After Offshore Leaks was published, Kristjánsson had contacted ICIJ about joining the project, but his calls and emails were lost in the avalanche of media requests Ryle fielded in the wake of publication. Then the wife of Iceland's president was found in Swiss Leaks. Kristjánsson sent a letter to ICIJ and got Sven Bergman, a longtime ICIJ member and award-winning investigative reporter in Sweden, to intercede on his behalf. When Kristjánsson learned that the Icelandic tax authorities were investigating the first lady, he decided to wait to see what they would do first.

Walker told Kristjánsson about the Mossfon data and Wintris Inc., the offshore company belonging to Sigmundur Gunnlaugsson, Iceland's prime minister, who had been elected on a platform of getting tough on the country's creditors and their offshore dealings. Icelanders were not aware that their prime minister was himself involved in the very activity he was castigating.

As Kristjánsson listened, time appeared to freeze before him. He watched as a vehicle drifted into the car wash. Kristjánsson knew his countrymen and their anger over the financial crisis. This news he now possessed could topple the Icelandic government.

Walker invited Kristjánsson to attend a preliminary meeting on the investigation to be held in Washington at the National Press Club on June 30. Kristjánsson discussed the trip with his wife, Brynja, who worked as a freelance accountant. The couple had children to support. Finances were tight. A plane ticket on short notice was expensive. If he joined the project, he would work without pay, at least in the beginning, and alone. He would be confronting not only Iceland's leader but the entire financial and political establishment of a relatively small country. Brynja did her best to stifle her fear, and said go for it.

THE IDEA BEHIND the Washington meeting was to brief a small group of committed partners who would investigate the data over the summer. In addition to the ICIJ team and the *Süddeutsche Zeitung* reporters, journalists with expertise on the biggest cases such as Iceland and Argentina were also invited. But what started out as a small gathering grew to more than fifty people.

Jóhannes Kristjánsson did not talk much at the Washington meeting, intimidated by journalists he recognized by reputation but did not know personally. Reporters from the BBC and *Le Monde* were there, as was Edouard Perrin, looking understandably glum. Less than two months earlier a Luxembourg prosecutor had indicted him for receiving the leak of the tax agreements. Economics reporter Kevin Hall and investigative editor James Asher, from the Washington bureau of the American news organization McClatchy, also attended. ICIJ's Michael Hudson had recommended partnering with McClatchy, whose Washington bureau was among the first to question the justification for the Iraq War. ICIJ also liked that McClatchy owned multiple newspapers across the country, including the *Miami Herald*. Oliver Zihlmann and Titus Plattner from Switzerland's Tamedia also came.

After group introductions, Bastian Obermayer and Frederik Obermaier presented some of what they knew. By this point *Süddeutsche Zeitung* had received 1.7 terabytes of Mossfon's data and expected another 500 gigabytes to arrive soon. It was the largest leak received by journalists in history. There were 7.4 million files. It was an astounding number—and turned out to be an undercount.

Frederik Obermaier reviewed some of the cases they had already found. The data contained information on arms traffickers, drug dealers, CEOs, and the megawealthy. Roldugin and Putin were mentioned, as was Iceland's Gunnlaugsson. Obermaier talked about the Báez case in Argentina and about the Israeli businessman Beny Steinmetz, who was under investigation for bribery over an iron-ore mine deal in Guinea. Mossfon had registered all the companies implicated by prosecutors in the court documents.

Bastian Obermayer then went into further detail about Mossack Fonseca itself. He discussed the personal background of the two founding partners and then drilled down into the firm's organization. The Germans had spent weeks trying to understand Mossfon's corporate structure. Mossfon had more than two hundred individual companies under its umbrella, divided by geography and purpose. For those who knew little about the firm, it was clear that the two German reporters were deep in the weeds.

Mar Cabra presented next. She introduced the ICIJ team, which in addition to the now three-person data team also included two talented young women, Cécile Schilis-Gallego from France and Emilia

Díaz-Struck from Venezuela, who handled everything from partner coordination to research. Rigoberto Carvajal had code-named the project "Prometheus." In addition to being the god who stole fire from Mount Olympus and gave it to mankind, Prometheus was also the name of one of the most powerful combat vessels in Starfleet.

Cabra introduced the Global I-Hub, a Facebook-like application where members of the project could log in securely and confidentially share the information they found in the data. The I-Hub would become a second home for reporters scattered across the globe to gather and communicate. It offered the kind of operational flexibility and digital security Mossfon could only dream about.

The last item on the agenda was among the most difficult—when to publish. Mariel Fitz Patrick, with the public television channel El Trece in Argentina, made an impassioned plea to allow the Argentineans to publish before October 25, the date of the country's presidential election. If the data included criminal activity that linked back to President Kirchner, they had to make that information public. It was a difficult conversation. Everyone in the room recognized the value of Fitz Patrick's argument, but the project was no longer about a single country. The reporters who had gathered in Washington were from all over the world. They could not publish until the reporting was ready.

By that point, the *Süddeutsche Zeitung* reporters had seen how difficult it was to process the data. They had given up on publishing in 2015. Rather than fight with their bosses, they did what reporters do all over the world—they strung them along. Ryle told them that once their editors saw the scale of the project and the amazing findings, they would come around to a new deadline. It was a leap of faith.

A week after the Washington meeting, Mossfon's lawyers submitted a declaration by Jürgen Mossack to the U.S. District Court in Las Vegas. Under penalty of perjury, Mossack declared that M. F. Nevada and Mossack Fonseca did not have a parent-subsidiary relationship. Mossack Fonseca did not "control the internal affairs or daily operations of M. F. Nevada."

The declaration proved insufficient to get Paul Singer to back off.

16

· COLLABORATION TRIUMPHS

Rita Vásquez could not stifle a sense of foreboding. It kept her awake on her overnight flight from Panama to Munich in early September 2015. When Vásquez gets nervous, she tends to giggle or smile maniacally. After Rolando Rodríguez, the head of investigations for Panama's *La Prensa* newspaper, told her about Prometheus, she laughed uncontrollably. Rodríguez then swore her to secrecy and made her sign ICIJ's confidentiality agreement.

Marina Walker had contacted Rodríguez to invite him and *La Prensa* into the project. A local partner in a tax haven was a delicate matter, but Rodríguez came highly recommended and *La Prensa* had a storied past. The newspaper was founded in 1980, in the teeth of the Torrijos dictatorship, by a group of returned exiles. The government forced *La Prensa* to close three times during the years of the dictatorship. Hard-hitting stories sent multiple reporters into exile.

In its first dozen years, the paper failed to earn a profit. Fearful vendors refused to sell it. Few dared advertise. The founders sold shares to raise capital. Mindful of the dangers of concentrated power, *La Prensa*'s organizational rules stipulated that no single person could own more than 1 percent of its stock. To be a *La Prensa* shareholder became a badge of honor. Share certificates were tangible representations of a common democratic vision. Ramón Fonseca was a shareholder. So was future president Ricardo Martinelli.

In the years after the fall of Manuel Noriega, the paper became complacent, but rampant corruption during the Martinelli administration reenergized its sense of mission. In 2012, La Prensa hammered Martinelli over the exaggerated costs of highway construction projects. A local building firm took offense at the allegations of bribery. Facing yet another exposé, the firm blocked the avenue leading to the paper's printing press with tractor-trailers in an attempt to physically prevent the story from getting out. In response, La Prensa's staff formed a human chain to carry the bales of newspapers past the blockade. As word of what was happening spread on social media, opposition politicians and neighbors joined the line. Around half past midnight, an inebriated Martinelli appeared on the scene, laughing. Video shows angry Panamanians surrounding him, yelling, "Thief!" He quickly departed. The blockade of trucks soon followed.

Vásquez was unique among the journalists in the project, and at La Prensa. In addition to being a deputy managing editor of the newspaper, she was also a lawyer who had worked for years in the British Virgin Islands for a midsize Panamanian law firm that provided offshore services. She knew that if her newspaper revealed the inner workings of one of Panama's top offshore providers, it would have a seismic impact in her tight-knit country. Even though it was far from the largest segment of the economy, much of Panama's political and economic elite worked in the offshore industry.

What also worried Vásquez was the personal toll that awaited her. She still had close friends in the business, some at Mossfon. She feared a fierce reaction.

Rodríguez had little to tell Vásquez about the project other than that they were going to Munich for a meeting hosted by Süddeutsche Zeitung. ICIJ expected more than one hundred top journalists from all over the world to attend. Oh, and by the way, he told Vásquez, you will be giving a presentation on how the offshore industry works.

On the morning of September 8, 2015, more than one hundred journalists gathered in the Sky Lounge conference room on the twenty-sixth floor of Süddeutsche Zeitung's modern glass-encased office building on the outskirts of Munich. They came from every continent save Antarctica. The Germans had tried to limit the meeting to eighty, which was the room's capacity, but as Walker and the ICIJ team picked participants, the list kept growing. It was like planning a wedding. There are certain family members you have to invite, and then all of sudden, you have a wedding of a hundred people, Mar Cabra recalled.

This particular wedding came with restrictions. In the past, cameramen had roamed freely at previous ICIJ project meetings to record the proceedings for documentaries that would be released concurrently with publication. Walker asked for moderation this time. She urged partners to keep in mind that some colleagues worked and lived in tough environments, and their appearance on camera could be dangerous. There were indeed people in the room who reported from countries whose leaders or other elites could be found in the Mossfon data, countries like Russia, Egypt, and Venezuela. Filming was limited to certain sessions and was to be avoided during strategy or case discussions. Those who did not want to appear were asked to make that known.

The editor in chief of *Süddeutsche Zeitung*, Wolfgang Krach, welcomed the journalists to the newspaper. Everyone went around the room introducing themselves. It was a United Nations of reporters, only this one functioned properly. Everybody was there for the same reason, with a similar motivation: to find the truth and hold the powerful accountable. For many of the reporters in the room, journalism was not merely a job but a calling. They came from countries with weak institutions and compromised politicians. The press was a bulwark against tyranny.

Krach beamed. Even Katharine Viner, the recently named editor in chief of the *Guardian*, had flown to Munich specifically for the meeting, in part to make amends with the Germans for the conduct of her predecessors during Offshore Leaks. That night, as the other journalists gathered for a meat-and-brew feast at an historic beer hall in the city's center, Viner, Krach, and Ryle dined at a fancy restaurant. Whatever remaining concerns Krach may have harbored over deadlines and the considerable time his star reporters had invested in the project evaporated once he saw the global community of journalists and heard their findings. The excitement was infectious. Ryle's strategy of letting events unfold had worked.

Obermayer, Obermaier, and Walker spoke after Krach. They reported that there were now 2.4 terabytes of data, and the material was still arriving. By the end of 2015, it would reach 2.6 terabytes. ICIJ would eventually calculate the number of files at 11.5 million, but this, too, would be a significant undercount. Many of the files were emails, which often came with multiple documents attached to them. Each email was counted as one file. Out of the more than 8 million files received by the time of the Munich meeting, in just six months ICIJ had managed to make 3.3 million of them searchable. It had required a technological leap for that to happen.

In the spring, not long after Cabra and Carvajal had returned from their trip to Munich with the data, ICIJ's Matthew Caruana Galizia recognized that it would be impossible to extract all the information from the millions of documents and make them searchable with just one computer. There were too many images. It would take at least two years. A radically new approach was needed.

Caruana Galizia found the answer in parallel processing. Rather than one giant computer churning through the data, they would employ multiple servers working collaboratively. At the height of the project, ICIJ had thirty-three Amazon cloud servers processing the data. Each server contained eight central processing units able to extract eight documents. When a CPU selected a document, the cue of documents froze so that it would be impossible for a different server to take the same file. Caruana Galizia designed a program that made this ballet of data extraction possible. A CPU grabbed a document— for example, an email with a PDF file as an attachment. The program indexed the text from the email and performed optical character recognition on the PDF. Then the machine extracted all the information from the PDF and indexed that as well, to ensure that every scrap of data from the email could be searched in Blacklight.

The data processing was analogous to the journalistic effort. By the Munich meeting, Prometheus was already the largest cross-border media collaboration ever undertaken. There were two hundred journalists involved, a number that by the end would swell to more than three hundred. They came from more than sixty-five countries and represented more than eighty media organizations. While English was the dominant language, the group covered twenty-five different tongues. They had already begun picking over the data, filling the I-Hub with their findings, and watching as their colleagues added details daily.

The German reporters presented a slide show of the world leaders found either in the data themselves or through relatives and cronies. Those new to the project gasped as photos of Vladimir Putin, Xi Jinping, Hosni Mubarak, Bashar al-Assad, the king of Saudi Arabia, Argentina's Kirchners, Iceland's Gunnlaugsson, the ruling family of Azerbaijan, and Nawaz Sharif, the prime minister of Pakistan, flashed on the screen. Sessions on specific cases then followed.

By the time Vásquez gave her presentation, she was freaked out by the scale of the findings. Her presentation was matter-of-fact, dry, and lawyerly. She ran through the history of Panama and its corporation and bank secrecy laws. The presentation ended with a slide that read, "They have resources . . . and will use them however they can. Lawyers doing what they do." After she finished, her fellow journalists swarmed her, scarcely leaving her alone for the rest of the conference. They even chased her into the bathroom asking questions. For the first time in her life, Vásquez felt what it was like to be on the other side.

Later in the day, Jóhannes Kristjánsson offered one of the most popular presentations. To demonstrate the hubris of Icelandic bankers in the lead-up to the financial crisis, Kristjánsson showed an over-the-top in-house video produced by the Icelandic bank Kaupthing called *Beyond Normal Thinking*. As synthesizers swelled, an announcer declared the bank's sky-is-the-limit philosophy, accompanied by images of Mother Teresa, Bill Gates, and Albert Einstein, along with clips from movies such as *The Matrix* and *Lawrence of Arabia*. Kristjánsson also showed an animation he had created for a news segment on the banks' market manipulation, which featured a Rube Goldbergian circular machine that sliced and diced loans.

Perhaps even more than world leaders, what stirred the crowd was the information on the globe's most popular sport, soccer. Hugo

Alconada Mon, a reporter and editor with Argentina's *La Nación*, gave a presentation on the preliminary findings. The greatest player in the game, Lionel Messi, was in the data through a company set up by his father. He was just one of dozens of high-profile sports figures who exploited the offshore world to escape taxes. The secrecy world was also used for more nefarious dealings involving sport. By the end of the project, the exposé would upend soccer's world governing body, the Fédération Internationale de Football Association, known as FIFA, which was already tarnished by scandal and governmental investigations.

In Munich, the team set a publication date of March 7, 2016—six months hence. On that day, all the partners would begin to drop their stories at a prearranged time. The Russians objected because the date conflicted with International Women's Day. The ICIJ team did not pay much heed initially to the concern, until they returned to Washington and realized how serious a holiday it was in Russia. Newspapers did not even publish. The date was pushed back by a week, to March 13.

Mar Cabra asked Ryle and Walker if they would have breakfast with her on the last morning they were in Munich. Throughout the meeting, Cabra had held tightly to a decision she had made over her summer holiday. Now she unburdened herself. She told Ryle and Walker that upon the conclusion of the project she was leaving ICIJ. Cabra considered ICIJ more like a family than a business, but she was too burned out to continue. Everybody was overworked, but neither Ryle nor Walker had seen this coming. Cabra started to cry. Ryle expressed sympathy. Both he and Walker had so many problems and challenges ahead, they were simply thankful six months existed to find a replacement.

THE BIENNIAL GLOBAL Investigative Journalism Conference was held a month later, in Lillehammer, Norway. Throughout the Mossfon project, ICIJ and its collaborators regularly attended conferences to give presentations and pick up awards for what had been their most successful project to date, the HSBC exposé Swiss Leaks, published nine months earlier. On the sidelines of the Lillehammer conference, the Prometheans stealthily met, trying hard not to tip off their fellow attendees, who were, by profession, inquisitive sorts. Will Fitzgibbon, an Australian-born ICIJ staffer who ran the organization's Africa desk, asked Cabra to meet with a handful of African journalists attending the conference. Africa had been largely absent from the Munich meeting; the participating news organizations had paid for their journalists to attend, but most African reporters could not afford the expense.

A pay-your-way approach was part of Ryle's innovation for ICIJ. Before he arrived, the organization often created the projects and then invited partners into them, sometimes even financing their participation. Under Ryle's leadership the collaborators participated in developing the projects almost from the outset, and in return their news organizations paid their own way. ICIJ then worked to find ways to include those who, because of either their financial situation or security considerations, could not participate as readily. And so a subsequent meeting was held in Johannesburg, with more than a dozen reporters from African countries including Senegal, Mali, Namibia, and Zimbabwe.

For ICIJ, the most consequential gathering at the Global Investigative Journalism Conference was held in a tucked-away meeting room at the Radisson Blu Lillehammer Hotel. It set in motion events that would radically reshape the future of the organization and sour much of 2016 for Ryle, at the very moment he achieved his greatest journalistic success.

As part of a three-year grant from the Netherlands-based Adessium Foundation, ICIJ was required to produce a report that discussed how ICIJ planned to grow. Ryle tapped an advisory board to help with the task. The group included ICIJ veterans such as Columbia journalism professor Sheila Coronel, the *Guardian*'s David Leigh, and Fredrik Laurin, an outspoken special projects editor for Swedish public television. In Lillehammer, Ryle and Walker presented their growth plan to ICIJ members for discussion.

The group wrestled with the issue of ICIJ's parent, the Center for Public Integrity. The ICIJ budget had grown from $600,000 to $1.8 million under Ryle, but CPI itself was in debt. To fill the gap, CPI appeared to be helping itself to money earmarked for ICIJ. CPI charged for a slew of services it provided ICIJ but not at market rates. The exact financial arrangements were opaque, invisible to Ryle and to the ICIJ staff. Increasingly, ICIJ did not even need CPI's services as it focused more on data and project management.

In January 2016, the group completed its report. "To create a genuine growth strategy for ICIJ one must now consider a different arrangement between ICIJ and its parent that includes a new management and financial arrangement," the report concluded. "ICIJ is at a crossroads in its history—to continue to grow it needs greater autonomy and flexibility."

Ryle and Walker were not proposing separation. Instead, they suggested a sort of "home rule" scenario. Rather than report to CPI's executive director, Ryle would answer to the CPI board, which would expand to add international members more in tune with ICIJ's mission. Under this organizational structure, ICIJ would continue as part of CPI but would be able to obtain services from whomever it chose, based on market rates. It would also do its own fund-raising. In return, ICIJ would pay an annual dividend to CPI.

Many of ICIJ's international partners who had gathered at the meeting in Lillehammer had given little consideration to how the organization actually functioned. Several opined that maybe it was time for a complete separation. Ryle dismissed the idea. There was value to being part of CPI, not least of all having the legal protection of an established American media organization.

Ryle, Walker, Laurin, and a few others then presented the growth plan to Peter Bale, CPI's chief executive officer. Bale had recently joined CPI after a stint as vice president and general manager of digital operations at CNN International. Laurin had never met Bale but was predisposed to like him because of his international background. That changed when Bale took offense at the suggestion that CPI was leeching off ICIJ. Bale told Laurin that if he wanted to understand the financials, he should look at CPI's annual report. Laurin grew angry. For ten years, he and his colleagues had worked to build ICIJ into a global brand, sacrificing time with their families because they believed in the stories and the idea of international cooperation between journalists. Now, in Laurin's opinion, Bale was talking like a politician, deflecting responsibility. The exchange grew heated.

Bale refused to submit the growth report to the CPI board for review. Instead, he created his own report, using numbers the ICIJ staff disputed. At this point, Sheila Coronel intervened. It was clear to her that ICIJ was financially carrying CPI, to the detriment of its own growth and development. Divorce appeared inevitable. She did an end run around Bale, submitting the report to the board as a letter from the advisory committee. A debate over the future of ICIJ quickly transformed into a personal dispute between Ryle and Bale. The board decided to support the man they had just hired.

Ryle knew that he could not fight this battle and simultaneously land the biggest cross-border journalism project in history. Even as angry emails and conversations on the topic ricocheted around them, he and Walker decided to shelve the debate until after the project was published. There was too much at stake.

As JÓHANNES KRISTJÁNSSON boarded his Icelandair flight in Munich to return home, he was recognized by a flight attendant. A fan of his journalism, she upgraded him to first class. It was a cherry on top of the Munich meeting—good feelings that would have to carry him through a long and lonely winter. There were few in Iceland with whom he could share the explosive information he possessed. Not only did the prime minister have a secret offshore company, but so did the finance minister and the minister of the interior.

As he worked on his stories, Kristjánsson cut off contact with all but his closest family members. He labored alone in his apartment and at a small summer cottage he and Brynja kept outside Reykjavík. As he parsed the Mossfon documents, mapping the stories on sheets of paper he taped to the walls, Kristjánsson covered the windows with dark material so the neighbors could not see inside. Occasionally he took his laptop to a harbor café where he passed the dwindling daylight hours watching the boats come in while he worked.

Money grew tight. Brynja's mother questioned her daughter's

choice in a husband. Brynja's friends worried that she had married a deadbeat: someone who did not work and seldom left the house. In order to bring in extra cash for the Christmas holidays, Kristjánsson agreed to write a newsletter for a church-run rehab and homeless shelter. He did it again around Easter but blew his deadline when Prometheus work interfered. He could not explain to his irate publisher that the church newsletter was being bumped for one of the biggest news stories in Iceland's history.

Kristjánsson's main refuge and support was the Global I-Hub, ICIJ's virtual newsroom, where he could exchange his findings and ideas with fellow Prometheans. He also received visits from colleagues who were quietly reporting their own Icelandic stories for the project. Ryan Chittum, a former *Wall Street Journal* reporter who worked for ICIJ on a contract basis, Bastian Obermeyer, and Sven Bergman from Swedish public television all made the trip that winter.

In December, Ryle took the opportunity of a London meeting to stop in Iceland on the way home so Kristjánsson could interview him for a documentary about the project. For his part, Ryle wanted to ensure the Icelandic reporter was not losing his mind or his marriage over the story. During meals and long coffees, Kristjánsson and Ryle discussed how to confront the prime minister. If they notified Gunnlaugsson about Wintris, the offshore company the prime minister and his wife held, before an interview, he would never agree to discuss the matter on camera. Gunnlaugsson might also try to cover his tracks in some way. However, Kristjánsson was uneasy with the idea of an ambush interview. Was it ethical in this circumstance?

Kristjánsson had employed hidden cameras for stories in the past. His philosophy was that if one could obtain the truth without questionable methods, that was obviously better. But if a little subterfuge was absolutely necessary to document reality, then so be it. Gunnlaugsson's reaction to the revelation about his secret offshore company, the very behavior he had built his political career railing against, was essential footage for the television program. The problem was that if Kristjánsson, known for hard-hitting investigative reporting, was the one to ask for an interview with the prime minister, Gunnlaugs-son would know immediately that something was afoot.

Ryle and Kristjánsson decided to enlist Sven Bergman, the Swedish television reporter. Bergman and his colleagues were interested in doing their own Iceland story. Swedish public television asked to interview Gunnlaugsson to discuss Iceland's handling of the financial crisis. The plan was for Kristjánsson to accompany the camera team as a local fixer. As soon as Bergman asked about Wintris, Kristjánsson would insert himself into the interview and ask the same question in Icelandic.

Bergman and his crew arrived a few days before the interview, which was scheduled for March 11, 2016. By this point, Kristjánsson had enlisted three Icelandic colleagues who would also be filming the interview for a program to air on Icelandic public television. In Kristjánsson's cramped living room they pushed aside the furniture to simulate the interview, gaming out likely reactions and responses. The consensus view was that the prime minister, who had been a television personality himself, would likely shrug off the questions.

After a lunch of fish and chips, the team went to the Minister's Residence at Tjarnargata, an old frame house with dormer windows where the prime minister held official meetings. Prior to rolling the cameras, Bergman succeeded at putting Gunnlaugsson at ease, talking about soccer and Sweden. The interview began broadly with Bergman asking about the 2008 financial crisis and Iceland's response. Slowly, Bergman drew closer to the question. He asked about recent reports that the Icelandic government had purchased "sensitive tax information," which was a reference to the Luxembourg Mossfon data. Bardi Stefánsson, one of Kristjánsson's cameramen, fought to keep his rickety camera tripod still on the wooden floor as his heart pounded. Gunnlaugsson said he wanted to make sure the public knew his government was "leaving no stone unturned."

Bergman asked what Gunnlaugsson himself thought about people having offshore companies in tax havens to hide assets. The prime minister said that in Iceland "we attach a lot of importance to everybody paying his share." The Swede then went in for the kill.

"Mr. Prime Minister, have you or did you have any connection yourself to an offshore company?"

For the first time, Gunnlaugsson started to stammer nervously as he delivered a confusing word salad of an answer. "It's an unusual question for . . . for an Icelandic politician to get. It's almost like being accused of something . . . But . . . I can confirm that I have never hidden any of my assets."

"Mr. Prime Minister, what can you tell me about a company called Wintris?" Bergman then asked.

A look of terror flashed over Gunnlaugsson's face. More rambling ensued. "I'm starting to feel a bit strange about this question," he said.

Bergman told Gunnlaugsson that his Icelandic partner had the details and would ask him further questions. Kristjánsson then fired a question at Gunnlaugsson in Icelandic.

Life seldom delivers moments when a single choice, made in an instant, determines the destiny of an individual and a country. Gunn-laugsson could have kept his calm and tried to talk his way out of the interview. Instead, he bolted from his chair and, after a few recrimi-nations flung at the journalists, fled the room through the first door he saw, which led into a kitchen. Kristjánsson and Bergman implored him through the closed door to come out and finish the interview, to no avail.

BACK IN SEPTEMBER in Munich, the ICIJ leadership began a conver-sation over what to name the project. Walker solicited input from the partners. Ryle wanted to get away from the "leak" motif, which had graced ICIJ's previous projects. He liked the alliteration of "Panama" and "Papers" as well as the allusion to Daniel Ellsberg's consequen-tial disclosure of the Vietnam-era Pentagon Papers in 1971. Vásquez and the *La Prensa* team were not happy, worried that the name would unfairly tar their entire country. This decision, like the publication date, ultimately rested with *Süddeutsche Zeitung* and ICIJ. Panama Papers won out.

In December, the deadline for publication was pushed further back, to two p.m. Eastern Daylight Time on Sunday, April 3, 2016. *Süd-*

deutsche Zeitung, with some embarrassment, had belatedly realized that March 13 conflicted with regional elections in Germany. Under the new deadline, journalists working on the project could start contacting people who created offshore companies for themselves or others to ask for comment on February 21. ICIJ requested they not refer to a global leak or collaboration, simply to say that they had seen documents that concerned the given company or companies. The approach to Mossack Fonseca itself would occur in two stages beginning March 6.

As winter turned to spring, John Doe was getting impatient. It had been close to a year since the first contact with Obermayer and still no story had been published. Weekly calls and email conversations between the Germans and ICIJ discussed how to handle the problem. Ryle had dealt with similar tensions from his source during Offshore Leaks. All Obermayer could do was offer reassurances to John Doe. These were not enough. John Doe contacted WikiLeaks to see if the organization would be interested in the files. With months of work by hundreds of journalists hanging in the balance, WikiLeaks failed to answer its tip line. The Mossfon files stayed with Prometheus.

In late January 2016, Brazilian federal police raided Mossfon's office in São Paulo. The operation was part of a fast-growing inquiry into bribery allegations involving the Brazilian construction firm Odebrecht, the state oil company Petrobras, and Brazil's top political leadership. Prosecutors issued arrest warrants for six people, at least three of them connected to Mossfon. In a press conference following the raid, Brazilian prosecutor Carlos Fernando dos Santos Lima accused one of the firm's employees of destroying documents. He described Mossfon as "a money-washing machine."

The firm responded with a statement declaring that Mossack Fonseca Brazil was independent of Mossack Fonseca in Panama. The Brazilian office had created the company in question at the request of an intermediary in 2005. Mossfon complied with all the due diligence standards in place at the time, the statement said.

Public attention to Mossfon's activities seemed to be growing by the day. The Brazilian partners in the project expressed alarm about losing their stories but promised to hold fast to the agreed-upon publication date. Ryle counseled calm as many wondered whether the largest journalism collaboration in history could remain a secret for two more months. Surely someone would break the embargo.

By early March, a few of Mossack Fonseca's clients informed the firm that reporters had contacted them about their Mossfon companies. Ramón Fonseca appeared on Panamanian television to defend the firm. On March 4, ICIJ sent Mossfon seventeen general questions, including this: *Had Mossfon, its affiliates or employees ever helped individuals launder money, evade taxes, or circumvent sanctions?* The letter asked the firm to respond by six p.m. on March 9. Soon after its receipt, Fonseca took a temporary leave of absence from his position in President Varela's government.

With thirty minutes to spare before the March 9 deadline, Carlos Sousa, Mossfon's public relations director, responded with a three-paragraph email. "We only incorporate companies, which just about everyone acknowledges is important, and something that's critical in ensuring the global economy functions efficiently," he wrote. "In providing those services, we follow both the letter and spirit of the law."

While Mossfon had been contemplating its answer, seven teams of television reporters in the project—from the United States, France, Germany, Denmark, and Finland—had come to Panama. The day after Sousa sent his email response, the television reporters staked out Mossfon's office. Nearly twenty reporters and producers, with ten cameras pointed to the door, demanded that someone come out and speak to them. After a while, Sousa came out and answered a few questions.

The next day Sousa, Jürgen Mossack, and another Mossfon lawyer paid a visit to *La Prensa*. Fonseca had contacted the paper's president to set up the meeting the week before but Mossack went in his stead. On the other side of the table were Rolando Rodríguez and *La Prensa*'s board chairman and managing editor. Mossack grew worried as he felt that the *La Prensa* participants refused to make eye contact. After declaring that his firm was being victimized by international journalists bent on sensationalism, Mossack said that he knew there was a reporter at *La Prensa* who was helping them. He physically described Rita Vásquez although he did not know her name. Mossack warned *La Prensa* of potential legal implications if they libeled the firm. He then invited Rodríguez to come to the office and learn more about what Mossfon actually did.

After some discussion, *La Prensa*'s leadership decided to assign a bodyguard to Vásquez. She worked late hours and they worried something might happen to her. It was an awkward fit. Even as Vásquez and her American husband, Scott Bronstein, were helping the foreign reporters, they were also entertaining friends who were visiting from the British Virgin Islands where they worked in the offshore business. They had put them off for most of the week while the reporters were in town. The day after the teams left, Vásquez and Bronstein invited their friends out to dinner. They passed off the bodyguard as an Uber driver. As the group headed to a restaurant, Bronstein looked in the front seat. Barely concealed in a bag by the driver was a handgun. No one else noticed.

17

THE WAVE BREAKS

Gerard Ryle and Marina Walker spent the last three weeks of Prometheus reassuring their partners.

In Iceland, Jóhannes Kristjánsson and his Swedish colleagues offered Prime Minister Sigmundur Gunnlaugsson another try after his disastrous interview. He declined. They also asked to speak with his wife, Anna Sigurlaug Pálsdóttir, who was listed as the owner of the couple's Mossfon company, Wintris. The journalists gave the pair a few days in which to respond.

An hour before the deadline lapsed, Pálsdóttir posted a confusing statement on her Facebook page. While it made no direct mention of the interview, she admitted to owning Wintris and claimed its existence was never hidden. All applicable taxes on the company's activities had been paid, she asserted. As Icelandic journalists learned about the company for the first time, they clamored for more information.

Russian president Vladimir Putin also chose the preemptive-strike approach. A detailed request-for-comment letter from ICIJ, *Süddeutsche Zeitung*, *Le Monde*, and others went to the Kremlin on March 23. It contained questions on topics such as Putin's connection to the Mossfon companies ostensibly owned by his old pal, the classical cellist Sergei Roldugin, and whether the Russian leader had ordered the murder of his former communications minister, a Moss-fon company owner himself, whose badly bruised, lifeless body had been found in November 2015 inside a Washington, DC, hotel room.

Five days later, Russian presidential spokesman Dmitry Peskov held a press conference to denounce the "honey-worded queries" from "an organization calling itself International Consortium of Investigative Journalists." The Kremlin spokesman warned that various media around the world planned to publish stories concerning off-shore companies allegedly connected to the president and "a large number of businessmen Putin has never seen in his life." The Russians appeared to be unaware the project was much bigger than Putin. Peskov, whose wife also had a company with Mossfon, blamed the yet-unseen revelations on a conspiracy driven by foreign intelligence services. The efficiency of their attacks would not be high, the spokesman promised, according to the government-controlled news agency Sputnik.

In Washington, Ryle dodged calls from media organizations fishing for information on what was in the offing. After several ICIJ partners expressed concern that these disclosures would imperil the project, Ryle batted down suggestions that they publish early. He insisted to worried editors and reporters that these early revelations would build interest. They should be happy, he told them, because Putin and Gunnlaugsson had tested the stories and they held up. Ryle stayed calm because he had been through this before in the previous leak investigations.

Mossack and Fonseca still did not realize what they were facing. There had been a leak, that much was clear, but its extent and how many media organizations were involved remained a mystery. Fonseca remembers shock at another list of forty-eight questions that ICIJ, *Süddeutsche Zeitung,* and the *Guardian* sent the firm. Queries about Jürgen Mossack's father being a Nazi and allegations that the firm had laundered money for an infamous English Brinks gold heist convinced the partners that the journalists were bent on sensationalism, not serious dialogue. These "idiotic" questions, as Fonseca described them, were starkly at odds with the partners' conception of themselves.

Mossack was semiretired. Fonseca was in the government. The partners viewed themselves as upstanding businessmen. They had never created companies for bank robbers; they had sold the companies to an agent in London, who in turn sold them to others. Whatever damage their companies had done in the world was neither their concern nor their responsibility, they believed.

That was about to change.

On Friday, April 1, the firm bowed to reality and sent a note to its clients about an unauthorized breach of its email server. Signed by marketing and sales director Carlos Sousa, the note acknowledged that the information had fallen into the hands of reporters, who had contacted the firm.

"We have responded in a general manner and have not provided details that would further expose confidential information," the note reassured its customers.

It was akin to closing the barn door after the horses had bolted, but the firm was not going to be held responsible for divulging information willingly themselves.

"Rest assured that we accord the highest priority to the safety and confidentiality of your information," the note continued. "We employ multiple layers of electronic security and limit access to files to selected individuals within our firm in order to prevent breaches."

A subsequent analysis of Mossfon's cybersecurity belied this assertion. Its biggest mistake was keeping its intranet, the company's internal database and communications, on the same server as its public-facing website. The firm compounded this error by not updating its software, even after security flaws and patches for them were publicly available. According to a story later published in *Wired*, the firm's content management system had at least twenty-five known vulnerabilities, some quite significant.

The day before publication, a blog in Malta connected the dots. Its author had seen a promo on a website for one of the partners, Finnish public television, discussing the upcoming Panama leaks. Walker and Ryle had granted a small number of the television partners permission to run promotional spots for their shows that could mention the collaboration, Panama, and the leak, but not the name Mossack Fonseca. In some cases, the TV shows were required to advertise their programs by law. The Malta blog then obtained the Mossack Fonseca client letter. Putting the two together, it ran a post with the headline, "Mossack Fonseca lets cat out of bag ahead of worldwide coverage of massive Panama Leaks data." Normally, this would be a minor inconvenience. Only in this case, the blogger was Daphne Caruana Galizia, the mother of ICIJ's data wrangler Matthew Caruana Galizia. As some partners grumbled, Matthew swore he had not told his mom about the project.

In Iceland, beyond the members of Jóhannes Kristjánsson's production company, Reykjavik Media, and his partner on the documentary, the daily news program *Kastijós*, few knew what was coming at the state television station where his report was to be broadcast. They had told the CEO of the station only the day before. The time slot—Sunday at six p.m.—was reserved for a children's program, one of the oldest on Icelandic television. Since everyone would publish across the world at the same time, the station preempted the program for a special report.

Kristjánsson insisted on being in the control room for the broadcast, a tradition he observed for all his broadcasts. As he sat in the booth, his eyes were bloodshot, his face blotchy from nervous exhaustion. He felt the weight of responsibility, not only to his Icelandic colleagues but to all the partners in ICIJ with whom he had worked so hard for the past nine months.

In Munich, *Süddeutsche Zeitung* had created a special microwebsite specifically for the project. It managed to jump the embargo by fifteen minutes to publish early. A few minutes later, at 1:49 p.m. EDT, Edward Snowden somehow found this microsite and linked to it on Twitter. Snowden's tweet to his millions of followers declared, "Biggest leak in the history of data journalism just went live, and it's about corruption." In London, the staff of the *Guardian* howled. Intentionally or not, the Germans had their revenge for Offshore Leaks. The *Guardian* hit publish on its stories. More than eighty media partners followed.

Kristjánsson watched the shocked expressions in the broadcasting room from the people who had not known the content of the program. More than 60 percent of the population of Iceland witnessed their panicked prime minister respond to the revelation of a secret offshore company by abruptly ending his interview and fleeing. Twitter and Facebook exploded. In the first twenty-four hours, ICIJ's website received more than six million page views.

JÜRGEN MOSSACK BEGAN to receive texts and emails from friends, family, and clients. As the messages and the stories piled on, one after the other, he felt bewildered. Mossfon was being connected to so many issues and notorious people. The remove he and Ramón Fonseca had long felt as their due was evaporating before their eyes. The partners quickly set up a damage control committee. They had already filed a criminal complaint in Panama about the suspected hacking. Now they hired an American consulting firm to help them respond to the media. But it wasn't until Mossack turned on the television and saw his life's work on every news channel that he realized the dimensions of what had just occurred. Fonseca grew ill and largely took to his house for a week. Two days after the first stories dropped, he formally resigned from his position with the Panamanian government. Mossack, who was due to become the president of the Rotary Club, withdrew his name from consideration.

At *La Prensa*, they had waited almost an hour after the other partners had published to put their own stories online. They wanted to report on the fact of the global investigation rather than breaking the story themselves and thereby risking legal jeopardy. In Panama, it is a crime to publish confidential emails or material derived from a theft. At the last minute, the paper's lawyers insisted the articles be written in the conditional tense to insulate *La Prensa* further. They also opted not to put the names of the authors on the stories. Nonetheless, the reaction was exactly as Vásquez had feared. Some of her friends dropped away or questioned her motives on Facebook. The defenders of the industry styled the "Panama Papers" as an attack against the entire country. *La Prensa*'s reporters were denounced in rival newspapers and threatened on Twitter.

Ramsés Owens had left Mossfon in 2011, after it became clear that Mossack and Fonseca would never promote him to partner. He was on a business trip to El Salvador when the stories broke. As his cell phone lit up, he hurried home. Several months earlier, Owens had been interviewed in his Panama office by *Süddeutsche Zeitung* reporter Frederik Obermaier, who had come to the country on a stealth reporting trip. Owens thought he was simply giving background on the industry. At the outset of the interview, Obermaier asked if a cameraman could tape the encounter. Always eager to please, Owens agreed. Now, back in his office, post-publication, Owens found Obermaier's business card. On it he scrawled in Spanish, "Avoid this person. He is the devil."

The day after Kristjánsson's report shook Iceland, Ólafur Hauksson, the special prosecutor investigating the banking crisis, was in his office when he noticed the cars. Reykjavík is not a bustling metropolis. Yet Hauksson watched as a line of vehicles as far as the eye could see made their way into the city. The call had gone out on Facebook. It was the last day of the Althingi, the Icelandic parliament, and organizers had urged Icelanders to congregate in the square in front of the parliament building. For Icelanders, who were still traumatized from the financial crisis, the Mossfon revelations felt as if a wound barely healed had been ripped open.

The story spread far beyond Iceland. Video of Gunnlaugsson's interview was featured on the *New York Times* website and in media around the world. Kristjánsson was inundated by interview requests. He took the big ones. Sven Bergman asked him to meet a cameraman in the square for a follow-up interview with Swedish television. Bergman wanted the crowd as a backdrop. Unable to find a parking place nearby, Kristjánsson and his wife, Brynja, made their way to the rendezvous spot on foot. The square was swollen with almost ten thousand people—the largest protest in the country's history. Icelanders in the crowd repeatedly waylaid the couple to congratulate Kristjánsson. For a man accustomed to directing the attention rather than receiving it, the praise made him deeply uncomfortable.

Two days later the prime minister resigned.

The following week, Kristjánsson and his family were watching the news on TV at home. His eleven-year-old daughter asked her mother why Iceland was having another election. Brynja replied,

"Well, it is partly because of your dad." At that moment, the enormity of what had occurred registered for Kristjánsson for the first time.

Gunnlaugsson was not the only official to step down over the Panama Papers. In Uruguay, Juan Pedro Damiani, whose law firm had done extensive work with Mossfon over the years, resigned from FIFA's ethics committee when it emerged that his firm had set up companies for a man under indictment in the United States for soccer corruption. FIFA's new president, the files revealed, had also been involved with some of the nefarious characters connected to the sport, although there was no evidence that he had acted illegally. Nonetheless, the Swiss federal police conducted raids on the Union of European Football Associations to collect evidence concerning the revelations. Meanwhile, the prosecutor in Geneva seized the Nahmads' Modigliani painting *Seated Man with a Cane*, stored in the Freeport while the prosecutor's office conducted their own investigation. Swiss authorities eventually gave the painting back.

Around the world government officials struggled to explain their connections to offshore companies revealed by the Mossfon files. Few did as poor a job at it as British prime minister David Cameron. Downing Street tried five separate stabs over the course of several days to answer the simple question of whether Cameron benefited from his father's offshore company, Panama-based Blairmore Holdings, which appeared to have been designed to avoid UK taxes. A spokesperson began with calling it "a private matter," which did not stand long. In the face of sustained press scrutiny, this answer was upgraded to "the prime minister doesn't own any shares." The next day this explanation turned into a statement that he and his family would not benefit in the future from the fund. After three days of prevarications, Cameron himself finally admitted that he had profited from his father's offshore business.

In Venezuela, the Communication Ministry sent a lengthy communiqué to the country's media advising them not to publish stories about the Panama Papers. "It should be noted that these documents are being used selectively for certain policy areas on an international scale," the memo warned, hinting darkly, as the Kremlin had, that the release came from the CIA.

The note sketched out an oddly self-incriminating conspiracy theory. The first round of stories might be a decoy, the ministry postulated. Once the Panama Papers received validation from the world's media, "new information will be published on senior officials of the National Government to justify the current attempt to increase interference and sanctions from the Obama administration, leaving us without room to maneuver before public opinion."

Chillingly, the memo also singled out by name Venezuelan reporters working for independent media organizations that had participated in the project.

Throughout the world, the publication of the Mossfon data fed into attacks on journalists and preexisting political and social dramas in various countries. Reporters and editors wrestled with what part of the data was in the public interest. In Europe and the United States, the dominant concern was taxes, and people evading them. In Latin America and Africa, tax was a vital issue, but it took second place to concerns about corruption and political repression.

In Argentina, a dozen years under the Kirchners had left behind a deeply polarized country. Much of the media, particularly television, was partisan and fiercely critical of anyone who disagreed with their position—for American audiences, imagine Fox versus MSNBC, times ten. The Panama Papers revelations served to deepen the country's cynicism, turning what should have been a journalistic triumph into a bitter experience for the journalists involved.

The Argentineans had not found Kirchner's money in the Mossfon data. This immediately raised suspicions from the anti-Kirchner side. Instead, on December 8, 2016, after a new round of material was uploaded into Blacklight, the journalists had stumbled upon the newly elected president, Mauricio Macri, who had defeated Kirchner's chosen successor and was to assume office two days hence. The scion of a wealthy industrialist, Macri was listed as a decadelong director of Fleg Trading, a company legally created by his father, which became inactive in 2009. Macri would later claim that he did not declare his participation in the company in government disclosure documents because it had failed to earn a profit. Kirchner supporters falsely accused reporters of deliberately withholding the information to favor Macri in the election. Others argued disingenuously that Macri's company simply proved that all politicians were equally dirty.

"The Kirchneristas accused us of trying to save Macri and the Macri people of trying to drown him," says Argentinean reporter Mariel Fitz Patrick.

Among Macri's supporters was the brother of ICIJ's Marina Walker. The mere fact that the project had dragged the Macri revelations into the light led to some angry family phone calls. ICIJ member Hugo Alconada, the investigations editor at *La Nación*, a newspaper that had been fiercely anti-Kirchner, saw the discovery as an opportunity to demonstrate the paper's independence and bolster its image in the eyes of readers. But this idea ran into trouble when the reporting team discovered that *La Nación* itself was in the data.

Alconada decided to publish a list of prominent Argentinean businessmen found in the files, in which he planned to include his own newspaper and an owner from a rival newspaper chain. His bosses nixed the idea, arguing that since the reporters had not proved the companies were up to anything illegal, it was inappropriate to publish the information. Alconada pointed out that ICIJ or its other partners would surely reveal the names anyway. The newspaper would lose even more credibility if it came out in another Argentinean publication first. He then threatened to quit if the paper suppressed the material. After Alconada's fellow editors added their names to the protest, the publisher relented, allowing the publication of the businessmen's names but running a separate note to readers on its own involvement.

In Ecuador, President Rafael Correa denounced the project participants on Twitter and rallied a troll army to send them a message. He helpfully included the reporters' social media accounts, which were then deluged with nasty comments. A dozen or so government supporters demonstrated outside *El Comercio* and *El Universo*, the two newspapers involved in the project.

As Panama's *La Prensa* had done, the Ecuadorian newspapers ran their stories without bylines and after everyone else had published.

The findings, sourced to ICIJ, revealed that the country's attorney general, the president's cousin (who was a former governor of the central bank), and the secretary of intelligence (who was a Mossfon intermediary) were in the data. The family that owned *El Universo* also had a Mossfon company. The owner himself had alerted Mónica Almeida, the Quito bureau chief leading the investigation for the newspaper, about the company. It had been created after President Correa had won a civil judgment against the paper that threatened to shut it down.

As part of his efforts to rein in the media, Correa had spearheaded the creation of the Orwellian-named Citizen Participation and Social Control Council a few years earlier. The council sent a letter to the newspapers demanding that the reporters appear before it on Monday, April 18, to hand over the Mossfon data and respond to questions. The reporters sent a letter the Friday before the meeting declining to appear and explaining that they did not have the data, ICIJ did. A showdown appeared imminent. But on the intervening Saturday, a 7.8 magnitude earthquake devastated the country. As the focus of the media and the government turned to the victims and the damage, the Monday meeting was quietly forgotten.

One of Correa's complaints about the Panama Papers was that the journalists had not posted all the data online. He suggested that important details were being hidden and he promised to acquire the entire set and make it public. ICIJ had never seriously considered releasing all the data. Many, if not most, of the people found in the database had committed no crime. There was little public-interest rationale for publishing personal information such as passports, bank account information, and emails filled with intimate details.

This explanation was insufficient for WikiLeaks, whose founder, Julian Assange, was holed up in Ecuador's embassy in London. The organization pounded ICIJ for not releasing the data. "If you censor more than 99% of the documents you are engaged in 1% journalism by definition," the group nonsensically tweeted. Matters took a more serious turn, when a television project partner mistakenly aired a Blacklight URL. Several quick-witted techies put the URL online and invited people to try to hack the site. Out of an abundance of caution, Mar Cabra had the site temporarily taken down and the URL changed, much to the dismay of journalists still working on stories who did not want to lose a minute with the data.

In Hong Kong, the indomitable Yuen-Ying Chan had lined up multiple partners for the project, meeting them separately in isolated spots around the University of Hong Kong before bringing them all together. In the individual meetings, she told them about the project and solicited commitments to collaborate. The collaborators included *Ming Pao*, *CommonWealth Magazine*, and the *South China Morning Post*. Once again the mainland Chinese government blocked the information.

The day after *Ming Pao* devoted its entire front page to its Panama Papers findings, the executive chief editor, Keung Kwok-Yuen, was fired. The paper's owners cited cost cutting to explain the decision, but the staff was unconvinced. Hundreds of reporters, editors, and free-speech activists rallied outside the building in protest. It was dubbed the "ginger protest," because many demonstrators held up pieces of the vegetable, the name of which in Cantonese sounds like the editor's surname.

TEN DAYS AFTER publication, Panamanian national police cordoned off the side street where Mossfon had its headquarters and searched the firm's offices for twenty-seven hours straight. Ramón Fonseca claims there were drug-sniffing dogs involved, but Javier Caraballo, the prosecutor in charge of the operation, insists no dogs were present. As the search progressed, a multinational collection of reporters and tourists camped out on the lawn in front of the building to watch the spectacle.

Caraballo confiscated copies of Mossfon's computer data and carried it back to a shabby set of offices in the public ministry building. It was a fool's errand. The prosecutor and his staff did not have the equipment, the subject-matter expertise, or the technical ability to make sense of the files, which had taken hundreds of investigative reporters a year to parse. And the prosecutor's job was also much more difficult. Unlike the reporters, Caraballo was looking for violations of Panamanian law that occurred within a strict statute of limitations.

Jürgen Mossack desperately wanted to respond to what he saw as misconceptions about his business, but he did not trust the journalists who were involved in the project. He sought out *Bloomberg News* and the *Wall Street Journal*, which he judged to be sober and reputable business news organizations. Despite interviews with these outlets, the partners could do little to counter the slow drip of new revelations from the files and the reactions of investigators and prosecutors throughout the world. In that first month alone, financial regulators, tax authorities, and prosecutors across the world from Mexico to Norway launched inquiries. Police in Peru and El Salvador raided their respective countries' Mossfon offices. European authorities pledged new cooperation to hunt down tax evaders. Preet Bharara, the U.S. attorney for the Southern District of New York, opened an investigation. Spain's minister of industry resigned after reporters caught him lying about his offshore companies.

A few days after the initial release, President Barack Obama gave a press conference on the topic from the White House briefing room. The administration had had advance warning that the stories were coming. Shortly before publication Ryle, along with McClatchy's Kevin Hall, had met with Treasury Department officials in the hope—ultimately unsuccessful—of getting an on-the-record comment about the Panama Papers.

Now, in the face of the tsunami of interest, Obama took to the podium to make a case for cracking down on corporate inversions, a tactic through which companies moved overseas to avoid taxes while still conducting most of their business in the United States. The scandal, Obama said, was not what was illegal, but what was legal. "Here in the United States, there are loopholes that only wealthy individuals and powerful corporations have access to," he said. "They have access to offshore accounts, and they are gaming the system. Middle-class families are not in the same position to do this. In fact, a lot of these loopholes come at the expense of middle-class families, because that lost revenue has to be made up somewhere."

The U.S. government had made some strides at trying to fix the problem. In 2010, Congress passed the Foreign Account Tax Compliance Act, known as FATCA, which, beginning four years later, required foreign financial institutions to report the holdings of U.S. clients upon request. To avoid being shut out of U.S. markets, foreign banks began to ask their American account holders if they were reporting to the IRS.

A month after the publication of the Panama Papers, the U.S. Treasury announced new rules for banks to govern how much information they needed to collect from their customers who used offshore companies to open accounts. The administration's actions had failed to live up to the president's lofty rhetoric. The rules had stalled for two years as the banking industry lobbied against them. Advocates charged that what now emerged from the process was a significant step backward.

Previously, U.S. banks had often tried to discover the actual owner of a company because they were worried about adverse consequences if the beneficiary was a terrorist or a criminal. They might not have written down the information but they knew it. Now the Treasury Department gave them permission not to know. Banks had to investigate the individual behind the company only if the person owned more than 25 percent. It also allowed the banks to stop their inquiry at the lawyer or intermediary.

A week after the first raid on Mossfon's headquarters, Caraballo conducted a similar operation on a warehouse where the firm stored hard copies of its documents. Investigators carried out bags of shredded documents, which the firm's spokesman described as trash destined for a recycler. After the bags were confiscated, they were piled onto an open flatbed truck. As the truck sped through a neighborhood near the warehouse, several of the bags flew off, bursting open and showering the streets with shredded confidential documents. Later that day, *La Prensa* reporters went door-to-door in the neighborhood collecting scraps of paper to see what the bags contained. What they found was already in the database.

BY THE END of the Panama Papers project, Mar Cabra had started meditating, eating properly, and exercising. She felt like she had finally found the right work-life balance. The project's success had also energized her, and she reconsidered her departure. While Ryle and

Walker had gone as far as to interview someone to replace her, when Cabra made no move to leave, they let the matter drop. Ryle secretly hoped she had changed her mind. He opted not to jinx it by raising the matter again.

In the beginning of May, Cabra spoke at the annual Neo4J conference, GraphConnect, in London. Neo4J was the open-source database system that underpinned Linkurious and much of what ICIJ did to make the leaked data accessible to journalists and the public. The conference attracted more than seven hundred techies. Cabra was now a veteran of speaking at journalism conferences, but this was the largest audience before which she had ever appeared. Two-thirds of the way through her presentation, she made a special announcement. ICIJ was going to put a database of all of Mossfon's companies online later that week. The crowd burst into spontaneous applause. Cabra smiled, thinking to herself, perhaps this is a bit of what it feels like to introduce a new iPhone.

ICIJ had already put the structured data for Offshore Leaks—the company names, shareholders, directors, addresses, and other information—online following that project. Now, they planned to add Mossfon's material. While in many cases, details on the actual owner of the company were not available, with the addition of the information from the Mossfon files, the database would contain more than 360,000 names of people and companies with links to more than two hundred countries and territories.

It was the largest collection in history of offshore companies and the people behind them. Thanks to Linkurious, users of the interactive database could visually see the connections among the companies, foundations, and trusts and the people involved in them. It allowed one to trace the role of banks, law firms, and accountants in setting up companies for the very wealthy.

For years, governments had debated fruitlessly over how much of this information should be made public. ICIJ had rendered the argument moot. It was making the information available for free. Government investigators, law firms pursuing claims, academics, the interested public—anybody could download the database or search on ICIJ's app.

Many of the tax havens and company incorporation hot spots had public-facing databases but they often charged for access or were difficult to navigate. In the months to come, ICIJ would receive leaks of the "public" databases of a number of these tax havens. They would throw this information into the database as well, augmenting it by many hundreds of thousands of companies.

For Mossack and Fonseca, this was the gravest betrayal of all. They had promised their customers secrecy, which they preferred to view as "privacy." Since they had convinced themselves that the vast majority of their customers were using companies legitimately, albeit sometimes to stretch tax laws, the disclosure of information about their activities was a gross violation of what they termed a human right to privacy. Even Rita Vásquez at *La Prensa* questioned the publication of the database. ICIJ made sure to have prominent disclaimers on its app to underscore that owning an offshore company was not illegal or an indication of criminal activity. Nonetheless, Vásquez feared that everybody found in the database would be tarred by being placed alongside the worst abusers of the system.

Three days before the release of the database, John Doe reemerged. When ICIJ's Rigoberto Carvajal named the Mossfon project Prometheus, he thought hard about John Doe. Prometheus stole fire from the gods to benefit humanity. As punishment, Zeus chained him to a rock in the Caucasus Mountains where day and night giant eagles tore at his liver. To the gods, he was a criminal and a thief; to humans, a hero. Carvajal worried that John Doe might suffer a similar fate of destruction, one experienced by so many whistle-blowers, for the selfless act of leaking a database that could have been sold for millions of dollars.

"I do not work for any government or intelligence agency, directly or as a contractor, and I never have," wrote John Doe.

An understanding of the material and the scale of the injustices contained therein is what motivated the leak. Mossfon knowingly and repeatedly violated myriad laws worldwide, John Doe asserted, noting Jürgen Mossack's misleading declaration in the Nevada court as an example. Mossfon's "founders, employees and clients should have to answer for their roles in these crimes, only some of which have come to light thus far," John Doe said.

The worst harm, John Doe seemed to suggest, was that Mossfon and the system within which it operated encouraged the growth of income inequality, "one of the defining issues of our time." It was a system that had led to "society's progressively diseased and decaying moral fabric." The firm had not worked in a vacuum, he observed: "It found allies and clients at major law firms in virtually every nation."

John Doe expressed willingness to cooperate with law enforcement to the extent possible. Since "whistleblowers and activists in the United States and Europe have had their lives destroyed by the circumstances they find themselves in after shining a light on obvious wrongdoing," that cooperation might be minimal.

But stopping the criminal behavior would be difficult as long as whistle-blowers were singled out for punishment because they had the guts to reveal what the powerful wanted to keep secret from the public. John Doe mentioned Edward Snowden, UBS's Bradley Birkenfeld, and the Lux Leaks whistle-blower Antoine Deltour, whom Luxembourg was hell-bent on convicting, along with the journalist Edouard Perrin, no matter how many trials it took.

"Until governments codify legal protections for whistleblowers into law, enforcement agencies will simply have to depend on their own resources or on-going global media coverage for documents," wrote John Doe.

The borderlines of the secrecy world, the distance between what is hidden and the public's right to know, was shifting quickly. "We live in a time of inexpensive, limitless digital storage and fast internet connections that transcend national boundaries," the anonymous leaker wrote. "It doesn't take much to connect the dots: from start to finish, inception to global media distribution, the next revolution will be digitized."

18

THE SECRECY WORLD ENTERS
THE WHITE HOUSE

The workday was just beginning in Turkey when Mehmet Ali Yalçındağ reached the nation's president by phone. Yalçındağ was calling from Trump Tower in Midtown Manhattan, where it was past midnight—the end of a long Election Night in November 2016. Yalçındağ had come to the hulking black skyscraper with the oversize gold letters above the entrance to show support for his business partner Donald J. Trump—on a night few but the true believers expected the brash real estate tycoon to emerge as the next president of the United States.

Despite a majority of the electorate viewing him unfavorably, the stars aligned for Trump: Mainstream Republicans, Democrats, and the media stumbled on how to handle an unconventional candidate. Trump faced a flawed and unpopular opponent in Hillary Clinton, who misread the electorate and ran a poor campaign. FBI director James Comey broke with precedent and inserted himself into the election, parceling out negative judgments and suggestive details on what turned out to be a fruitless Clinton email investigation. And Russian president Vladimir Putin launched a massive cyber-attack on the United States in an attempt to influence the outcome.

The Kremlin-backed attack included hacking the email server of the Democratic National Committee, flooding social media with fake news, and attempts to compromise individual state election databases. According to a declassified intelligence assessment, Putin targeted Democrats and the U.S. electoral system in part because he was furious over the Russian revelations contained in the Panama Papers. The details about the illicit cash flows swirling around the Russian leader had filled newspapers and news broadcasts worldwide. Putin blamed the damaging data leak on the Obama administration.

However, Putin's tilt toward Trump appeared to have been motivated by something deeper than a desire for revenge against Hillary Clinton and the Obama administration. Putin and Trump shared a similar zero-sum worldview and a penchant for operating in the shadows. Each man viewed the idea of a free press with contempt. They both believed that financial interests should be passed down to their children to create family dynasties. For years, Russian money helped keep Trump's business empire afloat. He and his campaign staffers maintained multiple business connections with Russian oligarchs closely allied to Putin.

Trump and Putin were also both conversant with the secrecy world, practiced hands at using anonymous companies to wall off their activities and keep their business affairs secret. During the campaign, Trump reported that he had 378 individual Delaware companies, but the full extent of his business dealings remained hidden. Trump was the first presidential candidate in forty years not to release his tax returns.

Though Donald Trump did not personally interact with Mossack Fonseca, the Trump Organization engaged in real estate transactions with Panama-based Mossfon companies as early as 1994. Real estate developers, buyers, and sellers have long operated in the secrecy world. Trump and his associates were no different. The Panama Papers reveal at least nine of his foreign business partners had connections to Mossfon. Several of Trump's business partners who used the secrecy world allegedly mixed legitimate businesses with illegal activities such as prostitution, bribery, and tax evasion. When asked about such allegations, Trump claimed ignorance.

Alexander Shnaider and Eduard Shyfrin, who developed the

Trump hotel in Toronto through a Guernsey company, conducted much of their business offshore and are shareholders of at least five companies in the Mossfon files. One company, Midland Resources Holding Limited, sold at least half of its shares in a steel plant to a collection of offshore companies acting as fronts for the Russian state-controlled bank Vnesheconombank, or VEB. The deal occurred as the developers battled cost overruns and delays on the condo-hotel development, which, like so many other Trump projects, ended in lawsuits and recriminations.

In his campaign and administration, Trump surrounded himself with people who were connected to the Panama Papers data. Trump's son-in-law, Jared Kushner, received financing from the Steinmetz family, who used multiple Mossfon companies and HSBC bank accounts. Kushner also did a $295 million real estate deal with Lev Leviev, an Israeli oligarch known as the "Diamond King," who had at least three Mossfon companies and a trust. Leviev was a business partner of Russian-owned Prevezon Holdings, which was implicated in the Magnitsky case, an alleged $230 million theft by Russian mobsters. Prevezon's assets were frozen by U.S. prosecutors while they investigated money laundering in the case. After the firing of U.S. Attorney Preet Bharara, the Trump Department of Justice abruptly settled with Prevezon for $5.9 million.

Trump's campaign chairman, Paul Manafort, had business relationships with two Russian oligarchs—gas billionaire Dmitry Firtash and metals magnate Oleg Deripaska, a confidant of Vladimir Putin—both of whom had offshore companies with the Panamanians. Sebastian Gorka, former deputy assistant to the president, appears to have written to the law firm in 1992 about a company he was researching for his employer. Mossfon provided Gorka with information on the company and then invoiced him $125. Gorka refused to pay, insisting that the inquiry had been "on a casual basis," and no fee had been discussed. Mossack did not pursue payment.

At Trump Tower on Election Night, Yalçındağ handed his cell phone to the new president-elect. Turkey's president, Recep Tayyip Erdoğan, thus became the first world leader to congratulate a still-stunned Donald Trump on his victory. Trump had spent the final hours of the evening glued to the television, in near silence. According to an account of the conversation between Trump and Erdoğan, procured by the Turkish journalist Amberin Zaman, the president-elect referred to Yalçındağ as his "close friend" and told Erdoğan that Yalçındağ was "your great admirer."

Trump's support was a fortuitous stroke for Yalçındağ, who was desperate to be in the Turkish president's good graces. Erdoğan had attacked his family's company, Doğan Holding, a sprawling financial empire with significant Turkish media and oil interests, several of which had Mossfon connections. Erdoğan's government had pursued Doğan over allegations of massive tax evasion and critical media coverage, levying billions of dollars in fines against the conglomerate.

Trump had long made a practice of consorting with dodgy characters for financial gain. News organizations reported that in New Jersey and New York he regularly conducted business with people connected to the Mafia. He had leased the site for his first casino from two men with Mob ties. Building unions known to be controlled by the Mob continued to service Trump's worksites, even when they went on strike elsewhere. Suffering no ill consequences for his sketchy associations, Trump doubled down when he was later forced to transform his business.

By the mid-1990s, Trump's bankruptcies and penchant for civil lawsuits dried up funding from most U.S. banks. He moved away from developing properties himself, focusing instead on selling his brand and seeking revenue abroad. He now licensed "signature" developments that bore his name and were built to his precise specifications. In the case of hotels, the Trump Organization would often manage the property for a percentage of the revenue. Outside the United States, he became even less picky about the origins of the money that came his way.

Following the 2016 election, Trump's foreign business entanglements escalated to national security and constitutional concerns. While his business partners hoped to profit in new ways from their relationship with the president of the United States, it became increasingly difficult to determine whether the Trump administration's actions were in the public interest or in pursuit of personal gain. At the same time, the White House, allied with a Republican Congress, pushed a new policy approach toward the secrecy world that better reflected their shared laissez-faire ideology.

During its eight years in office, the Obama administration had attempted to nudge government policy in the direction of increased transparency and oversight of the offshore system. In addition to signing the Foreign Account Tax Compliance Act in 2010, the administration tried to tamp down on states like Delaware, Nevada, and Wyoming that offered themselves as safe harbors for foreigners bent on tax evasion and criminal activity.

Faced with intense opposition from lawyers, bankers, and state officials, the Obama administration opted for baby steps to combat the problem. It passed a pilot project that forced real estate agents in Miami and New York to report the actual beneficial owners of property purchased with cash by an anonymous company, although the rule required only the names of those who owned 25 percent or more of the equity interest. In 2017, Treasury expanded the program. The Internal Revenue Service also issued a rule that foreign-owned limited liability companies based in the United States needed to obtain an Employee Identification Number (the corporate equivalent of a Social Security number, necessary for tax collection), to keep books and records available for inspection, and to designate a Responsible Person, who had control over the company.

Most important, the Obama administration had increased taxes on wealthy Americans. Trump and the Republican Party saw taxes, particularly on the wealthy, as theft by government edict to be eliminated whenever possible. Under Obama, efforts to increase funding for the resource-starved Internal Revenue Service, the frontline troops in the fight to stop Americans from evading taxes through the secrecy world, died in the face of Republican resistance. During the campaign, Trump praised himself for doing everything he could to escape paying taxes. When Clinton accused him of avoiding federal income tax for years, Trump responded, "That makes me smart."

Within weeks of Trump's inauguration, the new president and the Republican Congress signaled an end to Obama's approach to the secrecy world. In one of its first significant votes, Congress repealed an anticorruption measure that had forced oil, gas, and mining companies to file an annual report to the Securities and Exchange Commission detailing their payments to foreign governments where they did business. The intent of the original legislation had been to reduce bribery, and its abolition was a gift to the extractive industries that had helped fund the Republican Party's political campaigns through millions of dollars in contributions. The repeal could also benefit several of Trump's foreign business partners, who were heavily invested in the oil and mining industries.

Trump was already on record against efforts to tamp down on foreign corruption. In a phone-in appearance on CNBC in 2012, he called the Foreign Corrupt Practices Act, which forces U.S. companies to investigate the people with whom they do business to ensure that they are not cooperating with illegal activities, "a horrible law," which should be changed. "Every other country goes into these places and they do what they have to do," Trump said.

If American companies avoided bribery, "you'll do business nowhere," said Trump.

TRUMP WAS ALL smiles walking the red carpet at the Miss Universe pageant in Moscow in November 2013. His trip to Russia had gone amazingly well, even if Vladimir Putin was a no-show. The previous June, Trump had sounded like a besotted teenage girl when he speculated-via-tweet whether the Russian leader would attend. "Do you think Putin will be going to The Miss Universe Pageant in November in Moscow," Trump asked, "if so, will he become my new best friend?" Putin sent a decorative lacquered box and a personal note instead.

The real courtship, however, occurred on the sidelines. Trump's Russian business partners for the pageant were Aras and Emin Agalarov, a father-and-son team of billionaire real estate developers. Aras Agalarov was close to the Russian leader, having received Russia's Order of Honour the month before from Putin himself. During the trip, the Agalarovs and Trump discussed building matching apartment towers in Moscow.

In a meeting cohosted by Aras Agalarov, Trump met with a number of Russian oligarchs, including Putin's former economy minister Herman Gref, who ran Sberbank, Russia's largest state-controlled bank. After the trip, Trump boasted to *Real Estate Weekly*, "I have a great relationship with many Russians, and almost all of the oligarchs were in the room."

Trump had been trying to break into the Russian real estate market since the 1980s. He and his first wife, Ivana, traveled to Moscow in 1987, looking for a site to build a luxury hotel in a joint venture with the Soviet hotel and tourism agency, but the deal never took off. In 1996 he tried again, this time a condominium project in partnership with U.S. tobacco executives, also a bust. Less than ten years later, he signed a deal with Bayrock Group, an investment fund with connections to Russia, Kazakhstan, and Turkey, to explore building a Trump Tower in Moscow.

While this Russia project, once again, failed to come to fruition, Bayrock and Trump did complete several other deals. In Bayrock, Trump had found a willing if unsavory partner, one with plenty of links to the secrecy world and Mossfon. If Trump couldn't bring his business to Russia, Bayrock made it possible for Russian and Eastern European money to flow to him instead.

Bayrock was headed by Tevfik Arif, a former economist in the Soviet Ministry of Commerce and Trade. In a time when government officials and gangsters in the Eastern Bloc were carving up public goods, Tevfik and his brother Refik acquired the Aktyubinsk Chromium Chemicals Plant in Kazakhstan, a major producer of the chemical. (Chromium is an important component in steel products.) Tevfik Arif had business partnerships with Fettah Tamince, a relative of President Erdoğan, who owned the Turkish luxury hotel chain Rixos and maintained at least four Mossfon companies, some with interlocking shareholders. Arif had also branched out to America, redeveloping condominiums and a waterfront shopping center in Sheepshead Bay, Brooklyn.

In April 2000, Bayrock Holdings S.A. incorporated in the Bahamas, after which Arif established Bayrock companies in Delaware, Florida, and New York. He based Bayrock's operations out of the twenty-fourth floor of Trump Tower on Fifth Avenue. In the years before the 2008 financial crisis, Bayrock was awash in cash. When it needed more, money would magically appear. It was sent by his brother, according to a lawsuit filed in federal court in New York. Tevfik's brother Refik was based in Turkey, and his business interests ran through numerous Mossack Fonseca companies.

There were more than twenty-five companies connected to the Arif family in the Mossfon files, conducting a wide variety of business—everything from leasing private aircraft to selling chemicals to investing in real estate. The Arifs had operated in the secrecy world since at least 1996, creating layers of structures, with a Mossfon shell company even holding rights over Ravana, the Arif family foundation. Offshore companies tied to the family's primary business organization, the Doyen Group, were also linked to corruption in international soccer.

One of Bayrock's top employees was a former stockbroker and convicted felon named Felix Sater. Russian-born and Brooklyn-raised, Sater had served time for shoving a broken margarita glass into the face of a fellow patron in a barroom fight. After his release, he was involved in a Mafia-related $40 million pump-and-dump penny stock fraud in 1998. He managed to evade serious consequences for the crimes by turning confidential informant for the government. When questioned about Sater, Trump, who had traveled with him on at least one business trip, claimed to barely know him.

Trump joined forces with Bayrock in 2005, offering a brand name behind which Arif's money could coalesce. Their best-known project was Trump SoHo, a forty-six-floor hotel-condominium in one of Manhattan's trendiest neighborhoods. Trump announced the project on his television show, *The Apprentice*, in 2006. For the use of his name and input, Trump received a 15 percent cut of sales, with another 3 percent parceled out to two of his children, Ivanka and Donald Jr.

In 2007, Arif cut a deal with Iceland's FL Group for $50 million in financing for Trump SoHo and three other Trump-related projects, in return for future profits. Trump signed a document agreeing to the arrangement. FL Group was an international investment company surfing the Icelandic financial mania. Its principal Icelandic shareholders spun off offshore companies like a pinwheel, a number of them through Mossfon. FL Group would go belly up when the financial crisis exposed the fraud and self-dealing behind Iceland's economic miracle. A search of FL Group in the Mossfon files leads to substantial loans from Icelandic banks, a profligate Icelandic supermarket chain, investments in India, and Kaupthing's largest debtor in Luxembourg. Iceland's special prosecutor Ólafur Hauksson charged the company's former CEO, Hannes Smárason, with embezzlement of about $22 million in corporate funds, but the businessman was acquitted at trial.

A civil suit against Bayrock filed by a former employee, Jody Kriss, speculated that some of the money behind FL Group was Russian in origin. Kriss alleged that Bayrock operated for years through "a pattern of continuous, related crimes, including mail, wire, and bank fraud; tax evasion; money laundering; conspiracy; bribery; extortion; and embezzlement." He further alleged that the FL Group's investment in the Trump SoHo project was in fact a sale disguised as a loan, to avoid paying approximately $20 million in taxes. Bayrock denied the allegations. Trump insisted he had nothing to do with the financing, lending only his name.

"I don't know who owns Bayrock," Trump said in a deposition in 2011, despite having signed a document that stated clearly that FL Group was helping to finance the project. "I never really understood who owned Bayrock."

Another apparent investor in Trump SoHo through Bayrock, according to a company investment pamphlet, was Alexander Mashkevich, a Russian billionaire who was part of a trio of shareholders behind Eurasian Natural Resources Corporation (ENRC), a conglomerate with far-flung interests ranging from mining to construction. A spokesperson for Mashkevich says the billionaire never invested in Trump SoHo or Bayrock. The mining mogul was also close to Kazakhstan's president-for-life Nursultan Nazarbayev, whose grandson and other relatives had their own Mossfon companies. In 2011, the three principals behind ENRC—Mashkevich, Patokh Chodiev, and Alijan Ibragimov—were accused in Belgium of money laundering. The charges were subsequently dropped when they agreed to pay a settlement for an undisclosed sum without admitting wrongdoing.

ENRC had deep ties with Mossfon, dating to at least 2003, having connected with the law firm through a trust company in Guernsey in the Channel Islands. Some of ENRC's companies were involved in mining in Congo. In West Africa ENRC was implicated in a bribery investigation of the Israeli diamond magnate Dan Gertler, who also had Mossfon companies and HSBC Swiss bank accounts. Gertler denies any wrongdoing.

In 2014, the Guernsey intermediary, St. Peter's Trust, attempted to move fifteen ENRC companies directly to Mossfon. The law firm's compliance department reviewed the matter and discovered the companies were related to ENRC Limited, a joint venture between the trio of investors and the Kazakh government. All the people involved were PEPs. And ENRC had recently been delisted from the London stock exchange after a massive share price drop when investors bailed after a controversial mining deal with the Congolese president. The company faced multiple criminal investigations over corruption allegations in Kazakhstan and Africa. These were too many red flags, even for Mossfon. "Due to the adverse results found in the course of our investigations, the decision is, do not accept these companies under our administration," wrote one of the firm's compliance officers.

Trump SoHo was star-crossed from the start. The building site, it turned out, was on the grounds of a former African Methodist Episcopal church, and during construction, workers unearthed the bones of those buried in the churchyard, causing delays as those remains were disinterred and moved. A worker died on the job when he fell forty-two stories and was decapitated.

Before completion, Trump lied about how quickly the nearly four hundred units were selling, claiming the project had received thirty-two hundred applications when in fact only about sixty apartments had found buyers by the time the building opened in April 2010. Ivanka also fabricated sales figures, publicly stating that 60 percent of the units had sold. Angry buyers filed lawsuits alleging that the sales figures had been inflated. In a settlement in 2011, a number of the buyers received 90 percent of their deposits back. The developers had sold fewer than a third of the units by 2014, forcing the building into foreclosure where it was sold at auction.

Among the buyers for Trump SoHo condos were a family from Kazakhstan, the Khrapunovs, who in 2013 purchased three apartments for $3.1 million. The family is accused by the Kazakh city of Almaty of buying U.S. real estate through anonymous shell companies in order to launder hundreds of millions of dollars that Viktor Khrapunov allegedly stole while mayor of the city. The Khrapunovs deny the charges and claim they are dissidents, persecuted politically by the country's authoritarian ruler, President Nursultan Nazarbayev. The Khrapunov family also had control over several Mossfon companies that held property in Kazakhstan.

The Khrapunovs' son is married to the daughter of Mukhtar Ablyazov, a Kazakh oligarch accused, along with associates, of misappropriating $6 billion from the BTA Bank. While chairman of BTA, Ablyazov allegedly lent billions to shell companies that never paid the money back. On its website, BTA lists more than 786 offshore companies in which Ablyazov had an interest. Scores of these companies appear to be in the Mossfon files.

A few months after Trump SoHo opened, Tevfik Arif and the ENCR trio were aboard the *Savarona*, a 450-foot rented yacht, when Turkish police raided the boat because they suspected their involvement in prostitution. The men were accompanied by nine women between the ages of eighteen and twenty-three. Police had been surveilling Arif and his associates for months as they procured women, some as young as fifteen, for sex parties. All the men involved denied criminal intent. None of the girls agreed to testify. Prosecutors dropped the case.

Several years after the prostitution sting, Zamin Ferrous Limited, a Mossfon company whose director was one of Tevfik Arif's sons, sued ENRC over the disposition of $220 million that was tied up in a Brazilian mining deal. The two sides settled two years later.

In addition to the Trump SoHo, Bayrock also built what was to be called the Trump International Hotel and Tower Fort Lauderdale. Trump has a number of branded properties in the Sunshine State. The Fort Lauderdale project met a similar fate to the Trump SoHo. After the

2008 financial crisis, the developer stopped paying Trump, and the real estate mogul stepped away from the 298-unit condo-hotel. Lawsuits followed. The property defaulted on a $139 million loan, the bank foreclosed, and it was sold at auction.

Trump-branded properties in Florida found many customers among Russians. According to an analysis by Reuters, at least sixty-three individuals with Russian passports or addresses purchased almost $100 million's worth of properties in buildings that carried his name. A number of the buyers had Mossfon companies, including Andrey Truskov, the cofounder and principal of Absolute Group, LLC, one of the largest banks in Russia, with close ties to Putin.

Russians were such frequent buyers of condos in the Trump Ocean Club in Panama—a resort for which Donald Trump lent his name and had an operating agreement—that the sales force contracted with Mossfon for Russian translation services. The developer, Roger Khafif, used the firm for other matters as well. At one point in 2008, he asked Mossfon whether it had any experience getting visas for Iranians, since there were buyers with Iranian passports who were residents of the UK and wanted to purchase in Panama.

No single Florida real estate deal benefited Trump as directly as the sale of a Palm Beach mansion to the Russian billionaire Dmitry Rybolovlev. In 2004, Trump had purchased the spread in a bankruptcy auction for $41.4 million. He flipped the mansion to the oligarch four years later for $95 million. Rybolovlev probably never set foot inside the house. A few months after buying the property the billionaire became embroiled in a nasty divorce. Rybolovlev had several companies with Mossfon, which he insisted were for family planning purposes. His estranged wife claimed the structures were used to hide assets in the couple's divorce.[543] After the couple reached an undisclosed settlement, plans were approved to tear down the mansion.

As EARLY AS 2013, Mossfon knew key details about Anar Mammadov, a thirty-three-year-old businessman from Azerbaijan. Mossfon's compliance department ran Mammadov's name through World-Check, a paid database the firm employed to ascertain if its customers were sought by Interpol or mired in negative media coverage. The law firm possessed a copy of his passport. Mammadov provided signed Source of Wealth Declarations that revealed he was a PEP, a relative of an Azerbaijani public official, and even described the business expectations of his offshore entities, which were to hold property and for investment purposes.

Mossfon's due diligence showed that Anar's father was Ziya Mammadov, Azerbaijan's minister of transport. It also dredged up unflattering news articles. Anar Mammadov had become a billionaire off transportation concessions, public construction projects, and oil exploration. He claimed to have founded one of the country's most successful commercial development companies while he was still a teenager. The company, which was likely a front for his father, experienced explosive growth while Anar was studying full-time at the University of London. The Mammadov family specialized in no-bid state contracts and monopolies, and it owned Azerbaijan's largest taxi and bus companies.

The clips revealed that Anar did not appreciate journalists poking into his affairs. Azerbaijan consistently ranks at the bottom of press freedom indexes, and journalists there are beaten, imprisoned, and killed with regularity. Anar had sued two Azerbaijani opposition newspapers over their coverage. When reporters tried to take photos of luxury villas owned by Ziya Mammadov and other family members, they were stopped, their cameras were confiscated, and they were interrogated for three hours.

Ziya Mammadov "is notoriously corrupt even for Azerbaijan," a U.S. diplomat observed in a classified cable in 2009.

Given the brazen kleptocrats running Azerbaijan, the cable's claim for Mammadov's exceptional status was extraordinary. Situated north of Iran on the Caspian Sea, Azerbaijan once formed a strategic part of the Soviet Union. In 1969, Soviet premier Leonid Brezhnev appointed Heydar Aliyev, a top KGB official, to the post of First Secretary of the Central Committee of Azerbaijan's Communist Party. Aliyev would stay in power for two decades until Mikhail Gorbachev removed him over corruption allegations. When the Soviet Union collapsed, Azerbaijan gained its independence and became an oil-rich republic. After its first president was deposed in a coup, Aliyev slipped back into power. In October 2003, two months after his death, his son Ilham Aliyev won the election to replace him. The younger Aliyev then proceeded to coast from one overwhelming electoral victory to another. Such was the extent of the fraud that in 2013, the Azerbaijani election commission mistakenly released election results, the day before actual voting began.

Mossfon was undoubtedly well acquainted with Aliyev's corrupt petro-state, as the Azerbaijani leader's children owned Mossfon companies. Aliyev's daughters, Leyla and Arzu, controlled large chunks of the country's economy, including a bank, a phone company monopoly, a gold mine, and a construction firm. Leyla Aliyev was married for nine years to Emin Agalarov, one of Trump's business partners in Russia. The sisters had also amassed more than $140 million in luxury properties around the world, purchased through two Mossfon companies. After almost a decade, in 2013, Mossfon resigned as registered agent from one company after the British intermediary who set it up refused to provide newly required due diligence documents. For another Mossfon company, the intermediary, the London law firm Child & Child, failed to identify the two women as PEPs.

In the case of Anar Mammadov, Mossfon followed procedures exactly. It knew who and what he was. Nonetheless, the firm decided to sell him several companies, through an intermediary based in Guernsey. They classified Mammadov as a PEP and ordered "Enhanced Due Diligence," which, in practice, meant little.

Donald Trump also counted Anar Mammadov as a business partner. In 2012, Trump signed a licensing agreement with Mammadov's company, Garant Holdings, for a luxury condominium-hotel to bear the real estate mogul's name. The thirty-three-story building was already under construction in an isolated part of Baku, the capital of Azerbaijan. It was renamed the Trump International Hotel & Tower Baku. The project was publicly announced two years later in a company press release weighed down by superlatives:

"Trump International Hotel & Tower Baku represents the unwavering standard of excellence of The Trump Organization and our involvement in only the best global development projects," said Donald J. Trump, chairman and president of The Trump Organization. "When we open in 2015, visitors and residents will experience a luxurious property unlike anything else in Baku—it will be among the finest in the world."

Trump's people redesigned the building. He had the interior gutted and rebuilt to the organization's specifications. Ivanka Trump led the redesign. Reportedly, she personally approved every element from the wood paneling to the landscaping. Ivanka posted photos of herself on the job site wearing a hard hat, and produced a video extolling the project.

Unlike Mossfon, it is not clear if Trump did any due diligence on his Azerbaijani business partners. His spokesman has told reporters that Trump did a thorough vetting but declined to produce the due diligence documents or even say who undertook the review. Under the Foreign Corrupt Practices Act, Trump had a responsibility to investigate whether Anar Mammadov was getting his money illegally.

Allegations of bribery and corruption have long dogged Mammadov. During construction, contractors were apparently paid in sacks of cash. If Trump's team had looked closely, it would have found the WikiLeaks cable that details that the family was in bed with former elements of Iran's Revolutionary Guard. The cable revealed that Kamal Darvishi, a former general in Iran's Revolutionary Guard, had won at least eight major road construction and rehabilitation contracts in Azerbaijan from Ziya Mammadov. The diplomatic cable concluded, "We assume Mammadov is a silent partner in these contracts."

Trump and Mossfon were not the only ones to fall under the siren's sway of Anar Mammadov's money. Shortly before Mammadov signed his deal with Trump, he founded the Azerbaijan America Alliance, for which Dan Burton, a former Republican congressman from Indiana, acted as the front man. The Alliance spent more than $12 million showering cash on politicians in Washington, lobbying for them to be friendly to Azerbaijan. It held gala dinners attended by Speaker of the House John Boehner and met privately with Senator John McCain and House minority leader Nancy Pelosi. With the avalanche of money came fulsome praise for the corrupt and autocratic regime from both Democrats and Republicans in Congress.

When Azerbaijan's oil economy crashed in 2015, the party ended. The Azerbaijan America Alliance folded up shop, and Burton never received his final year's salary. Construction on Trump's Baku tower ceased. When he ran for president, Trump removed the project from his website. He would disclaim responsibility for anything having to do with the project, insisting that he had only licensed his name to it. The still-unfinished building remained an empty eyesore in Baku, the Trump moniker displayed prominently on its front.

WHEN TRUMP SPOKE with Turkish president Erdoğan on Election Night, he put in a plug for Ivanka. She was a big fan and supporter of Erdoğan, Trump told the Turkish president. On the call, he credited his daughter with the success of Trump's Turkey project, for which he had licensed his name.

Ivanka had been by her father's side when Trump Towers in Istanbul was dedicated in April 2012. The day before, Erdoğan had cut a ceremonial ribbon officially opening the building. The conjoined forty-story office and residential towers featured apartments, upscale shops, fitness areas, swimming pools, and a movie theater. "I was very excited when I met Mehmet Ali Yalçındağ and began to discuss this project four years ago," Ivanka Trump told Turkish media at the time. Donald Trump described the Doğan family, into which Yalçındağ had married, as "beyond partners . . . they've become very good friends."

During the U.S. election campaign, Erdoğan said he regretted coming to the building's opening ceremony and called for removing Trump's name from the towers because the U.S. presidential candidate had "no tolerance for Muslims in America." It appeared to be yet another example of the fraught relationship between the Turkish leader and the Doğan family.

The family patriarch, Aydın Doğan, had thrived for years by

playing political forces in Turkey off each other, primarily through his media holdings, particularly its daily newspaper *Hürriyet* and television channels CNN Türk and Kanal D. The conglomerate owned more than a dozen media properties in addition to real estate, financial services, and energy interests. He tried the same tactic against Erdoğan's AKP political party. Some of Doğan's media properties had attacked the AKP prior to the 2007 presidential elections, which the party won. Once Erdoğan consolidated single-party rule in Turkey, the strategy that had served Doğan so well in the past became a major liability.

In 2009, Doğan Holding was hit with a $2.5 billion fine for unpaid taxes, almost the company's entire value. Doğan publications also came under attack and intimidation, including calls for boycotts and physical assaults on journalists. In March 2016, the Turkish state prosecutor indicted Doğan and forty-six associates for criminal tax evasion that allegedly occurred between 2001 and 2007, when they were owners of Petrol Ofisi, a fuel distribution company.

Petrol Ofisi International Oil Trading Limited had been incorporated in the Bahamas in 2000 by a Jersey trust company. It was originally called Lysa Invest. Within a few years, the company moved to Mossfon. A report from Mossfon's London office on a meeting with Omer Iskefyeli, a director for the company who would later be indicted alongside Doğan, described the Petrol Ofisi Group as "the largest oil distribution company in Turkey with an annual turnover of £4 billion." One of the shareholders of the company, Mevlut Tufan Darbaz, was CEO of Doğan Holding.

The Bahamas company was one of several Mossfon companies connected to Doğan Holding. Three of Aydın Doğan's daughters had companies with the Panamanians, most of which went inactive in 2013, around the time that Erdoğan ratcheted up pressure on the family. One company that remained active, Glendoon Limited, was based in the Akara Building in the BVI. On a Source of Funds declaration, its principal beneficiary was listed as Imre Barmanbek, the deputy chairman of Doğan Holding. According to the form, its purpose was financial investments in capital markets.

In the face of Erdoğan's pressure, Aydın Doğan stepped down from running the family business. His daughter Arzuhan Doğan took his place as chairman. Her husband, Mehmet Ali Yalçındağ, was named CEO. Hacked emails released by WikiLeaks show how Yalçındağ worked hard to ingratiate himself with Erdoğan. He did this primarily through a back channel leading to Berat Albayrak, Erdoğan's son-in-law and the minister of energy, who many in Turkey believe is being groomed to succeed the president. The emails show that Yalçındağ tried to censor stories critical of Erdoğan in the Doğan media. In one of the emails, Yalçındağ described an anchor of his television station, CNN Turk, as "an enemy." Another email revealed that someone from a Turkish media organization forwarded to the energy minister a complete list of Turks and their companies found in the Panama Papers database that ICIJ has posted online.

Despite denying that he had written the emails, the WikiLeaks release forced Yalçındağ to resign from his position in the Doğan company. Erdoğan's relentless campaign against journalists in Turkey continued. As of August 2017, the Turkish government had arrested more than two hundred journalists and media workers. In the United States, Yalçındağ's business partner–turned–U.S. president, Donald Trump, also declared war on journalists and the media, castigating them as purveyors of "fake news."

EPILOGUE

Ramón Fonseca sat in his corner office in the Mossfon building in Panama City. It was early December 2016, eight months after the publication of the Panama Papers. Evidence of the firm's demise was all around him—in the empty offices throughout the building's warren-like interior, the packing boxes that cluttered his work space. The Mossack Fonseca sign by the building's entrance, which graced hundreds of television news reports, had been removed. After decades of existence, Mossfon was going out of business.

In the wake of the leak, the partners' original idea was to sell the firm to their employees. But by year's end there wasn't enough left to make a sale viable. The firm shuttered its asset management business, MAMSA. Government investigations and a decline in revenue forced the firm to close offices around the world, starting with Jersey, Gibraltar, and Wyoming. The firm was also forced to lay off more than a hundred employees.

Another cruel blow came in November, when the British Virgin Islands fined the firm $440,000 for lax internal controls, by far the largest sanction the country had ever levied. The Panama Papers had hit the BVI hard. Company incorporations in the jurisdiction dropped 30 percent during the first six months of 2016, compared to the previous year. The Financial Services Commission temporarily installed a monitor over Mossfon's BVI operations. The firm's focus switched from incorporating companies to performing due diligence on existing ones. In the sky blue Akara Building, the jewelry store the Flax family ran on the ground floor saw more customers than the suite of Mossfon offices upstairs.

Fonseca reminisced about the backwater he encountered in 1986, and how the arrival of Mossfon changed the BVI's fortunes. "They should build a statue to me instead of fining us," he said indignantly.

In Geneva, UBS sent a letter to Adrian Simon notifying him that it was closing Mossfon's bank account. The Geneva office had been a customer of UBS since the days of Antoni Guerrero in the 1990s. After some effort, Simon scheduled a meeting with his bankers. He was told that this was now a reputational issue for UBS; the bank had no choice but to terminate the relationship. The hypocrisy astounded Simon. He pointed out that UBS still had offshore companies registered with Mossfon. It didn't matter.

Paul Singer and his lawyers were not through with Mossfon in Nevada. What began with the theory of an Argentinean prosecutor in 2013 about Nevada companies laundering money for Lázaro Báez had spurred Elliott Management to file suit in Las Vegas and target Mossfon. In the end, no connection between Mossfon's Nevada companies and Báez was found, nor was any link discovered between the companies and Argentinean president Cristina Fernández de Kirchner. After Mauricio Macri's election, the new Argentinean government settled the sovereign debt case with Elliott Management for $2.4 billion.

However, the Panama Papers revealed the lengths to which Mossfon had gone to thwart the hedge fund's inquiry. In May, Elliott Management sued the Panamanians in federal court in Las Vegas for obstruction of justice. It demanded to be reimbursed for the costs incurred while trying to wrest information from the firm. Mossfon's motion to dismiss was denied. The two sides entered settlement talks, but Mossfon appeared to have little money left to make a settlement worthwhile.

Toward the end of 2016, Panama's attorney general, Kenia Porcell, removed Javier Caraballo, the prosecutor investigating the firm. With a history of prosecuting drug traffickers rather than financial crime, Caraballo was ill equipped to understand the data he had confiscated from the Mossfon offices. In his stead, Porcell tapped Rómulo Bethancourt, one of the leaders of the organized crime division, who had a background investigating money laundering. Prosecutors quickly focused on the firm's connections to a massive corruption scandal emanating from Brazil known as Lava Jato, Portuguese for Operation Car Wash.

At its center was Brazilian construction company Odebrecht, which had literally institutionalized the practice of bribery. Odebrecht created a special department called "the Structured Operations Sector" to funnel cash to local officials at home and abroad in order to win giant public works contracts. It paid for the bribes through cost overruns on its other projects. The money transited offshore companies—held by bearer shares to maintain anonymity—and secret Swiss bank accounts. During almost a decade ending in 2014, the firm paid about $3.3 billion in bribes to secure more than one hundred contracts in a dozen countries.

Mossfon had created dozens of shell companies in places like the BVI and Nevada that were implicated in the Lava Jato corruption probe, which in addition to Odebrecht also included the Brazilian state oil company, Petrobras. Mossfon insisted that it had done little more than sell the companies to intermediaries, but Panamanian attorney general Porcell claimed the firm had been more actively involved. Prosecutors developed a theory that the law firm had worked with a local bank to launder money as part of the scheme, an accusation Mossfon strongly denied. This information had not been part of the Panama Papers revelations.

On the morning of February 9, 2017, officials of the public ministry searched the homes of Jürgen Mossack and Ramón Fonseca. The two partners were then called in for questioning. Outside the public ministry, Fonseca, unshaven, his face contorted in anger, gave an impromptu press conference.

"We have kept quiet but this Oldebrecht case is the limit," he declared.

Fonseca defended the firm, arguing that the bankers and lawyers to whom it sold companies were to blame. Much of the business Mossfon did was with international banks like HSBC, Fonseca continued, before adding that HSBC had gotten the firm into a lot of trouble. He observed that there are more than ten thousand offshore companies involved with Lava Jato—why are they singling us out? he asked.

When a reporter interrupted, Fonseca told her to wait, he was getting to the good part.

He then related how as a member of President Juan Carlos Varela's government, he had heard things that made him believe that the administration was corrupt. Varela himself had accepted campaign contributions from Odebrecht—all legally, the president would later counter. Odebrecht had a strong bribery operation in Panama. Why were Panamanian prosecutors targeting Mossfon and not the lawyers who worked directly with Odebrecht?

"May I be struck down by lightning if I'm lying," said Fonseca theatrically. "They are looking for a scapegoat."

He accused Varela of failing to defend the financial system in Panama. "We have dropped our pants before the international institutions," he said contemptuously.

Fonseca claimed to have proof about government malfeasance that he would release at a later date. His forehead pinched in a frown, Fonseca shouted repeatedly, "I love my country!" as he and the pack of reporters moved toward the door of the public ministry.

If Fonseca was hoping for a reaction, it came swiftly. He and Mossack as well as another lawyer from the firm were denied bail and tossed in jail. Deemed flight risks, they remained incarcerated for more than two months while prosecutors gathered evidence. The partners were released on April 24 on bail of half a million dollars each. Fonseca is convinced the length of their jail stay was due to his outburst.

For Mossack, who marked his sixty-ninth birthday behind bars, the experience was traumatic. Apart from a few traffic tickets, he had never had a brush with the law, he said. Now he was being treated like public enemy number one for something that he felt many other companies routinely did. "We were one of a couple of thousand out-fits that were doing the same thing," he insisted a few months after his release.

Fonseca, by contrast, became more circumspect, trying to keep a low profile. He claimed to be coming to terms with what happened. "I am slowly recovering my spirituality and inspiration," he said in July. His law firm, however, which had employed about six hundred people at its height, was down to a staff of eighty as it wound down its business.

But he also knew the storm had yet to break. Journalists continued to pick over the material. The *New York Times*, after facing withering questions over why it had not been part of the collaboration, had talked its way into the project in May 2016, a month after the initial stories were published. Everyone could now see the utility and bene-fits of collaboration. The *Times* also recognized it could use the data-base in the same way it approached the WikiLeaks cables, as a resource to flesh out and develop future stories.

Panama's Porcell met with her counterparts from Europe and else-where to discuss investigations into Mossfon's activities. Prosecutors launched cases against individuals located in the material ICIJ released. In Pakistan, the ownership of Prime Minister Muhammad Nawaz Sharif's family of pricey London real estate through offshore companies triggered a judicial investigation that in the summer of 2017 resulted in a Supreme Court decision to remove him from office. ICIJ's online database enabled Europol, the EU's version of Interpol, to identify nearly thirty-five hundred individuals and companies with probable matches to suspected criminals.

Within a few months of publication, the European Parliament set up an inquiry committee into the Panama Papers revelations. For the next year, the committee held hearings probing every aspect of the offshore business. Once again, Eva Joly was a prominent member of the investigation.

GERARD RYLE DID not enjoy the euphoria from leading history's big-gest and most successful journalistic collaboration for very long. The financial difficulties of its parent, the Center for Public Integrity, had leached down to ICIJ. Ryle faced the prospect of serious budget cuts, even layoffs of employees. Then, in the summer of 2016, while on vacation in Australia, he learned there was a plan afoot to fire him.

Relations between Ryle and CPI's CEO, Peter Bale, had worsened after the publication of the Panama Papers. Bale had countered ICIJ's proposal for autonomy with one that offered little in return. It was not long before the two men had taken an active dislike toward each other. Two months after the release of the Panama Papers, the *New York Times* published a story about the financial woes of the two organizations. The *Times* noted the irony that despite the recent Panama Papers triumph, ICIJ was forced to part ways with three contract journalists and forgo three other budgeted positions. In the article, Bale accused his predecessor of saddling him with a deficit, which Bill Buzenberg denied.

By this point, relations between Bale and Ryle had deteriorated to the point where one of them had to go. The board began discussions about firing Ryle. It even interviewed a potential replacement. When Buzenberg and CPI's founder, Charles Lewis, found out, they were stunned. On August 24, Lewis sent an email to the board, from both him and Buzenberg, with the subject: "Wrong Solution to the Wrong Problem." It was "unfathomable" and defied "logic and credulity" that the board was "now seriously considering the termination of the immensely respected Director of ICIJ, Gerard Ryle," they wrote, after Ryle and his staff had "brought global acclaim and accolades to the Center/ICIJ." The two men warned the board that if it fired Ryle, the story would be huge news around the world. The biggest loser would be CPI "for its significant, suddenly quite public, potentially organization-ending missteps and misjudgments."

The ICIJ staff made it clear that they would quit en masse if Ryle was dismissed. Two major international funders to ICIJ, one of which also contributed to the CPI, also weighed in with their disapproval. The board eventually backed down, but the damage was done. From that point on, ICIJ's independence from CPI was a foregone conclusion. And on October 20, 2016, the two organizations issued a joint press release that CPI would spin off ICIJ.

Ryle, Marina Walker, and Mar Cabra spent the next several months standing up an entirely new organization, securing a fiscal sponsor and pledges from funders. It would take four more months of legal wrangling over intellectual property and funding before the divorce was finalized. The process sped up considerably after it was announced on November 15 that Bale was leaving CPI. The board's hand was forced after the CPI staff rebelled in the wake of the separation announcement. A new CEO, John Dunbar, the center's well-respected deputy director, was appointed to replace Bale.

On February 27, 2017, ICIJ officially went independent. Less than two months later, the organization's Panama Papers investigation was awarded the Pulitzer Prize for Explanatory Journalism and was also named a finalist in the International Reporting category.

"WE ARE NOT angels," Ramón Fonseca said from his emptying office in Panama City, "but we are not devils either."

Mossfon's founders know that the secrecy world that made them wealthy men continues to thrive. Even before the publication of the Panama Papers, company incorporations and secret bank accounts were finding new homes in Dubai and Singapore in reaction to the increased due diligence in the BVI and the loss of bank secrecy in Switzerland. The only difference was that it now cost more.

In a letter published on the company's website in April 2017, titled "From the Horse's Mouth," Jürgen Mossack noted that company formations worldwide had diminished by about 30 percent in Panama and many other places. "However," he pointedly observed, in "jurisdictions such as Delaware, Nevada and others located in the United States, where virtually no Due Diligence is required . . . incorporations are thriving."

AFTERWORD TO THE PAPERBACK EDITION

For weeks, the assassin spied on the occupants of the honey-colored house with the blue gate. In the early hours of October 16, 2017, he made his move. His objective, a gray Peugeot 108, was parked outside the gate. There was no need to jump the low wall encircling the property to plant the bomb.

Later that morning, Daphne Caruana Galizia and her son, Matthew, sat opposite each other at the dining room table, typing on their respective laptops. Matthew, a data journalist with the International Consortium of Investigative Journalists, was working on the final phase of ICIJ's Panama Papers sequel, codenamed "Athena." Daphne, as all in Malta knew her, was writing yet another in a series of blog posts accusing the prime minister's chief of staff, Keith Schembri, of corruption related to Pilatus, a Maltese bank.

Over nine years, in some twenty thousand posts, Daphne's blog, *Running Commentary*, had held the country's powerful to account in acid prose. During its tenure, the blog produced numerous scoops, including the news of the Panama Papers investigation. *Running Commentary* was gossipy, scalding, censorious, and frequently hyperbolic. Through a mix of freewheeling commentary and investigative journalism,

Daphne accused Malta's leaders of everything from money laundering to adultery, chronicling and exposing the small island's transformation into what one European finance official derisively called "the
Panama of Europe."

Daphne had been a battler her entire career, which included a stint
as the island's first bylined female columnist for a major newspaper.
Her pugnacious style met its perfect foil when the Labour government
took power in 2013. As a supporter of the opposition Nationalist Party,
Daphne was no fan of Labour, but her outrage grew as Prime Minister
Joseph Muscat quickly put the country up for sale. Daphne's disgust
soon encompassed the new leader of the Nationalist Party, whom she
accused of being implicated in a sex-trafficking and money-laundering
scandal.

Malta demonstrates how the secrecy world is a living, evolving
organism. When one avenue for hiding cash closes, a new one opens.
The Labour government and its lawyer-accountant enablers turned the
country into a European doorway for dirty money, just as a banking
crisis in Cyprus diminished that island's allure as a money-laundering
destination within the European Union. Malta's emergence as an outpost of the secrecy world underscored the resilience of the offshore
system and then became a call to action for the journalists seeking to
expose its abuses.

In its first seven months, the Labour government legalized the sale
of the country's passports. For less than a million dollars, one could buy
a Maltese passport and gain access to visa-free travel and banking
throughout the EU. Politically connected officials and businessmen from
Russia, Saudi Arabia, and the Philippines were among those to seize the
opportunity.

Daphne described the passport program as "super tacky," a vehicle for money laundering, and "financial heroin" for the Maltese government. Henley & Partners, the St. Kitts–based law firm that had
won the Maltese passport concession, threatened to sue Daphne for
libel over her frequent attacks, but not before first seeking permission
from the prime minister, according to a leaked email Daphne posted
on her blog. Daphne retaliated with a threat of her own: She would
take the Henley demand letters and use them to clean up after her

dog, she wrote on her blog. If the lawyers really pissed her off, she would then mail the letters back.

Offshore schemes inevitably need a bank to function. Malta had Pilatus. Henley's CEO had made the introduction between Prime Minister Muscat and Pilatus chairman and founder Ali Sadr Hasheminejad shortly after the prime minister was elected. Sadr, the son of an Iranian billionaire, held a St. Kitts passport courtesy of Henley & Partners. Chief of Staff Schembri then helped Pilatus get its Maltese banking license and in time would hold at least one account with the bank. After Pilatus received approval to operate, Muscat and Schembri, along with one of Malta's top money-laundering officials, attended Sadr's wedding at a luxury hotel in Florence, Italy.

Malta's passport buyers were steered to the bank, but the majority of the Pilatus capital came from the Azerbaijani elite. Major shareholders included the children of Premier Ilham Aliyev. The Azerbaijanis used Pilatus and a network of more than fifty shell companies to make secret investments throughout Europe. Azerbaijan's state-owned oil and gas company, SOCAR, also cut a deal with the Maltese government in 2015 to supply the island's gas for its power stations for a decade. On the selection committee was Brian Tonna, a local accountant who two years earlier had set up anonymous Mossack Fonseca companies for Schembri and a Labour energy minister. Tonna also deposited €100,000 into the chief of staff's Pilatus account. The money was to repay a loan, according to Schembri.

The publication of the Panama Papers offered an unprecedented insight into the wheeling and dealing of Malta's political class, prompting street protests on the island. In the wake of the revelations, Daphne archly observed that Muscat and his confederates had "hit the ground running" in 2013.

She then added another allegation: Egrant, a third Mossack Fonseca company created by Tonna, for which there was no listed beneficial owner, was secretly owned by Michelle Muscat, the wife of the prime minister. Daphne reported that Egrant had received $1 million from Ilham Aliyev's daughter. Muscat called the Egrant story "the biggest lie in Malta's political history." To date, her allegations have not been substantiated.

The prime minister seized on the scandal and called new elections. In June 2017, with Malta's economy booming, Muscat handily won reelection. Undaunted, Daphne continued to attract new tips. As the assassin crept toward the house, she was sitting on 680,000 leaked files that showed how Maltese consumers were paying substantially more than they should for their Azerbaijani gas.

Since the publication of the Panama Papers, Matthew Caruana Galizia could feel the cycle of allegations, heated rhetoric, and threats escalating around his mother. He had returned home in part out of concern for her safety.

At 2:35 p.m. on October 16, Daphne posted her final blog. It ended on a sour note. "There are crooks everywhere you look now," she wrote. "The situation is desperate."

Daphne had an appointment to sort out her finances at the local bank that afternoon. Her accounts had recently been frozen by a Maltese judge, a casualty from one of the forty-seven or so libel cases filed against her. Libel charges had become the weapon of choice of Malta's political and business class. Cases against Daphne accounted for about 90 percent of all the libel actions filed in Malta, according to her family.

Daphne's detractors had resorted to violence in the past. The family collie was found on the doorstep with its throat slit. Another dog was poisoned. A third, killed by shotgun. Once someone lit the front door afire. In 2005, a more serious arson attempt involved car tires filled with gasoline by the side of the house. The family was asleep inside. A tragedy was averted only because Matthew's brother Paul came home late that night and doused the flames. They then built the wall.

The attack on Daphne's bank account came courtesy of Christian Cardona, Malta's minister of the economy, and one of his aides. Daphne had taunted Cardona relentlessly for public drunkenness among other sins. One evening in January 2017, she published a "breaking news" story that Cardona and the aide were at that moment in a brothel in Germany, where they were guests of the German government for an economics conference.

Daphne had received a tip from inside the FKK Acapulco sex club outside of Düsseldorf, interrupting dinner at a pizza restaurant with her husband to take the call. A member of the Maltese diaspora happened to recognize Cardona, part of a group of informants Daphne playfully called her "international worldwide network of spies."

The source was close enough to identify the minister's tattoo in the shower room, Daphne wrote gleefully. She dubbed the ensuing scandal "Brothelgate." Daphne's initial post received almost 550,000 views, *Running Commentary*'s biggest audience for a single day. The minister vehemently denied the accusation that he and his aide had shared a prostitute, and he threatened to sue. Daphne responded with a blog post titled, "The drunken idiot is going to sue me when he knows full well that he was at the brothel and that all my details were correct."

Shortly before 3 p.m., Daphne left the house and walked to her car. Nearby was Alfred Degiorgio, the man who has been charged with placing explosives on the underside of the Peugeot. Using his disposable "burner" cell phone, Alfred called his brother George, whose job was to text a cell phone rigged to detonate the explosives. George awaited his brother's go-ahead from a cabin cruiser he owned called the *Maya* bobbing off Malta's Grand Harbour.

Over the years, police had charged the Degiorgio brothers with multiple crimes, ranging from possession of lock-picking tools to armed robbery and attempted murder, but they were always acquitted. We know about the calls and locations on October 16 because the police later triangulated their cell phones, a task made easier because the brothers used their personal cell phones concurrently with their burner phones, making their movements easy to track. That fateful morning, George, in a remarkable stumble, used his personal cell phone to buy more minutes for the burner phone so he could text the bomb trigger.

According to the police, Alfred's call to George disconnected quickly. When Daphne reached her car, she stopped, turned around, and went back into the house. She had forgotten her checkbook. Matthew and his mother shared a laugh over her forgetfulness.

When Daphne returned to the Peugeot. Alfred Degiorgio called his brother again. This time he kept the phone line open so George could hear what came next.

The car made it about one hundred meters down the road when George's text arrived. Eyewitnesses say Daphne survived the initial explosion but could not escape the vehicle. Seconds later the gas tank ignited, the fireball spreading body and car in pieces across an adjacent field. Matthew heard the explosion and ran barefoot to the scene where he saw the car aflame in the field and his mother's severed leg on the road.

A little more than a week after the assassination, ICIJ and its members published the results of the "Athena" project Matthew had been working on. Its public name: The Paradise Papers. The project was based on 1.4 terabytes of leaked data, almost half of which had been stripped from the corporate registries of nineteen offshore jurisdictions including Malta, the Bahamas, the Cook Islands, and Singapore. Many of the registries, while ostensibly public, were difficult or costly to access by outsiders.

Around 6.8 million files came from Appleby, a Bermuda-based offshore legal service provider. Appleby and its data were different from Mossack Fonseca and the Panama Papers. Whereas the upstart Panamanians were entrepreneurial risk-takers, their files filled with garrulously compromising emails, Appleby was the establishment. The firm had been founded in 1898 by Major Reginald Woodfield Appleby, who later became a commander of the Order of the British Empire. It boasted annual revenues of more than $100 million and membership in the elite trade group the Offshore Magic Circle. Appleby's correspondence was more circumspect than that of Mossack Fonseca, the leaked data incomplete and often in the form of spreadsheets.

After the Panama Papers, the offshore industry was willing to cut the Panamanians loose, casting them as outliers, a blemish on an otherwise law-abiding industry. And so the ICIJ and its partners felt a new focus was required. The story they now told explored a corruption that was systemic, where the scandal was what was legal. Unlike the Panamanians, Appleby worked with tens of thousands of Americans and top Fortune 500 companies—and still found time to create companies used by Ukrainian gangsters.

Appleby specialized in sophisticated corporate tax avoidance schemes—a lucrative business. By the end of 2016, some 322 Fortune 500 companies collectively held around $2.6 trillion offshore, which allowed them to avoid as much as $767 billion in U.S. federal taxes. The top destinations for U.S. multinationals to stash their cash were the Netherlands, Bermuda, Luxembourg, Ireland, Singapore, and Switzerland. In 2014, U.S.-controlled subsidiaries booked $96 billion in profits in Bermuda alone, an island with a GDP of just $6 billion.

The Appleby data showed how it was done. For example, the firm worked with the global sports brand Nike to route profits through limited partnerships in the Netherlands and subsidiaries in Bermuda. The various offshore strategies allowed Nike to avoid paying U.S. taxes on $12 billion in profits—legally.

Appleby also helped Apple reorganize its subsidiaries in a global tax avoidance shuffle. By 2018, the company had collected a staggering $269 billion in profits offshore, a giant pool of money held in corporate bonds, government debt, and mortgage-backed securities. Four years earlier, Appleby had assisted Apple in moving key subsidiaries to Jersey when an Irish tax dodge looked imperiled. During this period, Apple's offshore cash stockpile nearly doubled.

One of Appleby's biggest clients was Glencore, a Switzerland-based corporation that was the world's largest commodity trader, number 16 on the Fortune 500 with $173 billion in revenue. Glencore sought top-notch secrecy for its financial affairs, as it had a reputation for environmental contamination, tax evasion, and colluding with paramilitaries in Colombia and the Philippines. Appleby and a spinoff company called Estera created more than 107 offshore companies for Glencore, dedicating an entire room in its Bermuda offices to the commodity giant.

For years, journalists and human rights researchers wondered how Glencore managed to win lucrative copper and cobalt mining concessions in the Democratic Republic of the Congo at below market value. The Appleby data filled in the story of how the controversial Israeli diamond magnate Dan Gertler, a Mossack Fonseca client and a confidant of the country's leaders, facilitated the contract for Glencore through a complicated series of loans and payments. Gertler and Glencore deny that bribery was part of the equation.

The Appleby data also revealed that the U.S. secretary of commerce, Wilbur Ross, had failed during his confirmation to fully disclose that he owned a stake in a shipping firm that did business with Vladimir Putin's son-in-law. Ross was just one of many connected to President Donald Trump whose dealings were exposed in the Paradise

Papers, a reflection more of the ubiquity of the secrecy world than of any specific malfeasance. Most of these individuals were prominent Republican donors whose companies employed Appleby to avoid taxes. Democratic donors such as George Soros also appeared in the data.

Seven weeks after Daphne Caruana Galizia's murder, Maltese police arrested the Degiorgio brothers and an associate, Victor Muscat (no relation to the prime minister). The police recovered the burner phones in the bay outside a waterfront warehouse frequented by the Degiorgios. They also found DNA in cigarette butts the conspirators had left behind during their surveillance of the house. After an evidentiary hearing, the three men were jailed while awaiting trial. Maltese reporters noted that they acted unconcerned during their court appearances.

Few in Malta believe the men are the intellectual authors of the crime. So who ordered the murder?

There are a surfeit of suspects. The humiliated economy minister Christian Cardona has admitted to drinking at the same bar as the alleged killers. Two anonymous witnesses said they saw Cardona speaking with Alfred Degiorgio there, though the economy minister denies he ever met with any of the men. But Daphne's murderer could just as easily have been someone else whose dirty laundry had appeared in her blog or who believed it might. She was fierce and fearless, and such journalists are a threat to the powerful.

Two weeks after Daphne's murder, Laurent Richard, a French journalist with *Lignes Télévision*, launched a new reporting organization called Forbidden Stories to provide a secure place for investigative journalists working under threat to upload their source material confidentially. If anything happens to them, other journalists will be ready to complete their stories. "What is the point of killing a journalist if 10, 20 or 30 others are waiting to carry on their work?" Richard wrote in an op-ed in the *Guardian*.

With Daphne's murder, Forbidden Stories had a test case of sorts. It organized forty-five journalists from eighteen news organizations representing fifteen countries to investigate the murder and government corruption in Malta. Many of them had learned the art of collaborative journalism with ICIJ. The group included Maltese journalists as well. If the killers had hoped to silence her voice, the Daphne Project, as it was named, would work to ensure that this did not happen. In the coming months, the Daphne Project would break the stories of Cardona's alleged meeting with Alfred Degiorgio, the inflated Azerbaijani gas contract, and in-depth stories on the Maltese bank Pilatus and on Daphne herself.

Meanwhile, the U.S. Department of Justice unsealed a six-count indictment against Pilatus chairman Ali Sadr Hasheminejad and arrested him in Virginia. The indictment accused Sadr of helping Iran launder $115 million in payments from Venezuela prior to opening Pilatus. In Malta, banking regulators froze the bank's accounts.

At the end of 2017, President Trump and the Republican Congress enacted a $1 trillion tax cut that overwhelmingly favored corporations and the wealthy. Apple and other companies were rewarded handsomely for years of tax dodging. Instead of having to bring home its $269 billion at a tax rate of 35 percent, Apple was allowed to repatriate the money at 15.5 percent. The legislation also encouraged more secrecy, by providing incentives to real estate interests and hedge funds to form limited liability partnerships.

Meanwhile, dogged reporting, lawsuits, and indictments by Special Counsel Robert Mueller were slowly chipping away at the secrecy world activities of Donald Trump and his associates. The president's former campaign chairman Paul Manafort was indicted for money laundering through shell companies in Cyprus and then jailed over allegations of witness tampering. It was revealed that Trump's lawyer Michael Cohen had created a Delaware entity called Essential Consultants LLC to pay off the porn star Stormy Daniels in the weeks prior to the 2016 presidential election and that secret payments from other sources, including a Russian oligarch, were funneled through that same shell company. Reporters uncovered further evidence that Trump's franchised developments around the world were used by criminals for money laundering in the years prior to his election.

In May 2018, after years of campaigning by tax justice activists, the British parliament adopted a bill requiring overseas territories such as the British Virgin Islands and Bermuda to adopt public registries that would list the owners of all companies incorporated in their jurisdictions—and to do so by 2020. It was a sea-change for the secrecy world. The debate over the law cited the Panama Papers and the Paradise Papers as a motivating factor.

However, questions quickly surfaced about how the territories would respond, how such a law would be enforced, and whether this would simply drive illegal activity further underground. In Malta, Muscat's government moved forward with plans to make the island a center for cryptocurrencies like Bitcoin, which many fear has become a new frontier for money laundering.

By June 2018, tax authorities worldwide had collected more than $700 million in evaded taxes as a result of the Panama Papers. ICIJ estimated that more than 150 government and corporate inquiries in 79 countries had been launched in the first year alone. However, prosecutions in Panama itself presented the biggest personal threat to Jürgen Mossack, Ramón Fonseca, and their employees.

In March, Mossfon announced it was closing operations for good. The partners stopped giving interviews and largely vanished from public view. The move failed to quell the storm.

Three months later, Panamanian prosecutors detained seven of the firm's former employees as part of their investigation into corruption emanating from the Lava Jato scandal in Brazil. Ramsés Owens was among those charged, although he was already under house arrest for a separate investigation involving activities after he left the firm. When authorities went looking for Mossfon's top compliance officers, Sara Montenegro and Sandra Cornejo, they couldn't be found. Those implicated protested their innocence and insisted they had been singled out for practices common in the industry.

Then, on June 20, 2018, ICIJ and its partners published a stunning revelation: Mossfon had not sealed the leak after the initial publication of the Panama Papers in April 2016. The exfiltration of the firm's documents had continued. Journalists spent months perusing more than a million additional files covering the period from March 2016 to the end of 2017.

The new files showed what it was like inside the maelstrom. Mossfon was bombarded from all sides. Clients howled. Tax havens launched audits. Foreign governments demanded information. Mossfon frantically tried to comply with due diligence requirements it had never successfully enforced.

The firm filed suspicious activity reports to governments based on news stories drawn from Mossfon's own data, including for companies connected to Sergei Roldugin, the godfather of Vladimir Putin's eldest daughter. Mossfon's own reviews also uncovered new criminals and politicians who held the firm's companies.

In the face of demands for information, Mossfon conducted internal audits. The results were grim. Of the more than 28,500 active companies it had registered in the British Virgin Islands, the firm knew the names of the owners of just 28 percent. In Panama, where it had more than 10,500 active companies, the number was 25 percent.

Mossfon redoubled efforts to get the lawyers, accountants, and bankers who had originally requested their shell companies to provide the names of end users. After the leak, it became even harder to obtain the information.

"STOP ASKING WHAT YOU ALREADY HAVE and all governments THANKS TO MOSSACK can easily have," wrote one frustrated client. "This email will, probably, be intercepted like 11,600,000 other documents. I don't care."

Many customers simply moved their business to other offshore providers. In many cases where the firm could not get satisfactory answers, or where journalists had exposed questionable activities, Mossfon resigned as director or registered agent. After the firm informed one company belonging to the controversial Israeli diamond magnate Beny Steinmetz that it was resigning, the Steinmetz company financial controller emailed, "May I remind you that Mossack also had some extremely international bad press and we stayed a client."

Yet even in the midst of this chaos, the call of commerce continued. The files document efforts by Mossfon employees in Samoa and Panama to continue business under new names. The firm transferred Nevada and Wyoming shell companies to the Delaware-based firm American Incorporators Ltd. in return for referral fees. Invoices for company registrations no longer came from Mossack Fonseca, but little else had changed.

While Mossfon as a law firm was finished, the secrecy world endures.

—June 2018

NOTES

PROLOGUE

2   the U.S. Treasury issued a report: *National Money Laundering Risk Assessment 2015*, U.S. Department of the Treasury, June 12, 2015, https://www.treasury.gov /resource-center/terrorist-illicit-finance/Documents/National%20Money%20 Laundering%20Risk%20Assessment%20%E2%80%93%2006-12-2015.pdf.

2   In 2015, Delaware alone produced more than 128,000 LLCs: *Delaware Division of Corporations Annual Report 2015*, https://corp.delaware.gov/Corporations _2015%20Annual%20Report.pdf.

4   from $121.8 trillion in 2010 to $166.5 trillion in 2016: Jorge Becerra, Peter Damisch, Bruce Holley, Monish Kumar, Matthias Naumann, Tjun Tang, and Anna Zakrze- wski, *Global Wealth 2011: Shaping a New Tomorrow*, Boston Consulting Group, May 31, 2011, https://www.bcgperspectives.com/content/articles/financial _institutions_pricing_global_wealth_2011_shaping_new_tomorrow/; and "Global Private Wealth to Exceed $200 Trillion as the Rich Get Richer," Consultancy.uk, July 10, 2017, http://www.consultancy.uk/news/13650/global-private-wealth -exceed-200-trillion-as-the-rich-get-richer.

4   One recent study of three Scandinavian nations: Annette Alstadsaeter, Niels Johannesen, and Gabriel Zucman, "Tax Evasion and Inequality," preliminary draft paper, May 28, 2017, http://gabriel-zucman.eu/files/AJZ2017.pdf.

4   An estimated 8 percent of the world's household financial wealth: Annette Alstadsæter, Niels Johannesen, and Gabriel Zucman, "Who Owns the Wealth in Tax Havens? Macro Evidence and Implications for Global Inequality," National Bureau of Economic Research, September 2017, http://www.nber.org/papers /w23805.

4   the buyers of 58 percent of all property purchases: Ana Swanson, "How Secretive Shell Companies Shape the U.S. Real Estate Market," *Washington Post*, April 12, 2016, https://www.washingtonpost.com/news/wonk/wp/2016/04/12/how-secretive -shell-companies-shape-the-u-s-real-estate-market/?utm_term=.b75ad1498e76.

I: NAZIS AND RADICAL PRIESTS

5   an eighteen-minute corporate video: https://www.youtube.com/watch?v=iMtz
        -OBsSEI.

7   Erhard Mossack, a corporal in the Waffen-SS Skull and Crossbones division:
        Classified FBI document, Special Interrogation Report (CI-SIR No. 23) on Erhard
        Mossack, December 4, 1946, 105-HQ-9805-1, obtained by the International Con-
        sortium of Investigative Journalists, archived by the *New York Times*, https://
        www.documentcloud.org/documents/2791187-Erhard-Mossack
        -NationalArchives.html.

8   Erhard married and scraped together a living: Author interview with Jürgen
        Mossack, January 2017.

9   a declassified Central Intelligence Agency report: *Cable Re: Contact with and Possible
        Source from U.S. Military*, October 9, 1963. Agency: CIA. Record Series: JFK. File
        Number: 80T01357A. Released with deletions March 16, 1994.

9   His seven-year-old brother was first in his class: Author interview with Jürgen
        Mossack, January 2017.

10   Standard Oil registering its fleet of tankers in Panama in 1919: Armando Jose
        Garcia Pires, "The Business Model of the British Virgin Islands and Panama,"
        Institute for Research in Economics and Business Administration, SNF Project
        No. 6566, Working Paper No. 31/13 (paper published as part of a series by the
        Norwegian Center for Taxation), September 2013, http://www.snf.no/Files
        /Filer/Publications/A31_13.pdf.

10   "a big teddy bear": Author interview with Ramón Fonseca, Panama, August
        2016.

10   not to be a sheep like everyone else: Ramón Fonseca Mora en Gente de Mente
        PARTE 2, https://www.youtube.com/watch?v=qcIkW_K5GUA.

11   a de facto protectorate of the United States: "The 1903 Treaty and Qualified
        Independence," in *Panama: A Country Study*, ed. Sandra W. Meditz and Den-
        nis M. Hanratty, pp. 22–24 (Washington, DC: U.S. Government Publishing
        Office, 1987), http://countrystudies.us/panama/8.htm; and David McCullough,
        The Path Between the Seas: The Creation of the Panama Canal, 1870–1914 (New
        York: Simon & Schuster, 1977), pp. 392–93.

11   Fonseca's maternal grandfather, Ramón Mora: Sofia Izquierdo Valderrama,
        *Acción Comunal saluda a Lindbergh en español: Relatos de aventuras de Ramón E.
        Mora y sus hermanos de Acción Comunal* (Panamá: Editorial Círculo de Lectura
        de la USMA, 2002).

11   Arnulfo Arias: "The War Years," in *Panama: A Country Study*, ed. Meditz and
        Hanratty, p. 32, http://countrystudies.us/panama/12.htm.

12   There had been a priest in almost every generation of the Mora family: Izqui-
        erdo, *Acción Comunal saluda a Lindbergh en español*, p. 20.

12   50 percent of the children suffered from malnutrition: Eric Mansilla, "El caso
        Gallego y la extraña respuesta de la Guardia Nacional," *La Estrella*, June 14, 2015,
        http://laestrella.com.pa/panama/nacional/caso-gallego-extrana-respuesta
        -guardia-nacional/23872804.

13   Gallego had survived the fall: Seymour M. Hersh, "Why Democrats Can't Make
        an Issue of Noriega," *New York Times*, May 4, 1988, http://www.nytimes.com
        /1988/05/04/opinion/why-democrats-can-t-make-an-issue-of-noriega.html.

13   Fonseca kept a box of mixed human remains: Author interview with Ramón
        Fonseca, Panama, August 2016.

14   his body was dumped into a mass grave: Nimay González, "Hermana del Padre
        Gallego relata su búsqueda por conocer la verdad," *Telemetro* video, 28:25,

June 6, 2017, http://m.telemetro.com/nacionales/Hermana-Padre-Gallego
-busqueda-conocer_0_1033096948.html.

14   Upon completion of his law degree in 1976: https://www.martindale.com
/panama/panama/ramon-fonseca-m-1254354-a/.

15   Panama's corporation law was based on American corporate legislation:
Ricardo A. Durling, *La sociedad anónima en Panamá* (Panamá: R. A. Durling,
1986).

15   At first, Delaware permitted only certain local industries: "Law for Sale: A Study
of the Delaware Corporation Law of 1967," *University of Pennsylvania Law Review*
117, no. 6 (1969): 861–98, http://scholarship.law.upenn.edu/cgi/viewcontent.cgi
?article=6099&context=penn_law_review.

15   For a fee, they guaranteed they could round up enough votes: S. Samuel Arsht,
"A History of Delaware Incorporation Law," *Delaware Journal of Corporate Law* 1,
no. 1 (1976): 1–22.

16   Khashoggi embraced the benefits of offshore tax havens: Ronald Kessler, *The
Richest Man in the World: The Story of Adnan Khashoggi* (New York: Warner Books,
1988), 98, 253.

16   Donald Trump bought it: John Taylor, "Trump's Newest Toy," *New York*, July 11,
1988.

17   at least $450,000 of that found its way into bribes: Michael C. Jensen, "Northrop
Bribes of $450,000 for 2 Saudi Generals Reported," *New York Times*, June 5, 1975,
http://www.nytimes.com/1975/06/05/archives/northrop-bribes-of-450000-for-2
-saudi-generals-reported-northrop.html; and Associated Press, "Northrop Must
Pay Triad Arms Sale Commissions," *Los Angeles Times*, October 20, 1987, http://
articles.latimes.com/1987-10-20/business/fi-14604_1_arms-sale.

17   quickly maneuvered his way into power: "Torrijos' Sudden Death," in *Panama:
A Country Study*, ed. Meditz and Hanratty, pp. 59–64, http://countrystudies.us
/panama/21.htm.

2: TROPICAL PARADISES

19   Noriega's cooperation with drug cartels: Seymour M. Hersh, "Panama Strongman Said to Trade in Drugs, Arms and Illicit Money," *New York Times*, June 12,
1986, http://www.nytimes.com/1986/06/12/world/panama-strongman-said-to
-trade-in-drugs-arms-and-illicit-money.html.

19   International Monetary Fund and World Bank loans: "Cash Crisis Shuts Banks
in Panama: Financial Dilemma Blamed on U.S Economic Pressure," *Los Angeles
Times*, March 6, 1988, http://articles.latimes.com/1988-03-06/news/mn-705_1
_national-bank.

20   a sizable proportion of its budget: "Delaware State Budget and Finances," *Bal-
lotpedia*, https://ballotpedia.org/Delaware_state_budget_and_finances.

20   While actual industry practitioners in Delaware are few: *Economy at a Glance:
Delaware*, U.S. Department of Labor, Bureau of Labor Statistics, https://www.
bls.gov/eag/eag.de.htm#eag_de.f.p.

20   an outsize control over the political process: Nicholas Shaxson, *Treasure Islands*
(New York: St. Martin's Griffin, 2012).

20   According to Catholic legend, Saint Ursula was a princess: Ben Johnson, "Saint
Ursula and the 11,000 British Virgins," *Historic UK: The History and Heritage Accom-
modation Guide*, http://www.historic-uk.com/HistoryUK/HistoryofEngland/Saint
-Ursula-the-11000-British-Virgins/.

21   on display at the Smuggler's Cove Beach Bar: Sandra Phinney, "Tales from

Tortola ... Smugglers Cove," *sandraphinney.com*, January 5, 2011, http://sandraphinney.com/oddsnsods/tales-from-tortola-smugglers-cove/.

21   Paul Butler, a Wall Street tax attorney: Colin Riegels, "The BVI IBC Act and the Building of a Nation," *IFC Review*, January 3, 2014, http://www.ifcreview.com/restricted.aspx?articleId=7944&areaId=10.

21   Under the double tax treaty: Frith Crandall, "The Termination of the United States-Netherlands Antilles Tax Treaty: What Were the Costs of Ending Treaty Shopping," *Northwestern Journal of International Law and Business* 9, no. 2 (Fall 1988): 355–81, http://scholarlycommons.law.northwestern.edu/cgi/viewcontent.cgi?article=1258&context=njilb.

21   Tax *avoidance* ... Tax *evasion*: Craig Elliffe, "The Thickness of a Prison Wall—When Does Tax Avoidance Become a Criminal Offence?" *New Zealand Business Law Quarterly* 17, no. 4 (2011): 441–66, https://papers.ssrn.com/sol3/papers.cfm?abstract_id=1992652.

21   a BVI corporation for two wealthy Saudis: Jeff Gerth, "U.S. Is Opening Talks on Tax Haven Treaty," *New York Times*, January 15, 1982, http://www.nytimes.com/1982/01/15/business/us-is-opening-talks-on-tax-haven-treaty.html.

22   A fledgling tourist trade yielded a bit more than $42 million in 1985: "British Carribean Dependencies Economy—Historical Overview," http://www.photius.com/countries/british_virgin_islands/economy/economy.html.

22   "Something had to be done to replenish the coffers": "Video: The Story of the IBC Act," *Harneys* video, 4:52, http://micro.harneys.com/ibcact/.

22   no public registry of directors: "Law for Sale: A Study of the Delaware Corporation Law of 1967."

22   The BVI law passed in 1984: "R. T. O'Neal's Historic Move in HOA Unforgettable—Mrs. Flax," *Virgin Islands News Online*, May 20, 2014, http://www.virginislandsnewsonline.com/en/news/r-t-oneals-historic-move-in-hoa-unforgettable-mrs-flax.

23   In 1986, there were slightly more than twelve thousand people: Email with Ermin Penn, historian, the British Virgin Islands Tourist Board and Film Commission.

24   John Christensen was an economic adviser to Jersey: Interview with John Christensen, January 2017; and "John Christensen on Rocking the Boat in Jersey," *Tax Justice Network*, December 1, 2015, http://www.taxjustice.net/2015/12/01/john-christensen-reflections-of-a-whistleblower/.

24   Keith Flax, a local jeweler: "'Flax Craft' Fine Jewellery Store Reopens After 28 Years," *Virgin Islands News Online*, July 12, 2014, http://www.virginislandsnewsonline.com/en/news/flax-craft-fine-jewellery-store-reopens-after-28-years.

24   a close friend of both Romney and Peters: Author interview with Ramón Fonseca, Panama, August 2016; and funeral program for Cyril B. Romney, Wickham's Cay, British Virgin Islands, July 31, 2007, http://dspace.hlscc.org/jspui/bitstream/123456789/1808/1/Romney,%20Cyril%20Brandtford.pdf.

26   Adelina Mercedes Chavarria de Estribi: "Así viven los empresarios de papel," Connectas, http://www.abc.com.py/especiales/secretos-en-paraisos-fiscales/empresarios-de-papel-1467612.html.

27   "The signed blank documents": Ramón Fonseca, memo to Antoinette Stubbs, November 2, 1990.

28   Martin Kenney, a Canadian lawyer and fraud investigator: KPMG International, *Review of Financial Regulation in the Caribbean Overseas Territories and Bermuda* (London: Stationery Office, 2000).

28   The concept of the trust dates to feudal England: Brooke Harrington, *Capital With-out Borders: Wealth Managers and the One Percent* (Cambridge, MA: Harvard University Press, 2016), p. 39; and "In Trusts We Trust," *Tax Justice Network*, July 22, 2009, http://taxjustice.blogspot.ch/2009/07/in-trusts-we-trust.html.

29   a $50,000 fine or up to six months in prison: "Private Foundations," brochure, Mossack Fonseca, p. 5.

29   calling certain trust arrangements a "sham": Steve Meiklejohn, "Jersey: Sham Trust Finding Upheld in Jersey," *Mondaq*, March 4, 2009, http://www.mondaq .com/jersey/x/75470/Trusts/Sham+Trust+Finding+Upheld+In+Jersey.

29   "When our legitimate revenues are attacked": Franklin D. Roosevelt, "Message to Congress on Tax Evasion Prevention," June 1, 1937, http://www.presidency .ucsb.edu/ws/?pid=15413.

30   grew rich smuggling whiskey: Richard Oulahan and William Lambert, "The Scandal in the Bahamas," *Life*, February 3, 1967.

30   Meyer Lansky looked to the islands: Nicholas Shaxson, "The Truth About Tax Havens: Part 2," *Guardian*, January 9, 2011, https://www.theguardian.com /business/2011/jan/09/truth-about-tax-havens-two.

30   Together they concocted a system: Ronen Palan, Richard Murphy, and Christian Chavagneux, *Tax Havens: How Globalization Really Works* (Ithaca, NY: Cornell University Press, 2009).

30   Mossack was familiar with the Liberian ship registry: Author interview with Jürgen Mossack, January 2017.

30   The Liberians readily assented in return for a cut of the proceeds: Rodney Carlisle, "The 'American Century' Implemented: Stettinius and the Liberian Flag of Convenience," *Business History Review* 54, no. 2 (1980): 175–91.

31   A sparsely populated coral outcrop: http://www.niueisland.com/facts/.

32   Cross Trading, based in Niue, purchased the rights for Ecuadorian soccer matches: James Riach and Owen Gibson, "UEFA Offices Raided After Gianni Infantino Named in Panama Papers," *Guardian*, April 6, 2016, https://www.the guardian.com/news/2016/apr/06/uefa-offices-raided-swiss-police-panama -papers-gianni-infantino.

32   By 1994, the BVI hosted 136,112 companies: Secretary of State for Foreign and Commonwealth Affairs, *British Virgin Islands: Report of the Constitutional Commissioners 1993* (London: Stationery Office, 1994).

32   Mossfon accounted for more than 10 percent: Rigoberto Carvajal, analysis performed for the International Consortium of Investigative Journalists.

33   The BVI's population had more than doubled: Johnson, "Saint Ursula and the 11,000 British Virgins."

33   Today, the new BVI is a place: "BVI Community Board," https://www.facebook .com/groups/178954908878855/.

3: NAME OF THE GAME

35   Gordon had graduated from the State University of New York: Author interview with John Gordon, New York, July 2016.

35   Norman Island, the inspiration for Robert Louis Stevenson's *Treasure Island*: John Amrhein Jr., "Treasure Island: The Untold Story," http://www.treasureis landtheuntoldstory.com/.

36   one of the largest counterfeit software cases in the country's history: Rupert Steiner, "Police Investigate £2.5m Microsoft Forgery Racket," *Sunday Times*, December 26, 1999.

37   "He instructs us to resign as Directors": Fax from Ana Escobar to John Gordon, June 27, 1997.

37   "The two were idiots": Author interview with John Gordon, New York, July 2016.

37   the police seized thousands of copies of pirated Microsoft software: Steiner, "Police Investigate £2.5m Microsoft Forgery Racket."

38   "more unwanted and unneeded attention to all of us": Fax from John Gordon to Ana Escobar, February 17, 1998.

38   Two years later, police dropped criminal charges: "Computer Fraud Prosecution Is Dropped," *News* (Portsmouth, UK), March 12, 2002, http://www.portsmouth.co.uk/news/computer-fraud-prosecution-is-dropped-1-1275845.

39   "the highest possible degree of protection": Carmen Haughton and Ramsés Owens email to Brenda Estanislau, March 2006.

39   "The two things this accomplishes": Email from Wesley Long to Jennifer Mossack, February 9, 2008.

39   Fidentia went on to loot a survivors' fund: Barry Sergeant, "Living Hands Rescued," *Moneyweb*, March 5, 2007, http://www.moneyweb.co.za/archive/living-hands-rescued/; and Caryn Dolley, "I Don't Know What Happened to the Money," *Cape Times*, May 14, 2013, http://www.iol.co.za/capetimes/i-dont-know-what-happened-to-the-money-1515362.

40   Noriega's usefulness diminished: Stephen Knott, "George H. W. Bush: Foreign Affairs," Miller Center, University of Virginia, http://millercenter.org/president/biography/bush-foreign-affairs.

40   An Isle of Man newspaper report: "Panama's the Place to Be," November 1, 2001, https://web.archive.org/web/20130330113501/http://www.iomtoday.co.im/news/business/panama_s_the_place_to_be_1_1782652.

40   "You are an invisible man": Email from Mossfon Trust, July 25, 2007.

41   "We must take into account": Ramsés Owens, memo to Ramón Fonseca and Jürgen Mossack, October 19, 1998.

41   a population of less than twelve thousand: Jan Lahmeyer, "Liechtenstein: Historical Demographical Data of the Whole Country," *Populstat*, November 19, 2003, http://www.populstat.info/Europe/liechtsc.htm; and Tony Paterson, "Liechtenstein: Where the Missing Billions Go," *Independent*, February 26, 2008, http://www.independent.co.uk/news/world/europe/liechtenstein-where-the-missing-billions-go-787282.html.

41   creating a financial vehicle that anyone outside of Liechtenstein could use: Leo Zhang, "Trusts and Foundations: Protecting Your Wealth in Liechtenstein," *China Offshore*, http://www.chinainvestin.com/index.php/zh/china-offshore/supplements/trusts-and-foundations/1668.

42   there was almost no official record of a foundation's activities: Richard Murphy, "Why Is Liechtenstein a Tax Haven?" *Tax Research UK*, February 20, 2008, http://www.taxresearch.org.uk/Blog/2008/02/20/why-is-liechtenstein-a-tax-haven/.

43   Goodwin had bribed a fund manager: "Fidentia's Goodwin Goes to Jail," *News 24 Archives*, April 20, 2009, www.news24.com/SouthAfrica/News/Fidentias-Goodwin-goes-to-jail-20090420.

43   Goodwin was clearly a victim of circumstance: Steven Goodwin, Contact Report, Ramsés Owens, Mossfon Trust, March 18, 2007 (Contact Date: March 12, 2007).

43   The South African press dubbed him the "missing man": "Missing Man Features in Fidentia Indictment," *Mail & Guardian* (Johannesburg), February 13, 2008,

http://mg.co.za/article/2008-02-13-missing-man-features-in-fidentia
-indictment.

44   "In this manner officially and truthfully": Letter from Ramsés Owens, November 2003.

44   may have been Mexico's first narcotics billionaire: Dolia Estevez, "Was Mexican Fugitive Caro Quintero the First Billionaire Drug Lord?" *Forbes*, October 1, 2013, http://www.forbes.com/sites/doliaestevez/2013/10/01/was-mexican-fugitive-caro-quintero-the-first-billionaire-drug-lord/#14de129c3a25.

45   Mexican soldiers destroyed product likely worth several billion dollars: David Luhnow, "Mexico Finds Large Marijuana Farm in Baja California," *Wall Street Journal*, July 15, 2011, http://www.wsj.com/articles/SB10001424052702304521304576446441269265276.

45   Consumed by fury and paranoia: Paul Lieberman, "Agents Say Mexico Officials Stymied Raid," *Los Angeles Times*, May 23, 1990, http://articles.latimes.com/1990-05-23/news/mn-151_1_marijuana-raid.

45   In January 1985, the two friends mistakenly walked into the Crazy Lobster: United Press International, "Two Bodies Unearthed in Mexico Forest," *Los Angeles Times*, June 18, 1985, http://articles.latimes.com/1985-06-18/news/mn-3197_1_caro-quintero; and Jaime Ramírez Yáñez, "La caída de Rafael Caro Quintero," *El Economista*, August 9, 2013, http://eleconomista.com.mx/sociedad/2013/08/09/caida-rafael-caro-quintero.

45   A doctor was on call to keep the DEA agent alive: Héctor Aguilar Camín, "Narco Historias extraordinarias," *Nexos*, January 1, 2009, http://www.nexos.com.mx/?p=12886.

45   Caro Quintero boarded a Falcon executive jet: "Prime Suspect in Murder of U.S. Drug Agent Is Extradited to Mexico," *Los Angeles Times*, April 6, 1985, http://articles.latimes.com/1985-04-06/news/mn-18337_1_drug-trafficker.

45   the U.S. embassy suggested they deliver the papers to Pla Horrit: https://www.wikileaks.org/plusd/cables/1976SANJO00550_b.html.

45   On April 4, Costa Rican authorities arrested Caro Quintero: "Costa Rican Police Seize Suspect in the Slaying of U.S. Drug Agent," *New York Times*, April 5, 1985, http://www.nytimes.com/1985/04/05/world/costa-rican-police-seize-suspect-in-the-slaying-of-us-drug-agent.html.

46   Pla Horrit died on Christmas Eve in 2004: Tribunal Supremo de Elecciones, Consulta Civiles, Costa Rica.

46   a Mossfon lawyer sent an email to the partners: Rigoberto Coronado, email to Ramón Fonseca, Jürgen Mossack, and Chris Zollinger, March 18, 2005.

46   The Costa Rican government had given the committee: José Meléndez, "Sociedad de Mossack fue dueña de casa de Caro Quintero," *El Universal*, April 15, 2016, http://www.eluniversal.com.mx/articulo/mundo/2016/04/15/una-sociedad-de-mossack-fue-duena-de-casa-de-caro-quintero. The house is located in Vasquez de Coronado, San José, Costa Rica. See "Comité Olímpico Nacional de Costa Rica-CONCRC," *Facebook.com*, https://www.facebook.com/con.costarica/.

46   Before the United States could extradite him, he disappeared: Elaine Shannon, "A Drug Lord Walks Free in Mexico," *Los Angeles Times*, August 18, 2013, http://articles.latimes.com/2013/aug/18/opinion/la-oe-0818-shannon-camarena-quintero-mexico-20130818.

46   his name sits atop the DEA's list of fugitives: "DEA TOP Wanted Fugitives," U.S. Drug Enforcement Administration, https://www.dea.gov/fugitives.shtml.

4: RISE OF THE GLOBAL BANKSTERS

47   HSBC ordered more than twenty-three hundred companies from Mossfon: Rigoberto Carvajal, analysis performed for the International Consortium of Investigative Journalists.

48   Guerrero's top banking client was Luxembourg-based Safra Republic Holdings: Gerard Ryle, Will Fitzgibbon, Mar Cabra, Rigoberto Carvajal, Marina Walker Guevara, Martha M. Hamilton, and Tom Stites, "Banking Giant HSBC Sheltered Murky Cash Linked to Dictators and Arms Dealers," International Consortium of Investigative Journalists, February 8, 2015, https://www.icij.org /project/swiss-leaks/banking-giant-hsbc-sheltered-murky-cash-linked -dictators-and-arms-dealers; and Associated Press, "Swiss Leaks Show Deposit by Daughter of China's Ex-Premier," February 11, 2015, https://cn.nytimes.com /china/20150211/c11lixiaolin/en-us/.

49   a combined $56 billion in assets under management: Richard Roberts and David Kynaston, *The Lion Awakes: A Modern History of HSBC* (London: Profile Books, 2015), p. 332.

49   set a fire inside a waste basket in his Monte Carlo penthouse: Dominick Dunne, "Death in Monaco," *Vanity Fair*, December 2000, http://www.vanityfair.com /culture/2000/12/dunne200012.

49   Switzerland's bank secrecy: Sébastien Guex, "The Origins of the Swiss Banking Secrecy Law and Its Repercussions for Swiss Federal Policy," *Business History Review* 74, no. 2 (Summer 2000): 237–66.

50   In 1934, Switzerland made it a crime: Juliette Garside, "HSBC Files: How a 1934 Swiss Law Enshrined Secrecy," *Guardian*, February 8, 2015, https:// www.theguardian.com/business/2015/feb/08/hsbc-files-1934-swiss-law -secrecy.

50   based it in Hong Kong: Roberts and Kynaston, *The Lion Awakes*, p. 2.

50   a reputation as excessively conservative, secretive, and arrogant: Ibid., p. 430.

50   an opportunity for the wealth management industry: Ibid., p. 223.

51   Rumors that the bank served the criminal class: Gary Weiss, "The Mystery Man of Finance," *Bloomberg*, March 6, 1995, https://www.bloomberg.com/news /articles/1994-03-06/the-mystery-man-of-finance.

51   testifying before a committee of the House of Lords: Martin Arnold, "Former HSBC Chief Admits Mistakes over Acquisitions," *Financial Review*, July 15, 2015, http://www.afr.com/business/banking-and-finance/former-hsbc-chief -admits-mistakes-over-acquisitions-20150714-gichli.

51   Dedicating the resources needed to fix Republic: Roberts and Kynaston, *The Lion Awakes*, p. 340.

51   The deal was finalized a month after Safra's funeral: Paul M. Beckett, "Fed Approves HSBC's Acquisition of Republic New York for $9.9 Billion," *Wall Street Journal*, December 9, 1999, https://www.wsj.com/articles/SB9445062058 905250.

51   increasing assets under management to $122 billion: Roberts and Kynaston, *The Lion Awakes*, p. 227.

51   Prior to his death, Safra had shaved $450 million off the asking price: Andrew Anthony, "The Strange Case of Edmond Safra," *Guardian*, October 28, 2000, https://www.theguardian.com/theobserver/2000/oct/29/features.magazine47; and Noelle Knox, "Pending Bank Settlement Raises Questions of Timing," *USA Today*, November 15, 2001, http://usatoday30.usatoday.com/money/finance /2001-11-15-hsbc.htm.

52   slapped the bank with a $700 million fine: Jathon Sapsford, "Safra Accepts Less

Cash to Finish Republic Deal," *Wall Street Journal*, November 10, 1999, http:// www.wsj.com/articles/SB942250896962729313.

52   profits soared to $440 million: Roberts and Kynaston, *The Lion Awakes*, p. 406.

52   "The banks knew why they wanted to buy companies and for whom": Author interview with Adrian Simon, Geneva, September 2016.

52   "therapist, lightning rod, friend": Marie Maurisse, "HSBC Suisse, pour l'amour des femmes," *Le Temps*, February 10, 2015, https://www.letemps.ch/societe/2015 /02/10/hsbc-suisse-amour-femmes.

53   the former Grand Hôtel Bellevue: https://saentys.com/work/quai-wilson-37.

53   "The MEDIS accounts were disproportionately more often the subjects": Translation of interview with David Garrido by federal police in Brussels, October 29, 2014.

53   the Israeli billionaire Daniel Gertler: Elsa Buchanan, "DRC: Israeli Billionaire Dan Gertler Probed by UK Serious Fraud Office over Mining Deals," *International Business Times*, December 5, 2016, http://www.ibtimes.co.uk/drc-israeli -billionaire-dan-gertler-probed-by-uk-serious-fraud-office-over-mining-deals -1594961; and Uri Blau and Daniel Dolev, "Israeli Diamond Tycoons Listed in Leaked Panama Papers," *Haaretz*, April 7, 2016, http://www.haaretz.com/israel -news/1.713130.

53   another Israeli billionaire, Benjamin "Beny" Steinmetz: Silas Gbandia, Cooper Inveen, Khadija Sharife, Will Fitzgibbon, and Michael Hudson, "Diamond Mine with Offshore Ties Leaves Trail of Complaints," International Consortium of Investigative Journalists, July 25, 2016, https://panamapapers.icij.org/20160725 -sierra-leone-diamonds.html.

53   In 2016, he was arrested in Israel: Ian Cobain and Peter Beaumont, "Israeli Tycoon Beny Steinmetz Arrested over Guinea Bribery Claims," *Guardian*, December 19, 2016, https://www.theguardian.com/world/2016/dec/19/israeli-tycoon -beny-steinmetz-arrested-over-guinea-bribery-claims.

54   An Interpol alert for his arrest: Ryan Chittum, "Diamond Dealers in Deep Trouble as Bank Documents Shine Light on Secret Ways," International Consortium of Investigative Journalists, February 9, 2015, https://www.icij.org/project /swiss-leaks/diamond-dealers-deep-trouble-bank-documents-shine-light -secret-ways.

54   Michael Geoghegan began his HSBC career in 1973: Roberts and Kynaston, *The Lion Awakes*, p. 453.

54   "this was a special case for their senior executive": Fax from July le Feuvre to Manuela Fogarty, March 14, 1997.

54   a house in London's posh Kensington neighborhood: Holly Watt and David Pegg, "Former HSBC Boss Tried to Avoid Tax on £8m Kensington House," *Guardian*, April 7, 2016, https://www.theguardian.com/news/2016/apr/07/ex-hsbc-boss -michael-geoghegan-panama-papers-tried-to-avoid-tax-kensington-house.

54   Stuart Gulliver succeeded Geoghegan as HSBC's chief executive officer in 2010: Jill Treanor, "HSBC Chief Mike Geohegan Ousted After Brutal Boardroom Battle," *Guardian*, September 23, 2010, https://www.theguardian.com/business /2010/sep/23/hsbc-mike-geohegan-replaced-stuart-gulliver.

54   Gulliver had started his career as a relationship manager in 1981: Roberts and Kynaston, *The Lion Awakes*, p. 389.

54   Gulliver used the company to receive his HSBC bonuses: James Ball, Juliette Garside, David Pegg, and Harry Davies, "Revealed: Swiss Account Secret of HSBC Chief Stuart Gulliver," *Guardian*, February 23, 2015, https://www.the guardian.com/business/2015/feb/22/swiss-account-secret-of-hsbc-chief-stuart -gulliver-revealed.

55   Then they tried Tesler: Will Fitzgibbon, "Files Open New Window on $182-Million Halliburton Bribery Scandal in Nigeria," International Consortium of Investigative Journalists, February 10, 2015, https://www.icij.org/project/swiss-leaks/files-open-new-window-182-million-halliburton-bribery-scandal-nigeria.

56   in a Nigerian hotel parking lot: United States of America v. Jeffrey Tesler and Wojciech J. Chodan, Indictment, United States Southern District of Texas, February 17, 2009.

56   an election marked by violence, vote rigging, and fraud: "Nigeria: Political Violence & Elections, 02/03/03," Africa Action: Africa Policy E-Journal (University of Pennsylvania, African Studies Center), February 3, 2003, https://www.africa.upenn.edu/Urgent_Action/apic-020303.html.

57   Halliburton paid $35 million in a settlement: "Halliburton Settles Nigeria Bribery Claims for $35 million," CNN, December 21, 2010, http://www.cnn.com/2010/WORLD/africa/12/21/nigeria.halliburton/index.html.

57   But by 1998, both the United States and the United Kingdom had signed: Organisation for Economic Co-operation and Development, "Ratification Status as of May 2017," OECD Convention on Combating Bribery of Foreign Public Officials in International Business Transactions, http://www.oecd.org/daf/anti-bribery/WGBRatificationStatus.pdf.

57   "I relished the opportunity to talk": Sentencing Before the Honorable Keith P. Ellison, United States of America v. Jeffrey Tesler, U.S. District Court for the Southern District of Texas, Houston Division, No. H-09-CR-98-1, February 23, 2012.

57   to purchase 108 square miles in Namibia for a hunting reserve: Shinovene Immanuel, "Absentee Russian Landlord in Panama Papers," Namibian, May 13, 2016, http://www.namibian.com.na/index.php?page=archive-read&id=150709.

57   More than five hundred banks registered nearly 15,600 shell companies: "Giant Leak of Offshore Financial Records Exposes Global Array of Crime and Corruption," International Consortium of Investigative Journalists, https://panamapapers.icij.org/20160403-panama-papers-global-overview.html.

58   F. David Ford, the head of compliance for Republic: https://www.linkedin.com/in/f-david-ford-379ab87.

58   his wife was employed by the U.S. Justice Department: François Pilet and Marie Maurisse, "#Swissleaks: David Ford, l'homme de Washington," Hebdo, February 11, 2015, http://www.hebdo.ch/hebdo/cadrages/detail/swissleaks-david-ford-falciani-fraudeurs-narcodollars-cash-coke-diamants-arme.

58   Ford denies the allegation: Communication from F. David Ford to author, August 2017.

58   even surfaced in a Swiss newspaper: François Pilet and Marie Maurisse, "David Ford, L'homme de Washington," L'Hebdo, February 12, 2015, https://francoispilet.net/david-ford-lhomme-de-washington/.

58   Somewhere in Geneva was a covert CIA listening post: Glenn Greenwald, Ewen MacAskill, and Laura Poitras, "Edward Snowden: The Whistleblower Behind the NSA Surveillance Revelations," Guardian, June 11, 2013, https://www.theguardian.com/world/2013/jun/09/edward-snowden-nsa-whistleblower-surveillance.

59   By the end of 1953, they had devised a plan: Riggs Docs from CIA Reading Room—Secret Security Information, declassified, CIA Reading Room.

60   The island's ruler, France-Albert René: "President Steps Down After 27 Years," Los Angeles Times, April 15, 2004, http://articles.latimes.com/2004/apr/15/world/fg-briefs15.6.

60   fished the body of a Mafia soldier out of the swamps: The Association for Dip-
      lomatic Studies and Training Foreign Affairs Oral History Project, Ambassador
      David J. Fischer, interviewed by Charles Stuart Kennedy and Robert S. Pasto-
      rino, initial interview date March 6, 1998, p. 100.

60   "You are hereby instructed never to report": Ibid., p. 99.

60   eventually accounting for more than fifteen thousand companies: "Explore the
      Panama Papers Key Figures," International Consortium of Investigative Jour-
      nalists, https://panamapapers.icij.org/graphs/.

5: HOW TO BEAT THE GAME

61   Targeted at financial intermediaries, offshore professionals, and high-net-worth
      individuals: "Shorex 97: What Happened at Shorex 97?," http://web.archive.org
      /web/19980204222142/http://www.shorex.com/shx97.htm.

61   eighty exhibitors advertised their services: "Shorex 97: Exhibitors and Sponsors,"
      http://web.archive.org/web/19980204221914/http://www.shorex.com/exhib97
      .htm.

61   it was a "must be there" event: "Shorex 97: What Happened at Shorex 97?"

61   More than half the world's wealth was controlled offshore: "Press Release—The
      World Is Going Offshore at Shorex 97," October 3, 1997, http://www.mondaq
      .com/article.asp?article_id=2863.

62   The reactions of attendees to the agents ran from fear to befuddlement: Author
      interview with Joe West, New Jersey, February 2017.

62   A Cyprus exhibitor explained to the agents: Jay Adkisson, "Cyprus and the Death
      of an Offshore Haven," Forbes, March 25, 2013, http://www.forbes.com/sites
      /jayadkisson/2013/03/25/cyprus-and-the-death-of-an-offshore-haven/#3745fc6f130f.

63   links to President Richard Nixon and his Key Biscayne pal Bebe Rebozo:
      Anthony Summers, The Arrogance of Power: The Secret World of Richard Nixon
      (New York: Viking, 2000), p. 254.

63   The brass criticized the evidence collection: John F. Berry, "C. W. Deaton's Bril-
      liant Conceived Castle Bank Scam," Washington Post, April 3, 1977, https://
      www.washingtonpost.com/archive/business/1977/04/03/cw-deatons-brilliant
      -conceived-castle-bank-scam/50b4ad3d-3723-4e43-bcdd-4bd68ecbb2b4/?utm
      _term=.d2777c5222d9.

63   It would be more than a decade before the IRS focused on offshore tax abuse
      again: Author interview with Jack Blum, February 2017.

64   relatives were paid off the books through gifts of cars, boats, and other assets:
      David M. Razler, "Cracks in the Glass: The Wheaton Family Feud," Press of
      Atlantic City, June 6, 1993.

65   issued a stinging report in 1985: U.S. Senate Permanent Subcommittee on Investi-
      gations, "Crime and Secrecy: The Use of Offshore Banks and Companies Hearings
      Before the Senate Permanent Subcommittee on Investigations," 99th Cong.,
      1st Sess. (1985).

66   The broadcasts prompted a Department of Justice investigation: U.S. Senate Com-
      mittee on Finance, "Schemes, Scams and Cons: The IRS Strikes Back," 107th Cong.,
      2nd Sess., April 11, 2002, p. 47, https://www.finance.senate.gov/imo/media/doc
      /81637.pdf.

66   BCCI grew from $200 million in assets: Senator John Kerry and Senator Hank
      Brown, "The BCCI Affair: A Report to the Committee on Foreign Relations,
      United States Senate," 102nd Cong., 2nd Sess., December 1992, p. 40, https://
      info.publicintelligence.net/The-BCCI-Affair.pdf.

66   "godfather of Middle East Intelligence": Ibid., p. 290.

67   Another large shareholder, Abdul Raouf Khalil: Ibid., p. 38.

67   regulators yanked its license in 1991: Conrad de Aenlle, "Regulators Rally After BCCI Scandal," *New York Times*, November 23, 1991, http://www.nytimes .com/1991/11/23/your-money/23iht-m23e.html.

67   Organisation for Economic Co-operation and Development (OECD): http:// www.oecd.org/about/history/.

68   Delaware annually churned out more than a hundred thousand anonymous companies: Daniel Gross, "Listening to Delaware," *Slate*, November 7, 2003, http://www.slate.com/articles/business/moneybox/2003/11/listening_to _delaware.html.

68   All three were founding members of the OECD: Organisation for Economic Co-operation and Development, http://www.oecd.org/about/history/.

68   A seemingly infinite number of ways existed: "Money Laundering: Methods and Markets," in Peter Reuter and Edwin M. Truman, *Chasing Dirty Money: The Fight Against Money Laundering* (Washington, DC: Peterson Institute for International Economics, 2004), pp. 25–43.

69   billions of dollars in Russian capital flowed through it every month: Anthony B. van Fossen, "Money Laundering, Global Financial Responsibility, and Tax Havens in the Pacific Islands," *Contemporary Pacific* 15, no. 2 (Fall 2003): 237–75, https://scholarspace.manoa.hawaii.edu/bitstream/10125/13737/1/v15n2-237-275 .pdf.

69   selling Nauru bank licenses at $60,000 a pop: David Cay Johnston, "Pioneer of Sham Tax Havens Sits Down for Pre-Jail Chat," *New York Times*, November 18, 2004, http://www.nytimes.com/2004/11/18/business/pioneer-of-sham-tax-havenssits -down-for-prejail-chat.html.

69   they could get the same license for $5,000: Author interview with Jack Blum, February 2017.

69   accounted for 80 percent of the government's revenue: Martha M. Hamilton, "Panamanian Law Firm Is Gatekeeper to Vast Flow of Murky Offshore Secrets," International Consortium of Investigative Journalists, April 3, 2016, https:// panamapapers.icij.org/20160403-mossack-fonseca-offshore-secrets.html.

69   the foreign minister refused to meet him: Michael Field, "Pacific Islands Provided Fertile Ground for Panamanian Law Firm," *Nikkei Asian Review*, April 14, 2016, http://asia.nikkei.com/magazine/20160414-MEXICO-ASIA/Politics -Economy/Pacific-islands-provided-fertile-ground-for-Panamanian-law-firm ?page=1.

70   Mathewson had cooperated with the government to avoid a lengthy prison sentence: Ronald Smothers, "In Plea Deal, a Banker Outlines Money Laundering in Caymans," *New York Times*, August 3, 1999, http://www.nytimes.com /1999/08/03/us/in-plea-deal-a-banker-outlines-money-laundering-in-caymans .html.

72    $70 billion in tax revenue was lost each year: U.S. Senate Permanent Subcommittee on Investigations of the Committee on Governmental Affairs, "What Is the U.S. Position on Offshore Tax Havens?," 107th Cong., 1st Sess., July 18, 2001, https://www.gpo.gov/fdsys/pkg/CHRG-107shrg75473/html/CHRG -107shrg75473.htm.

72   controlled an estimated $5 trillion in assets: Minority Staff of the U.S. Senate Permanent Subcommittee on Investigations, "Private Banking and Money Laundering: A Case Study of Opportunities and Vulnerabilities," November 9–10, 1999, http://www.taxjustice.net/cms/upload/pdf/Report_Corresp .Banking.pdf.

72   The Money Laundering Abatement Act: Senate—Banking, Housing, and Urban

Affairs, S. 1920—Money Laundering Abatement Act of 1999, sponsored by Senator Carl Levin, November 10, 1999, https://www.congress.gov/bill/106th -congress/senate-bill/1920.

73   "Simply put, the guarantee of secrecy": Nancy Dillon, "Offshore Tax Dodge Probe IRS, Justice Checking into Bank Credit Card Accounts," *Daily News* (New York), March 26, 2002, http://www.nydailynews.com/archives/money/offshore -tax-dodge-probe-irs-justice-checking-bank-credit-card-accounts-article-1 .481851.

6: FULL SPEED

75   the European Union announced what it called a "savings directive": Charles-Henry Courtois, "The Impact of the European Commission on the Council of Ministers' Decisions in the Field of European Taxation," *International Public Policy Review* 2, no. 2 (November 2006): 26–47, https://www.ucl.ac.uk/ippr/journal /downloads/vol2-2/IPPR_Vol_2_No_2-2.pdf.

76   "we have before us a very positive outlook": Mossack Fonseca company newsletter, *MF Update: Mossfon Views on the Latest Developments*, issue 6, March 2003.

76   Mossack hired Zollinger as an assistant in 1997: Mario Stäuble, "Der Offshorepilot," *Tages Anzeiger*, April 27, 2015, http://www.tagesanzeiger.ch/wirtschaft /standard/Der-Offshorepilot/story/17029354.

76   In February 2004, Mossfon received a request: Letter to Mrs. Kelcine Smith-Evans from Loren Klein, February 2, 2004.

77   "We have noticed that too many clients of yours": Email from Sandra de Cornejo to John Gordon, February 12, 2004.

77   "I have read your message and find it very odd": Email from John Gordon to Sandra de Cornejo, February 12, 2004.

78   "MF had a tendency to be demanding for stuff then drop it": Email from John Gordon to author, March 2017.

79   Ramsés Owens met with executives from the Denmark-based Jyske Bank: Jyske Bank Private Banking contact report, Ramsés Owens, May 19, 2005.

79   Nordea Bank also helped customers circumvent the rule: Email from Roberth Josefsson, Wealth Planning, Nordea Bank to Jost Dex, May 24, 2005.

80   Niue maintained a lucrative trade in "900" sex telephone numbers: Tony Horwitz, *Blue Latitudes: Boldly Going Where Captain Cook Has Gone Before* (New York: Henry Holt, 2002), p. 228.

80   the BVI government was unconcerned: Email from Ana Escobar to Jürgen Mossack, et al., August 10, 2004.

80   Francisco Paesa Sánchez, an infamous Spanish intelligence agent and world-class opportunist: José María Irujo, "A Picaresque Life Amid the Halls of Power," *El País*, January 3, 2012, http://elpais.com/elpais/2012/01/03/inenglish/1325571644_850210.html; and Jesús Escudero and Will Fitzgibbon, "La 'resurreción' del espía Paesa provocó el caos en Mossack Fonseca," *El Confidencial*, April 5, 2016, http://www.elconfidencial.com/economia/papeles-panama/2016 -04-05/la-resurreccion-del-espia-paesa-provoco-el-caos-en-mossack-fonseca _1179183/.

81   citing fears that the notorious Spanish spy might tarnish its image: Will Fitzgibbon, "Spies and Shadowy Allies Lurk in Secret with Help from Offshore Firm," International Consortium of Investigative Journalists, April 5, 2016, https:// panamapapers.icij.org/20160405-spies-secret-offshore-companies.html.

81   Abacha had funneled some of his illicit money through Swiss banks: Swiss Federal Office of Justice, "Switzerland Provides Mutual Legal Assistance in the Abacha

Case," January 21, 2000, https://www.admin.ch/gov/en/start/dokumentation /medienmitteilungen.msg-id-22828.html.

82   "corporate governance in Russia!!!": Email from Manny Cohen to MF&Co, et al., September 23, 2005.

83   "I'd like to take advantage": Email from Ana Escobar to Jürgen Mossack, et al., September 27, 2005, translated from the original Spanish by author.

84   They had placed their money in a sure-fire fund run by Eugenio Curatola: Iván Ruiz, Maia Jastreblansky, and Hugo Alconada Mon, "'El Madoff argentino' estafó con un guiño de Mossack Fonseca," La Nación, May 15, 2016, http://www. lanacion.com.ar/1898918-el-madoff-argentino-estafo-con-un-guino-de-mossack -fonseca.

85   "the Argentinian Madoff": Ibid.

86   the firm tacked on an extra $20 charge: Email from Jochen Brandt to Mario Vlieg, April 17, 2007.

86   a report on the weapons trade: Sudan: Arming the perpetrators of grave abuses in Darfur, Amnesty International, November 16, 2004.

87   "People were supplying him with stuff": "British Arms Dealer Defends Attempts to Supply Sudan," Scotsman, November 18, 2004, http://www.scotsman.com /news/world/british-arms-dealer-defends-attempts-to-supply-sudan-1 -562489#ixzz42StHJTXx%C2%A0.

87   When they arrived in Kuwait, customs officials intercepted them and tipped off the British: "Arms Dealer Trapped by Shredder," BBC News, November 26, 2007, http://news.bbc.co.uk/2/hi/uk_news/england/kent/7113506.stm.

87   Knight was sentenced to four years in prison for arms trafficking: "Arms Dealer Jailed for Four Years," BBC, November 23, 2007, http://news.bbc.co.uk/1/hi /england/kent/7110160.stm.

7: THE NORTH STAR

88   the top 10 percent of wealth holders owning 85 percent of all household wealth: Credit Suisse Research Institute, Global Wealth Report 2014, October 2014, https://publications.credit-suisse.com/tasks/render/file/?fileID=60931FDE -A2D2-F568-B041B58C5EA591A4.

88   His cronies did not need a piece of paper signed by Putin: "Putin's Secret Riches," BBC, January 25, 2016, https://www.youtube.com/watch?v=LgDCRegyo7Q.

89   rumored to be one of the planet's wealthiest people: Adam Taylor, "Is Vladimir Putin Hiding a $200 Billion Fortune? (And If So, Does It Matter?)," Washington Post, February 20, 2015, https://www.washingtonpost.com/news/worldviews /wp/2015/02/20/is-vladimir-putin-hiding-a-200-billion-fortune-and-if-so-does -it-matter/?utm_term=.aa594b8bf90d.

89   senior KGB officials learned to manipulate offshore banks and companies: Author interview with Karen Dawisha, March 2016.

89   As a youth, Putin's ambition: Steven Lee Myers, The New Tsar: The Rise and Reign of Vladimir Putin (New York: Alfred A. Knopf, 2015), p. 62.

90   Medvedev has different offshore providers and his own network of school chums: Ivan Nechepurenko, "Kremlin Critic Says Russian Premier, Dmitri Medvedev, Built Property Empire on Graft," New York Times, March 2, 2017, https://www.nytimes.com/2017/03/02/world/europe/russia-dmitri-medvedev -aleksei-navalny.html.

91   to enter into a joint venture with the bank: Karen Dawisha, Putin's Kleptocracy: Who Owns Russia? (New York: Simon & Schuster, 2014), p. 64.

91   "Wide-scale infiltration of the Western financial system": U.S. House Committee on Banking and Financial Services, "Russian Money Laundering," 106th Cong., 1st Sess., September 21–22, 1999, http://www.archive.org/stream /russianmoneylaun00unit/russianmoneylaun00unit_djvu.txt.

91   The bulk of the Communist Party's shares of Bank Rossiya were transferred: Dawisha, *Putin's Kleptocracy*, p. 65.

91   Another early investor in Rossiya was Gennady Petrov: Karen Dawisha, *Putin's Kleptocracy: Who Owns Russia?* (New York: Simon and Schuster, 2014), p. 67.

92   Malyushin himself had a company with Mossfon: "Russia: A High Official Goes Offshore," Organized Crime and Corruption Reporting Project, April 3, 2016, https://www.occrp.org/en/panamapapers/high-russian-official-offshore/.

92   a long history of working in cooperation with the Russian mafia: "Putin Allies Aided by Russian Mafia in Spain," *Bloomberg*, June 30, 2015, https://www.bloomberg.com/news/articles/2015-06-29/putin-allies-aided-russian-mafia-in-spain -prosecutors-say.

92   paying $20,000 a month to the crime boss for reasons unknown: Ryan Chittum, Jake Bernstein, and Michael Hudson, "The Malefactors of Mossack Fonseca," International Consortium of Investigative Journalists, May 9, 2016, https:// panamapapers.icij.org/20160509-malefactors-criminals-offshore.html.

92   "the Ministry of Privileges": Myers, *The New Tsar*, p. 109.

92   about $30 million in kickbacks: Robin Munro, "Convicted Borodin Will Defy Swiss Court," *St. Petersburg Times*, March 19, 2002, http://star.worldbank.org /corruption-cases/sites/corruption-cases/files/documents/arw/Borodin _Switzerland_Conviction_StPetersburg_Times_Mar_19_2002.pdf.

93   An independent prosecutor, Yury Skuratov: Celestine Bohlen, "Fire Smoldering Under Kremlin Scorches Prosecutor Again," *New York Times*, April 3, 1999, http://www.nytimes.com/1999/04/03/world/fire-smoldering-under-kremlin -scorches-prosecutor-again.html.

93   indicted in a Swiss court on charges of money laundering in the Borodin case: Andrew Meier, "Russian Held in New York Was Putin's Mentor," *Time*, January 18, 2001, http://content.time.com/time/world/article/0,8599,95681,00.html.

93   "After the collapse of the Soviet Union": Author interview with Jürgen Mossack, June 2017.

93   teased Mossack that he should lighten up, the Cold War was over: Author interview with John Gordon, New York, January 2017.

94   Russia experienced a total net capital outflow of about $550 billion: "Russia: Massive Capital Flight Continues," EurasiaNet, April 30, 2015, http://www.eurasianet.org/node/73251.

94   a Mossfon company registered in the BVI named Southport Management Services Limited: "Treasury Sanctions Individuals and Entities Involved in Sanctions Evasion Related to Russia and Ukraine," U.S. Department of the Treasury, July 30, 2015, https://www.treasury.gov/press-center/press-releases/Pages /jl0133.aspx.

94   "They do not want to disclose details": Contact report Sequoia Treuhand Trust Reg, Dolan Laurence, March 6, 2013.

97   the former Siemens representative who was a major Bank Rossiya shareholder: Jack Stubbs, Andrey Kuzmin, Stephen Grey, and Roman Anin, "The Man Who Married Putin's Daughter and Then Made a Fortune," Reuters, December 17, 2015, http:// www.reuters.com/investigates/special-report/russia-capitalism-shamalov/.

98   earning at least $4 million from them between 2008 and 2011: Jake Bernstein,

Petra Blum, Oliver Zihlmann, David Thompson, Frederik Obermaier, and Bastian Obermayer, "All Putin's Men: Secret Records Reveal Money Network Tied to Russian Leader," International Consortium of Investigative Journalists, April 3, 2016, https://panamapapers.icij.org/20160403-putin-russia-offshore-network.html.

99   worth about $10 million a year in dividends to Roldugin: Ibid.

99   Direct investment by Russians in the BVI during this period increased eightfold: "Russians Park Money in British Virgin Islands," Wall Street Journal, August 16, 2013, http://blogs.wsj.com/emergingeurope/2013/08/16/russians-park-money-in-british-virgin-islands/?mg=id-wsj.

100   when the U.S. Treasury Department sanctioned the brothers: "Treasury Sanctions Individuals and Entities for Sanctions Evasion and Other Activities Related to Russia and Ukraine," U.S. Department of the Treasury, December 22, 2015, https://www.treasury.gov/press-center/press-releases/Pages/jl0314.aspx.

100   In 2016, Arkady Rotenberg placed first on the Forbes list: Roman Anin, Olesya Shmagun, and Dmitry Velikovskiy, "The Secret Caretaker," Organized Crime and Corruption Reporting Project, April 3, 2016, https://www.occrp.org/en/panamapapers/the-secret-caretaker/; and Bernstein et al., "All Putin's Men."

100   the younger Shamalov, barely thirty, managed to borrow about $1.3 billion: Stubbs et al., "The Man Who Married Putin's Daughter and Then Made a Fortune."

100   Russia has a GDP per capita of about $9,000: Julia Ioffe, "What Russia's Latest Protests Mean for Putin," Atlantic, March 27, 2017, https://www.theatlantic.com/international/archive/2017/03/navalny-protests-russia-putin/520878/.

101   the owners simply changed its name to MV Nerei: Anna Astakhova, "For the sake of maximizing profit from transportation, shipowners turned Russian seamen into slavery," Top Secret, June 3, 2015. Translated from Russian via Google Translate, https://www.sovsekretno.ru/articles/id/4824/.

101   The owners declared bankruptcy: "Database on Reported Incidents of Abandonment of Seafarers," International Labour Organization, December 19, 2016, http://www.ilo.org/dyn/seafarers/seafarersBrowse.details?p_lang=en&p_abandonment_id=194&p_search_id=130718104745; and "Thirteen Seafarers Stuck on Abandoned Ship Appeal for Help," Officer of the Watch, June 26, 2013, https://officerofthewatch.com/2013/06/26/thirteen-seafarers-stuck-on-abandoned-ship-appeal-for-help/.

102   were detained but to date have avoided trial or prison: "Former deputy Gleb Klokov used slave labor?," Translated from Russian via Google Translate, VladNews, April 22, 2013, http://vladnews.ru/2013/04/22/66986.html; "Suspected of using slave labor sailors on SS Veles taken in custody in Vladivostok," Translated from Russian via Google Translate, PortNews, April 22, 2013, http://xn—m1abcfge5eq.xn—p1ai/news/print/159116/.

8: THE ART OF SECRECY

103   The art trade in Switzerland is a multibillion-dollar business: Rachel A. J. Pownall, TEFAF Art Market Report 2017, European Fine Art Foundation (2017), p. 57, http://1uyxqn3lzdsa2ytyzj1asxmmmpt.wpengine.netdna-cdn.com/wp-content/uploads/2017/03/TEFAF-Art-Market-Report-20173.pdf.

103   the Geneva Freeport, more than 600,000 square feet of storage space: "Ports francs et entrepôts douaniers ouverts," Contrôle fédéral des finances (CDF), January 28, 2014, p. 34.

103   1.2 million pieces of art: Pownall, TEFAF Art Market Report 2017, p. 68.

103   everything from Roman antiquities to an estimated one thousand Picassos:

Graham Bowley and Doreen Carvajal, "One of the World's Greatest Art Collectors Hides Behind This Fence," *New York Times*, May 28, 2016, https://www.nytimes.com/2016/05/29/arts/design/one-of-the-worlds-greatest-art-collections-hides-behind-this-fence.html.

103   conservatively valued at more than $100 billion: Koltrowitz and Arnold, "Freeports Boom Highlights Risks of Shady Activities."

104   In 2016, Italian police pried open crates: Nick Squires, "Disgraced British Art Dealer's Priceless Treasure Trove Hidden in Geneva," *Telegraph*, February 1, 2016, http://www.telegraph.co.uk/news/worldnews/europe/switzerland/12134541/Disgraced-British-art-dealers-priceless-treasure-trove-discovered-hidden-in-Geneva.html.

104   Worldwide the art trade is valued at $30 billion annually: Pownall, *TEFAF Art Market Report 2017*, p. 26.

104   more than half of all art sales are private: Clare McAndrew, *TEFAF Art Market Report 2015*, European Fine Art Foundation (2015), p. 36, http://tbamf.org.uk/wp-content/uploads/2015/03/TEFAF2015.pdf.

106   Today more than 65 percent of the articles stored in the Geneva Freeport are art and antiques: Geneva Free Ports and Warehouses Limited, "Second Update," press conference presentation, June 8, 2016, http://geneva-freeports.ch/files/8714/7392/8901/dossier_presse_uk.pdf.

106   76 percent of collectors purchased art: Ibid.

106   prompted his friends to nickname him "Farouk": Susan Adams, "The Art of the Deal," *Forbes*, December 7, 2007, https://www.forbes.com/forbes/2007/1224/080.html.

106   an ostentatiously wealthy Egyptian ruler: Paul Crompton, "King Farouk's Fabulous Wealth," *Al Arabiya News*, January 30, 2014, http://english.alarabiya.net/en/perspective/features/2014/01/30/King-Farouk-s-fabulous-wealth-1977.html.

106   Joe Nahmad was willing, on occasion, to push the limits of the law: Adams, "The Art of the Deal."

107   the three brothers gained a reputation: Ibid.

107   Russian gambling ring run out of New York's Trump Tower: James Glanz, Randy Kennedy, and William K. Rashbaum, "Case Casts Harsh Light on Family Art Business," *New York Times*, May 16, 2013, http://www.nytimes.com/2013/05/17/arts/design/helly-nahmad-gallery-owner-indicted-in-gambling-case.html.

107   purchasing the pastel *Danseuses* by Edgar Degas: Jake Bernstein, "The Art of Secrecy," International Consortium of Investigative Journalists, April 7, 2016, https://panamapapers.icij.org/20160407-art-secrecy-offshore.html.

108   purchased an oil painting at auction at Christie's for $3.2 million: Nathaniel Herzberg (trans. Barbara Banks), "'Panama Papers': A Clearer Picture on the Hidden Modigliani," *Le Monde*, May 27, 2016, http://www.lemonde.fr/panama-papers/article/2016/05/27/panama-papers-a-clearer-picture-on-the-hidden-modigliani_4927569_4890278.html.

108   too young to have purchased the painting as claimed by Christie's: Ibid.

109   "an art world ambulance chaser": Michael Kaplan, "This 'Holocaust Hustler' Makes a Living Off of Nazi-Stolen Art," *New York Post*, July 2, 2016, http://nypost.com/2016/07/02/this-holocaust-hustler-makes-a-living-off-of-nazi-stolen-art/.

109   as much as $170 million: Robin Pogrebin and Scott Reyburn, "With $170.4 Million Sale at Auction, Modigliani Work Joins Rarefied Nine-Figure Club," *New York Times*, November 9, 2015, https://www.nytimes.com/2015/11/10/arts/with

-170-4-million-sale-at-auction-modigliani-work-joins-rarefied-nine-figure-club
.html.

110 "IAC did not have a corporate identity independent of its individual owner":
Judge Eileen Bransten, Court Transcript, Maestracci, Philippe, v. Helly Nahmad
Gallery, Inc., Supreme Court of the State of New York, April 24, 2017.

111 paintings by the likes of Picasso, Paul Cézanne, and Gustav Klimt: Juliette Garside, Jake Bernstein, and Holly Watt, "How Offshore Firm Helped Billionaire
Change the Art World for Ever," *Guardian*, April 7, 2016, https://www.the
guardian.com/news/2016/apr/07/panama-papers-joe-lewis-offshore-art-world
-picasso-christies.

111 A high-powered subsection of cultural New York: Carol Vogel, "Prized Picasso
Leads the Ganz Collection to a Record Auction of $206 Million," *New York
Times*, November 11, 1997, http://www.nytimes.com/1997/11/11/arts/prized
-picasso-leads-the-ganz-collection-to-a-record-auction-of-206-million.html.

113 Basil's death in 1994: Michael Moschos, "Obituary: Basil Goulandris," *Independent*, May 5, 1994, http://www.independent.co.uk/news/people/obituary-basil
-goulandris-1433953.html.

113 Chowaiki decided to give financial backing to the legal effort: Kelly Crow, "The
$3 Billion Family Art Feud," *Wall Street Journal*, June 30, 2016, https://www.wsj
.com/articles/the-3-billion-family-art-feud-1467326777.

113 Talara Holdings also put up a Chagall, *Le violoniste bleu*: "Marc Chagall—*Le Violoniste Bleu*," Sotheby's Impressionist and Modern Art Day Sale, May 6, 2015,
http://www.sothebys.com/en/auctions/ecatalogue/2015/impressionist-modern
-art-day-sale-n09341/lot.141.html.

114 "an elegy for a lost Golden Age": "Paul Gauguin—Mata Mua (In Olden Times),"
Museo Thyssen-Bornemisza, https://www.museothyssen.org/en/collection
/artists/gauguin-paul/mata-mua-olden-times.

114 housed more than a thousand paintings: Jonathan Kandell, "Baron Thyssen-
Bornemisza, Industrialist Who Built Fabled Art Collection, Dies at 81," *New
York Times*, April 28, 2002, http://www.nytimes.com/2002/04/28/nyregion
/baron-thyssen-bornemisza-industrialist-who-built-fabled-art-collection-dies
-81.html.

114 the baron's artworks were divided among thirty to forty companies: Rafael Mén-
dez, "Borja Thyssen usó una sociedad en Nevada para manejar cuentas bancar-
ias en Andorra," *El Confidencial*, September 4, 2016, http://www.elconfidencial
.com/economia/papeles-panama/2016-04-09/borja-thyssen-cuentas-andorra
-mossack-fonseca_1176959/.

114 masking her purchases through offshore companies as her husband did: Mar
Cabra and Michael Hudson, "Mega-Rich Use Tax Havens to Buy and Sell Masterpieces," International Consortium of Investigative Journalists, April 3, 2013,
https://www.icij.org/offshore/mega-rich-use-tax-havens-buy-and-sell
-masterpieces.

115 she split the company with Borja: Ángeles García, "Las cuentas secretas de
los Thyssen," *El País*, October 8, 2011, http://elpais.com/diario/2011/10/08
/revistasabado/1318024801_850215.html.

115 complained that all her liquidity is tied up in paintings: Chris Hastings, "Art
Expert Quits Museum in Fury at £25m Constable Sale," *Daily Mail*, June 30,
2012, http://www.dailymail.co.uk/news/article-2167024/Art-expert-quits-museum
-fury-25m-Constable-sale—Baroness-responsible-insists-needs-money-despite
-homes-125ft-yacht-700m-art-collection.html.

115 The Constable painting fetched $34 million: Cabra and Hudson, "Mega-Rich
Use Tax Havens to Buy and Sell Masterpieces."

9: THE VIKINGS LOSE THEIR FERRARIS

116   The nation's three leading banks had ballooned: Charles Forelle, "As Banking 'Fairy Tale' Ends, Iceland Looks Back to the Sea," *Wall Street Journal*, October 10, 2008, https://www.wsj.com/articles/SB122359763876821355.

116    $403,000 per man, woman, and child: Roger Boyes, *Meltdown Iceland: Lessons on the World Financial Crisis from a Small Bankrupt Island* (New York: Bloomsbury USA, 2009), p. 144.

117   Joly had taken a job with the Norwegian Agency for International Development: "Investigating Iceland's Financiers," *Financial Times*, November 13, 2009, https://www.ft.com/content/b4979f3a-cf2a-11de-8a4b-00144feabdc0.

117   Iceland was small enough where one could discover the real truth: Author interview with Eva Joly, Brussels, September 2016.

117   the scale of the crisis screamed for a response: Author interview with Ólafur Hauksson, Iceland, September 2016.

118   Landsbanki, which held the deposits of one in three Icelanders: Thor Bjorgolfsson, *Billions to Bust and Back: How I Made, Lost and Rebuilt a Fortune* (London: Profile Books, 2015), p. 214.

118   took out loans to fund a nationwide buying binge: Boyes, *Meltdown Iceland*, p. 90.

119   A father-and-son team: Bjorgolfsson, *Billions to Bust and Back*, p. 3.

120   "Like this we could provide our services much faster": Email from Jost Dex to MF&Co Legal Department, September 16, 2004.

121   the rating agency Fitch issued a negative grade for Iceland's economy: "Fitch Ratings Revises Iceland's Outlook to Negative," Central Bank of Iceland, February 21, 2006, http://www.cb.is/publications/news/news/2006/02/21/Fitch-Ratings-revises-Icelands-outlook-to-negative-/.

121   Landsbanki lent its own board members 40 billion kronur: Boyes, *Meltdown Iceland*, p. 160.

122   fraudulently boosting the bank's share price: "Sigurjón Þ. Árnason Sentenced to Three and a Half Years in Prison in the Ímon Case," *Kjarninn*, October 8, 2015, https://translate.google.com/translate?hl=en&sl=is&u=http://kjarninn.is/frettir/sigurjon-th-arnason-daemdur-i-thriggja-og-halfs-ars-fangelsi-i-imon-malinu/&prev=search.

122   Sheikh Mohammed bin Khalifa al-Thani, an investor from Qatar: Sigrún Davíðsdóttir, "The Al-Thani Story Behind the Kaupthing Indictment (Updated)," *Sigrún Davíðsdóttir's Icelog*, February 23, 2012, http://uti.is/2012/02/the-al-thani-story-behind-the-kaupthing-indictment/.

123   a fraud perpetrated by Kaupthing: Ibid.

124   Unemployment jumped from 2 percent to 10 percent in six months: Boyes, *Meltdown Iceland*, p. 187.

124   Born into a well-to-do Jersey family: Bibi van der Zee, "Holy Cow, Taxman! Featherweight Activist Battles the Dodgers," *Guardian*, July 7, 2011, https://www.theguardian.com/business/2011/jul/07/interview-john-christensen-tax-justice-network.

124   with the goal of researching the industry from the inside to expose its flaws: Author interview with John Christensen, January 2017.

125   to reveal the most prolific purveyors of financial secrecy: "And the Losers Are . . . ," *Tax Justice Network*, October 31, 2009, http://taxjustice.blogspot.com/2009/10/and-losers-are.html.

125   The release of the first index created a stir: "Financial Secrecy Index—What the Papers Said," *Tax Justice Network*, November 6, 2009, http://taxjustice.blogspot.com/2009/11/financial-secrecy-index-what-papers.html.

126   the Sovereign Society was responsible for at least sixty-nine Mossfon compa-
       nies: Kevin G. Hall, "Sovereign Society Fed Clients to Panama Papers Law
       Firm," *McClatchy*, June 1, 2016, http://www.mcclatchydc.com/news/nation
       -world/national/article80981417.html.

126   "Secure your wealth with an 82-year-old, proven, virtually 100% courtroom-
       proof structure": Sovereign Society, "The Most Effective Way to Build a 'Perma-
       nent Total Wealth Portfolio,'" March 15, 2008.

126   the Sovereign Society held a four-day conference at a swank resort in Bermuda:
       Matt Collins, "Mastering the Media Machine: Give 'Em the Story," *Sovereign
       Society*, March 20, 2009.

126   "But beware!!!": Email from Ramsés Owens to Aurie Escobar, April 13, 2009.

127   An American real estate tycoon: William Raymond Ponsoldt, Contact Report,
       Egbert Wetherborne, February 14, 2011.

127   federal prosecutors indicted Lockard for bank fraud and conspiracy: Indict-
       ment, United States of America v. Lance Lockard et al., U.S. District Court for
       the District of Alaska, Case 3:07-cr-00148-RRB, December 17, 2008.

128   "I want to know the entire history of this client": Email from Jürgen Mossack to
       Ramsés Owens et al., June 19, 2008, translated from original Spanish by author.

10: COMBING THE MONSTER

131   Birkenfeld and his colleagues had often traveled to America: CBS News,
       "Banking: A Crack in the Swiss Vault," December 30, 2009, http://www.
       cbsnews.com/news/banking-a-crack-in-the-swiss-vault/.

131   UBS bankers visited around thirty-eight hundred American clients: Lisa Jucca,
       "How the U.S. Cracked Open Secret Vaults at UBS," Reuters, April 9, 2010, http://
       www.reuters.com/article/us-banks-ubs-idUSTRE6380UA20100409.

131   "everyone who is attacking Swiss bank secrecy": Speech by Hans-Rudolf Merz,
       March 18, 2008. https://www.parlament.ch/en/ratsbetrieb/amtliches-bulletin
       /amtliches-bulletin-die-verhandlungen?SubjectId=13870.

132   In 2016, the Swiss changed their law to create a "serious tax offense": Bernhard
       Lötscher and Axel Buhr, "Tax Fraud to Become Predicate Offence to Money Laun-
       dering," International Law Office, August 31, 2015, http://www.internationalla
       woffice.com/Newsletters/White-Collar-Crime/Switzerland/CMS-von-Erlach
       -Poncet-Ltd/Tax-fraud-to-become-predicate-offence-to-money-laundering.

133   Kassim Tajideen, for being a financial contributor to Hizballah: U.S. Depart-
       ment of the Treasury, "Treasury Targets Hizballah Financial Network," Decem-
       ber 9, 2010, https://www.treasury.gov/press-center/press-releases/Pages/tg997
       .aspx.

133   the fund paid no UK taxes during thirty years of operation: Juliette Garside,
       "Fund Run by David Cameron's Father Avoided Paying Tax in Britain," *Guardian*,
       April 4, 2016, https://www.theguardian.com/news/2016/apr/04/panama-papers
       -david-cameron-father-tax-bahamas.

133   Mossfon's production had fallen by 82 percent: Rigoberto Carvajal, analysis for
       author.

134   Société Général switched the shareholders of the companies: Email from Jost
       Dex to Mossfon Trust Corporation, February 25, 2009.

136   "NOT their final clients . . . UNBELIEVABLE!": Email from Chris Zollinger to
       Adrian Simon, et al., September 30, 2010.

137   Zeller had come from a state-owned cantonal bank: https://www.credit-suisse
       .com/ch/en/about-us/governance/people/alexandre-zeller.html.

137   had repeatedly failed to live up to its obligations: Mark P. Sullivan, "Venezuela:

Political Conditions and U.S. Policy," Congressional Research Service, July 28, 2009, https://fas.org/sgp/crs/row/RL32488.pdf.

137   President Hugo Chávez's chief bodyguard and his wife: Tamoa Calzadilla, "Un matrimonio cercano a Chávez terminó con empresas en paraísos fiscales y cuenta en Suiza," Univision, April 1, 2016, http://www.univision.com/noticias/papeles-de-panama/un-matrimonio-cercano-a-chavez-termino-con-empresas-en-paraisos-fiscales-y-cuenta-en-suiza; and Alfredo Meza, "Adrián Velásquez: El edecán de Chávez que puso su dinero a buen resguardo," *Panama Papers Venezuela*, March 30, 2016, http://panamapapersvenezuela.com/adrian-velasquez/.

138   when a friend asked, "I have clients who have cash": Stéphane Joahny, " 'Virus' rebondit au Maroc," *Le Journal du Dimanche*, November 3, 2012, updated June 19, 2017, http://www.lejdd.fr/Societe/Actualite/L-affaire-Virus-rebondit-au-Maroc-573163.

138   a century-old inheritance stashed at HSBC in Switzerland: John Lichfield, "The Assistant Mayor, the Swiss Bank Accounts and the €350,000 of Moroccan Drugs Money," *Independent*, October 14, 2002, http://www.independent.co.uk/news/world/europe/the-assistant-mayor-the-swiss-bank-accounts-and-the-350000-of-moroccan-drugs-money-8210969.html.

139   may have laundered as much as €100 million a year: CBS News, "Banking: A Crack in the Swiss Vault."

139   one of the Central African Republic's accounts: U.S. Senate Permanent Subcommittee on Investigations, "Money Laundering and Foreign Corruption: Enforcement and Effectiveness of the Patriot Act," 108th Cong., 2nd Sess., July 15, 2004, p. 56.

139   the family of the president of Gabon: Majority and Minority Staff of the U.S. Senate Permanent Subcommittee on Investigations, "Keeping Foreign Corruption Out of the United States: Four Case Histories," February 4, 2010, p. 106.

140   HSBC's head of compliance publicly tendered his resignation: Jamie Grierson and Graeme Evans, "HSBC Boss David Bagley Resigns During US Senate Meeting After Money Laundering Revelations," *Independent*, July 17, 2012, http://www.independent.co.uk/news/business/news/hsbc-boss-david-bagley-resigns-during-us-senate-meeting-after-money-laundering-revelations-7953320.html.

140   allegations that HSBC laundered as much as 60 to 70 percent of the illicit money in Mexico: Majority and Minority Staff of the U.S. Senate Permanent Subcommittee on Investigations, "U.S. Vulnerabilities to Money Laundering, Drugs, and Terrorist Financing: HSBC Case History," July 17, 2012, p. 69.

140   An estimated 15 percent of the Cayman Islands accounts: Ibid., p. 283.

140   generating annual revenue of $26 million for HSBC: Ibid., p. 260.

140   sentenced to ten years in prison for tax fraud a few years earlier: "Miami Beach Hotel Developers Convicted of Tax Fraud," Southern District of Florida, U.S. Attorney, October 7, 2010, https://www.justice.gov/archive/usao/fls/PressReleases/2010/101007-01.html.

140   had as many as 895 companies with Mossfon: Marco Chown Oved and Robert Cribb, "Signatures for Sale," *Toronto Star*, January 26, 2017, http://projects.thestar.com/panama-papers/canada-signatures-for-sale/.

141   they owned a $1.2 million helicopter: Ashlea Ebeling, "Flatotel Father Son Team Get 10 Years for Tax Fraud," *Forbes*, February 4, 2011, https://www.forbes.com/sites/ashleaebeling/2011/02/04/flatotel-father-son-team-get-10-years-for-tax-fraud/#3cb02f63207c.

141   The Cohens were accused of opening bank accounts: "U.S. Vulnerabilities to Money Laundering, Drugs, and Terrorist Financing," p. 260.

141   froze the assets of Syrian businessman Rami Makhlouf: U.S. Department of the
       Treasury, "Rami Makhluf Designated for Benefiting from Syrian Corruption,"
       February 21, 2008, https://www.treasury.gov/press-center/press-releases
       /Pages/hp834.aspx.
142   head of Syria's feared civilian intelligence agency, the Mukhabarat: Ian Black,
       "Six Syrians Who Helped Bashar al-Assad Keep Iron Grip After Father's Death,"
       Guardian, April 28, 2011, https://www.theguardian.com/world/2011/apr/28
       /syria-bashar-assad-regime-members.
142   the European Union sanctioned Rami and Hafez Makhlouf: European Union,
       "Council Implementing Decision 2013/185/CFSP of 22 April 2013 implement-
       ing Council Decision 2012/739/CFSP Concerning Restrictive Measures
       Against Syria," http://eur-lex.europa.eu/legal-content/EN/TXT/?uri=CELEX%
       3A32013D0185.
143   "We have lost HSBC Geneva": Quoted in an email from Sandra de Cornejo to
       Ramón Fonseca et al., February 17, 2011.
143   In a six a.m. raid in Geneva: Fabiano Citroni, "Condamné pour blanchiment: 'Je
       me sens comme un paria,'" *Tribune de Genève*, June 11, 2013, http://www.tdg.ch
       /geneve/actu-genevoise/condamne-blanchiment-paria/story/19850613.
144   HSBC paid a record $1.9 billion in fines: Jill Treanor and Dominic Rushe,
       "HSBC Pays Record $1.9bn Fine to Settle US Money-Laundering Accusations,"
       Guardian, December 11, 2012. https://www.theguardian.com/business/2012/dec
       /11/hsbc-bank-us-money-laundering.
144   "I don't think HSBC was an anomaly": Author interview with Laura Stuber,
       Washington, DC, October 2016.

II: JOURNALISTIC FIREPOWER

146   His great-grandfather had been a prominent newspaper editor: Caelainn Barr,
       "Irish-Born Journalist Heads Up ICIJ Investigation into Offshore Account Hold-
       ers," *Irish Times*, April 6, 2013, http://www.irishtimes.com/news/irish-born
       -journalist-heads-up-icij-investigation-into-offshore-account-holders-1.1350791.
146   Journalism was about all he was qualified to do: Author interview with Gerard
       Ryle, July 2016.
147   In reality, it was a multimillion-dollar hoax: Gerard Ryle, "Rise of a Man with a
       Magic Mystery Pill," *Sydney Morning Herald*, January 8, 2007, http://www.smh
       .com.au/news/national/rise-of-a-man-with-a-magic-mystery-pill/2007/01/07
       /1168104867997.html?page=fullpage#contentSwap21.
148   The center put it on its mousepads: William E. Buzenberg, "Anatomy of a Global
       Investigation: Collaborative, Data-Driven, Without Borders," Harvard Ken-
       nedy School, Shorenstein Center on Media, Politics, and Public Policy, July 2015,
       https://shorensteincenter.org/wp-content/uploads/2015/07/Anatomy-of-a
       -Global-Investigation-William-Buzenberg.pdf.
148   Lewis envisioned a network: "About ICIJ," International Consortium of Inves-
       tigative Journalists, https://web.archive.org/web/19981201051259/http://icij
       .org:80/about/.
148   an American nonprofit whose initials sound like a U.S. intelligence agency:
       Author interview with Charles Lewis, July 2017.
148   "There was this thing in the air": Author interview with David Leigh, May 2017.
149   how Big Tobacco circumvented health laws and laundered money: "Big Tobacco
       Smuggling," International Consortium of Investigative Journalists, 2000–2001,
       https://www.icij.org/node/460/uk-considering-formal-investigation-cigarette
       -%20smuggling.

149   The initial story, published in January 2000: Duncan Campbell, "Big Tobacco Smuggling," *Duncan Campbell.org*, 2000–2001, http://www.duncancampbell.org /content/big-tobacco-smuggling.

149   The center was slow to adapt to the digital age: Mariah Blake, "Something Fishy?," *Columbia Journalism Review*, July–August 2012, http://archives.cjr.org /feature/something_fishy.php.

149   CPI's head Bill Buzenberg and the center's board: Ibid.

150   Global Investigative Journalism Conference: Speakers, Global Investigative Journalism Conference, October 11, 2011, https://web.archive.org/web /20111026070651/http://gijc2011.org:80/?page_id=19.

154   Australia's Paul Hogan, of *Crocodile Dundee* fame: Marina Walker Guevara, Nicky Hager, Mar Cabra, Gerard Ryle, and Emily Menkes, "Who Uses the Off-shore World," International Consortium of Investigative Journalists, April 16, 2013, https://www.icij.org/offshore/who-uses-offshore-world.

154   indicted Rich for tax evasion and racketeering: Eric N. Berg, "Marc Rich Indicted in Vast Tax Evasion Case," *New York Times*, September 20, 1983, http:// www.nytimes.com/1983/09/20/business/marc-rich-indicted-in-vast-tax -evasion-case.html.

154   Tony Merchant, Canada's "class action king": Frédéric Zalac, Alex Shprintsen, Zach Dubinsky, and Harvey Cashore, "Canadian Senator's Husband Shifted Money into Offshore Tax Havens," International Consortium of Investigative Journalists, April 3, 2013, https://www.icij.org/offshore/canadian-senators -husband-shifted-money-offshore-tax-havens.

154   He decided to contrast the findings with Putin's repeated calls: Roman Shley-nov, "Elites Undermine Putin Rail Against Tax Havens," International Consortium of Investigative Journalists, April 4, 2013, https://www.icij.org/offshore /elites-undermine-putin-rail-against-tax-havens.

155   Commonwealth appeared not to have known about the activities: Michael Hudson, Stefan Candea, and Marina Walker Guevara, "Caribbean Go-Between Provided Shelter for Far-Away Frauds, Documents Show," International Consortium of Investigative Journalists, April 4, 2013, https://www.icij.org/offshore /caribbean-go-between-provided-shelter-far-away-frauds-documents-show.

155   looked like a schooner's rigging: Bastian Obermayer, Frederik Obermaier, and Titus Plattner, "After Multi-Million Inheritance, Playboy Sachs Goes Offshore," International Consortium of Investigative Journalists, April 5, 2013, https:// www.icij.org/offshore/after-multi-million-inheritance-playboy-sachs-goes -offshore.

157   "The *Guardian* says, 'Shit tastes great'": Author interview with Mar Cabra, June 2016.

157   She was hooked, rejecting a promotion: Author interview with Giannina Seg-nini, June 2016.

158   Hudson was about to be laid off: Author interview with Michael Hudson, June 2016.

158   "None of this reflects our trust in your work": Michael Hudson, "Offshore Proj-ect: Writing Guidelines."

160   The website received more than six hundred thousand page views: Email to author from Hamish Boland-Rudder, July 28, 2017.

160   The *Washington Post* chose to publish its big story: Scott Higham, Michael Hud-son, and Marina Walker Guevara, "Piercing the Secrecy of Offshore Tax Havens," *Washington Post*, April 6, 2013, https://www.washingtonpost.com/investigations /piercing-the-secrecy-of-offshore-tax-havens/2013/04/06/1551806c-7d50-11e2 -a044-676856536b40_story_3.html.

161   Bill Buzenberg remembers three beefy IRS agents: Email to author from Bill Buzenberg, July 2017.

161   A month later the IRS put out a face-saving press release: "IRS, Australia and United Kingdom Engaged in Cooperative Effort to Combat Offshore Tax Evasion," Internal Revenue Service, May 9, 2013, https://www.irs.gov/uac/newsroom/irs-australia-and-united-kingdom-engaged-in-cooperative-effort-to-combat-offshore-tax-evasion.

12: PROFITABLE PRINCELINGS

162   offshore clients with addresses in Hong Kong and mainland China: Marina Walker Guevara, Gerard Ryle, Alexa Olesen, Mar Cabra, Michael Hudson, and Christoph Giesen, "Leaked Records Reveal Offshore Holdings of China's Elite," International Consortium of Investigative Journalists, January 21, 2014, https://www.icij.org/offshore/leaked-records-reveal-offshore-holdings-chinas-elite.

163   an exponentially larger amount of foreign direct investment: "China Foreign Direct Investment," Trading Economics, http://www.tradingeconomics.com/china/foreign-direct-investment.

164   the hidden wealth of the families of China's top leaders: David Barboza, "Billions in Hidden Riches for Family of Chinese Leader," New York Times, October 25, 2012, http://www.nytimes.com/2012/10/26/business/global/family-of-wen-jiabao-holds-a-hidden-fortune-in-china.html.

164   quickly banned access to the two news organizations: Keith Bradsher, "China Blocks Web Access to Times After Article," New York Times, October 25, 2012, http://www.nytimes.com/2012/10/26/world/asia/china-blocks-web-access-to-new-york-times.html.

164   They also opted not to renew a visa: "Visa Issue in China Forces Out Times Reporter," New York Times, December 31, 2012, http://www.nytimes.com/2013/01/01/world/asia/times-reporter-in-china-is-forced-to-leave-over-visa-issue.html.

164   Chan was one of the original foreign journalists at the Harvard meeting: https://www.icij.org/journalists/ying-chan.

165   One of its reporters, Luo Changping: "Luo Changping: Journalist—China (Integrity Award)," Transparency International, November 8, 2013, https://www.transparency.org/getinvolved/awardwinner/luo_changping; and Chris Buckley, "After a Journalist's Prodding, China Investigates a Top Official," New York Times, May 12, 2013, http://www.nytimes.com/2013/05/13/world/asia/china-eyes-liu-tienan-an-official-challenged-by-a-journalist.html?_r=0.

166   two most popular jurisdictions for Hong Kong's elite: Author interview with Jürgen Mossack, January 2017.

167   "To lower the political risks": "Gong Enguang: Corporate Overseas Investment Is Mainly Concerned About Legal Risks," Sina Finance, April 26, 2015, http://finance.sina.com.cn/hy/20150426/143022046771.shtml.

169   "Austin, be very careful": Email from Ramsés Owens to Austin Zhang, et al., May 14, 2008.

169   offered a similar service to Marianna Olszewski: Eric Lipton and Julie Creswell, "Panama Papers Show How Rich United States Clients Hid Millions Abroad," New York Times, June 5, 2016, https://www.nytimes.com/2016/06/06/us/panama-papers.html.

170   Portcullis TrustNet: Walker Guevara et al., "Leaked Records Reveal Offshore Holdings of China's Elite."

171   a grandfatherly reformer concerned with the well-being of the poor: "Who's Who in China Leaks," International Consortium of Investigative Journalists, January 22, 2014, https://www.icij.org/blog/2014/01/whos-who-china-leaks.

171   Deng Jiagui, a successful developer: "Excellence Effort Property Development Limited," International Consortium of Investigative Journalists, https://offshoreleaks.icij.org/nodes/158037.

171   The other half was owned by a pair of real estate tycoons: "Excellence Group Wins Two Shenzhen Qianhai Plots for $2 Billion," Bloomberg, July 27, 2013, https://www.bloomberg.com/news/articles/2013-07-27/excellence-group-wins-two-shenzhen-qianhai-plots-for-2-billion.

171   A senior engineer: China Power International Development Limited, "Resignation of Chairman and Non-Executive Director and Appointment of Chairman," January 2, 2008, http://www.irasia.com/listco/hk/chinapower/announcement/a22350-ehkse(e).pdf.

171   Her interests have also strayed into other lucrative activities: Malcolm Moore and Raf Sanchez, "Daughter of 'Butcher of Tiananmen Square' Brokered Secret Deal for Insurance Giant," Telegraph, October 10, 2013, http://www.telegraph.co.uk/news/worldnews/asia/china/10370547/Daughter-of-Butcher-of-Tiananmen-Square-brokered-secret-deal-for-insurance-giant.html.

171   She was a director of two TrustNet companies: https://offshoreleaks.icij.org/nodes/52627.

171   her HSBC Swiss bank account held almost $2.5 million: Sneha Shankar, "Li Xiaolin, Former Chinese Premier Li Peng's Daughter, Hid Over $2M in HSBC Swiss Account," International Business Times, February 10, 2015, http://www.ibtimes.com/li-xiaolin-former-chinese-premier-li-pengs-daughter-hid-over-2m-hsbc-swiss-account-1811000.

171   none was more notorious than Bo Xilai: "Burst Balloons," Economist, August 4, 2012, http://www.economist.com/node/21559933; and Jamil Anderlini, "Bo Xilai: Power, Death and Politics," Financial Times, July 20, 2012, https://www.ft.com/content/d67b90f0-d140-11e1-8957-00144feabdc0.

171   As mayor of Dalian in the 1990s: "China: A Princeling Who Could Be Premier," Bloomberg, March 15, 2004, https://www.bloomberg.com/news/articles/2004-03-14/china-a-princeling-who-could-be-premier.

171   "Fog City": Pete Brook, "World's Fastest-Growing Megalopolis Hides in Fog," Wired, August 25, 2010, https://www.wired.com/2010/08/chongqing/.

172   Wang Lijun, the star of Iron-Blooded Police Spirits: Pin Ho and Wenguang Huang, A Death in the Lucky Holiday Hotel: Murder, Money, and an Epic Power Struggle in China (New York: PublicAffairs, 2013), p. 22.

172   They administered electric shock treatment: "Tiger Chains and Cell Bosses: Police Torture of Criminal Suspects in China," Human Rights Watch, May 13, 2015, https://www.hrw.org/report/2015/05/13/tiger-chairs-and-cell-bosses/police-torture-criminal-suspects-china; and Tom Phillips, "Gu Kailai 'Painted Neil Heywood as Crystal Meth–Dealing Drug King Pin,'" Telegraph, December 20, 2012, http://www.telegraph.co.uk/news/worldnews/asia/china/9758503/Gu-Kailai-painted-Neil-Heywood-as-crystal-meth-dealing-drug-king-pin.html.

172   "Corruption is the Party's mortal wound": John Garnaut, "The East Is Still Red," Foreign Policy, August 22, 2013, http://foreignpolicy.com/2013/08/22/the-east-is-still-red/.

172   a fortune in kickbacks: Alexa Olesen, "Leaked Files Offer Many Clues to Offshore Dealings by Top Chinese," International Consortium of Investigative Journalists, April 6, 2016, https://panamapapers.icij.org/20160406-china-red-nobility

-offshore-dealings.html; and Jeremy Page and Noémie Bisserbe, "French Villa Linked to Fallen China Leader," *Wall Street Journal*, August 6, 2013, https://www .wsj.com/articles/SB10001424127887323420604578650071253073626.

172   The school cost about £30,000 a year: Anderlini, "Bo Xilai: Power, Death and Politics."

174   He was the director of two companies and the shareholder of another: https:// offshoreleaks.icij.org/nodes/102672.

174   *Caijing*'s deputy investigative editor, Luo Changping: Zhang Hong, "Hard-Hitting Caijing Editor Luo Changping Removed from Post: Sources," *South China Morning Post*, November 27, 2013, http://www.scmp.com/news/china /article/1367171/hard-hitting-caijing-editor-luo-changping-removed-post -sources.

13: FOLLOW THE LEAKS

176   scrambled after the release of Offshore Leaks: Kimberley Porteous, Michael Hudson, and Sasha Chavkin, "Release of Offshore Records Draws Worldwide Response," International Consortium of Investigative Journalists, December 4, 2014, https://www.icij.org/blog/2013/04/release-offshore-records-draws-world wide-response.

176   "crisis of confidence": Sasha Chavkin, "Tax Havens Face Crisis in Wake of Offshore Leaks, Report Says," International Consortium of Investigative Journalists, November 26, 2013, https://www.icij.org/blog/2013/11/tax-havens-face -crisis-wake-offshore-leaks-report-says.

177   Spain's *El País* printed a list of Spanish HSBC account holders: Manuel Altozano, "La primera 'lista Falciani,'" *El País*, April 21, 2013, http://politica.elpais.com /politica/2013/04/21/actualidad/1366522419_772068.html.

177   Mar Cabra wrote a story in *El Confidencial*: C. Hernanz and Mar Cabra, "El rastro de españoles en la lista Falciani conecta con el 'paraíso' de las Islas Vírgenes Británicas," *El Confidencial*, April 22, 2013, http://www.elconfidencial.com/espana /2013-04-22/el-rastro-de-espanoles-en-la-lista-falciani-conecta-con-el-paraiso -de-las-islas-virgenes-britanicas_205648/.

177   In 2006, Falciani was tapped: Juan Luis Sánchez, "¿Quién es Falciani? ¿Qué sabe Falciani?," *El Diario*, December 18, 2012, http://www.eldiario.es/economia /falciani-HSBC-quien_0_80842176.html.

177   he downloaded the data for himself: Titus Plattner and Oliver Zihlmann, "La vraie histoire d'Hervé Falciani," *Le Matin Dimanche*, February 15, 2015, http:// enquete.lematindimanche.ch/falciani/.

178   he would use the money to leave his wife and autistic daughter: Ibid.

178   the BND had purchased a DVD for almost €5 million: "Massive Tax Evasion Scandal in Germany: The Liechtenstein Connection," *Der Spiegel*, February 16, 2008, http://www.spiegel.de/international/business/massive-tax-evasion-scandal -in-germany-the-liechtenstein-connection-a-535768.html.

181   Panama: "Latest FATCA News from Bahamas, Cayman Islands, U.K., U.S.; Panama 'Immobilizes' Bearer Shares," *Gunster*, August 19, 2013, https://gunster .com/alerts/latest-fatca-news-from-bahamas-cayman-islands-u-k-u-s-panama -immobilizes-bearer-shares-3/.

181   the Seychelles: "The Seychelles: Bill Amending the International Business Companies Act 1994," *LCG International*, http://www.lcg-international.net/IBC -Companies-are-no-longer-pe.949.0.html.

182   In May, the BVI Financial Services Commission contacted Mossfon: https:// offshoreleaks.icij.org/nodes/10062310.

182   the Mubaraks (including another son, Gamal) were arrested: Associated Press, "Egypt Court Orders Release of Hosni Mubarak's Sons," *Guardian*, October 12, 2015, http://www.theguardian.com/world/2015/oct/12/egypt-court-hosni -mubarak-sons-gamal-alaa-release-corruption-conviction; and Greg Botelho, "Egypt Court Rejects Mubarak's Bid to Throw Out Corrupt Sentence," CNN, January 9, 2016, http://www.cnn.com/2016/01/09/middleeast/egypt-mubarak -corruption-appeal/.

182   "You don't think when Mubarak walks through the door": Author interview with Jürgen Mossack, May 2017.

183   Mossfon was able to provide the true owner's name for just five of those requests: David Pegg and Helena Bengtsson, "British Virgin Islands Failed to Crack Down on Mossack Fonseca," *Guardian*, April 4, 2016, https://www.the-guardian.com/news/2016/apr/04/british-virgin-islands-failed-to-crack-down -on-mossack-fonseca-panama-papers.

183   about thirty of the firm's shell companies: Email from Sandra de Cornejo to Josette Roquebert, et al., August 8, 2013.

183   a group of mostly elderly tourists boarded the *Ethan Allen*: "More Lawsuits Filed in Capsizing of *Ethan Allen*," *North Country Gazette*, February 19, 2016, http://www.northcountrygazette.org/articles/021906BoatLawsuits.html.

183   The Coast Guard later determined: National Transportation Safety Board, "Marine Accident Report: Capsizing of New York State-Certificated Vessel *Ethan Allen*, Lake George, New York, October 2, 2005," July 25, 2006, https:// www.ntsb.gov/investigations/AccidentReports/Reports/MAR0603.pdf.

183   There were forty-seven aboard: Richard Pérez-Peña, "21 Die in Sinking of Tourist Boat in Adirondacks," *New York Times*, October 3, 2005, http://www.nytimes .com/2005/10/03/nyregion/21-die-in-sinking-of-tourist-boat-in-adirondacks .html.

184   His body was found the next day: "Police: LG Drowning Was Suicide," *Post Star*, September 14, 2009, http://poststar.com/news/local/police-lg-drowning-was -suicide/article_d2a184bb-3cec-56c3-b020-876bf1cc4181.html.

184   it would appear that the removals had happened prior to his conviction: Email from Sandra de Cornejo to Josette Roquebert, et al., August 8, 2013

184   the French television journalist Edouard Perrin struck gold: Author interview with Edouard Perrin, August 2016.

184   Richard Murphy, an accountant and cofounder of the organization: http:// www.internationaltaxreview.com/Article/3288256/Richard-Murphy.html.

185   Richard Brooks, a former investigator: https://www.theguardian.com/profile /richard-brooks.

185   Kohl had run Sociétés 6: Matthew Karnitschnig and Robin van Daalen, "Business-Friendly Bureaucrat Helped Build Tax Haven in Luxembourg," *Wall Street Journal*, October 21, 2014, https://www.wsj.com/articles/luxembourg -tax-deals-under-pressure-1413930593.

185   There were hundreds of companies: Leslie Wayne, Kelly Carr, Marina Walker Guevara, Mar Cabra, and Michael Hudson, "Leaked Documents Expose Global Companies' Secret Tax Deals in Luxembourg," International Consortium of Investigative Journalists, November 5, 2014, https://www.icij.org/project /luxembourg-leaks/leaked-documents-expose-global-companies-secret-tax -deals-luxembourg.

185   The agreements themselves were often quite complex: "12 LuxLeaks Diagrams That Will Make Your Head Spin," *Guardian*, November 7, 2014, https://www .theguardian.com/business/gallery/2014/nov/07/12-luxleaks-diagrams-that -will-make-your-head-spin.

185   the Illinois-based pharmaceutical company Abbott Laboratories: Wayne et al., "Leaked Documents Expose Global Companies' Secret Tax Deals in Luxembourg."

185   the Australian division of the Swedish furniture giant IKEA: Neil Chenoweth, "Why IKEA's Australian Profits Are Mostly Tax Free," International Consortium of Investigative Journalists, November 6, 2014, https://www.icij.org/project /luxembourg-leaks/why-ikeas-australian-profits-are-mostly-tax-free.

185   reduce its tax burden in the places where it actually earned the profits: Wayne et al., "Leaked Documents Expose Global Companies' Secret Tax Deals in Luxembourg."

185   On April 21, 2010, he had been exceptionally efficient: Omri Marian, "The State Administration of International Tax Avoidance," *Harvard Business Law Review* 7, no. 1 (2017): 1–65, http://www.hblr.org/wp-content/uploads/2017/06/The-State -Administration-of-International-Tax-Avoidance.pdf.

186   Many of these firms also took advantage of laws: Jan Kleinnijenhuis, "Is Your Head Spinning? 5 Tips to Understand the 'Lux Leaks' Files," International Consortium of Investigative Journalists, November 10, 2014, https://www.icij.org /project/luxembourg-leaks/your-head-spinning-5-tips-understand-lux-leaks -files.

186   His hourlong report for the program *Cash Investigations*: "Paradis Fiscaux, les petits secrets des grandes entreprises," https://www.youtube.com/watch?v =123_Ll6AVtM.

14: TROUBLE AHEAD, TROUBLE BEHIND

191   all the way to the U.S. Supreme Court: Ken Parks, Nicole Hong, and Brent Kendall, "Supreme Court Sides with Holdout Creditors Appeal in Argentina Debt Case," *Wall Street Journal*, June 16, 2014, https://www.wsj.com/articles/u-s -supreme-court-rejects-argentina-appeal-in-sovereign-debt-case-1402926119.

192   "freedom, sovereignty, or dignity": "Argentina's Vulture, Paul Singer, Is Wall Street Freedom Fighter," *Bloomberg*, August 8, 2014,

192   video testimony of alleged associates of Báez: Santiago Pérez and Taos Turner, "In Argentina, Mix of Money and Politics Stirs Intrigue Around Kirchner," *Wall Street Journal*, July 28, 2014, https://www.wsj.com/articles/in-argentina -mix-of-money-and-politics-stirs-intrigue-around-kirchner-1406601002.

192   The illicit loot was destined for foreign bank accounts: "Jorge Lanata mostró la ruta del dinero de Lázaro Báez," *La Nación*, April 15, 2013, http://www.lanacion .com.ar/1572765-lanata-mostro-la-ruta-del-dinero-de-lazaro-baez.

192   Báez allegedly sent it back to the Kirchners: Hugo Alconada Mon, "Báez 'alquiló' los tres hoteles de los Kirchner por $14,5 millones," *La Nación*, December 17, 2013, http://www.lanacion.com.ar/1648473-baez-alquilo-los-tres-hoteles -de-los-kirchner-por-145-millones.

194   one of Mossfon's most prolific nominees: Tomás Ocaña, "La oficinista de las 11,000 empresas," Univision, April 2, 2016, http://www.univision.com/noticias /papeles-de-panama/la-oficinista-de-las-11-000-empresas.

194   Paul Singer's team then sought to depose Patricia Amunategui: NML Capital, Ltd. v. The Republic of Argentina, United States District Court, Nevada, Case no. 2:14-cv-492-RFB-VCF, Videographed Deposition of Patricia Amunategui, September 11, 2014.

195   "I'm worried about 'Miss Patricia'": Luis Martínez, email to Ernesto González et al., September 17, 2004, https://www.documentcloud.org/documents/2792783 -160403-background-02.html.

195   Gerard Ryle and Marina Walker replicated it for the HSBC investigation: https://www.icij.org/project/779/partners.

196   from Ian Fleming: https://www.ajb007.co.uk/topic/45912/swiss-bank-account -references-in-the-bond-films-and-novels/.

196   to Robert Ludlum: http://allthetropes.wikia.com/wiki/Swiss_Bank_Account.

196   approximately $1.36 billion in unpaid taxes: Martha M. Hamilton, Jakob Sor-genfri, and John Hansen, "New Countries Seek HSBC Data and Undeclared Cash," International Consortium of Investigative Journalists, February 23, 2015, https://www.icij.org/project/swiss-leaks/new-countries-seek-hsbc-data-and -undeclared-cash.

197   Linkurious downloaded it to create a product demonstration: Jean Villedieu, "Analysing the Offshore Leaks with Graphs," *Linkurious*, May 27, 2014, https:// linkurio.us/blog/analysing-the-offshore-leaks-with-graphs/.

197   Botín's company, North Star Overseas Enterprises Inc.: https://projects.icij.org /swiss-leaks/people/emilio-botin.

198   Clicking on each: Jean Villedieu, "How the ICIJ Used Linkurious to Reveal the Secrets Hidden in the Swiss Leaks Data," *Linkurious*, June 18, 2015, https:// linkurio.us/blog/how-the-icij-used-linkurious-to-reveal-the-secrets-hidden-in -the-swiss-leaks-data/.

198   A French government investigation: M. Christian Eckert, Information Report to the National Assembly, p. 19.

198   the Belgian diamond dealer Emmanuel Shallop: Mario Stäuble, "Das sagt die HSBC über ihre Geschäftspraxis," *Basler Zeitung*, February 8, 2015, http://bazonline.ch /schweiz/swissleaks/Das-sagt-die-HSBC-ueber-ihre-Geschaeftspraxis/story /23435911.

199   Shallop was found guilty in the Belgian Court of Appeals: United Nations Secu-rity Council Committee Established Pursuant to Resolution 1572, *Final Report of the Group of Experts on Côte d'Ivoire*, April 27, 2011.

199   A UN-sponsored court: "S Leone War Crimes Trio Convicted," Al Jazeera, Feb-ruary 25, 2009, http://www.webcitation.org/68rsEYVOi.

199   He received a $12 million loan from the state bank: Gustavo Olivo Peña, "Del caso Arturo del Tiempo, en RD todo 'se esfumó,' sólo quedó la torre Atiemar," *Acento*, February 14, 2014, http://acento.com.do/2014/actualidad/1164513-del -caso-arturo-del-tiempo-en-rd-todo-se-esfumo-solo-quedo-la-torre-atiemar/.

199   It would take the publication of the HSBC files: Daniele Grasso, Ryan Chittum, Jake Bernstein, and Michael Hudson, "Los negocios sucios de Mossack Fon-seca con delincuentes y convictos españoles," *El Confidencial*, May 10, 2016, http://www.elconfidencial.com/economia/papeles-panama/2016-05-10 /papeles-panama-papers-criminales-convictos-delincuentes-mossack-fonseca _1197210/.

200   "I never had any problems with Juncker": Karnitschnig and van Daalen, "Business-Friendly Bureaucrat Helped Build Tax Haven in Luxembourg."

201   to investigate Luxembourg's tax agreements: Julie Levy-Abegnoli, "Juncker Faces Further 'LuxLeaks' Probing," *Parliament Magazine*, January 16, 2015, https://www. theparliamentmagazine.eu/articles/news/juncker-faces-further-luxleaks-probing.

201   One of its vice chairs was Eva Joly: "EP Tax Evasion Investigation Kicks Off; Proper Inquiry Must Be Swiftly Ramped-Up," *Sven Giegold*, February 26, 2015, http://www.sven-giegold.de/2015/ep-tax-evasion-investigation-kicks-off -proper-inquiry-must-be-swiftly-ramped-up/.

201   The committee was scathing: Levy-Abegnoli, "Juncker Faces Further 'LuxLeaks' Probing."

201　He easily beat back a no-confidence vote: Philip Blenkinsop, "EU'S Juncker Survives No-Confidence Vote over Tax Deals," Reuters, November 27, 2014, http://www.reuters.com/article/us-eu-juncker-idUSKCN0JB13Q20141127.

202　the military security contractor Blackwater: Richard Lardner, "Blackwater Hires PR Giant in Image Siege," USA Today, October 5, 2007, https://usatoday30.usatoday.com/news/washington/2007-10-05-2348857332_x.htm.

202　Blackwater lost its State Department contract: Charley Keyes, "Source: Firm to Take Over Blackwater/Xe's Iraq Contract," CNN, April 1, 2009, http://www.cnn.com/2009/POLITICS/04/01/us.iraq.security/.

202　which had Mossfon companies in the BVI: Adam Weinstein, Catherine Dunn, Miriti Murungi, and Fusion Investigative Unit, "Panama Papers Include One of U.S.'s Biggest Wartime Military Contractors," Fusion, April 13, 2016, http://fusion.net/story/289615/panama-papers-leak-military-contractor-triple-canopy/.

203　Geneva's lead prosecutor, Olivier Jornot: Hamish Boland-Rudder, "HSBC's Geneva Office Raided as Swiss Open Investigation," International Consortium of Investigative Journalists, February 18, 2015, https://www.icij.org/blog/2015/02/hsbcs-geneva-office-raided-swiss-open-investigation.

203　The bank would pay $43 million: Joshua Franklin and Stephanie Nebehay, "HSBC to Pay $43 Million Geneva Money Laundering Settlement," Reuters, June 4, 2015, http://www.reuters.com/article/us-hsbc-tax-swiss-idUSKBN0O K1G220150604.

15: FORTUNE FAVORS THE BOLD

205　Commerzbank, Germany's second-largest bank: Labutes IR, "Commerzbank Is a Value Trap," Seeking Alpha, November 9, 2016, https://seekingalpha.com/article/4021438-commerzbank-value-trap.

205　Commerzbank insisted that the inquiry dealt with ancient history: Bastian Brinkmann, Hans Leyendecker, Bastian Obermayer, and Klaus Ott, "Wie Fahnder gegen das System Luxemburg losschlagen," Süddeutsche Zeitung, February 25, 2015, http://www.sueddeutsche.de/wirtschaft/ermittlungen-wegen-steuerhinterziehung-wie-fahnder-gegen-das-system-luxemburg-losschlagen-1.2366065.

206　"We are talking about a big fish here": Bastian Brinkmann, Katrin Langhans, and Bastian Obermayer, "Datenleck erschüttert Offshore-Dienstleister in Panama," Süddeutsche Zeitung, February 25, 2015, http://www.sueddeutsche.de/wirtschaft/kanzlei-mossack-fonseca-datenleck-erschuettert-offshore-dienstleister-in-panama-1.2365907.

206　to sell compact discs to the government of North Rhine–Westphalia: Edward Taylor, Matthias Inverardi, and Mark Hosenball, "Special Report: How Germany's Taxman Used Stolen Data to Squeeze Switzerland," Reuters, November 21, 2013, http://www.reuters.com/article/us-germany-swiss-datatheft-specialreport-idUSBRE9AK0GT20131121.

206　paying $1.14 million for the information: Sean Sinico, "Germany Probed Mossack Fonseca Before Panama Papers Leak," DW, April 6, 2016, http://www.dw.com/en/germany-probed-mossack-fonseca-before-panama-papers-leak/a-19166145.

206　Germany was not the only customer for the data: Hans Leyendecker, Bastian Obermayer, and Klaus Ott, "Steueraffäre erschüttert Commerzbank," Süddeutsche Zeitung, February 25, 2015, https://web.archive.org/web/20150226064048/http://www.sueddeutsche.de/wirtschaft/luxemburg-steueraffaere-erschuettert-commerzbank-1.2366678.

207   Commerzbank paid a €17 million fine: "Commerzbank zahlt 17 Millionen Euro
        Bußgeld," *Frankfurter Rundschau*, October 14, 2015, http://www.fr.de/wirtschaft
        /dossier/commerzbank/steuerhinterziehung-commerzbank-zahlt-17-millionen
        -euro-bussgeld-a-429348.

207   in a book he coauthored with fellow *Süddeutsche* reporter Frederik Obermaier:
        Bastian Obermayer and Frederik Obermaier, *The Panama Papers: Breaking the
        Story of How the Rich and Powerful Hide Their Money* (London: Oneworld Publica-
        tions, 2016).

208   bank transfer information for almost $500 million in gold: Frederik Obermaier, Bas-
        tian Obermayer, and Jan Strozyk, "Searching for Gold," *Süddeutsche Zeitung*, n.d.,
        http://panamapapers.sueddeutsche.de/articles/570e7bb4a1bb8d3c3495bb08/.

210   interviewed Switzerland's own Christoph Zollinger: Mario Stäuble, "Der
        Offshorepilot," *Tages Anzeiger*, April 27, 2015, http://www.tagesanzeiger.ch
        /wirtschaft/standard/Der-Offshorepilot/story/17029354.

211   a slick, albeit unintentionally comical, promotional video: " 'Spirit of Panama'—
        ein Bobteam auf Mission," *SRF* video, 9:38, January 16, 2012, http://www.srf.ch
        /play/tv/sportlounge/video/spirit-of-panama-ein-bobteam-auf-mission?id
        =f839d563-832e-4be4-aa21-d84ff07f2a3c.

212   Fonseca went on television and called the president an autocrat: "Ramón Fon-
        seca Mora Fired After Defending Panameñista Position on Television News
        Program," *Panama Guide*, May 30, 2011, www.panama-guide.com/article.php
        /20110530164555784; and interview with Ramón Fonseca.

212   where he faces criminal charges over misuse of public money: Curt Anderson,
        "Judge: Panama Ex-President Should Be Extradited from US," Associated Press,
        August 31, 2017, https://www.washingtonpost.com/national/judge-panama-ex
        -president-should-be-extradited-from-us/2017/08/31/d872dad8-8e89-11e7-9c53
        -6a169beb0953_story.html?utm_term=.4b3d4cb6141f.

214   Jóhannesson would essentially be suing himself: Paul Fontaine, "How a Tycoon
        Almost Sued Himself," *Reykjavík Grapevine*, January 14, 2013, https://grapevine.is
        /news/2013/01/14/how-tycoon-almost-sued-himself/.

218   one of the most powerful combat vessels in Starfleet: http://memory-alpha
        .wikia.com/wiki/Prometheus_class.

16: COLLABORATION TRIUMPHS

219   Rita Vásquez could not stifle a sense of foreboding: Author interview with Rita
        Vásquez, Panama, August 2016.

220   *La Prensa's* staff formed a human chain: Rubén Polanco, "Concerns Raised over
        TCT Decision," *La Prensa*, July 16, 2015, http://www.prensa.com/in_english
        /TCT-corprensa_21_4256034357.html.

220   Video shows angry Panamanians: https://www.youtube.com/watch?v=CzK
        -1Az8s4s.

220   a midsize Panamanian law firm that provided offshore services: http://sucre.net/.

220   much of Panama's political and economic elite worked in the offshore industry:
        Michael Hudson, Will Fitzgibbon, Emilia Díaz-Struck, and Sol Lauría, "Panama's
        Revolving Door Shows Global Challenge of Offshore Reform," International Con-
        sortium of Investigative Journalists, December 19, 2016, https://panamapapers
        .icij.org/20161219-panama-offshore-reform-challenge.html.

221   It was like planning a wedding: Author interview with Mar Cabra, August 2016.

222   Caruana Galizia found the answer in parallel processing: Author interview
        with Matthew Caruana Galizia, July 2016.

223   an over-the-top in-house video: https://www.youtube.com/watch?v=Rkz-hjpch38.

223   an animation he had created: Jóhannes Kr. Kristjánsson, "Alleged Market Manipulation of Kaupthing Bank," December 2011, https://vimeo.com/41317731.

226   "To create a genuine growth strategy for ICIJ": "Making a Difference: How ICIJ will Continue Changing the World of Investigative Journalism," Growth Plan, Final Draft, ICIJ, January 2016.

226   vice president and general manager of digital operations at CNN International: "Change of Leadership at the Center for Public Integrity," Center for Public Integrity, November 15, 2016, https://www.publicintegrity.org/2016/11/15/20470 /change-leadership-center-public-integrity.

227   Now, in Laurin's opinion, Bale was talking like a politician: Author interview with Fredrik Laurin, November 2016.

227   Not only did the prime minister have a secret offshore company: Frederik Obermaier and Bastian Obermayer, "A Storm Is Coming," *Süddeutsche Zeitung*, n.d., http://panamapapers.sueddeutsche.de/articles/56fec0cda1bb8d3c3495adfc/.

227   He labored alone in his apartment: Author interview with Jóhannes Kristjánsson, Iceland, September 2016.

228   For his part, Ryle wanted to ensure the Icelandic reporter: Author interview with Gerard Ryle, Washington, DC, October 2016.

229   the Minister's Residence at Tjarnargata: https://eng.forsaetisraduneyti.is/ministry /ministers-residence/.

231   The Mossfon files stayed with Prometheus: "Panama Papers Source Offers Documents to Governments, Hints at More to Come," International Consortium of Investigative Journalists, May 6, 2016, https://panamapapers.icij.org/20160506 -john-doe-statement.html.

231   "a money-washing machine": Rolando Rodríguez B., "Mossack Fonseca Employees Face Charges in Brazil," *La Prensa*, January 28, 2016, http://www.prensa.com /in_english/Mossack-Fonseca_21_4403019655.html.

231   The firm responded with a statement: "Mossack Fonseca—Announcement Regarding Clarification of Media Reports," https://mossfon.wordpress.com/2016 /02/15/mossack-fonseca-announcement-regarding-clarification-of-media -reports/.

232   paid a visit to *La Prensa*: Author interview with Rolando Rodríguez, Panama, August 2016.

233   Bronstein looked in the front seat: Author interview with Scott Bronstein, Panama, August 2016.

17: THE WAVE BREAKS

234   Pálsdóttir posted a confusing statement on her Facebook page: Anna Sigurlaug Pálsdóttir, Facebook post, March 15, 2016, https://www.facebook.com/AnnaStellaP /posts/10154071610940559.

234   A detailed request-for-comment letter: Bernstein et al., "All Putin's Men."

235   "honey-worded queries": "Kremlin: Some Mass Media Prepare Outspoken Pre-Planned Attack Against Putin," Tass, March 28, 2016, http://tass.com/politics /865567.

235   Peskov, whose wife also had a company with Mossfon: https://www.occrp.org /en/panamapapers/persons/peskov/.

235   The efficiency of their attacks would not be high: "Kremlin Warns of Wave of False Media Reports on Putin in the Works," *Sputnik International*, March 28, 2016, https://sputniknews.com/russia/201603281037083084-kremlin-putin-false -media-reports-world/.

236   A subsequent analysis of Mossfon's cybersecurity: Mark Maunder, "Mossack Fenseca Breach—WordPress Revolution Slider Plugin Possible Cause," *Wordfence*, April 7, 2016, https://www.wordfence.com/blog/2016/04/mossack -fonseca-breach-vulnerable-slider-revolution/.

236   at least twenty-five known vulnerabilities: Matt Burgess and James Temperton, "The Security Flaws at the Heart of the Panama Papers," *Wired*, April 6, 2016, http://www.wired.co.uk/article/panama-papers-mossack-fonseca-website -security-problems.

237   "Mossack Fonseca lets cat out of bag": "Mossack Fonseca Lets Cat Out of Bag Ahead of Worldwide Coverage of Massive Panama Leaks Data," *Running Commentary: Daphne Caruana Galizia's Notebook*, April 2, 2016, https://daphnecaruanagalizia .com/2016/04/mossack-fonseca-let-cat-bag/.

237   "Biggest leak in the history of data journalism": Edward Snowden, Twitter post, April 3, 2016, https://twitter.com/snowden/status/716683740903247873 ?lang=es.

238   ICIJ's website received more than six million page views: Email to author from Hamish Boland-Rudder, July 28, 2017.

239   the largest protest in the country's history: Jessica Durando, "Thousands Call for Iceland PM to Resign After Panama Papers Leak," *USA Today*, April 4, 2016, https://www.usatoday.com/story/news/world/2016/04/04/panama-papers -iceland-reaction-prime-minister/82622674/.

240   FIFA's new president, the files revealed: Michael W. Hudson, "Panama Papers Spark High-Level FIFA Resignation and Swiss Police Raid," International Consortium of Investigative Journalists, April 6, 2016, https://panamapapers.icij .org/20160406-uefa-raid-fifa-resignation.html.

240   the Swiss federal police conducted raids: "Panama Papers: UEFA Offices Searched by Swiss Police," BBC, April 6, 2016, http://www.bbc.com/sport/football/35981302.

240   seized the Nahmads' Modigliani painting: Martha M. Hamilton, "Contested Modigliani Seized from Freeport as Swiss Open Investigation," International Consortium of Investigative Journalists, April 11, 2016, https://panamapapers .icij.org/blog/20160411-swiss-art-freeport-search.html.

240   After three days of prevarications, Cameron finally admitted: Robert Booth, Holly Watt, and David Pegg, "David Cameron Admits He Profited from Father's Panama Offshore Trust," *Guardian*, April 7, 2016, https://www.theguardian.com /news/2016/apr/07/david-cameron-admits-he-profited-fathers-offshore-fund -panama-papers.

240   "It should be noted that these documents": "For Communication Media, 'Panama Papers,'" Ministerio del Poder Popular para la Comunicación, Venezuela, April 4, 2016, translated by the author.

241   Macri was listed as a decadelong director of Fleg Trading: https://offshoreleaks .icij.org/nodes/15002701.

242   "The Kirchneristas accused us": Author interview with Mariel Fitz Patrick, June 2017.

242   *La Nación* itself was in the data: "La Nación a sus lectores," *La Nación*, April 10, 2016, http://www.lanacion.com.ar/1887983-la-nacion-a-sus-lectores.

242   allowing the publication of the businessmen's names: Iván Ruiz, Maia Jastreblansky, and Hugo Alconada Mon, "Panamá Papers: Aparecen grandes empresarios locales," *La Nación*, April 19, 2016, http://www.lanacion.com.ar/1890675 -panama-papers-aparecen-grandes-empresarios-locales.

242   government supporters demonstrated outside *El Comercio* and *El Universo*: "Panama Papers: Harassment of Journalists in Ecuador and Venezuela Must

End," IFEX, April 22, 2016, https://www.ifex.org/ecuador/2016/04/22/panama _papers/.

243   the country's attorney general, the president's cousin: "Panama Papers: The Power Players," International Consortium of Investigative Journalists, https:// panamapapers.icij.org/the_power_players/.

243   As part of his efforts to rein in the media: Freedom House, "Freedom of the Press 2015: Ecuador," https://freedomhouse.org/report/freedom-press/2015 /ecuador.

243   "If you censor more than 99% of the documents": Timothy Bertrand, "WikiLeaks Had Some Snarky Tweets About the Panama Papers," Social News Daily, April 7, 2016, http://socialnewsdaily.com/62059/wikileaks-panama-papers-tweets/.

243   Several quick-witted techies put the URL online: narkopolo, Twitter post, April 5, 2016, https://twitter.com/nark0polo/status/717473567286411266.

244   Hundreds of reporters, editors, and free-speech activists: "Hundreds Join Protest over Sacking of Ming Pao Editor," Hong Kong Free Press, May 2, 2016, https://www.hongkongfp.com/2016/05/02/hundreds-join-protest-sacking -ming-pao-editor/.

244   the "ginger protest": Ibid.

244   Caraballo confiscated copies of Mossfon's computer data: Martha M. Hamilton and Emilia Díaz-Struck, "Panama Police Raid Mossack Fonseca as Global Fall-out Continues," International Consortium of Investigative Journalists, April 13, 2016, https://panamapapers.icij.org/20160413-panama-raids-mossack-fonseca .html; and "MP asegura archivos de Mossack Fonseca," La Prensa, April 14, 2016, http://impresa.prensa.com/panorama/MP-asegura-archivos-Mossack-Fonseca _0_4460553901.html.

245   He sought out Bloomberg News and the Wall Street Journal: Kejal Vyas, "Co-Founder of Mossack Fonseca Defends Law Firm at Center of 'Panama Papers,'" Wall Street Journal, April 7, 2016, https://www.wsj.com/articles/co-founder-of-mossack -fonseca-defends-law-firm-1460004583?tesla=y&mg=prod/accounts-wsj.

245   European authorities pledged new cooperation: "Five EU Nations Agree Tax Crackdown in Wake of Panama Leak," BBC, April 15, 2016, http://www.bbc.com /news/business-36052142.

245   Preet Bharara, the U.S. attorney for the Southern District of New York: Rupert Neate, "Panama Papers: US Launches Criminal Inquiry into Tax Avoidance Claims," Guardian, April 19, 2016, https://www.theguardian.com/business/2016 /apr/19/panama-papers-us-justice-department-investigation-tax-avoidance.

245   Spain's minister of industry resigned: Raphael Minder, "Spain's Industry Minister Steps Down over Panama Papers Revelations," New York Times, April 15, 2016, https://www.nytimes.com/2016/04/16/world/europe/panama-papers -spain.html.

246   only if the person owned more than 25 percent: David Dayen, "The Obama Administration's Panama Papers Misfire: Why New Rules to Curtail Global Tax Avoidance Could Actually Make Things Worse," Salon, May 10, 2016, http:// www.salon.com/2016/05/10/the_obama_administrations_panama_papers _misfire_why_new_rules_to_curtail_global_tax_avoidance_could_actually _make_things_worse/.

246   Investigators carried out bags of shredded documents: Katherine Chang and Jorge E. Quirós, "Allanan depósitos de Mossack Fonseca en Parque Lefevre," TVN Noticias, April 22, 2016, https://www.tvn-2.com/nacionales/judicial/MP -allananamiento-depositos-Mossack-Fonseca_0_4466553360.html.

247   users of the interactive database could visually see the connections: Marina

Walker Guevara, "ICIJ Releases Database Revealing Thousands of Secret Offshore Companies," International Consortium of Investigative Journalists, May 9, 2016, https://panamapapers.icij.org/blog/20160509-offshore-database-release .html.

248   Carvajal worried that John Doe might suffer a similar fate: Email to author from Rigoberto Carvajal, June 2017.

248   "I do not work for any government or intelligence agency": "Panama Papers Source Offers Documents to Governments, Hints at More to Come," International Consortium of Investigative Journalists, May 6, 2016, https://panamapapers.icij .org/20160506-john-doe-statement.html.

18: THE SECRECY WORLD ENTERS THE WHITE HOUSE

250   Yalçındağ was calling from Trump Tower: Paul Blumenthal, "Trump Touted His Turkish Business Partner in a Call with President Erdogan," *Huffington Post*, November 23, 2016, http://www.huffingtonpost.com/entry/donald-trump -turkey-business_us_5836188ae4b01ba68ac41d9f.

251   furious over the Russian revelations contained in the Panama Papers: "Intelligence Report on Russian Hacking," *New York Times*, January 6, 2017, https:// www.nytimes.com/interactive/2017/01/06/us/politics/document-russia -hacking-report-intelligence-agencies.html.

251   378 individual Delaware companies: Kevin G. Hall, Franco Ordoñez, and Vera Bergengruen, "What Panama Papers Say—and Don't Say—About Trump," *McClatchy DC*, April 29, 2016, http://www.mcclatchydc.com/news/nation-world /national/article74789322.html.

251   real estate transactions with Panama-based Mossfon companies as early as 1994: Letter from Rana Hunter Williams to Process Consultants Inc., September 6, 1994.

252   Russian state-controlled bank Vnesheconombank, or VEB: Ben Protess, Andrew E. Kramer, and Mike McIntire, "Bank at Center of U.S. Inquiry Projects Russian 'Soft Power,'" *New York Times*, June 4, 2017, https://www.nytimes.com /2017/06/04/business/vnesheconombank-veb-bank-russia-trump-kushner.html

252   the developers battled cost overruns and delays on the condo-hotel development: "Trump's Name May Not Stay on Toronto Tower as Push for Buyers Begins," *Financial Post*, November 25, 2016, http://business.financialpost.com/personal -finance/mortgages-real-estate/trumps-name-may-not-stay-on-toronto-tower -as-push-for-buyers-begins/wcm/b7732a42-835e-462b-81ee-cca2c16c2f20.

252   who had at least three Mossfon companies and a trust: Wendy Dent, Ed Pilkington, and Shaun Walker, "Jared Kushner Sealed Real Estate Deal with Oligarch's Firm Cited in Money-Laundering Case," *Guardian*, July 24, 2017, https://www .theguardian.com/us-news/2017/jul/24/jared-kushner-new-york-russia-money -laundering.

252   the Trump Department of Justice abruptly settled with Prevezon for $5.9 million: Jose Pagliery, "Russian Money-Laundering Details Remain in the Dark as US Settles Fraud Case," CNN, May 13, 2017, http://www.cnn.com/2017/05/13 /world/prevezon-settlement/index.html.

252   gas billionaire Dmitry Firtash: Adam Weinstein and Laura Juncadella, "Trump Campaign Manager's Ukrainian Clients Have Panama Papers Connections," *Fusion TV*, July 22, 2016, http://fusion.net/story/328264/paul-manafort-trump -campaign-panama-papers-connection/.

252   metals magnate Oleg Deripaska: Adam Weinstein and Laura Juncadella, "Trump Campaign Manager's Ukrainian Clients Have Panama Papers Connections,"

Fusion, July 22, 2016, http://fusion.net/story/328264/paul-manafort-trump
-campaign-panama-papers-connection/.

252   appears to have written to the law firm in 1992: Letter to Yolanda De Azcarraga
from Sebastian Gorka, August 20, 1992.

253   According to an account of the conversation between Trump and Erdoğan:
Amberin Zaman, "From Trump to Erdogan: My Daughter Ivanka Is Your Big
Fan and Supporter," *Diken,* November 10, 2016, http://www.diken.com.tr
/trump-erdogan-gorusmesi-kizim-ivanka-sizin-buyuk-hayraniniz-ve
-taraftariniz/.

253   regularly conducted business with people connected to the Mafia: Michael
Rothfeld and Alexandra Berzon, "Donald Trump and the Mob," *Wall Street Journal,*
September 1, 2016, https://www.wsj.com/articles/donald-trump-dealt-with-a
-series-of-people-who-had-mob-ties-1472736922.

253   Building unions known to be controlled by the Mob: Ibid.

253   dried up funding from most U.S. banks: Anupreeta Das, "When Donald Trump
Needs a Loan, He Chooses Deutsche Bank," *Wall Street Journal,* March 20, 2016,
https://www.wsj.com/articles/when-donald-trump-needs-a-loan-he-chooses
-deutsche-bank-1458379806.

253   their relationship with the president of the United States: Dan Alexander, "In
Trump They Trust: Inside the Web of Partners Cashing In on the President,"
Forbes, March 20, 2017, https://www.forbes.com/sites/danalexander/2017/03/20
/in-trump-they-trust-inside-the-global-web-of-partners-cashing-in-on-the
-president/#2a7573987605.

254   a pilot project that forced real estate agents in Miami and New York: Louise
Story, "U.S. Will Track Secret Buyers of Luxury Real Estate," *New York Times,*
January 13, 2016, https://www.nytimes.com/2016/01/14/us/us-will-track-secret
-buyers-of-luxury-real-estate.html.

254   needed to obtain an Employee Identification Number: "United States Tax Alert,"
Deloitte, International Tax, December 20, 2016, https://www2.deloitte.com
/content/dam/Deloitte/global/Documents/Tax/dttl-tax-alert-united-states
-6038a-20-december-2016.pdf.

254   Congress repealed an anticorruption measure: Tim Fernholz, "Republicans
Want US Oil Companies to Keep Their Payments to Corrupt Governments
Secret," *Quartz,* February 2, 2017, https://qz.com/901494/republicans-will
-repeal-cardin-lugar-and-let-us-oil-companies-hide-their-payments-to-corrupt
-governments-again/.

255   "you'll do business nowhere": "Trump: Dimon's Woes & Zuckerberg's Prenup-
tial," CNBC video, May 15, 2012, http://www.cnbc.com/video/2012/05/15/trump
-dimons-woes-zuckerbergs-prenuptial.html?play=1.

255   "Do you think Putin will be going to The Miss Universe Pageant": Donald J.
Trump, Twitter post, June 18, 2013, https://twitter.com/realdonaldtrump/status
/347191326112112640?lang=en.

255   Putin sent a decorative lacquered box: Tom Hamburger, Rosalind S. Helderman,
and Michael Birnbaum, "Inside Trump's Financial Ties to Russia and His
Unusual Flattery of Vladimir Putin," *Washington Post,* June 17, 2016, https://
www.washingtonpost.com/politics/inside-trumps-financial-ties-to-russia-and
-his-unusual-flattery-of-vladimir-putin/2016/06/17/dbdcaac8-31a6-11e6-8ff7
-7b6c1998b7a0_story.html?utm_term=.a39ebca741c0.

255   having received Russia's Order of Honour: "Vladimir Putin Decorated Aras
Agalarov with the Order of Order," *Crocus Group,* October 29, 2013, http://
crocusgroup.com/press-center/news/752/.

256   "I have a great relationship with many Russians": Julie Strickland, "The Don-

ald, Sapir Mull Bringing Trump Soho to Moscow," *Real Deal*, November 12, 2013, https://therealdeal.com/2013/11/12/the-donald-sapir-execs-mull-bringing-trump-soho-to-moscow/.

256   a condominium project in partnership with U.S. tobacco executives: Hamburger, Helderman, and Birnbaum, "Inside Trump's Financial Ties to Russia."

257   Ravana, the Arif family foundation: Email from Jason Vella Tabone to Mossack Fonseca & Co, Subject: Rosetti Overseas Ltd, September 27, 2013.

257   linked to corruption in international soccer: Michael Bird, Zeynep Sentek, and Craig Shaw, "Football Leaks: Kazakh Moguls, the Pal of Donald Trump, Teen Models and the Yacht of the 'Father of the Turks,'" *Black Sea*, December 16, 2016, https://theblacksea.eu/index.php?idT=88&idC=88&idRec=1274&recType=story.

257   a Mafia-related $40 million pump-and-dump penny stock fraud in 1998: Ibid.

257   When questioned about Sater: Rosalind S. Helderman and Tom Hamburger, "Former Mafia-Linked Figure Describes Association with Trump," *Washington Post*, May 17, 2016, https://www.washingtonpost.com/politics/former-mafia-linked-figure-describes-association-with-trump/2016/05/17/cec6c2c6-16d3-11e6-aa55-670cabef46e0_story.html?utm_term=.4ba08dce702d.

257   Their best-known joint project was Trump SoHo: Associated Press, "City Backs 46-Story Trump Condo-Hotel Project in SoHo," *Daily News* (New York), September 23, 2007, http://www.nydailynews.com/news/city-backs-46-story-trump-condo-hotel-project-soho-article-1.242953.

257   Trump received a 15 percent cut of sales: Ruth Sherlock and Edward Malnick, "Donald Trump May Go Before Court over Tax Deal That Deprived US Treasury of Millions of Dollars," *Telegraph*, August 7, 2016, http://www.telegraph.co.uk/news/2016/08/07/trump-may-go-before-court-over-deal-that-deprived-us-treasury-of/.

257   in return for future profits: Gary Silverman, "Trump's Russian Riddle," *Financial Times*, August 14, 2016, https://www.ft.com/content/549ddfaa-5fa5-11e6-b38c-7b39cbb1138a.

258   embezzlement of about $22 million: Vala Hafstad, "Panama Papers Expose Icelandic Executive," *Iceland Review*, May 13, 2016, http://icelandreview.com/news/2016/05/13/panama-papers-expose-icelandic-executive; and Eygló Svala Arnarsdóttir, "Former FL Group CEO Acquitted in District Court," *Iceland Review*, February 18, 2015, http://icelandreview.com/news/2015/02/18/former-fl-group-ceo-acquitted-district-court.

258   "I don't know who owns Bayrock": Silverman, "Trump's Russian Riddle."

258   conglomerate with far-flung interests ranging from mining to construction: Mike McIntire, "Donald Trump Settled a Real Estate Lawsuit, and a Criminal Case Was Closed," *New York Times*, April 5, 2016, https://www.nytimes.com/2016/04/06/us/politics/donald-trump-soho-settlement.html.

258   whose grandson and other relatives had their own Mossfon companies: Vlad Lavrov and Irene Velska, "Kazakhstan: President's Grandson Hid Assets Offshore," OCCRP, April 4, 2016, https://www.occrp.org/en/panamapapers/kazakh-presidents-grandson-offshores/.

259   an undisclosed sum without admitting wrongdoing: William MacNamara and Stanley Pignal, "Case Against Three ENRC Oligarchs Settled," *Financial Times*, August 17, 2011, https://www.ft.com/content/95f8ecc4-c8dd-11e0-a2c8-00144feabdc0.

259   "Due to the adverse results": Email from Mossack Fonseca & Co to St. Peters Trust, May 22, 2014.

259   on the grounds of a former African Methodist Episcopal church: Michael Idov, "Trump Soho Is Not an Oxymoron," *New York*, March 30, 2008, http://nymag .com/news/features/45591/index2.html.

260   forcing the building into foreclosure where it was sold at auction: Craig Karmin, "CIM Group to Take Control of New York's Trump SoHo Hotel-Condo," *Wall Street Journal*, November 20, 2014, https://www.wsj.com/articles/cim -group-to-take-control-of-new-yorks-trump-soho-hotel-condo-1416513457.

260   The Khrapunovs deny the charges: Tom Burgis, "Dirty Money: Trump and the Kazakh connection," *Financial Times*, October 19, 2016, https://www.ft.com /content/33285dfa-9231-11e6-8df8-d3778b55a923.

260   accused, along with associates, of misappropriating $6 billion: Emma Farge and Martin de Sa'Pinto, "Swiss Interrogate Kazakh Oligarch Ablyazov's Extended Family," Reuters, August 7, 2013 http://www.reuters.com/article/us-swiss -ablyazov-khrapunov-idUSBRE9760XG20130807; and "Hogan Lovells Secures Success in UK Supreme Court for BTA Bank in Ablyazov Fraud Case," October 22, 2015, https://www.hoganlovells.com/news/hogan-lovells-secures-success-in-uk -supreme-court-for-bta-bank-in-ablyazov-fraud-case.

260   BTA lists more than 786 offshore companies in which Ablyazov had an interest: *List of Assets in which MKA has an Ownership Interest*, BTA Bank website, http://bta.kz/files/AssetslistnewBTAsite.pdf

260   suspected their involvement in prostitution: Bird, Sentek, and Shaw, "Football Leaks."

260   sued ENRC over the disposition of $220 million: Margareta Pagano, "Zamin Ferrous and ENRC Heading for Bitter High Court Battle," *Independent*, December 10, 2014, http://www.independent.co.uk/news/business/news/zamin-ferrous-and -enrc-heading-for-bitter-high-court-battle-9916113.html.

260   the Trump International Hotel and Tower Fort Lauderdale: Michael Sallah and Michael Vasquez, "Failed Donald Trump Tower Thrust into GOP Campaign for Presidency," *Miami Herald*, March 12, 2016, http://www.miamiherald.com/news /politics-government/election/article65709332.html.

261   any experience getting visas for Iranians: Email from Marie Williams to Sara Montenegro, June 26, 2008.

261   the billionaire became embroiled in a nasty divorce: Will Fitzgibbon, "How the One Percenters Divorce: Offshore Intrigue Plays Hide and Seek with Millions," International Consortium of Investigative Journalists, April 3, 2016, https:// panamapapers.icij.org/20160403-divorce-offshore-intrigue.html.

261   plans were approved to tear down the mansion: Michael Crowley, "Trump and the Oligarch," *Politico*, July 29, 2016, http://www.politico.eu/article/donad -trump-and-the-oligarch-russia-dmitry-rybolovlev-house-vladimir-putin-us -presidential-election-america-2016/.

262   Azerbaijan's largest taxi and bus companies: Nushabe Fatullayeva, "Azerbaijan: Insider Deals Thrive in Ministry," OCCRP, April 1, 2013, https://www.occrp.org /en/investigations/1907-azerbaijan-insider-deals-thrive-in-ministry.

262   they were stopped: "Police Prevent Staff of Opposition Newspaper from Working," Reporters Without Borders, August 3, 2010, https://rsf.org/en/news/police -prevent-staff-opposition-newspaper-working.

262   "is notoriously corrupt even for Azerbaijan": https://wikileaks.org/plusd/cables /09BAKU175_a.html.

263   mistakenly released election results: Max Fisher, "Oops: Azerbaijan Released Election Results Before Voting Had Even Started," *Washington Post*, October 9, 2013, https://www.washingtonpost.com/news/worldviews/wp/2013/10/09/oops

-azerbaijan-released-election-results-before-voting-had-even-started/?utm
_term=.6d3f537e3bfd.

263   Aliyev's daughters, Leyla and Arzu: Miranda Patrucic, Eleanor Rose, Irene Vel-
        ska, and Khadija Ismayilova, "Azerbaijan First Family's London Private Enclave,"
        OCCRP, May 10, 2016, https://www.occrp.org/en/panamapapers/azerbaijan-first
        -familys-london-private-enclave/.

263   "Trump International Hotel & Tower Baku represents the unwavering standard
        of excellence": "Trump Hotel Collection Announces Trump International Hotel,"
        PR Newswire, November 4, 2014, http://www.prnewswire.com/news-releases
        /trump-hotel-collection-announces-trump-international-hotel—tower-baku
        -281425361.html.

264   every element from the wood paneling to the landscaping: Adam Davidson,
        "Donald Trump's Worst Deal," *New Yorker*, March 13, 2017, http://www.new
        yorker.com/magazine/2017/03/13/donald-trumps-worst-deal.

264   contractors were apparently paid in sacks of cash: Ibid.

264   The Alliance spent more than $12 million showering cash on politicians: Ilya
        Lozovsky, "How Azerbaijan and Its Lobbyists Spin Congress," *Foreign Policy*,
        June 11, 2015, http://foreignpolicy.com/2015/06/11/how-azerbaijan-and-its
        -lobbyists-spin-congress/.

265   with Senator John McCain and House minority leader Nancy Pelosi: Kevin
        Sullivan, "For A President Trump, Global Real Estate Deals Present Unprece-
        dented Gray Areas," *Washington Post*, May 30, 2016, https://www.washingtonpost
        .com/politics/for-a-president-trump-global-real-estate-deals-present
        -unprecedented-gray-areas/2016/05/30/beac0038-15fa-11e6-aa55-670cabef46e0
        _story.html?utm_term=.14613dce37fe.

265   Burton never received his final year's salary: "Azerbaijan's Key Lobbyist in
        Washington, Dan Burton, Refuses to Protect Country's Interests Citing Non-
        payment," *Panorama.am*, March 3, 2016, http://www.panorama.am/en/news
        /2016/03/03/Dan-Burton/1538734.

265   She was a big fan and supporter of Erdoğan: "Diken Reports Call Between
        President-Elect Trump and President Erdogan of Turkey," *Hsquared Magazine*,
        November 11, 2016, http://hsquaredmagazine.com/2016/11/11/diken-reports
        -call-between-president-elect-trump-and-president-erdogan-of-turkey/.

265   The conjoined forty-story office and residential towers: "Real Estate Portfolio:
        Istanbul, Turkey," http://www.trump.com/real-estate-portfolio/istanbul/trump
        -towers/.

265   "I was very excited when I met Mehmet Ali Yalçındağ": "Trump Towers Istan-
        bul," *Istanbul View*, http://www.istanbulview.com/trump-towers-to-open-luxury
        -shopping-mall-in-istanbul/.

265   "beyond partners": Kevin Sullivan, "Trump's Foreign Network," *Washington
        Post*, January 13, 2017, http://www.washingtonpost.com/sf/world/2017/01/13
        /trumps-foreign-network/?utm_term=.8c58c6f5e967.

266   a $2.5 billion fine for unpaid taxes: "IPI Troubled by Tax Case Targeting Turkey
        Media Owner," International Press Institute, July 8, 2016, https://ipi.media/ipi
        -troubled-by-tax-case-targeting-turkey-media-owner/.

266   "the largest oil distribution company in Turkey": General Comments, Petrol
        Ofisi International Oil Trading Ltd., September 23, 2003.

266   its principal beneficiary was listed as Imre Barmanbek: Source of Funds/Wealth
        Declaration, November 5, 2015.

267   how Yalçındağ worked hard to ingratiate himself with Erdoğan: Amberin Zaman,
        "WikiLeaks Dump Casts Rare Light on Erdogan Inner Circle," *Al-Monitor*,

December 6, 2016, http://www.al-monitor.com/pulse/originals/2016/12/erdogan
-albayrak-wikileaks.html#ixzz4m5CoQZu.

267   a complete list of Turks and their companies: https://wikileaks.org/berats-box
/emailid/27681.

EPILOGUE

268   the partners' original idea was to sell the firm: Author interview with Ramón
Fonseca, Panama City, August 2016.

268   the British Virgin Islands fined the firm $440,000: British Virgin Islands
Financial Services Commission, Enforcement Action, http://www.bvifsc.vg
/Publications/EnforcementAction/tabid/378/ctl/EnforcementSummary/mid
/1188/actionId/17069/language/en-AU/Default.aspx.

268   Company incorporations in the jurisdiction dropped 30 percent: "British Virgin Islands: Have They Cleaned Up Since the Panama Papers?," Transparency International, October 14, 2016, https://www.transparency.org/news
/feature/british_virgin_islands_have_they_cleaned_up_since_the_panama
_papers.

269   "They should build a statue to me": Author interview with Ramón Fonseca,
Panama City, December 2016.

269   UBS still had offshore companies registered with Mossfon: Author interview
with Adrian Simon, Geneva, September 2016.

269   In May, Elliott Management sued the Panamanians: Taos Turner and Santiago
Pérez, "Paul Singer's New Target: Mossack Fonseca," Wall Street Journal, June 7,
2016, https://www.wsj.com/articles/paul-singers-new-target-mossack-fonseca
-1465326566.

270   the firm paid about $3.3 billion in bribes: Paulo Prada, "Brazil's Odebrecht Paid
$3.3 Billion in Bribes over a Decade: Reports," Reuters, April 15, 2017, http://
www.reuters.com/article/us-brazil-corruption-odebrecht-idUSKBN17H0MW;
and Rolando Rodríguez B., "Questions Answered About Odebrecht Bribes," La
Prensa, June 9, 2017, http://www.prensa.com/in_english/perdio-juego-Odebrecht
_21_4776482306.html.

270   gave an impromptu press conference: Catherine Perea, "Fonseca Mora se des-
vincula de caso Odebrecht y señala a Varela," Telemetro, February 9, 2017,
http://m.telemetro.com/nacionales/Fonseca-Mora-desvincula-Odebrecht
-Varela_0_998000997.html#.

271   on bail of half a million dollars each: "Mossack and Fonseca Released from Jail,"
Panama Today, April 24, 2017, http://www.panamatoday.com/panama/mossack
-and-fonseca-released-jail-4176.

272   "We were one of a couple of thousand outfits": Author interview with Jürgen
Mossack, June 2017.

272   to identify nearly thirty-five hundred individuals and companies: David
Pegg, "Panama Papers: Europol Links 3,500 Names to Suspected Criminals,"
Guardian, November 30, 2016, https://www.theguardian.com/news/2016/dec
/01/panama-papers-europol-links-3500-names-to-suspected-criminals.

273   "Wrong Solution to the Wrong Problem": Email from Charles Lewis to Peter Bale
et al., August 24, 2016.

273   a joint press release that CPI would spin off ICIJ: "Center for Public Integrity to
Spin Off ICIJ," International Consortium of Investigative Journalists, October 20, 2016, https://www.icij.org/blog/2016/10/center-public-integrity-spin
-icij.

274   Bale was leaving CPI: "Change of Leadership at the Center for Public Integrity,"

Center for Public Integrity, November 15, 2016, https://www.publicintegrity.org /2016/11/15/20470/change-leadership-center-public-integrity.

274   "incorporations are thriving": Jürgen Mossack, "Tax Avoidance and Tax Evasion by Clients," *From the Horse's Mouth (Jürgen Mossack's Letters from Preventive Detention)*, April 10, 2017, http://mossfonmedia.com/wp-content/uploads/2017 /05/From-the-Horses-Mouth-10.April_.2017.pdf.

AFTERWORD TO THE PAPERBACK EDITION

275   corruption related to Pilatus: Daphne Caruana Galizia, "That crook Schembri was in court today pleading that he is not a crook," *Running Commentary*, October 16, 2017, https://daphnecaruanagalizia.com/2017/10/crook-schembri-court -today-pleading-not-crook/.

276   "the Panama of Europe": Giorgia Pacione, "Malta branded 'Panama of Europe' after anonymous tip-off," *Italia Oggi*, May 12, 2017, https://www.euractiv.com /section/economy-jobs/news/malta-branded-panama-of-europe-after -anonymous-tip-off/.

276   sex-trafficking and money-laundering scandal: "Adrian Delia files fourth libel case against Daphne Caruana Galizia," *Malta Independent*, August 29, 2017, http:// www.independent.com.mt/articles/2017-08-29/local-news/Adrian-Delia-files -fourth-libel-case-against-Daphne-Caruana-Galizia-6736178416.

276   among those to seize the opportunity: Lorenzo Bagnoli, "The Dubai-ification of Malta," The Organized Crime and Corruption Reporting Project, March 5, 2018, https://www.occrp.org/en/goldforvisas/the-dubai-ification-of-malta.

276   "financial heroin" for the Maltese government: Daphne Caruana Galizia, "Government now dependent for revenue on sale of Maltese citizenship," *Running Commentary*, November 16, 2016, https://daphnecaruanagalizia.com/2016/11 /government-now-dependent-revenue-sale-maltese-citizenship/.

276   a leaked email Daphne posted on her blog: Daphne Caruana Galizia, "BREAKING/Prime Minister and chief of staff use @josephmuscat.com addresses to deal secretly with Henley & Partners chairman, who addresses them as "Keith and Joseph" (in that order),"*Running Commentary*, May 31, 2017, https://daphnecaruana-nagalizia.com/2017/05/prime-minister-chief-staff-use-josephmuscat-com -addresses-deal-secretly-henley-partners-chairman-addresses-keith-joseph -order/.

277   she would then mail the letters back: Daphne Caruana Galizia, "No wonder Henley & Partners have broken out into a cold sweat," *Running Commentary*, May 12, 2017, https://daphnecaruanagalizia.com/2017/05/no-wonder-henley -partners-broken-cold-sweat/.

277   shortly after the prime minister was elected: Stephanie Kirchgaessner and Juliette Garside, "How Joseph Muscat's glittering political career lost its lustre," *The Guardian*, April 23, 2018, https://www.theguardian.com/politics/2018/apr /23/joseph-muscat-malta-political-career-lost-lustre.

277   held a St. Kitts passport courtesy of Henley & Partners: Videoconference with Henley & Partners, European Parliament, Strasbourg, March 14, 2018.

277   would hold at least one account with the bank: Ivan Camillieri, "Pilatus account only used to buy passport: New Zealand billionaire," *Times of Malta*, March 27, 2018, https://www.timesofmalta.com/articles/view/20180327/local /pilatus-account-only-used-to-buy-passport-new-zealand-billionaire.674606.

277   a luxury hotel in Florence, Italy: Kirchgaessner and Garside, "How Joseph Muscat's glittering political career lost its lustre."

277   secret investments throughout Europe: Jacob Borg, "Pilatus Bank used by Azeri

elites to move millions into Europe," *Times of Malta*, April 23, 2018, https://www .timesofmalta.com/articles/view/20180423/local/pilatus-bank-used-by-azeri -elites-to-move-millions-into-europe.677236.

277   On the selection committee was Brian Tonna: Jacob Borg, "Watch: Schembri, Mizzi, advisers Nexia BT sat on power station selection committee," *Times of Malta*, April 25, 2018, https://www.timesofmalta.com/articles/view/20180425 /local/watch-schembri-mizzi-advisers-nexia-bt-sat-on-power-station-selection .677397.

277   The money was to repay a loan: Camillieri, "Pilatus account only used to buy passport: New Zealand billionaire."

277   had "hit the ground running" in 2013: Daphne Caruana Galizia, "PANAMA PAPERS: This is the third (mysterious) company associated with Schembri's and Mizzi's," *Running Commentary*, April 11, 2016, https://daphnecaruanagalizia .com/2016/04/panama-papers-third-mysterious-company-associated -schembris-mizzis/.

277   Daphne reported that Egrant had received $1 million: Helena Grech, "DCG uploads alleged text showing Egrant declaration of Trust, Michelle Muscat named," *Malta Independent*, April 21, 2017, http://www.independent.com.mt /articles/2017-04-21/local-news/DCG-uploads-alleged-text-showing-Egrant -declaration-of-Trust-Michelle-Muscat-named-6736173317.

278   she was sitting on 680,000 leaked files: Tim Diacono, "680,000 Documents Leaked to Daphne Project Originate From Electrogas," *Lovin Malta*, April 27, 2018, https:// lovinmalta.com/news/680-000-documents-leaked-to-daphne-project-originate -from-electrogas.

278   "The situation is desperate": Daphne Caruana Galizia, "That crook Schembri was in court today pleading that he is not a crook."

278   90 percent of all the libel actions filed in Malta: Tim Diacono, "WATCH: Caruana Galizia Brothers: 'We Watched Our Mother's Assassination Unfold in Slow Motion'," *Lovin Malta*, January 22, 2018, https://lovinmalta.com/news/watch -caruana-galizia-brothers-we-watched-our-mothers-assassination-unfold-in -slow-motion.

278   They then built the wall: Stephen Grey, "The Silencing of Daphne," Reuters, April 17, 2018, https://www.reuters.com/investigates/special-report/malta-daphne/.

278   at that moment in a brothel in Germany: Daphne Caruana Galizia, "BREAK-ING/Malta's Economy Minister, Labour Party deputy leader in German brothel tonight," *Running Commentary*, January 30, 2017, https://daphnecaruanagalizia .com/2017/01/breakingmaltas-economy-minister-labour-party-deputy-leader -german-brothel-tonight/.

279   Daphne wrote gleefully: Daphne Caruana Galizia, "BROTHELGATE: Naked government minister has shoulder tattoo," *Running Commentary*, January 31, 2017, https://daphnecaruanagalizia.com/2017/01/brothelgate-naked-government -minister-shoulder-tattoo/.

279   Daphne responded with a blog post: Daphne Caruana Galizia, "The drunken idiot is going to sue me when he knows full well that he was at the brothel and that all my details were correct," *Running Commentary*, January 31, 2017, https:// daphnecaruanagalizia.com/2017/01/idiot-going-sue-knows-full-well-brothel -details-correct/.

279   they were always acquitted: Ivan Martin, "Watch: Three accused of Daphne Caruana Galizia murder as widower looks on," December 5, 2017, https://www .timesofmalta.com/articles/view/20171205/local/three-to-be-arraigned-over -caruana-galizia-murder.664956.

280   the elite trade group the Offshore Magic Circle: "Offshore Law Firm Appleby

Explained (Briefly)," ICIJ, November 5, 2017, https://www.icij.org/blog/2017/11/offshore-law-firm-appleby-explained-briefly/.

280   Ukrainian gangsters: "Paradise Papers: Ukraine crime gang hid proceeds in luxury London flats," BBC Panorama, April 23, 2018, http://www.bbc.com/news/uk-43823962.

280   some 322 Fortune 500 companies collectively held around $2.6 trillion offshore: "Fortune 500 Companies Hold a Record $2.6 trillion offshore," Institute on Taxation and Economic Policy, March 28, 2017, https://itep.org/fortune-500-companies-hold-a-record-26-trillion-offshore/.

281   to avoid paying U.S. taxes on $12 billion in profits: Simon Bowers, "How Nike Stays One Step Ahead of the Regulators," ICIJ, November 6, 2017, https://www.icij.org/investigations/paradise-papers/swoosh-owner-nike-stays-ahead-of-the-regulator-icij/.

281   a staggering $269 billion in profits offshore: Simon Bowers, "What to look for from Apple's big updates this month," ICIJ, February 1, 2018, https://www.icij.org/blog/2018/02/what-to-look-for-from-apples-big-updates-this-month/.

281   Apple's offshore cash stockpile nearly doubled: Simon Bowers, "Leaked Documents Expose Secret Tale Of Apple's Offshore Island Hop," ICIJ, November 6, 2017, https://www.icij.org/investigations/paradise-papers/apples-secret-offshore-island-hop-revealed-by-paradise-papers-leak-icij/.

281   number 16 on the Fortune 500 with $173 billion in revenue: "Fortune Global 500 2017: These Are the Companies Shaping the World," Fortune, http://fortune.com/global500/glencore/

281   dedicating an entire room: Will Fitzgibbon, Bastian Obermayer, Frederik Obermaier, Edouard Perrin, Petra Blum, Oliver Zihlmann, "Room Of Secrets Reveals Glencore's Mysteries," ICIJ, November 5, 2017, https://www.icij.org/investigations/paradise-papers/room-of-secrets-reveals-mysteries-of-glencore/.

281   bribery was part of the equation: Ibid.

282   Cardona speaking with Alfred Degiorgio: Jacob Borg, "Chris Cardona's presence at bar 'frequented by murder suspect' flagged by magistrate," Times of Malta, April 17, 2018, https://www.timesofmalta.com/articles/view/20180417/local/cardona-presence-at-bar-frequented-by-murder-suspect-flagged-to.676636.

282   Richard wrote in an op-ed in the Guardian: Laurent Richard, "A warning to the corrupt: if you kill a journalist, another will take their place," The Guardian, April 16, 2018, https://www.theguardian.com/commentisfree/2018/apr/16/reporter-murdered-daphne-caruana-galizia-malta.

283   the Daphne Project would break the stories: The Daphne Project, The Organized Crime and Corruption Reporting Project, https://www.occrp.org/en/thedaphneproject/.

283   helping Iran launder $115 million in payments from Venezuela prior to opening Pilatus: "Iranian National Arrested For Scheme to Evade U.S. Economic Sanctions by Illicitly Sending More Than $115 Million From Venezuela Through The U.S. Financial System," U.S. Department of Justice, March 20, 2018, https://www.justice.gov/opa/pr/iranian-national-arrested-scheme-evade-us-economic-sanctions-illicitly-sending-more-115.

283   banking regulators froze the bank's accounts: John O'Donnell, "Malta freezes Pilatus bank's operations after chairman's arrest," Reuters, March 22, 2018, https://www.cnbc.com/2018/03/22/reuters-america-malta-freezes-pilatus-banks-operations-after-chairmans-arrest.html.

283   Apple was allowed to repatriate the money: Simon Bowers, "What to look for from Apple's big updates this month."

283   to form limited liability partnerships: Miles Weiss, "New Hedge-Fund Tax

Dodge Triggers Wild Rush Back Into Delaware," Bloomberg, February 14, 2018, https://www.bloomberg.com/news/articles/2018-02-14/new-hedge-fund-tax -dodge-triggers-wild-rush-back-into-delaware.

283   money laundering in the years prior to his election: Peter Fritsch and Glenn R. Simpson, "The Business Deals That Could Imperil Trump," *New York Times*, April 21, 2018, https://www.nytimes.com/2018/04/21/opinion/sunday/trump -business-mueller-money-laundering.html.

284   to make the island a center for cryptocurrencies: Kai Sedgwick, "Malta Prime Minister Welcomes Binance to Its 'Blockchain Island,'" Bitcoin.com, March 23, 2018, https://news.bitcoin.com/malta-prime-minister-welcomes-binance-to-its -blockchain-island/.

284   collected more than $700 million in evaded taxes: Cecile S. Gallego, "Panama Papers investigations bring more than $700 million back onshore," ICIJ, June 26, 2018, https://www.icij.org/blog/2018/06/panama-papers-investigations-bring -700-million-back-onshore/.

284   more than 150 government and corporate inquiries: Will Fitzgibbon and Emilia Diaz-Struck, "Panama Papers have had historic global effects—and the impacts keep coming," The Center for Public Integrity, December 1, 2016, https://www .publicintegrity.org/2016/12/01/20500/panama-papers-have-had-historic -global-effects-and-impacts-keep-coming.

284   In March, Mossfon announced: "Comunicado de Cierre de Operaciones," Mossack Fonseca, March 14, 2018.

284   they couldn't be found: Olmedo Rodriguez, "Fiscal detiene a siete personas por caso Mossack Fonseca," *La Prensa*, May 23, 2018, https://impresa.prensa.com /panorama/Fiscal-detiene-personas-caso-MF_0_5036496409.html.

284   more than a million additional files: Will Fitzgibbon, "New Panama Papers Leak Reveals Firm's Chaotic Scramble to Identify Clients, Save Business Amid Global Fallout," ICIJ, June 20, 2018, https://www.icij.org/investigations/panama-papers /new-panama-papers-leak-reveals-mossack-fonsecas-chaotic-scramble/.

285   the firm knew the names of the owners: Nicholas Nehamas, "'A Mickey Mouse operation': How Panama Papers law firm dumped clients, lost Miami office," *Miami Herald*, June 20, 2018, http://www.miamiherald.com/latest-news/article213423514 .html.

285   "I don't care": Fitzgibbon, "New Panama Papers Leak Reveals Firm's Chaotic Scramble to Identify Clients, Save Business Amid Global Fallout."

285   "we stayed a client": Email from Johan Van den Braber to Mossack Fonseca & Co. (Companies Internal Administration), January 25, 2017.

285   in return for referral fees: Kevin G. Hall, "New Panama Papers leak shows U.S. oddly inactive," *McClatchy*, June 20, 2018. http://www.mcclatchydc.com/news /nation-world/world/article213380974.html.

ACKNOWLEDGMENTS

In May 2015, Michael Hudson, a senior editor at the International Consortium of Investigative Journalists, told me that ICIJ had launched a project for which I might be a good fit. He wouldn't reveal the details on the phone. Instead, he encouraged me to travel to Washington, DC, to meet with Gerard Ryle and Marina Walker, ICIJ's director and deputy director.

On the walk to lunch, Ryle told me about the Prometheus Project, a massive data leak ICIJ was in the process of receiving. The material afforded an unprecedented view into the secrecy world. It had the potential to topple governments. By meal's end I was on board, not realizing the subject would consume my life for more than two years.

What followed was one of the most enjoyable professional experiences I've had in twenty-five years as a journalist. The material was endlessly fascinating. For someone governed by his curiosity, there was a new find to be discovered around every corner. But what elevated it beyond a reporting gold mine was the collaboration.

I soon found myself working with some of the best investigative journalists from around the world. Most already knew one another from previous ICIJ collaborations. They were open and helpful and as excited by the material as I was. We were united by a common purpose and a shared creed. We all believed we were toiling in the public interest. The material we uncovered was information an informed citizenry needed to have. The challenge was more difficult for some than others. Many of the reporters faced considerable obstacles at home, including hostile governments, a skeptical public, and economic pressures.

In the end, more than 370 journalists labored on the Panama Papers. They worked in nearly three dozen languages. Without their effort, this book would not be possible. They tilled many of the fields before I got to them. While I cannot name all who deserve to be mentioned, I am grateful for the work of each and every one.

Despite schedules that would kill normal people, the incredible folks behind ICIJ found time to speak with me for this book and amiably tolerated my extensive follow-up questions. In particular, a grateful thank-you to Gerard Ryle, Marina Walker Guevara, Michael Hudson, Mar Cabra, Rigoberto Carvajal, Matthew Caruana Galizia, Emilia Díaz-Struck, Alexa Olesen, Giannina Segnini, Sheila Coronel, Yuen-Ying Chan, Michael Rothberg, Charles Lewis, Bill Buzenberg, Peter Bale, Hamish Boland-Rudder, Will Fitzgibbon, Cécile Schilis-Gallego, Martha Hamilton, and Miguel Fiandor.

A special thank-you to Ryan Chittum, a crackerjack investigative reporter, who provided invaluable research help.

The Panama Papers would not have been possible without the courageous decision of the editors and reporters at *Süddeutsche Zeitung* to share the leaked files with hundreds of reporters. They made everything that came afterward possible and deserve special recognition.

One of the unfortunate aspects of a secret leak investigation is the inability to approach the subjects early in the project. Despite having access to more than 11.5 million documents from Mossack Fonseca, when we published on April 3, 2016, I still felt as if the full story of the firm and its principals was incomplete. Who were the human beings beneath the caricatures? What did they make of the secrecy world and their place within it? What was it like to build a global business and then watch it unravel? Filling in those missing pieces is part of the reason I undertook this book.

Both Ramón Fonseca and Jürgen Mossack agreed to speak with me in the belief that I was truly interested in trying to understand their perspective. While I am sure they will not agree with everything contained herein, I hope their confidence was not misplaced. My thanks also to Adrian Simon and Rosemarie and Keith Flax.

I traveled to six different countries in the process of writing this book. Along the way, many people took time to educate me about the secrecy world and the journalism around it.

In the British Virgin Islands, Ermin Penn, Martin Kenney, and Penny Haycraft all provided invaluable insights on their lovely tropical home.

Across the Atlantic in volcanic Iceland, Jóhannes Kr. Kristjánsson was a constant resource. Special thanks also to Brynja Gísladóttir, Ólafur Hauksson, Bardi Stefánsson, Aðalsteinn Kjartansson, and Grímur Jón Sigurðsson.

In Switzerland, Titus Plattner and Oliver Zihlmann not only provided invaluable information about their country and their journalistic exploits but kindly opened their homes to me. Thanks also to the other stalwarts of the Tamedia crew, Alexandre Haederli and Catherine Boss, for their time and insights.

Additional thanks in Europe to Edouard Perrin, Jacob Borg, David Leigh, John Christensen, Eva Joly, Fredrik Laurin, Sven Bergman, Sébastien Heymann, James Palmer, Ron Sofer, Jan Martínez Ahrens, Jan Strozyk, and Petra Blum.

In Panama, Rita Vásquez and Scott Bronstein were indefatigable in their assistance. Also thanks to Rolando Rodríguez, Rodrigo Noriega, Rafael Pérez Jaramillo, Ramón Ricardo Arias, and Gian Castillero. I owe a second trip to Panama to an invitation to speak at the 2016 International Anti-Corruption Conference. On the sidelines of the conference, Mónica Almeida, Hugo Alconada Mon, Paul Radu, and Nicholas Shaxson were all generous with their time and input.

Closer to home, John Gordon was thoughtful, patient, and forthright. Joe West was kind enough to rummage through memories of trials and triumphs he had tried to forget. Ezra Chowaiki provided keen-eyed observations of the art market. Additional thanks to Keith Fogg, Brad Berman, and Frank Smyth.

I was extremely fortunate to be able to speak with Jack Blum, Elise Bean, and David Weber for this book. They are walking encyclopedias of the secrecy world, money laundering, and efforts to regulate such activities. I only wish I had more time to learn at their feet.

Much of the good that is in this book comes from the folks listed above. Any errors I reserve for myself.

I also want to thank my talented wife, Eve, who, in addition to keeping me sane, helped with everything from research to editing. Thanks also to my agents David Patterson and Howard Sanders and to my lawyer George Sheanshang. Paul Golob at Henry Holt was an enthusiastic and patient editor. And to the Park Slope Food Coop, thank you for the forbearance.

There are a number of people I cannot mention because they spoke to me on condition of anonymity. You know who you are. I am grateful for your trust and insight.

None of the leak investigations detailed in this book would have been possible without people turning the information over to reporters because they felt the public needed to know. These leakers risked everything. They are the true heroes of this narrative. Chief among them is the person or persons known as John Doe. Thank you.

INDEX